INSIDERS' GUIDE® TO

DALLAS & FORT WORTH

HELP US KEEP THIS GUIDE UP-TO-DATE

We would love to hear from you concerning your experiences with this guide and how you feel it could be improved and kept up-to-date. Please send your comments and suggestions to:

editorial@GlobePequot.com

Thanks for your input, and happy travels!

INSIDERS' GUIDE® SERIES

INSIDERS' GUIDE® TO
DALLAS &
FORT WORTH

JUNE NAYLOR

WITH JUDY WILEY

INSIDERS' GUIDE

GUILFORD, CONNECTICUT
AN IMPRINT OF GLOBE PEQUOT PRESS

All the information in this guidebook is subject to change. We recommend that you call ahead to obtain current information before traveling.

INSIDERS' GUIDE ®

Editorial Director, Travel: Amy Lyons
Project Editor: Ellen Urban
Layout artist: Kevin Mak
Text design: Sheryl Kober
Maps by XNR Productions Inc. © Morris Book Publishing, LLC

ISBN: 978-0-7627-5313-0

Printed in the United States of America
10 9 8 7 6 5 4 3 2 1

CONTENTS

Preface xiv

How to Use This Book 1

Area Overview 2

History 8

Getting Here, Getting Around 13

Accommodations 20

Restaurants 37

Nightlife 70

Shopping 85

Attractions 106

The Arts 123

Parks and Recreation 133

Spectator Sports 148

Kidstuff 155

Annual Events 167

Day Trips and Weekend Getaways 176

Relocation and Retirement 187

Education and Child Care 197

Health Care and Wellness 206

Media 213

Worship 217

Index 223

Directory of Maps

Dallas vii

Dallas–Fort Worth viii

Fort Worth ix

Fort Worth Cultural District x

Stockyards District xi

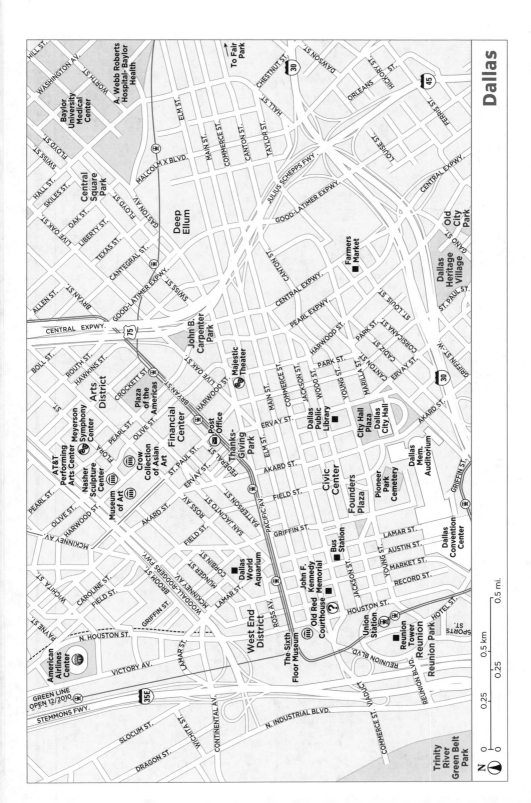

Dallas

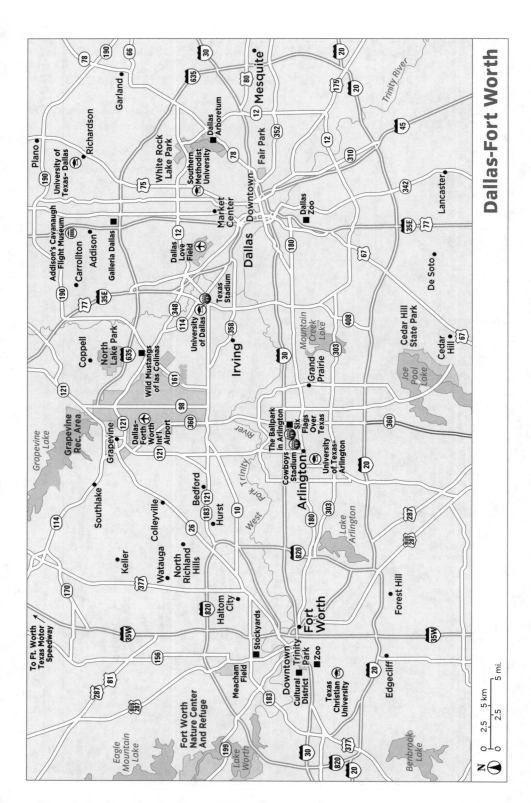

Dallas-Fort Worth

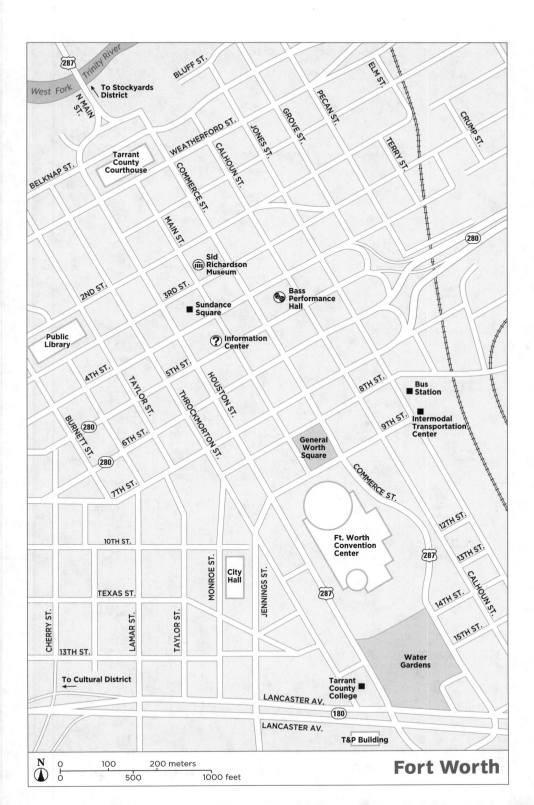

Fort Worth

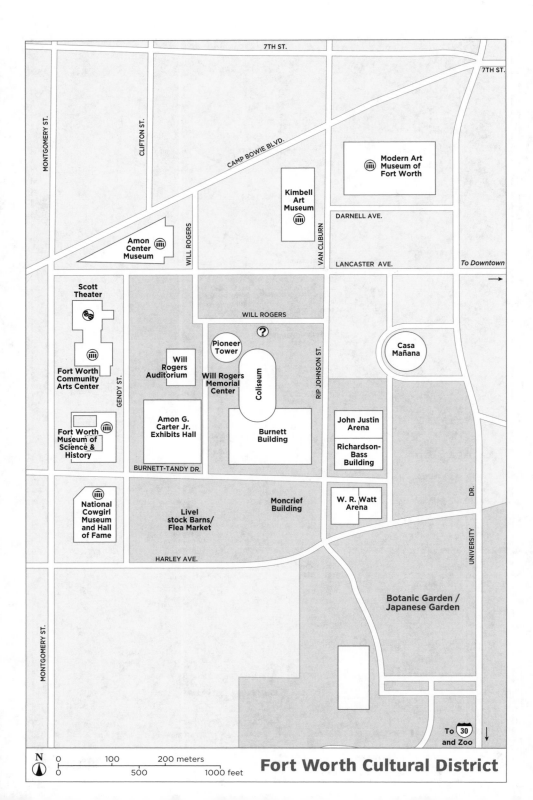

Fort Worth Cultural District

N

| 0 | 100 | 200 meters |
| 0 | 500 | 1000 feet |

7TH ST.

7TH ST.

MONTGOMERY ST.

CLIFTON ST.

CAMP BOWIE BLVD.

WILL ROGERS

VAN CLIBURN

Modern Art Museum of Fort Worth

Kimbell Art Museum

DARNELL AVE.

Amon Center Museum

LANCASTER AVE.

To Downtown

Scott Theater

WILL ROGERS

Pioneer Tower

?

Casa Mañana

Fort Worth Community Arts Center

GENDY ST.

Will Rogers Auditorium

Will Rogers Memorial Center

Coliseum

RIP JOHNSON ST.

Fort Worth Museum of Science & History

Amon G. Carter Jr. Exhibits Hall

Burnett Building

John Justin Arena

Richardson-Bass Building

BURNETT-TANDY DR.

National Cowgirl Museum and Hall of Fame

Live stock Barns/ Flea Market

Moncrief Building

W. R. Watt Arena

DR.

UNIVERSITY

HARLEY AVE.

MONTGOMERY ST.

Botanic Garden / Japanese Garden

To 30 and Zoo

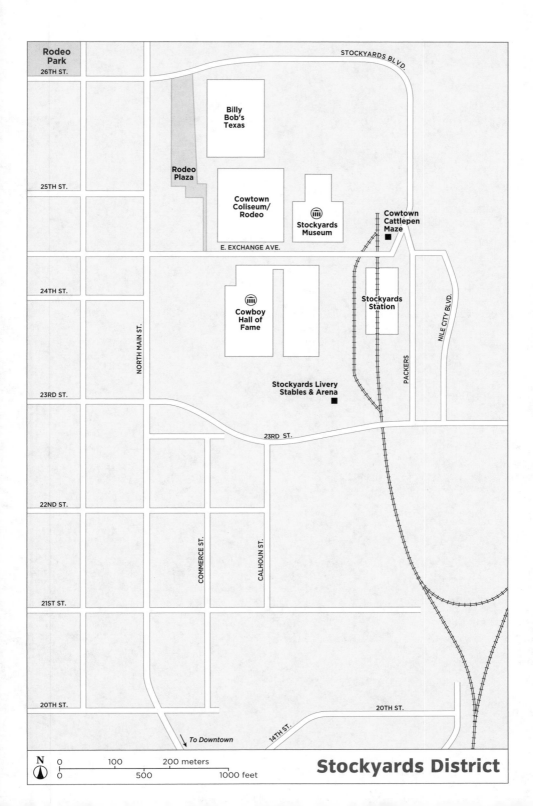

Stockyards District

ACKNOWLEDGMENTS

Having spent my lifetime in the Dallas–Fort Worth area and having written about it for more than 20 years, I've been blessed to know some of the most interesting locals and fortunate to meet newcomers who now feel as at home here as I do. Learning what the veteran and novice Texans like and enjoy in this area has helped make this book possible.

A great deal of gratitude goes to the Dallas Historical Society and to the Fort Worth Museum of Science and History, two wonderful sources of information. I'm deeply grateful to my friends at the Dallas Convention and Visitors Bureau, especially Phyllis Hammond and her staff, and to the Fort Worth Convention and Visitors Bureau, notably Kelly Campbell and Leigh Lyons.

This guide came together only because of the dedication of two exceptional young women who provided endless research and enthusiastic writing: Katie Flodder in Dallas and Callie Cox in Fort Worth. Their diligence, good humor, and faith made this job a joy, and I hope we can work together again. And without the clever words and fast footwork of friend, colleague, editor, and all-around wonderful person Judy Wiley, the eleventh hour wouldn't have been bearable.

Finally, my editor, Amy Lyons must have been heaven-sent. Without her support and guidance, you wouldn't be reading this now.

ABOUT THE AUTHOR

June Naylor, a sixth-generation Texas and Fort Worth native, has written about travel and food since 1984, primarily with the *Fort Worth Star-Telegram*, where she served as assistant travel editor for 10 years. She is currently the newspaper's dining critic and a regular contributor to the travel section, while writing features for other publications, such as *American Way* and *Texas Highways*. She is the author of several Texas guidebooks, such as the award-winning *Texas Off the Beaten Path*® (Globe Pequot Press) and *Quick Escapes*® *Dallas/Fort Worth* (Globe Pequot Press). She serves on the board of the Society of American Travel Writers and was a founder of the Association of Women Journalists. A cookbook author, June also leads culinary touring programs.

PREFACE

Welcome to Dallas–Fort Worth, the tandem cities that make up one of the nation's largest metropolitan areas. Maybe you're just here for a weekend or you're planning to settle for a lifetime; either way, you'll find plenty in the way of amusement, cultural enrichment, and quality of life. The best of Texas is showcased in the DFW area, from sophisticated arts and shopping to the thrill of professional sports and the foot-stomping good times enjoyed since the days of the Wild West.

This pair of cities—each a county seat, Dallas in Dallas County and Fort Worth in Tarrant County—sits atop a region of Texas called Prairies and Lakes, and you can bet your ten-gallon hat that this huge hunk of landscape dominating the top of Texas is easily the state's most diversely juicy stretch of real estate.

Although the two appear on a map as though they might be as cozy as two peas in a pod, they're as different as Canada and Mexico. Thirty miles of freeway lie between the two downtowns, but it's not uncommon to meet people who rarely make the drive from one to another. And that's a shame, because as those who do divide their time between the two can tell you, Dallas and Fort Worth exude a certain yin and yang, ably reflecting that intriguing dual personality of the Lone Star State, that of the sleek 'n' sassy socialite and the rough-and-tumble cowpoke.

Dallas, the largest banking center in the Southwest, constantly changes costumes in her many roles as Southern belle, fashionable urban babe, steely business titan, and contemporary artist. Established as a humble trading post on the Trinity River in 1841, Big D (as it's long been known) has aged gracefully and stylishly into a city brimming with cultural diversity and a proliferation of artistic pastimes. Within the Dallas Arts District (largest of its kind in the nation) are the Dallas Museum of Art, the Morton H. Meyerson Symphony Center, and the Frank Lloyd Wright–designed Dallas Theater Center. Every indulgent pursuit is met in Dallas, which has more shopping centers per capita than any major city in the nation, and four times more restaurants (from Ethiopian to Moroccan and Romanian to Pakistani) per person than even New York City.

Fort Worth brings the Old West to life, but with generous doses of fine arts on the side. Part of this city's appeal lies in the fact that a city nicknamed "Cowtown" boasts a surprising number of world-class art museums, a performing arts center named one of the world's 10 best, and remarkable zoo. The Stockyards National Historic District is a perfectly preserved center of Wild West, cattle-driving heritage, where you can see a rodeo every weekend and hear such crooners as Willie Nelson and Robert Earl Keen play at the world's largest honky-tonk. Sundance Square, with its wealth of restaurants, galleries, shops, theaters, and nightspots, has been called the hottest downtown in Texas, too.

The duo connects the eastern and western halves of the state, looking north toward the plains and south toward the magnificent Hill Country. The Red River lies just north and the two cities straddle various branches of the mighty Trinity River that weaves through the ranch and farm country that surrounds the metro sprawl. Just outside of Dallas and Fort Worth, you'll find charming hamlets with cute town squares and fishing holes, wildflower meadows and old railroad towns, comfortably complementing DFW's urban appeal, replete with architectural wonders, internationally renowned art collections, one of the world's largest airports, and major universities.

If you're a sports fan, you'll find yourself spoiled rotten by a healthy selection of professional football, basketball, hockey, baseball, car racing, horse racing, and rodeo in the Dallas–Fort Worth area. If you're an outdoors fiend, you'll be pleased with plentiful in-town parks, as well as impressed by nearby jewels such as Dinosaur Valley, Lake Whitney, Cedar Hill, Mineral Wells, and Ray Roberts state parks.

Between Big D and Cowtown, you'll find plenty to like—twice as much as you probably expected.

HOW TO USE THIS BOOK

If you're new to town, either as a visitor or resident, this book will familiarize you with the area. Even if you've been to Dallas–Fort Worth before, this guide will point you to places, diversions, and resources you never knew existed. Although it's not the only book you'll ever need to learn these two cities and the entire metro area, it's a great source of information that will help you along the way.

You'll see that the material is compartmentalized into logical sections. If you're trying to wrap your head around the area's past and present, read the Area Overview and History sections. If you're driving to town and need to get a sense of the freeway systems, check out Getting Here, Getting Around. For your lodging and dining selections, read through the Accommodations chapter, followed by Restaurants. There's plenty of material, too, on shopping, festivals, arts, outdoor fun, day trips and getaways, education, child care, health care, and worship in appropriate sections.

Take note of the Close-Up sidebars, those separate essays that provide deeper background on specific destinations and points of interest. Look also for Insiders' Tips, (marked with an), the short items that give you special direction or helpful details.

Keep in mind that no book can provide every answer for everyone. You'll find Web sites herein that can give you up-to-the-moment information when you need it, and be ready to adjust your schedule when necessary. Keep in mind that the famously changing Texas weather can sometimes wash out your plans at the last minute, so it's always good to have a backup idea at the ready.

AREA OVERVIEW

If your passions run to urban delights, spend your time in Dallas and Fort Worth, friendly rivals with utterly different personalities. Dallas, the ninth-largest city in the nation, is the showy and chic retailing and financial industry giant with every ethnic dining offering imaginable, while the easygoing, cattle-driving Fort Worth, the 13th-largest city in the country, is home to a national historic district and a surprising stash of world-class art museums.

A thriving metropolis on the edge of the Great Plains that has been embracing visionaries, dreamers, and pioneers for more than 150 years, Dallas merges Southern hospitality with modern sophistication. The landscape has changed dramatically from the 1800s, when trappers, traders, cowboys, and westward-bound pioneers pulled into town, but Dallas remains a place where enterprising people gather to share their grand ideas and stake claims on new frontiers of business and enterprise.

In Fort Worth, there's a popular barbecue-and-beer joint where servers wear T-shirts declaring, "Life's too short to live in Dallas." The slogan captures an attitude held dear to longtime residents of Cowtown, although they will admit to enjoying a shopping, dining, and nightlife trip to Dallas. Newcomers pay little mind to the friendly sparring, finding that the laid-back attitude in Fort Worth strikes a happy balance with the progressive daily pace that characterizes Dallas.

The similarities between the two include a stunning rate of business and population growth, in spite of a sluggish recent economy; a shared passion for their pro sports teams, including the Dallas Cowboys, whose new billion-dollar stadium is now in Tarrant County instead of Dallas; and a great pride in being Texan. In truth, a lot of Dallasites and Fort Worthians realize that the two cities go hand-in-hand, each offering essential parts that add up to a grand whole.

BUSINESS AND INDUSTRY

Dallas–Fort Worth grew from a trading and supply point to a banking center (Dallas) and military center (Fort Worth) in fairly quick order, and business growth has remained steady, if not rapid. *Fortune* magazine reported in 2008 that DFW ranks second in metropolitan areas for revenue generated by Fortune 500 companies. Interestingly, the Texas Workforce Commission reports that DFW's 200 largest employers comprise less than half of 1 percent of all firms in the region but account for 26.2 percent of the region's employment. In spite of the difficult economy of 2008 and 2009, business leaders have expressed optimism that because the area's industry composition is diversified the area will perform ahead of the national average.

Real estate and construction, manufacturing, retailing and trade, transportation, utilities, energy exploration, communications and information services, health care and education, and leisure and hospitality pay much of the wages for the area workforce. Primary employers are led by AMR Corporation (American Airlines' parent company), based in Fort Worth, followed by (among others) the Dallas Independent School District, Texas Health Resources in Arlington, Baylor Healthcare System in Dallas, UT-Southwestern Medical Center in Dallas, Texas Instruments in Dallas, and JCPenney Company in Plano. Business has been very good for some industrious types: titans with national name recognition include Jerry Jones and Mark Cuban, billionaires who own the Dallas Cowboys and the Dallas Mavericks, respectively.

COWBOY CULTURE

The roots of western heritage run deep beneath the North Texas soil, and Fort Worth enjoyed its share of the Wild West period. Cattle-driving became important business in Texas after the Civil War, and the Chisholm Trail was considered the most important cattle path used to move cows—mostly longhorn—from Texas to the shipping point at Abilene, Kansas. More than 1.5 million head of Texas cattle were driven over the Chisholm between the Civil War and 1873, passing right through Fort Worth. Cowboys would take a load off in Fort Worth, getting a hot meal, card game, drink of whiskey, and maybe some warm companionship in a district called Hell's Half-Acre. Nearby, the National Stockyards Historic District marks an area where the cattle—after the trail-drive period—were penned and slaughtered. There's a wealth of cowboy history on display there, and a live competition rodeo happens in Cowtown Coliseum every weekend.

When fences were employed to create ranches, the trail days were finished. Ranches grew north and west from Fort Worth, and many of the cattle barons kept mansions in the city. Many of the legendary ranches remain, as do a few of those mansions, overlooking the Clear Fork of the Trinity River. The cattle (and oil) barons began collecting art with their riches, and these collections eventually gave way to some of the more extraordinary art museums in the nation. One is the Sid Richardson Museum in downtown Fort Worth, housing one of the (if not the single) foremost collections of works by famed western artists Frederic Remington and Charles Russell. There are a number of Remingtons and Russells also at the Amon Carter Museum, named for the colorful, late newspaper publisher whose pride in Fort Worth knew no bounds. He was known to travel to New York on business, walk into a hotel lobby, and shout, ``Hooray for Fort Worth! Hooray for West Texas!" He coined a catchy phrase, part of which is still carried on the front page of the Star-Telegram: "Fort Worth is where the West begins, and Dallas is where the East peters out." Carter was responsible for establishing the Will Rogers Memorial Center, named for his good friend, where some of the nation's greatest equestrian and livestock events are staged today. Next door, the National Cowgirl Museum and Hall of Fame pays homage to women who helped shape the West.

Dallas saw some cattle-driving action when a branch of the Shawnee Trail, called the Sedalia and Baxter Springs Trail, came through town en route to markets up north. The city pays homage at Pioneer Park, found downtown, where an enormous bronze depiction of a cattle drive, complete with cowboys on horseback, brings the period to the present, larger than life. Said to be the largest bronze of its kind in the world, it sits exactly where the trail passed through. For live cowboy action, the Mesquite Rodeo, a short drive east of downtown Dallas, is your destination.

i Average rainfall in the Dallas–Fort Worth area most months is less than 3 inches. The rainiest month, on average, is May, with 5.3 inches, and the driest is January, with 1.89 inches.

SPORTS

If you're a sports fan, you'll think you've found heaven on earth in Dallas–Fort Worth. (If you're not, you may find yourself annoyed at the level of fanaticism here.) Most of all, people live for Sunday between August and December, hoping the Dallas Cowboys will return to their Super Bowl glory, having taken the title five times. In 2009, the Cowboys began playing in their new, billion-dollar stadium in Arlington, which will host the Super Bowl in 2011. Next door to the Cowboys' stadium is the Ballpark in Arlington, where the Texas Rangers play Major League Baseball from April through September. In Dallas at the American Airlines Center, on the northwest corner of downtown, the Dallas Mavericks play basketball and the Dallas Stars play hockey in front of enthusiastic crowds. Soccer fans will head to Frisco to see FC Dallas play MLS opponents, and you can stay in Frisco also to see the Rough Riders, a Double-A baseball team in the Texas League, one of the Rangers' farm teams. If you like golf, you'll love the month of May when the Byron Nelson tournament in Dallas and the Colonial tournament in Fort Worth bring PGA pros to town.

SHOPPING

It's a fact––Dallas has more shopping centers per capita than any other major U.S. city. And truthfully, the acquisition of pretty things ranks as an art form in North Texas. And why not? The man who wrote the book on retailing, the late Stanley Marcus, remains glorified at the magnificent flagship store in downtown Dallas. You can't find a finer collection of stores with famous names like Chanel and Armani than those in tiny, historic Highland Park Village in Dallas. At NorthPark Center, you'll be wowed by 235 stores and restaurants, including Neiman Marcus, Nordstrom, and Barney's New York, and by designer shops, such as Burberry, Ed Hardy, Kate Spade, and Roberto Cavalli. The Galleria, anchored by Saks Fifth Avenue, Macy's, and Nordstrom, has dozens of specialty stores, too. In Fort Worth, a Neiman Marcus anchors Ridgmar Mall, and you'll find a Nordstrom at NorthEast Mall in Hurst. Great boutique shopping awaits in Dallas in the Knox-Henderson area and in Inwood Village and in Fort Worth along Camp Bowie Boulevard and West Seventh Street.

DINING AND NIGHTLIFE

Dallas's dining scene has gathered increasing national attention in recent years, thanks to a mix of celebrity chefs, interesting bistro destinations, and a solid ethnic selection. Recently, southwestern cuisine pioneer Dean Fearing, who made the Mansion on Turtle Creek a must-visit place among American restaurants, stole headlines again upon opening his own place, Fearing's, inside the new Ritz-Carlton. Almost immediately, John Mariani wrote in *Esquire* magazine that this was the best new restaurant in the country, an opinion soon repeated in *Newsweek* by Julia Reed.

Fearing's colleague and friendly competitor, Stephan Pyles, was another of the founders of Southwestern cuisine. His namesake restaurant on the edge of downtown Dallas remains a favorite, and their friend Wolfgang Puck has given Dallas another boost by opening Five Sixty atop Reunion Tower. But throughout Uptown, the Park Cities, Oak Cliff, North Dallas, Addison, Frisco, and Plano, you'll find intriguing places that win loyal patrons on their own merit. Dallas certainly has its share of Mexican food, steaks, and barbecue, but there's a good assortment also of French, Italian, Caribbean, Latin American, Spanish, Japanese, Thai, Vietnamese, and Indian food, too. When you need comfort, Dallas can spoil you with home cooking and soul food, as well.

Fort Worth's restaurant choices may be somewhat less plentiful than those in Dallas, but it's not without its share of noteworthy dining options. Chefs who have brought crowds to their dinners at the James Beard House in New York include Jon Bonnell of Bonnell's Fine Texas Cuisine and Tim Love of Lonesome Dove, two of Fort Worth's prominent eateries. Grady Spears of Grady's and Louis Lambert of Lambert's both offer exceptional Texas fare, as does Brian Olenjack of Olenjack's Grille in Arlington. Famous destination dining options include Kincaid's Hamburgers, Angelo's Barbecue, and Joe T. Garcia's Mexican Restaurant, all of which have enjoyed exposure in national media. In Sundance Square, popular restaurants include Reata, which presents ranch cuisine, and Piranha Killer Sushi, a favorite for Asian dishes. In the Cultural District, exceptional dining is found at Lanny's Alta Cocina Mexicana and at Eddie V's Prime Seafood and Steaks. Good hole-in-the-wall eating is done at Fred's Texas Café in the Cultural District, at El Asadero near the Stockyards, and at Tu Hai, a Vietnamese cafe in Haltom City.

Nightlife in the DFW area ranges from ubertrendy places like ghostbar at the W in Dallas's Victory Park to country-western friendly at Billy Bob's Texas, the world's largest honky-tonk, found in the Fort Worth Stockyards. There's everything in between, too, from pretty wine bars to good old dive bars.

i Be cautious about using your cell phone while driving. State law allows cities and counties to ban cell phone use in school zones, and cities like Dallas and Fort Worth have done so, levying hefty fines on violators.

TOURISM AND CONVENTIONS

Dallas loves its tourists and convention visitors. In 2007, the last year for which figures were available at press time, the Dallas area hosted 29 million visitors who spent about $8.9 billion in the area. There were 603 conventions, which accounted for a $1.05 billion impact. In Fort Worth, too, tourism and conventions mean big business. Research shows that 5.4 million visitors come to town annually and represent what the convention bureau describes as 10.1 million days. That figure includes those who stayed in a hotel, attended an event at the Fort Worth Convention Center, attended a major attraction, or attended a major event. These visitors had an economic impact of $1.2 billion in one year.

MUSEUMS AND THE ARTS

It surprises even Dallasites to learn that Big D claims the largest contiguous urban arts district in the United States. Sprawling over the northern rim of downtown, the assemblage of museums and performance halls impresses with architecture and artistic content. Not long ago, *New York Magazine* even cited Dallas as having a superb set of offerings for art fans. In Fort Worth, the Cultural District holds five outstanding museums, warranting its nickname of "museum capital of the southwest." Between the two cities, there is every sort of art gallery you can imagine, as well as an abundant selection of opera, symphony, chamber orchestra, jazz, ballet, and contemporary dance performances. And between the two, you'll find a staggering roster of names from the architecture world, with icons such as Louis Kahn, Philip Johnson, Renzo Piano, I. M. Pei, and Tadao Ando creating the renowned museums here.

LANGUAGE AND DIVERSITY

English is the official language, of course, but you'll easily hear Spanish, Vietnamese, and Korean spoken. The African-American and Hispanic populations are significant, naturally, and there are 16 different Asian nationalities represented among the North Texas population. In the area nearest the airport, particularly in Euless, there's a large Tongan population. This has grown in the past 30-plus years after American Airlines moved its headquarters to the area and brought in hired workers from Tonga as baggage handlers. In much of the culture here, the Tongan customs remain strong. The gay and lesbian community is substantial in the DFW area, as Dallas boasts the sixth-largest gay population in the country.

GOVERNMENT

Dallas and Fort Worth are each governed by a city manager–council system; there are 14 district representatives and a mayor. In Fort Worth, there is a mayor and eight district representatives.

Vital Statistics

Texas governor: Rick Perry

Dallas mayor: Tom Leppert

Fort Worth mayor: Mike Moncrief

Population: Dallas, 1,210,390; Dallas metro area, 4,153,727; Fort Worth, 702,850

Area (square miles): Dallas, 384.7; Fort Worth, 350

Nickname: Dallas, Big D; Fort Worth, Cowtown

Average temperature low/high: Dallas, January 34/54; July 75/96. Fort Worth, January 41/61, July 75/96

Annual average rainfall/days of sunshine: Dallas, 33.3 inches/232 days; Fort Worth, 31.56 inches/232 days

Year founded: Dallas, 1841; Fort Worth, 1849

Texas statehood: 1845

Major universities: In Dallas, Texas A&M University (TAMU)-Commerce; Texas Woman's University, Denton; the University of Texas at Arlington (UTA); the University of Texas at Dallas; the University of Texas Southwestern Medical Center at Dallas; University of North Texas (UNT), Denton; Dallas Baptist University; Southern Methodist University; University of Dallas. In Fort Worth, Southwestern Baptist Theological Seminary, Tarrant County College, Texas Christian University, University of North Texas Health Science Center, Texas Wesleyan University

Major area employers: In Dallas, Exxon Mobil, Electronic Data Systems, JCPenney, KimberlyClark, Centex, Texas Instruments, Dean Foods, Southwest Airlines. In Fort Worth, Lockheed Martin, American Airlines, Bell Helicopter Textron, Burlington Northern Santa Fe Railroad, Pier 1 Imports, Radio Shack

Famous natives: From Dallas, Jessica Simpson, Boz Skaggs, Angie Harmon, Owen and Luke Wilson, Dr. Phil McGraw. From Fort Worth: Larry Hagman, Bob Schieffer, Roger Miller, Spanky McFarland, Liz Smith, Dan Jenkins

State/city holidays:
January 1, New Year's Day
Third Monday in January, Martin Luther King Day
Third Monday in February, Presidents' Day
March 2, Texas Independence Day
March/April (varies), Good Friday
March/April (varies), Easter
Last Monday in May, Memorial Day
June 19, Emancipation Day
July 4, Independence Day
First Monday in September, Labor Day

September (varies), Rosh Hashanah

October (varies), Yom Kippur

Second Monday in October, Columbus Day

November 11, Veterans Day

Fourth Thursday in November, Thanksgiving Day

December 25, Christmas Day

Resources:

Dallas Convention and Visitors Bureau, Visitors Center, 100 South Houston St., Dallas, (214) 571-1300, www.visitdallas.com

Greater Dallas Chamber of Commerce, 700 North Pearl St., Suite 1200, Dallas, (214) 746-6600, www.dallaschamber.org

Fort Worth Convention and Visitors Bureau, Visitor's Center, 400 Throckmorton St., Fort Worth, (817) 336-8791 or (800) 433-5747, www.fortworth.com

Major airports and interstates: Dallas is accessed by DFW Airport, halfway between Dallas and Fort Worth, and by Love Field, a short drive north of downtown Dallas. Dallas is reached from the north and south by Interstate 45 and Interstate 35E and from the east and west by Interstate 20 and Interstate 30. Fort Worth is reached by Dallas/Fort Worth International Airport, and by ground from Interstate 30 and Interstate 20, running east and west, and Interstate 35W, running north and south.

Public transportation: Bus and light rail service, Dallas Area Rapid Transit (DART) Customer Information Center (routes, schedules, and trip planning assistance), (214) 979-1111, www.dart.org; trolley service, McKinney Avenue Transit Authority, (214) 515-7272, www.mata.org. In Fort Worth, bus service and light rail are operated by the T (bus) and Trinity Railway Express (TRE), (817) 215-8600, or visit www.the-t .com and www.trinityrailwayexpress.org.

Driving laws: Drivers must be 16 to obtain a driver's license. Seat belts must be worn by passengers in the front seats of cars and trucks and all children under the age of four in any part of a car or truck. Hefty fines are levied for failure to comply. Typical speed limit on city streets is 30 to 40 mph and on the freeways, 60 mph. Away from the metropolitan area, the maximum speed limit is usually 70 mph. Turning right at a red light is allowed unless signs say otherwise. HOV lanes are for cars with at least two passengers in the car during the rush hours mentioned in the sign. For details, visit www.txdps .state.tx.us.

Alcohol laws: The legal drinking age in Texas is 21. Beer and wine purchases may be made after noon on Sunday in Texas, and there is no hard liquor purchased in stores on Sunday. Liquor stores are open between 10 a.m. and 9 p.m. Monday through Saturday. The Texas legal limit for blood alcohol is 0.08. No open containers of alcohol are permitted in moving vehicles. For more information, visit www.tabc .state.tx.us.

Daily newspapers: *Dallas Morning News* and the *Fort Worth Star-Telegram*.

Sales tax: 8.25 percent on retail purchases.

Time and temperature information: Dallas, 214-844-6611; Fort Worth, 817-844-4444

HISTORY

While Dallas and Fort Worth do not offer the sort of lengthy history that you find in Chicago, Atlanta, and other vibrant cities, the two offer two backstories, nevertheless. And what DFW lacks in longevity, the area makes up for with colorful anecdotes. When settlers got here and put down roots, they came armed with wagonloads of determination and strong spirit. Perhaps they came with some vision, too: the traders establishing a post laid groundwork for the financial and marketing center Dallas would become, and Fort Worth's cattle kings provided a foundation that would give Fort Worth its enduring ranching heritage.

DALLAS HISTORY

The Big D got off to something of an inauspicious start in 1839, when a Tennessee lawyer named John Neely Bryan traveled from Arkansas to survey a spot for a trading post at three forks of the Trinity River. He found a good river crossing, perfect for his business catering to Native Americans and settlers. Trouble was, by the time Bryan returned from settling his affairs in 1841, a treaty had removed the Native Americans—and therefore, half his customers. So he decided on a permanent settlement instead. And with that, the bragging began.

Bryan invited settlers at Bird's Fort, 22 miles northwest, to his town, and according to the Dallas Historical Society, "agents" from another colony "bragged on the new town," and attracted still more settlers. By then, it was named Dallas, but for whom no one is quite sure. Bryan named it after a friend, whose identity is uncertain to this day, according to the society.

It is certain, though, that Dallas County was named after U.S. Vice President George Mifflin Dallas when it was established in 1846 in a log cabin courthouse. The little settlement along the river grew from 430 people in 1850 to 2,000 a decade later. Though the Civil War years of 1861 to 1865 were hard times, Dallas grew again during Reconstruction, drawing Southerners in search of rich farmland.

With 1872 came the railroad, and the population swelled to more than 7,000—outlaws among them. Belle Starr sold stolen horses; Doc Holliday opened a dentist's office, turned to gambling, and had to leave town after killing a man in 1875.

The late 1800s saw bank closings, dropping cotton prices, and a departing population, followed by renewed growth at the turn of the century and establishment of Dallas landmarks: a Federal Reserve Bank opened in 1911, and Southern Methodist University in 1915. World War I established Love Field for aviation training, and the Army trained soldiers at Camp Dick, on Fair Park.

And then the bragging really began. While the rest of the nation was suffering through the Great Depression in 1930, Columbus Marion "Dad" Joiner struck oil 100 miles east of the city. Businesses formed or moved to Dallas, banks made loans for oilfield development, and the Big D was the financial hub for the oil boom across all of Texas and Oklahoma. Big bucks also meant big fun when the city was chosen for the Texas Centennial Exposition, a $25 million affair that attracted 10 million visitors.

And the big money kept on coming. Chance Vought, now Vought Aircraft Industries, moved its headquarters to Dallas in 1948, starting a business trend that drew more than 626 companies by 1974, including Texas Instruments and Mary Kay Cosmetics, Inc. Dallas/Fort Worth International Airport opened the same year.

Camp Bowie Boulevard

The roadway reaching westward from Fort Worth's Cultural District might be only about 9 miles in length, but its history spans almost 90 years. The most exciting time for the venerable Camp Bowie Boulevard of late, however, is the boom that it's enjoying right now.

The rash of restaurant openings on the "new" stretch of the street—that's the one west of Interstate 30, roughly where the vintage brick runs out—is downright dizzying. Suddenly there's a fresh selection of Asian dining, as well as a modern steakhouse, a snazzy soul food joint that melds Harlem with New Orleans, and a couple of watering holes that will pair sustenance with your sipping, too.

Named for the Army's 36th Infantry Division camp established for mobilizing troops in World War I, the boulevard was a grand thoroughfare that bisected the west side of town from northeast to southwest. Initially called Arlington Heights Boulevard, its name was changed in 1919 to honor the camp's soldiers. A trolley line served the road, carrying passengers along what's now the median, and the bricks—manufactured out west in Thurber for use here and on Exchange Avenue in the Stockyards and Austin's Congress Avenue—were laid by the early 1930s.

From its old red brick genesis to its conclusion near the Tarrant County line, Camp Bowie Boulevard continues to feed Fort Worth in monumental ways. The wonderful Rockyfeller's, a hamburger dinette, and the Old Swiss House, Cowtown's leading continental restaurant of the period, are but distant memories, but longtime favorites like the Original Mexican Restaurant and Kincaid's are still going strong. You'll find yourself well fed, too, at more recent arrivals that have made happy homes within historic buildings, and at new kids on the block that bring diversity and contemporary variety to this vintage corner of town. Good shopping awaits along the boulevard, too.

But on November 22, 1963, the city and the nation stopped in their tracks. President John F. Kennedy was assassinated during a motorcade through downtown Dallas, and the man accused of killing him, Lee Harvey Oswald, was gunned down two days later by local nightclub owner Jack Ruby. Visitors today can see the Kennedy Memorial, built in 1970. The Sixth Floor Museum, in the book depository from which Kennedy was believed to have been shot, opened in 1989.

The city was on the national radar in the 1970s, but for less serious reasons: The TV series *Dallas* debuted in 1978, riveting the nation with Texas soap opera on a grand scale, and the Dallas Cowboys became known as "America's Team," winning their first Super Bowl in 1972. Baseball's Texas Rangers came to the area the same year, the Mavericks brought basketball in 1980, and the Dallas Stars arrived with hockey sticks in 1993.

With the big-name sports teams attracting thousands of clamoring fans, Dallas spent the '80s and '90s becoming a good host to visitors both inside and outside the ballparks: The West End restaurant and entertainment district opened in the '80s, as well as an arts district that includes the Dallas Museum of Art, Nasher Sculpture Center, and Morton H. Meyerson Symphony Center.

Today's Dallas is a vibrant, cosmopolitan city—a far cry from the camp John Neely Bryan started in 1841. With a population of about 2.4 million in July 2008, according to the U.S. Census, the city has become a sophisticated destination with a big heart—big hair not required. For more details on Dallas history and sports, visit the Dallas Historical Society at www.dallashistory.org or www.dallascowboys.com.

FORT WORTH HISTORY

First an army camp, then a stage stop, Fort Worth had a hardscrabble beginning before it grew up into today's Cowtown, which boasts one of Texas's great downtown scenes, still patrolled on horseback.

Major Ripley S. Arnold established Camp Worth—named after U.S. Army General William Jenkins Worth—on the banks of the Trinity River in June 1849. By August, he moved it to a bluff, and the War Department officially named it Fort Worth the same year. The army evacuated to forts farther west in 1853, and settlers took over. John Peter Smith (for whom the public hospital is named today) started a school with 12 students. Businesses opened—a general store, a flourmill—and the Butterfield Overland Mail used Fort Worth as a western terminus on the way to California by 1856. A bitter county seat war (the other contender was Birdville, Texas, to the east) delayed courthouse construction until 1860. It was finished in the 1870s, only to burn down in 1876.

The Civil War and its aftermath drove the population down to a sparse 175 in the 1860s, but by 1872 the town had three general stores. Incorporated in 1873, the city was beginning to look good to cowboys, tired and hot from long cattle drives on the Chisholm Trail to Abilene, Kansas. Barrooms like Tom Prindle's Saloon and Steele's Tavern were a welcome sight. But Hell's Half Acre, reportedly quite a bit bigger than half an acre—also attracted unsavory types, and allegedly sheltered desperados. Residents fed up with the lawlessness elected a marshal in 1876.

i Fort Worth was named to the 2009 list of America's Dozen Distinctive Destinations by the National Trust for Historic Preservation.

The name Cowtown caught on, and so did "Queen City of the Prairie." By 1900, eight railroads rolled through the town, which was becoming a center for cattle buyers and more businesses including liquor wholesalers, dry goods stores, more stage lines, and meatpacking companies. Three packing companies founded by Fort Worth businessmen, including the Fort Worth Stockyards Co., were open when the railroads—and a $100,000 incentive put together by citizens—attracted two big names: Armour and Co., and Swift and Co. The first livestock were slaughtered in the new plants in 1903. By 1909, the city limits encompassed nearly 17 square miles.

The town had seen six newspapers come and go, but a seventh—the *Fort Worth Star-Telegram*—started in 1909 and is still reporting the news today. Publisher Amon Carter Sr. was a key player in Fort Worth's growth—besides publishing the daily newspaper, Carter had his hand in oil and real estate.

World War I brought the U.S. Army's Camp Bowie, plus three training fields for the Army Air Force. And the city grew, stretching city limits to more than 61 square miles by 1924. The aviation industry, grew, adding Braniff Airways and American Airlines based at Meacham Field in 1927. Carswell Air Force Base opened during World War II in 1948.

By the 1950s, the city was home to Texas Christian University, Texas Wesleyan College, and Southwestern Baptist Theological Seminary. The Modern Art Museum, originally chartered as part of the Fort Worth Public Library and Art Gallery in 1892, opened in a new building as the Fort Worth Art Center in 1954. The Amon Carter Museum opened in 1961, and the Kimbell Art Museum in 1972.

Downtown Fort Worth came to life in 1998 with the opening of Bass Hall, a remarkably beautiful world-class venue that is home to the Van Cliburn International Piano Competition every four years.

In 2000, a devastating tornado struck downtown, leaving the streets filled with shattered glass and twisted metal. Bank One Tower, a part of the city's skyline, suffered some of the worst

Close-up

Timeline

1841: John Neely Bryan starts a permanent settlement that will become Dallas at three forks of the Trinity River.

1846: Dallas County is established.

1849: Major Ripley S. Arnold sets up Camp Worth, which is later officially named Fort Worth.

1860: Fort Worth wins a county seat war with Birdville, and courthouse construction starts.

1865: Texas slaves are freed on June 19, and many African Americans come to Dallas because of its prosperity after the Civil War.

1872: Dallas's first passenger train, the Houston and Texas Central, rolls into the city.

1873: The city of Fort Worth is incorporated.

1900: Fort Worth has eight railroads.

1903: First livestock slaughtered at Fort Worth's Armour and Swift packing plants.

1908: The Great Flood of Dallas kills five people, leaves 4,000 homeless and causes damage estimated at $2.5 million.

1909: Amon Carter Sr. founds the *Fort Worth Star-Telegram*.

1911: A Federal Reserve Bank opens in Dallas.

1915: Southern Methodist University opens in Dallas.

1927: Meacham Field opens and offers commercial passenger airline service in Fort Worth.

1930: Columbus Marion "Dad" Joiner strikes oil 100 miles east of Dallas.

1948: Major industries begin to set up headquarters in Dallas, and in Fort Worth, Tarrant Field Air Drome becomes Carswell Air Force Base.

1963: President John F. Kennedy is assassinated in Dallas.

1972: The Dallas Cowboys win their first Super Bowl, defeating the Miami Dolphins.

1979: Voters approve a Dallas arts district.

1991: The *Dallas Times Herald* closes, leaving the *Dallas Morning News* as the city's only newspaper.

1998: Nancy Lee and Perry R. Bass Performance Hall opens in downtown Fort Worth.

2000: A tornado devastates downtown Fort Worth.

2001: American Airlines Center, home of the Dallas Mavericks, Stars, and Desperados, opens in Dallas.

2002: The new Modern Art Museum of Fort Worth opens in a building designed by Japanese architect Tadeo Ando.

2006: Texas's first W Hotel opens in Victory Park, a $6.5 billion planned development to include luxury condos, hotels, retail stores, and apartments.

2009: Five Sixty by Wolfgang Puck opens in the revolving Reunion Tower, adding a new culinary star to the Dallas skyline.

2011: Dallas–Fort Worth to host Super Bowl XLV at Cowboys Stadium, Arlington.

damage, but was eventually left standing and converted into luxury condominiums.

The Fort Worth Art Center became the Modern Art Museum of Fort Worth in 1987 and moved into a stunning new building designed by architect Tadeo Ando in 2002, a serene and important addition to the city's cultural district.

i Discover the new downtown Fort Worth Information Center, located at 508 Main St. in the historic Jarvis building. This new high-tech, high-impact visitor experience will feature many different options to obtain information, from a personal concierge, prominently displayed brochures, a wall-sized illuminated map, computer stations, video screens, and a 47-inch touch-screen device, appropriately named Molly (she's Fort Worth's cow mascot), the first of its kind in the nation for a convention and visitors bureau. Visit www .fortworth.com.

Today the city is the 17th largest in the U.S., with a population of 702,850, according to the Fort Worth Convention and Visitors Bureau. Hell's Half Acre is no more, but that doesn't keep anyone from having a good time in Cowtown.

For more on Fort Worth's history and culture, check the Texas State Historical Association (www.tshaonline.org); Amon Carter Museum (www.cartermuseum.org); Kimbell Art Museum (www.kimbellart.org); or the Modern Art Museum of Fort Worth (www.themodern.org).

Shoot-out at the White Elephant Saloon

Each year on September 8, Fort Worth's White Elephant Saloon in the Stockyards National Historic District celebrates the most famous and last Old West gunfight to take place in the old Fort Worth neighborhood. Actors re-create the incident that occurred in front of the White Elephant Saloon (then located nearby, on Main Street) on February 8, 1887.

Because the area had become a dangerous place, thanks to the outlaws who loved to spend time here, the town hired T. I. "Longhair Jim" Courtright—marksman, Civil War hero, former marshal, and private detective—to keep order. His illustrious career ended in a duel with gambler Luke Short, who owned the White Elephant and was a friend to Wyatt Earp, Bat Masterson, and Doc Holliday. Courtright's gun jammed, costing him his life, but a subsequent investigation declared the duel legal.

Courtright was buried near the Stockyards at Oakwood Cemetery, which you can find nearby at Grand Avenue at Gould Street, as was Short, who died in 1893 of natural causes. Other notables you'll find buried in the same cemetery include General Winfield Scott, Jim Miller, the gunman who killed the famous lawman Pat Garrett, and various cattle barons who settled Fort Worth.

GETTING HERE, GETTING AROUND

The Dallas–Fort Worth area lies at the northern gateway to Texas, just over an hour's drive (in light traffic, of course) south of the Red River, which separates Texas from Oklahoma. You'll need about four hours, however, to drive due east to the Louisiana state line and some 9 to 10 hours to make the long haul due west to the New Mexico state line. If you want to head down to the Mexican border, it's about a 7-hour drive southwest to Laredo (Texas)/Nuevo Laredo (Mexico) and a 10- to 11-hour drive straight south to the towns of McAllen (Texas)/Reynosa (Mexico) and Brownsville (Texas)/Matamoros (Mexico).

Driving to other important and favorite destinations in Texas takes no small amount of time. Allow yourself a minimum of three hours to drive down I-35 to Austin, a little over four hours along I-35 to San Antonio, and four to five hours on I-45 to Houston. It's about five hours along smaller highways to Lubbock and six to seven to Amarillo. A trip to Big Bend National Park, one of the greater wonders of Texas, is about a 10-hour drive.

Within Dallas–Fort Worth lies a significant web of freeways to learn. One of the trickier parts of the system is the dual naming of Interstate 35. As this major artery courses from north to south, it splits above the Dallas–Fort Worth area at Denton, with the half called I-35E running down through Dallas and the other, I-35W, running through Fort Worth. The two meet again to become one below the Metroplex at the town of Hillsboro leading toward Waco, Austin, and San Antonio. You also need to know that in Dallas, I-35E is called Stemmons Freeway, and in Fort Worth, I-35W is called the North Freeway north of downtown or the South Freeway south of downtown.

In Dallas, the other big freeways are I-635, known as LBJ Freeway, looping around Dallas from Mesquite on the east and northwest through North Dallas and Coppell to DFW Airport; Highway 183/121, called Carpenter Freeway, running from midtown to Irving; I-30, an east-west artery south of downtown called R. L. Thornton Freeway; Highway 75, connecting downtown with North Dallas, Richardson, Plano, and Frisco, called Central Expressway; I-45, reaching southward from downtown and called Julius Schepps Freeway; and Highway 161, a toll road extending from Irving northeast to Plano, called the President George Bush Turnpike. Another toll road is the all-important Dallas North Tollway, connecting downtown with North Dallas, Plano, and Frisco. If you work and play in or near downtown, you'll get to know Spur 366, mostly called the Woodall Rogers, which connects I-35/Stemmons Freeway with Highway 75/Central Expressway.

Fort Worth is less complicated, although its current growth spurt could change that status. For now, I-30W, which cuts through the center of town and reaches west toward Aledo, is called the West Freeway; and I-20, which connects the south side with Arlington and Mansfield, is called Loop 820. Highway 183, reaching northeast from downtown to the airport through Hurst, Euless, and Bedford, is the Airport Freeway. Highway 121 runs from the Airport Freeway northward to Grapevine, Colleyville, and Southlake, and Highway 377 reaches southwest from Fort Worth to Benbrook and Granbury.

BY AIR

Dallas/Fort Worth International Airport

Situated 20 miles from downtown Dallas and 17.5 miles from downtown Fort Worth, DFW Airport is larger than the island of Manhattan and one of the world's busiest with more than 1,900 flights daily. Its territory touches the cities of Irving, Grapevine, and Fort Worth, and it's reached via I-635, Highway 183, and Highway 114 from the east and Highway 183 and Highway 114 from the west. The home airport for American Airlines, you'll find American's flights arriving and departing Terminals A, B, C, and D; all international flights are served through Terminal D, the newest and most beautiful, filled with impressive shopping, dining, and art.

Find a USO Center at Gate B15; an airport chaplain's office at Gate D21; Western Union at B30 and D15; currency exchange at D11, D22, D 24 and D36; and Travelers Aid at B30 and D15. Hotels on airport property include the Grand Hyatt and the Hyatt Regency DFW. If you find yourself at the airport and without some of the techy stuff you need, there's help at kiosks and shops around the airport: Airport Wireless is a store found at A36 and B10; Apple Electronics Automated Shopping is found at B29, C28, and E11; Best Buy Express is at A33, B12, C8, C31, D24, and E33; Brookstone, D20 and D27; InMotion Entertainment, D10, D31, and E16; Samsung, C27; Sony Electronics Automated Shopping, A13, C11, and D20.

Fort Worth's T offers rail service to DFW Airport from Dallas and Fort Worth via the Trinity Railway Express (TRE), with scheduled rail service provided Monday through Saturday. Passengers board the Trinity Railway Express at any of the following train stations located throughout the Metroplex: Union Station, Medical/Market Center, South Irving, and West Irving in Dallas County and at Hurst/Bell, Richland Hills, and ITC and T&P platforms in Tarrant County. Exit the train at CentrePort/DFW Airport Station and take a DFW Airport bus to the remote parking area and another bus to your terminal. A single-trip ticket between the CentrePort/DFW Airport Station and all stations east is $2.50; a single-trip ticket to stations west of CentrePort/DFW Airport Station is $1.50. For more information, call (214) 979-1111 or visit www.trinityrailwayexpress.org.

Flight Times to DFW

Atlanta 2 hours	New Orleans 1.5 hours
Austin 45 minutes	New York 3.25 hours
Boston 3.75 hours	Phoenix 2.5 hours
Chicago 2.5 hours	St Louis 1.75 hours
Denver 2 hours	San Diego 3 hours
Honolulu 8.5 hours	San Francisco 3.25
Houston 1 hour	hours
Las Vegas 3 hours	Seattle 4.5 hours
Los Angeles 3 hours	Washington D.C. 2.75
Miami 3 hours	hours

DFW Airport Parking

In addition to valet parking, you'll find ample parking next to each of the terminals. In addition, there are Express Parking lots just to the north and south of the terminals, with shuttles that pick you up at your parking space and drop you at one of several points in your chosen terminal; and Remote Parking lots lying north and south of the terminals, with shuttles serving a central station at either lot. For current parking availability, call (972) 973-7275. Off-premises parking includes The Parking Spot, (972) 915-3672; Fasttrack Airport Parking, (866) 922-7275; and Park 'n Fly, (972) 471-1194.

Love Field Airport

The city's first commercial air facility, in the heart of Dallas and close to downtown, remains an important Dallas portal. It's home to Southwest Airlines, which offers 121 direct flights daily to Texas, Louisiana, Arkansas, Oklahoma, New Mexico, Mississippi, Alabama, Missouri, and Kansas destinations and to points across the nation through myriad connection points. Love is also served by American Eagle, Continental Express, and ExpressJet. The airport is at 8008 Cedar Springs Rd., (214) 670-7275 or (214) 670-6080, www.dallas-lovefield.com.

Useful Phone Numbers at DFW Airport

Lost and found, 972-574-4420
Valet parking, 972-574-2407
Emergency, 911
Non-emergency police/fire, 972-574-4454
U.S. Customs, 972-973-9825

Commercial Airline Reservation Phone Numbers
Air Canada, (888) 247-2262
Air Tran Airways, (800) 247-8726
Alaska Airlines, (800) 252-7522
American Airlines, (800) 433-7300
British Airways, (800) 247-9297
Continental Airlines, (800) 525-0280
Delta Airlines, (800) 221-1212
Frontier, (800) 432-1359
KLM, (800) 225-2525
Korea Air, (800) 438-5000
Lufthansa, (800) 645-3880
Mexicana, (800) 531-7921
Midwest Airlines, (800) 452-2022
Sun Country Airlines, (800) 359-6786
TACA, (800) 535-8780
United, (800) 241-6522
US Airways, (800) 428-4322

Love Field Airport Parking
Terminal parking includes 7,500 spaces in the ample garage. If you have a Toll Tag, you can pay through your account. For more parking info, call (214) 670-PARK or Park Company of America at (214) 350-4881. Off-site parking includes the Parking Spot, (214) 350-2410.

Car Rentals
The major rental companies are represented at DFW Airport and Love Field, with many city offices, too.
Advantage Rent-A-Car, arac.com, (800) 777-5500
Alamo, www.alamo.com, (877) 222-9075

Avis Budget Group, www.avis.com, (800) 230-4898
Dollar, www.dollar.com, (800) 800-3665
Enterprise Rent-A-Car, www.enterprise.com, (800) 261-7331
Hertz, www.hertz.com, (800) 654-3131
National, www.nationalcar.com, (877) 222-9058
Thrifty, www.thrifty.com, (888) 400-8877
DFW Elite Auto Rental offers exotic and executive cars; www.dfweliteautorental.com, (817) 869-0776

i DART (Dallas Area Rapid Transit) is due to add a station at Dallas Love Field Airport and at the hospital district, near Parkland Hospital and the Children's Medical Center, in 2010. In 2013, DART will complete its $3.3 billion expansion, adding 45 miles of light-rail lines and a new station at DFW Airport.

Shuttle Service
Shuttles between downtown Dallas or Fort Worth and DFW Airport are typically $40 and up.
Super Shuttle, www.supershuttle.com, (800) 258-3826
Yellow Checker Shuttle, www.yellowcheckershuttle.com, (972) 222-2000

Taxi Service
Taxi fares between DFW Airport and downtown Dallas or Fort Worth are usually $40. Taxi fare between downtown Dallas and Love Field is about $20. The prominent cab company is Yellow Cab, (214) 426-6262, www.dallasyellowcab.com. Another is Cowboy Cab Company, (214) 428-0202, www.cowboycab.com.

Car and Limo Service
360 Limo, Inc., www.360limo.com, (214) 348-9898
Book-a-Limo International, www.bookalimo.com, (800) 266-5254
E3 Worldwide Transportation, www.dfwtransit.com, (214) 473-8181
ExecuCar, www.execucar.com, (800) 410-4444
Premier Transportation Services, www.premierofdallas.com, (214) 351-7000

(Q) Close-up

Seven Great Reasons to Get to DFW Airport Three Hours Before Your Flight

Thanks to the spectacular new Terminal D and the magnificent new Skylink rail system, you can enjoy flying to and from DFW again.

Terminal D's two concessions "villages," separated into north and south zones and each measuring 40,000 square feet, provide you with luxuries found in cool airports like those in Detroit and Minneapolis–St. Paul. Even jaded road warriors might admit that DFW has entered an enviable era with the opening of Terminal D.

Arrive early and take in an exceptional meal with a great glass of wine and even get in some superb shopping. This terminal, with its sixty retail spaces, is so sleek and art-filled that you'll almost forget you're in an airport. Even if you're flying out of one of the other terminals, check your bags, get through security, hop on Skylink, and zip over to Terminal D to dawdle here before your flight to any destination. When it's time for you to board, hop back on Skylink and zoom to your terminal in three minutes flat.

No need to feel guilty spending your hard-earned money at the airport, either: A vast majority of the vendors are locally based, and all are required to keep their prices no more than 10 percent above "street" rates.

Star Concessions general manager Linda Mazzei, says the majority of customers seem surprised that there's "real food" at the airport now, and they seem mighty pleased, too. "We get a more worldly clientele who want something better," she says.

So why not avoid the stress and head to the airport early? Even if you don't have much time, all restaurants will box up your food for your flight. Here are seven ways to make the most of your time in TD, as it's sometimes called.

1. Pamper yourself with an 18-ounce "cowboy" rib eye steak at Cool River Cafe. Taking in a meal at this Las Colinas outpost, one of several full-service restaurants in TD, will instantly make you forget you've come to the airport. Even as you pick up the deceptive-looking flatware—it's plastic, as required for security reasons, but is a heavy, shiny, and silver version that looks a lot nicer than you'd think—you'll feel like your fairy godmother came to cook your supper. Perfectly seasoned and topped with a nest of skinny, crisp onion rings, this is a steak to remember. Yes, it will set you back a little more than $34, but this impossibly tender Black Angus cut is a silken wonder that slices easily, even with plastic. North Village, near D25.

2. Scoop up the freshest guacamole within miles. At Cantina Laredo, a full-service restaurant with a great view from its second-floor balcony perch, you can start lunch or dinner with a lush avocado dip, made fresh to order, so there's none of that awful preservative taste. Fresh, warm chips come alongside, but you may want to supplement your order with a platter of carne asada or a bountiful spinach salad topped with grilled chicken (not the prefab kind, hooray!), Mexican cheeses, roasted almonds, and a raspberry chipotle dressing. The house specialty, a Casa Rita, is made with freshly squeezed lime juice, Cointreau, and Sauza Silver. North Village, on the Mezzanine, near D27.

BY RAIL

Amtrak serves Dallas at Union Station and Fort Worth at the Jones Street station. From Dallas you can travel northeast to St. Louis and Chicago and south to San Antonio on the Texas Eagle route; from Fort Worth, you can do the Texas Eagle or head up to Oklahoma City on the Heartland Flyer. Visit www.amtrak.com or call (800) USA-RAIL.

3. Rustle up a cowboy meal at Reata. The best seller at the Fort Worth and Alpine locations of this western-style favorite has long been the tenderloin tamales, and the new TD location is no exception. The presentation involves the splitting open of the tamale, which is topped with a dollop of Mexican crema and a sprinkling of pico de gallo. A good pairing is the sumptuous tortilla soup, filled with shreds of chicken, slices of fresh jalapeños in the broth, and crispy strips of corn tortillas. Other popular picks are stacked chicken enchiladas, the signature chicken-fried steak, and chocolate cobbler for dessert. Don't overlook a Cowboy Cosmo, blending Grey Goose L'Orange with Cointreau and fresh lime juice. North Village, Mezzanine, near D33.

4. Belly up to the Blue Mesa Taco & Tequila Bar. This fast-casual rendition of a Fort Worth/ Southlake favorite for New Mexico–inspired Southwestern cuisine sells a mean steak relleno taco, filled with marinated skirt steak, roasted poblanos, and the signature queso blanco. Burritos come filled with pulled pork and black beans, and nachos can be topped with grilled carnitas. You can wash all those down with a top-shelf margarita, made with fresh lime juice, Cointreau, and premium tequila. North Village, near D31.

5. Get your Irish up at Tigin Pub. If you'd like a side of rugby on TV with a pint of Smithwick's Ale and a hearty platter of superb bangers and mash, this cozy tavern is a destination that will feel like home within about 30 seconds of your arrival. Pull up a stool at the magnificent old wooden table at the center of the pub (like the bar and other furnishings, all millwork was done in Ireland and shipped here) and settle in for a visit with fellow voyagers destined to be your pals. Like you, they're probably torn between other temptations, such as corned beef and cabbage boxty and the Irish breakfast, which includes eggs, sausages, rashers (bacon), black and white pudding, baked beans, tomatoes, and brown bread. South Village, near D20.

6. Before hopping your flight, sip a flight at La Bodega. At the world's second winery in an airport—owner Gina Puente-Brancato opened the first La Bodega in DFW's Terminal A a decade ago—you can relax over a wine tasting at the long wooden bar or you can buy a bottle and sit on the pretty La Bodega patio. Either way, you can enjoy tapas plates of appetizers such as smoked salmon and platters laden with cheeses and sausages while enjoying La Bodega's own vintages, such as private reserve merlot and cabernet sauvignon blends that have won a number of awards. La Bodega also pours and sells wines from thirty Texas wineries, as well as elegant gifts such as Riedel stemware, wine decanters, leather-clad flasks, and gourmet goodies such as fig confit sauce. The shop feels much more like a bistro, thanks to a decor enhanced by artwork on loan from Milan Gallery in Fort Worth. South Village, near D14.

7. Shop here, leaving more free time once you reach your destination. You can get a suit tailored at Malla Sadi Men's Boutique, an exclusive full-service men's store whose original location is in the tony area of Dallas's Oak Lawn retail area, which also sells fragrances, gloves, sweaters, and ties, in the South Village, near D12. You can cowboy up at Buckaroo Duty Free, a two-story store that brings Fort Worth to the airport with a big and unprecedented selection of western gear, along with the typical beauty products, liquors, and Godiva chocolates you'd expect at duty free; in the North Village, near D28. Two Brookstone stores, in the North Village nearest gates D24 to 30 and in the South Village near D18, sell MP3 accessories, noise cancellation headphones, and cushy travel blankets and pillows.

IN TOWN

Trolleys

In Dallas, you ride for free on the McKinney Avenue Trolley (www.mata.org, 214-855-0006), which operates vintage cars daily through the Uptown neighborhood from 7 a.m. Monday through Friday until 10 p.m. Sunday through Thursday and until midnight on Friday and Saturday.

ℹ️ The T, Fort Worth's public bus system, stages its Clean Air Bike Rally each year in late September at Fort Worth Trinity River Park. It is free for bicycle riders of all ages and skills. The first 1,000 cyclists to register for the event receive a free bike rally T-shirt. Registration for the bike rally is required and is encouraged ahead of time at www.cleanairbikerally.eventbrite.com.

In Fort Worth, Molly the Trolley runs vintage-style cars on routes taking you around downtown (free) and to the Stockyards ($1.50 one-way). Schedules vary according to day and season; www.mollythetrolley.com, (817) 215-8600. Choose from three Molly routes:

- Downtown Get Around—this is a free line, operating daily between 7 a.m. and 11 p.m. from late May through November.

Love Field Airport and Southwest Airlines

Long before there was Dallas/Fort Worth Airport, Dallas was well-served by Love Field, begun as a World War I army airfield in 1914. It was named for Lieutenant Moss L. Love, who was killed during a training flight at San Diego, California, on September 4, 1913. In 1927 the city of Dallas purchased 167 acres of the field for $325,000 for use as a private airport, and passenger service to San Antonio and Houston began the next year. Love became an army field again in 1942 and served during World War II as headquarters for the United States Air Transport Command. The military greatly expanded these facilities, and by 1964 Love Field was the largest air terminal in the Southwest.

Love took a big backseat to DFW Airport when it opened in the early 1970s and only Southwest flew from Love Field. In fact, the Civil Aeronautics Board ordered all carriers to use the new airport, but Southwest refused to do so and won a subsequent lawsuit in the matter. Today Love is plenty busy, thanks to the ever-growing prominence of Southwest.

Dallas-based Southwest Airlines operates as a leading domestic carrier providing mostly short-haul, high-frequency, low-fare flights. Begun in 1971, it served three Texas cities, Dallas, Houston, and San Antonio, and was known for its flight attendants in hot pants. Today, the airline operates more than 500 Boeing 737 planes serving 67 cities from coast to coast.

Passengers love the friendly flight attendants—who no longer wear hot pants— and ease of using Dallas Love Field, the airline's home airport. And it's the people behind the airline that make it interesting: More than 1,000 married couples work for Southwest, and the airline boasts a high number of familial relationships, including a mother, father, and daughter who are all Southwest flight attendants, as well as a family in Chicago that has more than 15 family members working for the airline.

Southwest also has a cool community program called Adopt-A-Pilot. More than 500 classrooms across the country adopt a Southwest Airlines Pilot for a four-week educational and mentorship program. Pilots volunteer their time to their classrooms and correspond from the "road" via e-mail and postcards. Kids in schools can chart the pilot's course through an official U.S. route map, and they record daily flying statistics sent by their pilot in the provided Adopt-A-Pilot curriculum.

i Because parking at the Cowboys Stadium in Arlington can be pricey and hard to come by, the T, Fort Worth's bus system, offers a welcome option. Take the Cowboys Coach to the brand-new Cowboys Stadium for all regular season home games. It's just $5 to park at the T&P lot off Vickery Boulevard and $5 for a round-trip ticket to ride. Shuttles will begin departing two hours before kickoff and return as each bus is filled. Visit www.the-t.com.

- Stockyards Shuttle—$1.50 one way, Saturday only, between downtown and the Stockyards.
- Sundance Lunch Line—free, downtown route, 11 a.m. until 2 p.m. weekdays.

When the vehicle approaches, check the overhead sign above the windshield to be sure you're boarding the right trolley. Passenger shelters and trolley stop signs are located along the routes. For your safety, drivers stop only at designated trolley stops. Use the map that shows available routes.

Light-Rail and Bus Service

In Dallas, DART (Dallas Area Rapid Transit) provides service between downtown and several suburban areas via light-rail and bus. For schedules, routes, and fares, call (214) 979-1111 or visit www.dart.org.

In Fort Worth, the TRE (Trinity Railway Express) provides light-rail service between downtown and the suburbs northeast, DFW Airport, and downtown Dallas, as well as bus connections all over town. For details, call (817) 215-8600 or visit www.the-t.com.

Horse-Drawn Carriage

In Dallas, try Belle Starre Carriages, www.carriage tour.net, (214) 855-0410 or (972) 734-3100. In Fort Worth, contact Classic Carriages, www.classic carriages.net.

Driving Tips

Driving in the metroplex can be a hair-raising experience whether you're a seasoned city driver or not. Dallas traffic moves fast and the freeways may seem inexplicable when you're new in town. Pay close attention to your GPS or directions, and be ready to change lanes and merge quickly on the big interchanges.

One of the most puzzling issues is I-35, which is split into I-35E and I-35W south of the Metroplex around Hillsboro. The I-35E fork goes through Dallas, where it takes on the name R. L. Thornton Freeway south of I-30, and Stemmons Freeway north of I-30. The I-35W fork runs on up to Denton, where the freeway becomes one again.

Parking in downtown Dallas is just difficult. You'll more than likely wind up paying at a parking lot unless you have plenty of time to search for a meter.

Both parking and driving in Fort Worth are considerably easier. Do keep an eye out for one-way streets in both cities—the downtown areas have many of them.

Rush hour starts backing up traffic on most major freeways around 4:30 p.m., or as early as 3:30 p.m. on Friday. It can actually save you time to stay put until 6 p.m.

Speed limits vary from 55 to 65 mph on the freeways. Watch them. State and city police are abundant, and they will be watching you.

Also be cautious about using your cell phone while driving. State law allows cities and counties to ban cell phone use in school zones, and some cities including Dallas and Fort Worth have done so.

ACCOMMODATIONS

The hotel scene in Dallas–Fort Worth differs little from most metropolitan areas. In other words, whatever you want, you can find. If you seek simple and modestly priced lodging, it is widely available. The high-end variety is in plentiful supply, too, from traditional and elegant to modern and sleek. Of course, you can find everything in between, as well.

The majority of Dallas's most popular lodgings are downtown and in the nearby Uptown area, as these are in demand among convention attendees and tourists. The hotels along Stemmons Freeway serve the Dallas market buyers and Design District patrons, but the downtown and Uptown hotels are nearby, too. North Dallas tends to offer chain hotel options in various price ranges, with a couple of luxury choices, such as the Four Seasons and Omni hotels, in the Las Colinas area. Boutique hotel choices are growing in Dallas, with the bulk in downtown and nearby.

In Fort Worth, luxury lodging is comparatively limited to the Renaissance Worthington, the Ashton, and the Omni, but more hotels are expected in the next few years. The boutique hotel scene is smaller than it should be in a city of this size, but a few new properties in this category are on the horizon.

Note that pet policies differ among the hotels; some allow pets and will charge an extra deposit or fee, while others limit pets according to size or forbid certain breeds. Ask each hotel about policies.

With only noted exceptions, all hotels are ADA-compliant, with some offering a greater degree of accessibility. Many hotels are becoming smoke-free, but a few still offered smoking rooms at press time. All hotels noted here offer cable TV and telephones in rooms.

Price Code Key

$.................... up to $100
$$ .... $101 to $150
$$$ .... $151 to $225;
$$$$ .... more than $225

HOTELS AND MOTELS

Dallas Downtown

THE ADOLPHUS $$$–$$$$
1321 Commerce St., Dallas
(214) 742-8200, (800) 221-9083
www.hoteladolphus.com
The Adolphus looks and feels like a palace, and for good reason: Built in 1912 as a secondary residence for beer baron Adolphus Busch, the hotel has hosted the likes of Queen Elizabeth II and Norway's King Olaf V, among a long list of dignitaries. Everything about the 21-story Adolphus broadcasts baroque, from the ornately framed portraits and fantastic tapestries and upholstery in public spaces to the grand, Queen Anne–style decor in 422 rooms, including 16 suites. You'll enjoy luxurious bedding, complimentary wireless Internet, luxurious marble bathrooms, flat-screen TVs and DVD players, and, in suites, a choice of garden terraces, entertaining areas, and full-kitchen options. There is a limited, on-site fitness center or the option of (for-fee) passes for the nearby Texas Club, with full fitness facilities. Extensive meeting spaces are available, and the business center includes computer and laptop workstations, color printers, office equipment rental, and desktop publishing. Finest among the

Queen for a Day

The Adolphus Hotel in downtown Dallas makes you feel like royalty, and there's a good reason. Built by beer king Adolphus Busch, the hotel was designed to be his Texas home, and he wanted a place of Edwardian elegance. Everything about it screams baroque, from the heavy, ornate frames around portraits to the Flemish tapestries, Louis XV chairs, and a Victorian Steinway that once belonged to the Guggenheims. Schedule an afternoon tea and see what it feels like to be treated like a queen.

Adolphus offerings, on top of elegant afternoon tea service, is the sublime experience of dining in the widely acclaimed French Room, a restaurant with ceiling murals and sparkling chandeliers. In addition, there's the Bistro Bar and Lobby Living Room; and Walt Garrison Rodeo Bar and Grill. A block from the hotel is Neiman Marcus, which co-hosts with the Adolphus the children's Christmas parade bringing 350,000 spectators downtown.

FAIRMONT HOTEL $$-$$$
1717 North Akard St., Dallas
(214) 720-2020, (800) 257-7544
www.fairmont.com/dallas
One of downtown's landmark hotels, this venerable favorite sets a luxurious tone with its timelessly appealing marble lobby. All 545 rooms and suites impress with Italian decor and cozy pillow-top mattresses, just for starters. Guests already enrolled in the hotel's complimentary President's Club receive exclusive perks such as high-speed Internet and a private reception desk. Specials include an affordable Romance Package, with a presentation of champagne and strawberries on arrival and rose-petal turndown service and breakfast in bed. The fitness center

features Techno cardio machines, and there's a 24-hour business center to go with ample meeting space; the outdoor pool even has its own bar. In 2008, the hotel's famous Pyramid Restaurant and bar got a trendy, modern look after a major renovation.

HOTEL BELMONT $$-$$$
901 Fort Worth Ave., Dallas
(866) 870-8010
www.belmontdallas.com
Here's one of the coolest lodgings to open in Dallas in recent years, although it's not entirely new. This laid-back, mid-century-modern hotel made its original debut in 1946 immediately east of downtown in Oak Cliff and was the work of renowned architect Charles Stevens Dilbeck, whose handiwork is seen in the neighborhood and in the Park Cities. The Belmont got new life a couple of years ago with a magnificent renovation, delivering 68 chic rooms and suites in four buildings, the Moderne Building, the Garden Rooms, the Bungalows, and the Loft Suites; rooms have views either of the pretty gardens or the Dallas skyline. No two are alike, but all are rich with local art and marvelous retro furnishings and colorful fabrics. Ask about rooms with sunken tubs, adjoining bedrooms, or private terraces. The BarBelmont is a neighborhood lounge where you sip wine or martinis, enjoy afternoon snacks, and listen to live music on Thursday evening. Smoke is the hotel restaurant, a snappy redo of the old coffee shop, complete with a great cocktail and wine menu, as well as a lusty Sunday brunch. There's a beautiful swimming pool on-site, as well as a superb health club and meeting rooms.

HOTEL INDIGO $$-$$$
1933 Main St., Dallas
(214) 741-7700
www.ichotelsgroup.com
A 1925 structure built by Conrad Hilton has borne many a hotel name on its doors through the years. Most recently a Holiday Inn called the Aristocrat, it enjoyed a thorough makeover two years ago to become one of a few of this new brand. As the Indigo's emblem is a nautilus shell, the theme

throughout evokes ideas of the beach and ocean, and the color schemes incorporate a range of soothing blues. There are 170 rooms, including 59 suites, on 13 floors. Oversized beds and pillows are lovely, and the glass-encased spa-style shower is a plus. Hardwood floors and area rugs make it feel less like a typical hotel. Some rooms have refrigerators, and there's room service and a concierge, too. The 24-hour fitness center is small, but the equipment is good quality. There's a business center and a small supply of meeting space. There's free transportation within a 3-mile radius, which includes some Uptown restaurants and the Meyerson Symphony Center.

HYATT REGENCY $$–$$$
300 Reunion Blvd. East, Dallas
(214) 651-1234, (888) 591-1234
www.dallasregency.hyatt.com
Having undergone an extensive renovation recently, this shiny hotel with the sparkling ball-topped tower offers 397 rooms, including 20 suites, with most of the suites including kitchenettes. Amenities include in-room safe, in-room fax, Portico bath products, morning newspaper delivery, coffeemakers, and the availability of a business plan that includes Internet access, breakfast, phone calls, and clothes pressing. Rooms offer exceptional city views and comfortable beds. The vast lobby has dining and a bar, as well as a Starbucks cafe. There is a third-floor outdoor pool and a sundeck with Jacuzzi; a 24-hour fitness center; and extensive supply of convention space, meeting rooms, and business services. Guests are in easy walking distance of Dealey Plaza, the Sixth Floor Museum, and the Convention Center. Atop the famous tower, a stunning new restaurant called Five Sixty by Wolfgang Puck brings a new element of Asian-influenced glamour to Dallas dining.

THE JOULE $$$$
1530 Main St., Dallas
(214) 748-1300
www.luxurycollection.com
A Starwood property, the Joule opened in 2008 after an extensive makeover of the 1920s Dallas National Bank building rendered 129 rooms and suites. The renovation by New York architect Adam D. Tihany offers modern lines filled with black-and-white photos by son Bram Tihany, a designer who gave the rooms a posh, contemporary feel with lacquered wood surfaces and dark-tiled showers. There's a 20th-floor, $5,000-per-night penthouse suite with two bedrooms, two terraces, a pool table, and an entertaining kitchen. The lobby is a piece of artwork in itself: There's rotating black iron gear meant to evoke the age of oil in Dallas's heritage, and in the adjacent Charlie Palmer Restaurant, there are gold turbines in the ceiling, making you think that Howard Hughes might walk through the door any moment. A wine cellar offers an extensive selection, along with retail prices for takeaway bottles. The hotel pool sits on a cantilevered rooftop, surrounded by clear walls for a view of the city. A fitness center, 24-hour concierge, and meeting rooms are on-site, too.

MAGNOLIA HOTEL $$–$$$
1401 Commerce St., Dallas
(214) 915-6500, (888) 915-1110
www.magnoliahoteldallas.com
Within a 29-story building that was the city's tallest at its 1922 opening, the charming boutique hotel takes its name from the Magnolia Petroleum Company that called this skyscraper home. That company became Mobil Oil and its lighted red Pegasus on top became Dallas's signature symbol. This 330-room hotel retains original pieces of decor, such as gold-leaf and copper details and chandeliers in the lobby, and offers a variety of room types with few duplicating one another. Guest rooms feature wireless Internet access, large baths with soaking tubs, refrigerators, and premium Egyptian linens, and suites include full-size kitchens and sitting rooms. A recent $3 million update spruced up furnishings and decor in guest rooms and meeting rooms. An on-site fitness center includes Jacuzzi tubs, and a club lounge gives guests a place to read; have a cocktail, snacks, and breakfast; and play billiards. There's complimentary transportation around downtown on weekdays.

SHERATON DALLAS HOTEL $$$
400 North Olive St., Dallas
(214) 922-8000, (800) 444-2326
www.sheratondallashotel.com
Formerly the Adams Mark, this hotel was originally a Sheraton that has come full circle. It's the largest hotel in Dallas, with 1,840 rooms and more than 230,000 square feet of meeting space. A $90 million renovation produced new guest rooms with separate seating areas, LCD flat-screen TVs, and iPod docking stations. On the Sheraton Club level, guests are treated to complimentary breakfast, hors d'oeuvres, and drinks in the evening, and business services, such as copier, fax, and printer use and complimentary office supplies. There are indoor and outdoor swimming pools, and the hotel is connected to the Plaza of the Americas, with its indoor ice-skating rink. Dining choices include the Draft Media Sports Lounge, Peets Coffee & Tea, Chill and the Kitchen Table Restaurant and Lounge. Perhaps best of all, there's a DART light-rail stop in front of the hotel.

THE W $$$-$$$$
2440 Victory Park Lane, Dallas
(214) 397-4100
At the heart of Victory Park, The W faces the American Airlines Center on the northwest corner of downtown and the edge of the Arts District and Uptown. There's a waterwall in the lobby and a terribly chic lobby bar. Flat-screen TVs, iPod docking stations, Bliss spa products, rain showers, spa robes, and ultra-modern decor define the contemporary style of guest rooms. Within the hotel are two major destinations, Tom Colicchio's Craft restaurant and the crazy-busy nightspot called ghostbar. Pets are welcomed with a little red carpet, pet bed and turndown gift, food bowls, and litter boxes. There's a pool bar, too. This hotel caters to a young, chic crowd and is not as much for people seeking quiet pampering.

Dallas Uptown

HOTEL ZAZA $$$$
2332 Leonard St., Dallas
(214) 468-8399, (800) 597-8399
www.hotelzaza.com/dallas

Fascinating and quirky while altogether fashionable, the ZaZa wins fans as much for overall style in 154 rooms as its concept suites, such as the Bohemian, Erotica, Far East, and Rock Star, some of which have private kitchens or large terraces. Enormously popular for weddings and corporate events, it's a good place to entertain or take a pampered vacation. A fabulous spa is on-site, and there's a special pet menu for dog lovers, too. Celebrity guests have included George Clooney, Kate Hudson, Alex Rodriguez, and Lance Armstrong. The Urban Oasis is ZaZa's pool and patio party site, open even in winter with its enclosed tents and a covered pool. The Dragonfly is a popular restaurant, and the hotel offers its Magic Carpet Ride, a car service taking guests to destinations within a 5-mile radius.

RITZ-CARLTON $$$-$$$$
2121 McKinney Ave., Dallas
(214) 922-0200, (800) 542-8680
www.ritzcarlton.com
Among the newer additions to Dallas's luxury hotel inventory, the Ritz takes chic to the next level in Uptown. Within a few months of opening, it made all the top travel magazine lists of the best, hottest, and most luxurious places to stay. There are 218 rooms and 52 suites, all with the ultimate in decor and amenities, and with numerous meeting facilities and services. Guests have immediate access to the Arts District and downtown, and the hotel sits right on the McKinney trolley line. There's a fabulous spa with an extensive menu of treatments, and Fearing's is the most widely acclaimed restaurant in the city.

THE ROSEWOOD MANSION ON TURTLE CREEK $$$-$$$$
3411 Gillespie St., Dallas
(214) 559-2100, (888) 767-3966
www.mansiononturtlecreek.com
A true Dallas legend, the Mansion began as an elegant 1925 home that a member of the famous Hunt oil family bought and converted into a world-renowned restaurant with a widely respected hotel attached. Sitting on five acres in an old Turtle Creek neighborhood roughly two

minutes from downtown, the hotel offers 143 exceptionally comfortable and chic rooms, each with different decor. Guests love the full-service concierge, who finds everything for guests from tailors and hairstylists to dentists, theater tickets, and dinner reservations. The bar is the ideal place to unwind after a long day or to listen to piano music in the evening, and the restaurant suits a power lunch duo as well as a celebratory dinner crowd.

THE STONELEIGH HOTEL $$–$$$
2927 Maple Ave., Dallas
(214) 871-7111
www.stoneleighhotel.com
Opened as the Stoneleigh Court Hotel in 1923, this was the tallest residence hotel west of the Mississippi at the time. The 11-story brick beauty—a favorite of celebrities over the years, from Lauren Bacall and Bob Hope to Tom Cruise and George Strait—has had almost as many lives under various management companies than Dallas has plastic surgeons. Recently, however, it reopened after a $36 million transformation that makes it unequivocally the most gorgeous hotel in North Texas, if not the whole state. There are 170 grand guest rooms and suites, all given updated looks but with distinct Art Deco inspiration, and each with a stunning amount of space in bedroom, bath, sitting room, and closet. The spa is a special version of exquisite, with signature products and services. There's a pool to come, but for now you can chill happily in the lovely bar, which bridges the divine lobby space and the contemporary but ever-so-elegant restaurant, Bolla. In the latter, Iron Chef competitor and James Beard Award nominee David Bull, formerly of the Driskill Hotel in Austin, produces tasting menus of updated Italian fare.

WARWICK MELROSE $$–$$$
3015 Oak Lawn Ave., Dallas
(214) 521-5151
www.warwickmelrose.com
A 1924 landmark in the old Oak Lawn neighborhood that lies adjacent to Uptown, the Melrose exudes an old-world feel the moment you walk

A Star-Studded Landmark

A member of the National Trust for Historic Preservation's "Historic Hotels of America," the Stoneleigh Hotel has been a prestigious Dallas landmark since opening in 1923. Architect F. J. Woerner designed it in the Beaux Arts style, giving Dallas its first luxury high-rise, which was the tallest west of the Mississippi at the time. If you wanted to gawk at stars through the years, you'd come to the Stoneleigh, where the guest register has included everyone from Frank Lloyd Wright, Lauren Bacall, and Judy Garland to LeAnn Rimes, Oliver Stone, and Tom Cruise. A magnificent renovation in 2008 restored the beauty to its proper luster, with a chic spa and graciously hip dining room and bar.

into the marble lobby. Even the standard rooms are oversized, meaning you'll be more than comfortable. The hotel has 184 rooms and 21 suites, along with ample meeting space. Locals are particularly fond of the Library Bar, a favorite watering hole with live piano music. The Landmark Restaurant continues to be a popular place for upscale American food.

Dallas Market Center

DALLAS MARRIOTT SUITES
MARKET CENTER $$–$$$
2493 North Stemmons Freeway, Dallas
(214) 905-0050
www.marriott.com
A 265 all-suite hotel now has 42-inch flat-screen televisions and luxury down comforters in all rooms, which give you separate living and sleeping spaces and a pull-out sofa, in addition to the bed, which is a boon for families. If you're on the

concierge floor, you're treated to a breakfast in the morning and cocktails in the evening in a private lounge. Shuttles to Love Field are free, as is transport to sites within 5 miles of the hotel. Allie's American Grille, Verandah Lounge, and a Starbucks are on property, and there's an outdoor pool and modest meeting spaces.

EMBASSY SUITES MARKET CENTER $$
2727 Stemmons Freeway, Dallas
(214) 630-5332
www.embassysuites.com
Recent renovations at this 224-suite property produced new bedding, living room furniture, wall treatments, and granite countertops, all within the signature, two-room spaces that come with in-room fridge and microwave. Guests all get complimentary breakfast in the morning and cocktails and snacks in the late afternoon. Embassy Kiosks take the stress out of travel with speedy self-serve check in/out, and you can print boarding passes and check flight information. There's complimentary shuttle serve to Love Field and to sites within 3 miles of the hotel. The casual Polo Rose Steakhouse is found in the atrium.

HILTON ANATOLE $$-$$$
2201 Stemmons Freeway, Dallas
(214) 748-1200, (800) 445-8667
www.hilton.com
One of the largest hotels in the Southwest, with more than 1,600 rooms and 130 suites, the Anatole remains a prime meeting destination in Dallas's market area. But the Anatole is about comfort, too, as there's a no-smoking policy throughout the 45-acre grounds. A $58 million makeover upgraded the room decor and amenities and added a spectacular new V-Spa at the popular Verandah Club fitness center that also has three swimming pools, basketball courts, and a boxing gym. There's a world-class art collection throughout the property, including pieces from ancient China and works by Pablo Picasso, and magnificent dining at the 27th-floor restaurant called Nana.

North Dallas and Irving

FOUR SEASONS HOTEL
AND RESORT $$$$
4150 North MacArthur Blvd., Irving
(972) 717-0700, (800) 819-5053
www.fourseasons.com/dallas
Some well-traveled, demanding patrons vow that this is the finest among all Dallas-area lodgings, and why not? Home to the prestigious Byron Nelson Classic, a favorite stop on the PGA tour, this hotel perhaps surpasses the Four Seasons' reputation for extraordinary service and lovely, luxurious decor. Its 397-room spread with 20 suites almost baffles you with its selection of room types. Even the moderate rooms have sitting areas, for example, and the deluxe premium variety overlook the golf courses and have large balconies. The Tower Suite comes with a baby grand piano and wood-burning fireplace, and the Payne Stewart Suite (named in memory of a favorite local PGA star) is penthouse in style, with dining or meeting space to accommodate 14. Villas afford the most privacy, each with 560 square feet of living space, indoor garden courtyard, and golf or pool views. Tournament Players Club (TPC) golf course is among the top courses in Texas, and there's a massive sports club, too, with indoor tennis courts and racquetball and squash courts, indoor running track, half basketball court, indoor heated pool, and personal training available. There are outdoor tennis courts, along with a new family pool, a lap pool, and the spa pool, the latter attached to a full-service, European-style spa with an elaborate menu of treatments. The Café on the Green is the hotel's wonderful dining room; the Terrace Lounge is a good place for cocktails, snacks, and soft music; and 19 is the pub. Wine lovers will be gratified to know that one of the few master sommeliers in Texas is on staff at the Four Seasons.

HILTON PARK CITIES $$$
5954 Luther Lane, Dallas
(214) 368-0400, (800) 445-8667
www.hilton.com
This 224-room hotel may be larger than the typical boutique lodging, but it offers that intimate

🔍 Close-up

Hotel Spas

Among the bonuses in the recent Dallas hotel boom is the addition of spas to the lodging landscape. Several hotels offer lovely spas under their umbrellas; here's a look at the very newest available.

Bliss Dallas—Victory
W Dallas, 16th floor
440 Victory Park Lane, Dallas
(877) 862-5477
www.blissworld.com
Watch a movie during your manicure and abandon yourself to the brownie buffet after a long drive or flight to Dallas at this rightfully well-respected—and aptly named—aerie of pampering. Done in a theme of clouds against clear Bliss blue with clean white contemporary lines, the spa offers tons of trademark targeted treatments like "thinny thin chin" ($45) involving microcurrents and masks for those who hate their necks, or "fatgirlslim" ($150) designed to prepare you for the form-fitting cocktail dress you're slipping into later. They're also reportedly really good with a plain pedicure, using good old-fashioned patience to carefully smooth off calluses. Your improvements are delivered with Bliss twists like manicure tools on conveyor belts to your station, which is equipped with a flat-screen TV, DVD player, rhythm and blues music, and a brownie buffet in a 5,100-square-foot spa with nine treatment rooms.

The Ritz-Carlton Dallas Spa
2121 McKinney Ave., Dallas
(214) 922-0200
www.theritzcarlton.com
This being the only Ritz in Texas and all—the hotel itself a vision of creamy brocades and crisp contemporary touches—the spa is the only place in the state to get Prada Beauty treatments, performed by experts with special training. These start at $195 for an exfoliating body facial and go up to $375 for the men's facial peel. The 12,000-square-foot spa has, among other things, a Vichy treatment room, two VIP/couples rooms, and 12 treatment rooms with their own showers, so privacy is part of the package. Manicures, or "Solar Hand Therapy," start at $55. If travel or house-hunting really stresses you out, go for the "Texas Eight-Hand Massage," a synchronized, 50-minute rubdown by four therapists, $415.

Mokara Spa
Omni Fort Worth Hotel
1300 Houston St., Fort Worth
(817) 350-4123
www.omnihotels.com
Go up to the pool level, above the bustle of Cowtown's newest downtown luxury hotel for peace, quiet, and Texas-style pampering, like the Pecan and Brown Sugar Manicure ($40) that will leave you feeling as pretty as a slice of pecan pie without the calories. Besides the usual couples rooms and treatments for men and women, Mokara has a special menu for teens 14 to 17. The services include a "Clear Skin Facial" ($70); "School Stress Massage" ($45); and teen manicure ($25). If your teen has arrived in Cowtown pale (horrors) from lack of Texas sun, the sunless "Sun Kiss" spray tanning treatment is $60.

feel nonetheless. Sitting in Dallas's prestigious University Park neighborhood next to the fashionable Preston Center shopping center and beside the Dallas North Tollway, it's a well-located, quiet lodging. NorthPark shopping is nearby as well. Rooms on the Executive Floor give you access to complimentary breakfast, hors d'oeuvres, and cocktails. There's a coffee cafe off the lobby, as well as the Tuscany-inspired Opio restaurant. Two swimming pools and a fitness center are on-site, too.

HOTEL LUMEN $$$–$$$$
6101 Hillcrest Ave., Dallas
(214) 219-2400
www.hotellumen.com

This Park Cities property is a Kimpton Hotel, opened in 2007 following a brave redo of a nondescript 1960s motor hotel gone to neglect. Facing Southern Methodist University, the four-story luxury hangout offers 52 rooms and suites flooded with light, especially in the two-story windows in the lobby. The look is minimalist and modern, with rooms awash in blue and cream; several rooms overlook the campus. Bedding features cushy, goosedown duvets; baths have granite countertops and glass-enclosed showers. Suites have separate sitting areas. Behind the lobby is Social, a cozy, sleek restaurant and bar. Room service is available in the evening, and Internet connection is free. There are flat-screen TVs with DVD and CD players in rooms, and fridges and microwaves are provided on request. Meeting rooms are available and business services can be provided, too. Across the street, SMU is home to an extraordinary art collection at the Meadows Museum.

HOTEL PALOMAR $$$–$$$$
5300 East Mockingbird Lane, Dallas
(214) 520-7969
www.hotelpalomar-dallas.com

Another Kimpton hotel, this impressive overhaul of a dated and drab Hilton ended a style drought in the lodging landscape of North Central Expressway. Calling itself the "first luxury urban resort," the Palomar offers 198 rooms, includ-ing 18 one-bedroom suites. Luxury bedding, LCD flat-screen TV, DVD/CD player, free Internet access and French press coffee on request, and L'Occitane bath amenities are standard. Exhale, the on-site spa, is worth the trip alone for mind-body fitness classes and therapeutic skin and body treatments, including acupuncture and cupping. There's much to like at two restaurants, including the original Trader Vic's, home of the mai tai and Polynesian dishes; and Central 214, starring regional American cuisine, with outdoor dining an option. There's a wealth of business and meeting services, and you're just across the street from shopping and the Angelika film theater in Mockingbird Station. If you want to go downtown, the DART rail station is a block away.

NYLO DALLAS $$$
1001 West Royal Lane, Irving
(972) 373-8900, (866) 391-NYLO
www.nylohotels.com

A super-chic hotel near DFW Airport feels as though it was cut out of Manhattan and dropped in the North Texas plains. You'll find an intriguing mix of urban design and earth-friendly operations with all the boutique hotel joys—and you'll wonder if Austin Powers is hiding around the corner. Among pleasant and pampering offerings are allergy-friendly bedding in the 200 guest rooms—here, they are called lofts—and access to a fabulous gym. A 7,500-square-foot courtyard comes outfitted with two heated pools, cabanas, fire pits, and an outdoor bar, too. Complimentary goodies include bottled water in guest rooms, local and domestic long distance phone calls, Wi-Fi throughout the entire hotel, fax and copying services, and shuttle service to the airport. The groovy restaurant called the Loft specializes in sushi, sesame-seared ahi tuna, and Dr Pepper–braised short ribs, as well as a multitude of drink specials.

OMNI MANDALAY LAS COLINAS $$–$$$
221 East Las Colinas Blvd., Irving
(972) 566-0800, (800) 843-6664
www.omnihotels.com

One of a pair of posh properties in Las Colinas urban center, a collection of corporate buildings, shops and restaurants in Irving, the Omni Mandalay lies on Lake Carolyn and near Mandalay Canal. If you're in need of pampering, check out the Sweet Tea Body Gloss at Mokara Spa; if you're after a nice evening dinner, Trevi's is your destination. The hotel's guest rooms are large and include sitting areas, and the Presidential Suite has a fireplace, a grand piano, two bedrooms, and a balcony with patio seating. Families can look into booking a kids' fantasy suite with a connecting room for parents. Another option is Get Fit Guest Room with an in-room treadmill and healthy menu options.

WESTIN AT THE GALLERIA $$$–$$$$
13340 Dallas Parkway, Dallas
(972) 934-9494
www.westin.com/galleriadallas
A weekend packed with retail therapy is filled with sweet dreams at this Westin, which is attached to the Galleria Dallas. The 448-room hotel with 19 suites spoils you with those famous Heavenly Beds and Heavenly Showers, and there's a great gym on-site, too. There's a new executive lounge on the 21st floor, as well.

i In September 2009, the City of Dallas broke ground on the Omni Dallas Convention Center Hotel, which was backed by the sale of nearly $500 million in revenue bonds. The 1,000-room hotel will open on eight downtown acres in early 2012, with skybridge access to the convention center. The new Omni will feature a signature restaurant, lounges, shopping, a high-end Mokara Spa, pool deck, and other features. For business groups, there will be some 80,000 square feet of flexible meeting space, with a 33,500-square-foot Senior Ballroom, a 16,500-square-foot Junior Ballroom, 10,000 square feet of usable outdoor area, and Internet access throughout.

Fort Worth Downtown

BLACKSTONE MARRIOTT COURTYARD $$–$$$
601 Main St., Fort Worth
(817) 885-8700, (800)-321-2211
www.marriott.com
Right in Sundance Square, this historic property sits four blocks from the Convention Center and about 10 minutes from the historic Stockyards. Built as the Blackstone Hotel in 1929, the 23-story structure bears a strong Art Deco facade; the interior has been extensively remodeled and retrofitted with modern design and decor. There's free wireless in public areas, a rooftop swimming pool, mini-gym, and meeting rooms. Pets are allowed with a deposit. Dining is found on the ground floor at Corner Bakery.

i The Blackstone Hotel in downtown Fort Worth, now a Marriott Courtyard, recalls the city's 1920s boom years. Designed by Mauran, Russell & Crowell of St. Louis, who also designed the Galvez in Galveston and the St. Anthony in San Antonio, it is noteworthy for its unusual stepped, spired top. Author Judith Singer Cohen, who wrote *Cowtown Moderne,* called it the only true New York–style skyscraper in Texas. It functioned as a Hilton from 1952 until 1962, and then the hotel sat empty from 1982 until 1999, when Marriott took over and made it pretty again. Although the rooms are modern, the overall look of the Blackstone is yesteryear.

EMBASSY SUITES $$–$$$
600 Commerce St., Fort Worth
(817) 332-6900
www.embassysuites1.hilton.com
A great location a block from Bass Hall and Sundance Square, this all-suite property sits just four blocks from the Convention Center. Each of the 156 suites gives you a separate living room with fireplace and bedroom with Bose stereo and MP3 connection, and both rooms have plasma TVs. Jacuzzi tubs are standard, and bath products are

either Neutrogena or Bath and Body Works brand. There's free wireless in public areas, a free hot breakfast, and nightly happy hour. Swimming pool and fitness center are on-site, too. The 24/7 Embassy BusinessLink Business Center is complimentary with stay. New to the hotel is Thai Tina's, a wonderful Asian restaurant with a pretty bar area.

HILTON FORT WORTH $$–$$$
815 Main St., Fort Worth
(817) 870-2100, (800) HILTONS
www1.hilton.com

Facing the Convention Center, this historic building lies a few blocks from Bass Hall. Its sad claim to fame is that this, when open as the Texas Hotel, was the last place President John F. Kennedy slept in 1963; he delivered a speech to an enthusiastic breakfast crowd and then another outside the hotel on the morning of November 22 before departing for Dallas. Recently renovated at a cost of $10 million, the hotel is a handsome structure with free wireless Internet in public areas and rooms; guest rooms are equipped with Bose stereos and LCD flat-panel TVs, along with clock/radios with MP3 connection. The 1,200-square-foot Presidential Suite has a parlor area and connecting king and double guest room, dining and conference area, and a wet bar. Executive level rooms give you access to the lounge where breakfast and happy hour are offered on weekdays. Pets are accepted, but a deposit is required. The business center, open 24 hours, serves the conference and meeting clientele. There's everyday dining at Café Texas and a full steakhouse experience at Ruth's Chris.

i John F. Kennedy spent his last night in Fort Worth at the old Texas Hotel, now a Hilton, a redbrick landmark facing the Fort Worth Convention Center. Before he left on his fateful trip a few minutes east in Dallas, the President spoke to a crowd in a light November rain outside the hotel. Nearly 47 years later, he will finally be honored when city boosters erect an 8-foot-tall bronze of Kennedy in General Worth Square, one block from the hotel. The privately funded statue was crafted by Texas sculptor Lawrence M. Ludtke.

HOLIDAY INN EXPRESS HOTEL
AND SUITES $$
1111 West Lancaster Ave., Fort Worth
(817) 698-9595, (888) 465-4329
www.ichotelsgroup.com

People looking for a place to stay near the Medical District, downtown, and the Cultural District should give this place some consideration. It's an older property that received a thorough renovation in 2008, but it remains low on the frills scale. There are 132 guest rooms and 24 suites on four floors with free Internet access. There's a free breakfast for all guests, and there's a swimming pool and fitness center, too. A small meeting space is available as well.

HOTEL ASHTON $$$$
610 Main St., Fort Worth
(817) 332-0100, (866) 327-4866
www.theashtonhotel.com

Sitting on the bricked stretch of Main Street a block from Sundance Square, this vintage (circa 1890) office building has been converted to become Fort Worth's first boutique hotel. The 39 oversized guest rooms and suites come equipped with the signature Ashton king-size beds, complimentary wireless, sitting and work areas, Bose stereo systems and iPod docking stations, and Gilchrist & Soames bath products. The signature suites have living rooms, perfect for entertaining. The hotel welcomes small pets; ask about deposit fees. There's a small selection of meeting rooms. Off the lobby, the new 610 Grille serves contemporary American cuisine, and a small bar serves as a good place to unwind at day's end. Afternoon tea is a specialty here, and art fans will appreciate the collection of paintings from the Fort Worth Circle, a group of local artists working between the 1930s and 1960s.

i The Fort Worth Convention Center recently underwent a $75 million expansion and renovation. It now offers 253,226 square feet of exhibit space; 41 breakout rooms for maximum flexibility (with a total of 58,849 square feet of meeting room space); and a 28,160-square-foot ballroom and 13,500-seat arena.

Close-up

End-of-Summer Deals and Packages

A quick staycation in one of Dallas's pretty hotels could be just the break you need. Here are some typical summer-end deals, usually good through Labor Day.

Hotel Belmont
901 Fort Worth Ave., Dallas
(214) 393-2300 or (866) 870-8010
www.belmontdallas.com

The renovated, classic 1940s courtyard hotel perched on a hilltop just west of downtown looks like it came from a Hollywood film set. More than a dozen different room designs include garden rooms and suites and loft suites and bungalows, each offering garden, pool, or downtown views. The restaurant, Smoke, offers all sorts of regional foods cooked over hardwood fires. In addition, there's stylish eating and drinking to be done in BarBelmont, and sometimes you'll find a hotel poolside party in progress. The Belmont Health Club can help you get rid of some indulgence guilt.

When you're ready, the hotel staff will shuttle you over to the nearby Bishop Arts District, a trendy little neighborhood in Oak Cliff with some fifty restaurants and boutiques. The American Airlines Center and Victory Park are in easy reach, as is the Dallas Museum of Art.

The Weekend Steal Deal Package in 2009 offered a third night free if you stay Friday and Saturday night, starting at $109 per night for a standard and topping out at $199 for a suite. If you just want to stay one night and add a champagne breakfast, you standard room plus the meal is $157.

Four Seasons Hotel and Resort
4150 North MacArthur Blvd., Irving
(972) 717-0700
www.fourseasons.com/dallas

Unless you've stayed at this Las Colinas retreat, home to the Byron Nelson Golf Classic, you wouldn't realize it offers one of the finest spas in the country. The spa will cost you, but all guests can use the fabulous fitness facility (a favorite workout spot of Jessica Simpson's) for free, as well as lounge by the lagoon-like main pool or at the new family pool, complete with a sand beach. There are 34 new Club Villa rooms overlooking the golf course, bringing the villa total to 124 and the overall guest room count to 431.

If you're into food and wine, you'll be spoiled by Chef Katie Natale, who sources fresh ingredients from local suppliers and staff sommelier James Tidwell, a friendly wine expert who's one of just four master sommeliers in Texas. But if you want to wander around, take your camera and go photograph *The Mustangs of Las Colinas,* the largest equestrian sculpture in the world. The bronze of nine wild mustangs crossing a granite stream in Williams Square Plaza is gorgeous, day and night.

The typical summer Spa Getaway rate starts at $360 for superior room and includes a massage, facial or mani/pedi for one, along with breakfast buffet for two. There's a three-for-two deal in which you get a third night free if you pay for two consecutive nights. Rates start at $225 for a moderate room with a golf course view, small balcony, marble bathroom with deep soaking tub; with the third night you wind up averaging $150 per night. Or book the Summer Escape Package, in which you get a moderate room for $195 and a 25 percent discount on room charges and meals, plus free meals for kids under 12.

Hotel Palomar
5300 East Mockingbird Lane, Dallas
(214) 520-7969, 800-KIMPTON
www.hotelpalomar-dallas.com

A superchic Kimpton Hotel, the Palomar is the clever reinvention of a 1960s Hilton on North Central Expressway. It helped make the boutique hotel genre familiar in Dallas, and provides luxury bedding and French press coffee in your room. On-site, Exhale is the top-rate spa, and there are two restaurants, the original Trader Vic's, where sipping mai tais has never been more fun; and Central 214, where chef Blythe Beck makes food an adventure.

You're right across from Mockingbird Station, where you can blow the better part of a day shopping at Urban Outfitters and the Gap and seeing a film at the eight-screen Angelika, a theater showing mostly indie films. Vapiano and Urban Taco are among new hit restaurants there.

The Palomar's last Summer Playground Package was a hoot: If you could Hula-hoop at the front desk for one minute, your room rate was half-price. If you could Hula-hoop for just 20 seconds, you got a free room upgrade, with drinks and snacks included at happy hour. Playground rates start at $199.

NYLO Dallas
1001 West Royal Lane, Irving
(972) 373-8900, (866) 391-NYLO
www.nylohotels.com
A new and very hip lodging, the NYLO meshes urban styling, green construction and practices, and boutique sensibilities to deliver upscale lodging near the airport. There's a very nice gym and 200 guest rooms (called lofts) that feature allergy-friendly environs. There's a 7,500 square-foot courtyard with two heated pools, cabanas, fire pits, and an outdoor bar, too.

NYLO's drinking and dining spaces include a sushi bar, game room, and library. Menu intrigues include sesame-seared ahi tuna, white bean hummus with grilled flatbread, Dr Pepper–braised beef short ribs, and Thai curry spring chicken. If you want to sip your way through your staycation, check out happy hour specials, such as $2 off specialty cocktails, $5 selected wines by the glass, half-price sushi and sashimi on Monday, and half-price selected apps on Wednesday. Itch-

ing to venture out? Check out La Buena Vida and other wineries in downtown Grapevine, less than 10 minutes away. Summer rates start at about $79 on weekends and $139 weekdays.

Stoneleigh Hotel
2927 Maple Ave., Dallas
(214) 871-7111
www.stoneleighhotel.com
A grande dame in Big D, this 1923 residential hotel in Uptown was graced by the interior design of New York's Dorothy Draper and beloved by stars like Katherine Hepburn and Andy Warhol in its lengthy heyday. When a bit too well worn, the Stoneleigh underwent a massive $36 million restoration that returned her to delicious glory. Within the 11-story beauty are 170 magnificent guest rooms and suites with Deco-inspired looks, including teal, cinnamon, aqua, and ivory detailing; original crown and door moldings; soaring windows; and vintage (but lovely) bathrooms. Do your mind and body a favor and book some time in the Stoneleigh's wonderful spa, where summer specials typically include a warm aromatherapy oil upgrade on Tuesday with any booked massage; an organic sugar foot scrub with a 25-minute focused massage, a $99 combo deal on Wednesday; and a free 20-minute mini-facial on Thursday or a $70 full facial upgrade. Just be sure to book a table for dinner at Bolla, where weeknight deals often include a four-course dinner for $40. If you want something simple, head across the street for one of the famous burgers and a pint of ale at the Stoneleigh P, a former pharmacy and favorite watering hole since the 1970s.

The Dallas Deluxe package includes one night in a premier guest room, champagne at arrival, valet parking, and Wi-Fi, starting at $189; and the Deep in the Art of Texas Package includes one night in a premier guest room, two tickets to the Nasher Sculpture Center and to the Dallas Museum of Art, transportation to both museums, valet parking, and Wi-Fi, starting at $199.

OMNI HOTEL $$$$
1300 Houston St., Fort Worth
(817) 535-6664, (800) 444-OMNI
www.omnihotels.com

Considered the official Convention Center hotel, this beautiful new addition to the downtown landscape is much more. A meeting facility in itself, the stone-and-glass masterpiece commands attention with its contemporary design and its wealth of offerings. There's an abundance of contemporary western art in public spaces that appears to be specially selected for this setting. Of interest to those who try to travel in healthful manner, the hotel offers an in-room fitness option with a Get Fit Kit, and there's a healthy meal option at each of the hotel's dining facilities. On site, the Mokara Spa (www.mokaraspa .com/fortworth) will spoil you, as will the fitness center, swimming pool, and pool bar. Suites offer kitchenettes; the largest suite is 1,825 square feet with living and entertainment rooms, formal dining, and a large guest bathroom. Regular guest rooms come with a jack pack, which allows most portable electronics to connect with the flat-screen TV. There's the Omni Sensational Kids Program, too. Restaurants at the Omni include Bob's Steak and Chop House; Cast Iron, the everyday restaurant; the Wine Thief, a quiet, dark spot for wine, cognac, and small plates; Whiskey and Rye, a sports lounge with light and hearty dining; and a Starbucks.

RENAISSANCE WORTHINGTON $$$–$$$$
200 Main St., Fort Worth
(817) 870-1000, (800) HOTELS-1
www.marriott.com

Perhaps the perfect Fort Worth location, with an address on Sundance Square, the Worthington is your pick if you want to be close to Bass Performance Hall and lots of shopping and dining. It was the city's first four-diamond hotel and its 504 newly renovated rooms keep it atop the list of desirable stays. Sleek styling in the public rooms and guest rooms offer a bit of western chic in the detail, and it's a generally warm, welcoming place. There's wireless Internet connection in the public areas and guests pay a fee for daily wireless and local and long-distance phone calls in the rooms. On site, find Vidalias, the three-meals-a-day restaurant with upscale southern cuisine; the Lobby Bar, with drinks and appetizers; a coffee lounge; and a fitness center with indoor and outdoor pools and workout facilities. There are pet policies in place and, like at most hotels, cribs are available, and you can inquire about babysitting. A full-service business center serves the ample (57,000-square-foot) meeting-space area of the hotel.

SHERATON DOWNTOWN $$–$$$
1701 Commerce St., Fort Worth
(817) 335-7000, (800) 325-3535
www.starwoodhotels.com/sheraton

A half-block from the Convention Center at the south end of downtown, this extensively renovated hotel manages to offer an interior that's both warm and sleek. There are 431 guest rooms with pretty new wooden furnishings and modern art, as well as big flat-screen TVs and Bliss bath products; Club Level rooms give you access to the lounge with free breakfast and happy hour. In addition to a 24-hour fitness center, there's Spa Beaubelle, an 8,000-square-foot luxury spa with yoga room and Pilates studio and six treatment rooms; you can book in-room massage here, too. Dogs are accepted, with proper deposit, and doggie beds are offered. A business center is available, offering 22,000 square feet of meeting space. Off the lobby, find the steakhouse and sports bar called Shula's 347 Grill.

Fort Worth Stockyards

HYATT PLACE FORT
WORTH STOCKYARDS $$–$$$
132 East Exchange Ave., Fort Worth
(817) 626-6000, (888) 492-8847
www.stockyards.place.hyatt.com

Found at the east end of the Stockyards, next to Stockyards Station, this is a great place to stay with family who want to make a weekend of the Stockyards' horseback riding, guided tours, shopping, and dining. A modern, new lodging, this has complimentary high-speed Wi-Fi Internet in public spaces and an Internet room with free access to computers and printers. There's a swimming pool and fitness center, too. Each guest room is equipped with the Hyatt Plug Panel and a 42-inch flat-panel HDTV in the media/entertainment center. Meeting facilities are on-site, as is a business center. The continental breakfast is free and a hot breakfast is available for purchase.

STOCKYARDS HOTEL $$–$$$
109 East Exchange Ave., Fort Worth
(800) 423-8471
www.stockyardshotel.com
Perhaps the crown jewel of the National Historic Stockyards District, this pretty old hotel sits in the thick of the Stockyards' attractions. Billy Bob's Texas is a three-minute walk, Cowtown Coliseum is next door, and the White Elephant is across the street. Originally opened in 1907, the hotel bears a National Historic Register marker and has long been known for its big lobby and pure Old West atmosphere. Renovated in recent years, the inn features 52 rooms and suites with Victorian, Western, Native American, and mountain man themes. Several suites are named for characters, including Butch Cassidy, Davy Crockett, Geronimo, and Bonnie and Clyde. There's wireless Internet, modern electronics, mini-bars, and in-room safes. Pets are welcome with a deposit. Meeting services and catering are offered, too.

Fort Worth Cultural District
COURTYARD BY MARRIOTT ON UNIVERSITY $$
3150 Riverfront Dr., Fort Worth
(817) 335-1300, (800) 321-2211
www.marriott.com
Across the street from the Residence Inn, this newer property faces the Trinity River and is just a few blocks from the Botanical Garden. There are indoor and outdoor swimming pools and a small fitness center, and suites offer separate living rooms. The Courtyard Café serves a breakfast buffet and offers a menu. There are two small meeting rooms and a business center. There's no elevator, but the staff will help with luggage.

RESIDENCE INN $$
1701 South University Dr., Fort Worth
(817) 870-1011, (800) 331-3131
www.marriott.com
Here's a perfectly located hotel if you're planning to spend time at Texas Christian University, in the Cultural District, or visiting the Fort Worth Zoo. Situated on the Trinity River bank and alongside its jogging trails, the apartment-like motel offers free wireless in public areas, a swimming pool, fitness center, and free hot breakfast and happy hour. Pets are accepted with a deposit, and there are business center services. Ask about grocery shopping service.

RESIDENCE INN FORT WORTH CULTURAL DISTRICT $$–$$$
2500 Museum Way, Fort Worth
(817) 885-8250, (800) 331-3131
www.marriott.com
Situated midway between downtown and the Cultural District next to Trinity Park, this is one of the first businesses located in a new multipurpose development called So7 (South of Seventh). You'll find free wireless in public areas and free wired Internet in the guest rooms and suites, the latter with full kitchens. A fitness room is on-site, along with a swimming pool and a courtyard barbecue area. Bring your pets, but be prepared to pay a nonrefundable deposit. There's a business center, meeting space, and shuttle service for destinations within 5 miles. The hotel offers a grocery-shopping service, and there's a free hot breakfast and weekday happy hour.

Fort Worth, DFW Airport
GAYLORD TEXAN $$$–$$$$
1501 Gaylord Trail, Grapevine
(817) 778-2000
www.gaylordhotels.com/gaylord-texan
You'll know you're in Texas when you enter the Gaylord, because everything here is larger than life. At the center of the massive complex is a facade of the Alamo, and pathways leading to various meeting areas, guest rooms, and a multitude of restaurants and shops that emulate

San Antonio's famous River Walk. There are 1,511 luxurious guest rooms, including 127 suites. Each room offers wireless Internet, two phones, in-room coffee, refrigerator, double vanities, and a laptop charger in the safe. Dining includes the posh Old Hickory Steakhouse for Black Angus beef, artisanal cheeses, and a remarkable wine list; Southwestern cuisine in a courtyard setting at Ama Lur; Texan Station, a sports fans' dream, with two bars and a 52-foot screen; the Riverwalk Café, the everyday family restaurant; and Glass Cactus, a nightclub overlooking Lake Grapevine and offering the largest list of tequilas in the state.

GRAND HYATT DFW $$–$$$$
2337 South International Parkway, Fort Worth
(972) 973-1234
www.granddfw.hyatt.com
Attached to the new, glitzy international termi-nal, Terminal D, this exceptional hotel caters to the well-heeled globe-trotter. Sleek and sophis-ticated, it became instantly popular for special, sound-proofed rooms and a good sleep in the primo Hyatt Grand Beds. The bathrooms are fabulous, with granite detail and separate showers and soaking tubs. Meeting facilities are numerous, and there is a full spa, rooftop swimming pool and a fitness center with excellent equipment. Food gets special attention at this Hyatt, starting with an intriguing Epicurean Studio Weekend offering, allowing you and your spouse or a pal to take hands-on cooking lessons in a fabulous hotel kitchen and tour the nearby wineries in Grape-vine. The Grand Met features an iTaste menu that customizes wine, cheese, and chocolate tasting programs. M Lounge is a friendly bar and Moka is the hotel's coffee/pastry shop.

GREAT WOLF LODGE $$–$$$
100 Great Wolf Lodge, Grapevine
(817) 488-6510
www.greatwolf.com
Just about five minutes from the airport is this 400-room property that is all about keeping moms, dads, and kids happy. Suites sleep from four to eight guests, and each suite has styling that includes

granite countertops and mini-refrigerators. Kids sleep in their own "wolf den," a cave-like area with bunk beds, movies, and Nintendo on their own flat-screen LCD TV. Parents hang out in their own part of the suite, with a queen bed and full-size sleeper sofa. When it's playtime, the options are mind-boggling: There's Fort Mackenzie, a four-story interactive treehouse water fort where everyone gets soaked on 12 different levels, complete with slides, bridges, soaker buckets, and more. For teens, there's the gr8_space, with Internet access, iPod and other mp3 docking stations, all sorts of gaming options, and video watching. An arcade is on-site, too, and for moms (and dads) who need to really chill, there's a full-service Aveda spa, with massage, manicure, pedicure, facial, and more on the menu. Be sure to ask for packages, many of which may include special room deals at slower times of the year and may be combined with spa and meal options, too.

HYATT REGENCY DFW $$–$$$
International Parkway
P.O. Box 619014
DFW Airport
(972) 453-1234, (888) 591-1234
dfwairport.hyatt.com
The first of two Hyatt properties to open at Dallas/Fort Worth Airport, this one has been frequently renovated to remain contemporary. Only when the flashy new Grand Hyatt opened across the way did this one seem a bit dated. Nevertheless, it's a good hotel with everything you'd need if you're here on a layover or wanting to spend the night before a very early-morning flight. There's wireless Internet access, of course, and each guest room has a desk in a work area for the business traveler. Suites come with one, two, or three bedrooms with dining/conference area and kitchenette, too. There are business and meeting facilities on-property, as well as a swimming pool and updated fitness center. Fine dining is at the pricey Mister G's, which offers an unexpectedly impressive wine cellar; Jacob's Spring Grille is the everyday restaurant, and there's a coffee bar and Aces Lobby Bar, with a sports theme, on-site, too.

INNS AND BED-AND-BREAKFASTS

Dallas

BAILEY'S UPTOWN INN $$$–$$$$
2505 Worthington St., Dallas
(214) 720-2258
baileysuptowninn.com
You can walk to galleries, bistros, and pubs along the brick-paved McKinney Avenue from this well-located, contemporary town house built in 2003 in the historic State-Thomas neighborhood in Uptown. Simple but handsome and cheerful, the inn's six tasteful guest rooms with private baths offer equal doses of comfort, security, and value for the business traveler and the solo or duo leisure visitor seeking convenience and quiet. The Blue Room offers a Jacuzzi, and several rooms offer a writing desk, fireplace, or porch. You'll like the pleasant reading area in the downstairs living room; satellite TV in guest rooms and wireless Internet connection throughout; full breakfast weekdays, continental-plus on weekends; guest services including theater tickets, dinner reservations, and limo bookings; modest business services; and daily housekeeping. There are no ADA-compliant rooms.

DAISY POLK INN AND COTTAGE $$–$$$$
2917 Reagan St., Dallas
(214) 522-4692
www.dailypolkinn.com
Tucked into the heart of Cedar Springs, the city's fashionable gay neighborhood near Uptown, this charming inn offers three cozy rooms with private baths in the 1904 Arts & Crafts–style home and three more in the spacious, newly renovated guesthouse to the rear. International business travelers and weekend retreaters seeking an affordable getaway will appreciate the thoughtful composition of New England, French, and New Orleans antiques that add up to a tidy and immensely comfortable lodging, especially with heated floors, full kitchen, and laundry facilities in the cottage. You'll find wireless Internet and flat-screen TVs with DVD players throughout;

wine and cheeses upon arrival; better bath amenities; fabulous parlors and dining spaces; daily housekeeping and individual room security; an innkeeper helpful with reservations and tickets to museums and events; wonderful baked goods in the morning; and good proximity to better dining and an excellent bar in nearby Melrose Hotel, a few steps away. The only caveat is that the rundown apartments across the street are an eyesore, but they're expected to be torn down within a year or two. There's no wheelchair access for the main house, and the main house bathrooms are a bit cramped.

> **i** More than 70,000 hotel rooms are available in the Dallas area, and 1 in 11 Dallas-area workers is employed in the hospitality industry.

HOTEL ST. GERMAIN $$$$
2516 Maple St., Dallas
(214) 871-2516
www.hotelstgermain.com
The spirit of vintage New Orleans, imbued with hints of Paris, awaits within a richly renovated manse on a swanky stretch of Uptown once known as Millionaires' Row. Elegant parlors exude old world gentility and shabby-chic sophistication in antique furnishings, exquisite roses in silver bowls, and the burnish of candlelight. Ideal for romantic liaisons, the seven private, secure suites offer luxurious furnishings, fresh flowers, fireplaces, TV/CD-DVD players hidden within armoires, Internet connection, and thoughtfully prepared bathrooms, with Bulgari amenities and plush robes. Here, you have immediate access to museums, galleries, restaurants, and shopping; a multilingual staff that serves champagne, fruit, and cheese at arrival and arranges tickets, reservations, transportation, and limited business services; a 24-hour butler that will escort guests to rooms at any hour; automatic ice bucket refills; twice-daily housekeeping; full breakfast on fine china en suite, in the dining room, or on the terrace; and an elaborate, seven-course dinner served by reservation. There are no ADA-compliant rooms, however.

Fort Worth

ETTA'S PLACE $$–$$$
200 West Third St., Fort Worth
(817) 255-5760, (866) 355-5760
www.ettas-place.com

Named for Etta Place, the alleged girlfriend of the Sundance Kid, this little bed-and-breakfast inn became a hit in Fort Worth's Sundance Square long before boutique inns were commonplace. Smack in the middle of downtown, the comfortable lodging with 10 efficiency suites—each with kitchenette, sitting areas, big private baths, cable TV, Internet access, and robes—brings a homey but polished feel to the urban stay. Furnishings include antique chairs, writing desks and bed, quilts and lace sheets, wood-and-iron tables, and wicker chairs. Best is the honeymoon suite, with the most seclusion, as well as a Jacuzzi tub for two and glassed-in shower. Whatever you'd like, from champagne and chocolate-covered strawberries, car service, or carriage rides to massage or flower arrangements, Etta's can arrange. Shopping awaits in all corners of Sundance Square, and nearby dining includes Reata, a half-block away, and Grace, Del Frisco's, Vidalias, and Mi Cocina.

MISS MOLLY'S IN THE
STOCKYARDS $–$$$
109 West Exchange Ave., Fort Worth
(817) 626-1522
www.missmollyshotel.com

Cowtown's first B&B, this cute excerpt from the Old West puts you in the midst of the historic Stockyards fun. Occupying the second floor of a 1910 building, the space has served as a proper boarding house and then a brothel. A sense of days past holds steady with the absence of TVs and telephones in each of the seven guest rooms, all of which features period and replica antiques. Decor themes include cowboy, rodeo, oil boom, and railroad era, and all rooms open onto a main parlor area. Only Miss Josie's Room, the one said to have been the madame's quarters when girls rented their bedrooms by the hour, offers a private bath. The others share hall bathrooms, with iron bathtubs and pull-chain toilets. If you like a good ghost story, this is your place; Miss Molly's is said to be one of the most active paranormal places in Texas. If you like a good, simple steak with a cold beer, head downstairs to the Star Café, a friendly eatery just below the inn.

TEXAS WHITE HOUSE $$–$$$
1417 Eighth Ave., Fort Worth
(817) 923-3597, (800) 279-6491
www.texaswhitehouse.com

Found within a handsome 1910 home near the Medical District on Fort Worth's South Side, this B&B makes a good choice if you seek something quiet. There's a wraparound porch where you can sit with coffee in the morning or a good book on a temperate afternoon, and there's space for business meetings, too. The hosts will arrange food and drink if you want a catered gathering. You can stay in one of three large guest rooms in the main house, each with private baths and seating areas, or in one of two suites in the carriage house, which offers fireplaces, whirlpool tubs, large sitting areas, private entrance, small fridges, and microwaves. There's a full breakfast daily with stay; for other meals, nearby choices include Esperanza, Chadra Mezza Grill, Ellerbe Fine Foods, Benito's, Lili's Bistro, and Cat City Grill.

RESTAURANTS

Some people find it surprising that Dallas has more restaurants per capita than even New York City, but this shouldn't be hard to swallow. Texans love good food and Texas restaurateurs know how to put it on a plate.

Of course, you'll find an ample supply of places in the Dallas/Fort Worth metroplex that fall into what we like to call the Texas Trilogy—that's beef, barbecue, and Tex-Mex. Burger places have grown in number exponentially in the past few years, and the population of steak restaurants shows no sign of slowing, the economy be damned. As our Hispanic population grows and the popularity of Tex-Mex food increases among all palates, our supply of food with flavors from south of the border appears bottomless.

Although DFW doesn't have any Italian heritage, the depth of good Italian dining appears to be getting better. The availability of really good pizza has improved dramatically in recent years, as have options in sushi and other Asian dining. Other ethnic food has come along lately, too, with Middle Eastern a prime example.

We're still really big on comfort food in Texas; some folks call it country food, others think of it as Southern cooking, and many people just consider it good home-cooking that Grandma provided. We have our share of celebrity chefs, too, and most of them are heading up what are commonly called upscale American dining venues.

There's far more good stuff to eat than we could possibly cover here, so this is a selective, rather than a comprehensive, guide. One thing is for sure—you won't go hungry here.

Up until recently, Dallas has been a strict dress-for-dinner kind of city. But Chef Dean Fearing defied the Dallas coat-and-tie dinner protocol when he declared his Fearing's restaurant at the Ritz-Carlton, Dallas would have no dress code. His former restaurant at the Mansion at Turtle Creek also has done away with the dress code in order to be more inclusive. That said, you can't stroll into these fine dining establishments in your sneakers and tank tops, even if this is Texas.

You still would not be embarrassed at all in a coat and tie, but for men, nice jeans, a stylish shirt, and good shoes are fine. Similarly for women, you can't go wrong with a dress, but nice jeans with heels and a chic, tasteful top won't attract any stares of the wrong kind.

Price Code Key

The price key symbol found in each listing is the approximate price for a meal for two including an appetizer, entree, nonalcoholic beverage, and dessert. Where restaurants have a wide variety of entrees, you'll find a price range with the listing.

$	Less than $25
$$	$26 to $45
$$$	$46 to $70
$$$$	more than $70

DALLAS AREA

American Casual

BREAD WINNERS　　　　　　　　　　　$$
3301 McKinney Ave., Dallas
(214) 754-4940
www.breadwinnerscafe.com
This is a trendy but personable cafe in bustling Uptown, found within an early 20th-century pharmacy building that feels very New Orleans in style. Stop by for a relaxed breakfast, a professional

lunch, or a candlelit dinner. The menu is full of eclectic and healthy items, including 20 different salads. Try brunch specialties such as beef brisket hash with eggs or Julio's Huevos.

CAFE BRAZIL $$
3847 Cedar Springs Rd., Dallas
(214) 461-8762
www.cafebrazil.com

Open 24/7, this rather Boho coffee shop serves up a mean Mexican omelet and a lovely plate of crepes stuffed with spinach, onion, tomato, and feta. The pulled pork sandwich deserves attention, and your sweet tooth will be satisfied with an order of chocolate chip or butterscotch chip pancakes. The coffee, as you might guess by the name, is primo. (Check the Web site for nine other locations in town.)

i The Greater Dallas Restaurant Association, a local chapter of the Texas Restaurant Association, has more than 1,000 members and is one of the largest trade associations in Dallas. The GDRA provides more than $100,000 annually in scholarships to further culinary education in North Texas, and it supports a program called FSPrep in 22 schools in North Texas. FSPrep combines nationally accredited culinary arts instructional materials into a user-friendly resource for secondary level teachers, offering a well-rounded approach to culinary education benefiting students, teachers, schools, and parents.

DRAGONFLY AT THE HOTEL ZAZA $$$
2332 Leonard St., Dallas
(800) 597-8399
www.hotelzazadallas.com

Inside the hipper-than-thou hotel in Uptown, this dining room urges you to start brunch with a Wake Up Call, a cocktail blending Grey Goose L'Orange, mango, and fresh lime juice. That pairs nicely with lobster-mushroom-tarragon omelet or blueberry pancakes. At dinner, try the grilled quail with salsa verde as an appetizer, followed by the pan-seared scallops with parsnip puree and braised fennel.

THE DREAM CAFÉ $$
2800 Routh St., Dallas
(214) 954-0486
www.thedreamcafe.com

A favorite for breakfast but superb at lunch and dinner, too, this longtime staple in the Quadrangle served organic, natural foods in a hip setting way before such a concept was fashionable. Try Grady's Omelet, with smoked salmon (lox), spinach, tomato, and herb cream cheese; the signature Cloud Cakes, fluffy ricotta pancakes topped with fresh strawberries and crème fraîche; or Sonoma Squash, roasted acorn squash stuffed with brown rice, pecans, currants, shallots, and goat cheese.

THE GRAPE $$$
2802 Greenville Ave., Dallas
(214) 828-1981
www.thegraperestaurant.com

Fiercely loyal patrons from the surrounding M Street neighborhood frequent this trend-proof, Lower Greenville gem at least twice a week, and everybody else wishes they could. Tables on the quintessential urban bistro's sidewalk are delightful but the dark, intimate inside seating is irresistible for romantic duos. Smart staffers help diners navigate an inspired wine list that's packed with unusual and very affordable finds, as well as the exceptional by-the-glass choices. Don't miss the signature mushroom soup, nor specials, such as grilled ahi tuna dusted in cumin and topped with caper butter.

HATTIE'S $$
418 North Bishop Ave., Dallas
(214) 942-7400
www.hatties.com

Sophisticated southern charm makes this delightful stop in Bishop Arts District a neighborhood hit. Thick tomato soup with grilled cheese and buttermilk fried chicken salad are lunch favorites, while dinner winners are bacon-wrapped meat loaf and pulled pork over grits. It's a popular date place and reservations are strongly recommended.

Close-up

Fabulous French Fries

If you truly love french fries, you know they're far more than a side item. This favorite edible has evolved into a glorious gastronomic experience, whether you're talking about the most simple burger-stand sort, with salt and ketchup, or gussied up in fancy restaurants, with elegant oils and herbs. And just ask anyone who's watching what they eat: they're likely to give up about 40 other sinful foods before they'd pass up a handful of good fries.

Here's a look at some of the best fries in Dallas–Fort Worth.

Brix Pizza & Wine Bar (2747 South Hulen St., Fort Worth; 817-924-2749; www.brixpizzeria .com): Hell's Kitchen Fries, a creation by owner-chef Daniele Puleo, are a regular cut, not too thin but just crispy outside, tossed with crumbled gorgonzola (blue cheese) with a little heavy cream. He runs the works under the salamander (broiler) briefly to get everything really hot, then drizzles about a tablespoon of Tabasco sauce over the plate before serving. Enjoy these with Brix's Palermo panini, a sandwich from the hot wood oven stuffed with grilled chicken, mozzarella, bacon, avocado, lettuce, and tomato.

Café Modern (Modern Art Museum of Fort Worth, 3200 Darnell St., Fort Worth, 817-840-2157; www.themodern.org): Executive chef Dena Peterson changes the menu frequently, so you're just as likely to find her whipping up fries tossed with garlic butter, herbes de Provence, smoked salt, smoked paprika, or truffle salt. She'll also do a tempura-battered sweet potato fry dusted in black sesame seeds, along with an assortment of dipping sauces. Order them with a grilled sirloin burger on jalapeño-cheddar bun or with one of the grilled fish dishes.

Tillman's Roadhouse (324 West Seventh St., Oak Cliff [Dallas]; 214-942-0988; and 2933 Crockett St., Fort Worth; 817-850-9255; www.tillmansroadhouse.com): The Trio of Fries features a third of the fries treated with parmesan and black pepper; a third with a dusting of an ancho-poblano chile powder blend; and the remaining third sprinkled with smoked sea salt. On the side, there's a house-made catsup, or tomato puree, plus a horseradish mayo flavored with bread and butter pickles. Chef Dan Landsberg's threesome is so popular that nearly every table of diners orders these every day. Get them with the venison Frito pie, chipotle barbecued ribs, or a prickly pear margarita.

HIBISCUS $$$
2927 North Henderson Ave., Dallas
(214) 827-2927
www.hibiscusdallas.com

A comfortably chic spot for dates, impressing the parents, or hanging with pals, this dinner place offers treasures like maple-glazed quail with blue cheese–pebbled slaw, osso bucco with gremolata and foie gras, and chile-coated Pacific snapper. Crowds tend to be huge on weekends, so plan accordingly.

HIGHLAND PARK PHARMACY $
3229 Knox St., Dallas
(214) 521-2126

Little has changed through the years at this 1912 pharmacy, which has an authentic soda fountain that takes you back—way back. Breakfast is served daily—pecan waffles are a big seller—but it's the lunch that everyone loves. Get a grilled pimento cheese sandwich or chicken salad sandwich; in cold weather, the chili's fine. Be sure to leave room for a chocolate malt or a Coke float.

⊘ Close-up

Highland Park Pharmacy

Many are the Dallasites who make a happy return to a childhood haunt called the Highland Park Pharmacy. Most climb on a swivel stool at the soda fountain counter and order the classic chicken salad sandwich, served on wheat toast. Legions of regulars have made that choice a best-seller since a Mr. H. S. Forman opened his pharmacy in 1912. Anchoring the corner of Knox and Travis streets in what's called old Highland Park, the brick facade whose color is that of yellowed newspaper has changed not one bit.

Neither has much inside, for that matter. Pharmacy manager Mary Duncan says the counter and stools are original; they've just been recovered through the years. "We even have one of the old cash registers on display—but it doesn't work anymore."

The pharmacists still fill prescriptions in back and you can still buy specialty health and beauty goods, but it's the enduring breakfast, lunch, and sweets that bring the crowds craving a taste of childhood, a hint of uncomplicated moments.

Longtime customers bring their little ones in today, and most are agog at the cinnamon rolls that are as big as their faces. Those go well with chocolate milk, made with real chocolate syrup, as do the pecan waffles.

The real regulars are those who visit the pharmacy every day, says Duncan, who notes that some patrons will eat meals there twice daily. Some of these octogenarians will even hire a taxi or personal driver to bring them daily for breakfast and then either lunch or early supper.

Duncan says that when weather turns bad, the pharmacy will deliver meals to their regulars. "They're pretty sweet. They love telling us stories of coming here since they were children. As we lose one, it really does hurt."

Most of the old-timers count the Palm Beach as their favorite nosh at the soda fountain. A grilled pimento cheese on rye, this specialty offers a crunchy exterior and smooth, cool interior. Nobody knows why it bears its name, but it's probably got something to do with the sandwich's perfect pairing with a handmade chocolate malt, altogether a sinfully rich adventure from start to finish.

Duncan says that the only menu changes through the years have been additions, such as egg salad sandwich, Frito chili pie, chili dogs, pinto beans, freshly baked cookies, and a breakfast sandwich of egg, cheese, and bacon. The pharmacy has changed hands only three times through the years—the owners are now Sonny Williams and his wife Gretchen Minyard Williams, she of the grocery family—and nobody has found reason to remove anything from the menu. Top-sellers remain grilled cheese, chicken salad sandwich, and the Palm Beach, along with ice cream sodas and milk shakes.

Those lunch items are offered all day, right until closing. Breakfast, which can be anything from scrambled eggs with a toasted bagel to even eggs Benedict, is served weekdays until 11 a.m. and until 1 p.m. on Sunday. And if you're worried that the Palm Beach craving will hit at night, you can pick up containers of pimento cheese, along with chicken, ham, tuna, and egg salad, to go.

The busiest day, naturally, remains Saturday, when the soda fountain counter is crowded and the scattered tables with chairs stay full, too. Service can be brisk, and loitering to soak in the nostalgia is a bit tricky. It's better to go on a mid-afternoon on a Tuesday or Wednesday, when the pace is slack and you can dawdle over a Coke float. Find HP Pharmacy at 3229 Knox St., Dallas, (214) 521-2126.

PARIGI $$$
3311 Oak Lawn Ave. #102, Dallas
(214) 521-0295
www.parigirestaurant.com
Catering to a well-heeled Uptown crowd, this is the ideal bistro stop for patrons en route to art galleries or a symphony performance. Cozy and urbane, the room features sleek lines and big, vivid paintings, along with a fanciful menu and clever wine pairings. Tuck into a plate of greens topped with sesame and soy-marinated beef with dried mango, toasted peanuts, and an Asian vinaigrette, or go for the heartier lamb loin stuffed with eggplant, currants, feta, and pine nuts.

THE PORCH $$$
2912 North Henderson Ave., Dallas
(214) 828-2916
www.theporchrestaurant.com
Part corner bistro, part neighborhood watering hole, this hot spot attracts a young, upwardly mobile crowd to hang at the bar, sit on the patio, or camp at tables for hours. They come for appetizers like steamed mussels and chicken liver mousse, and to nosh on the sensational burger and the mustard-crusted salmon. Specialty drinks include a blueberry martini.

SAN FRANCISCO ROSE $$
3024 Greenville Ave., Dallas
(214) 826-2020
www.sanfranciscorose.com
Since 1977, this funky little saloon has been a destination for burgers, nachos, pizza, and salad, and there's a terrific, super-casual Sunday brunch. The Rose is a darn good place to watch ball games on TV. The patio is pet-friendly, and there's free Wi-Fi, as well. Bring someone you're comfortable hanging with, but know that it's a family-friendly joint, too.

SUZE $$$
4345 West Northwest Highway, #270, Dallas
(214) 350-6135
www.suzerestaurant.net
This small restaurant cultivates a neighborhood feel with its two small dining areas where you'll see that regulars know the staff as if they're family members. New American dishes and inventive desserts change frequently with whatever market discoveries intrigue chef Gilbert Garza. Lamb is usually a favorite, but look for interesting fish plates, too. The wine selection is small, but you can find something you like.

American Upscale

ABACUS $$$$
4511 McKinney Ave., Dallas
(214) 559-3111
www.kentrathbun.com
You'll find some intriguing Asian ideas in this solid American delight from celebrity chef Kent Rathbun. Seared yellowtail with taro chips is pleasing, as is the signature lobster shooter appetizer. For something a little more stout, try the aged bone-in rib eye.

BOLLA AT THE STONELEIGH $$$$
2927 Maple Ave., Dallas
(214) 871-7111
www.stoneleighhotel.com
David Bull offers Italian influences on seriously elegant food inside one of the most gorgeous hotels in Texas. Striped bass with potato croquette, braised beef short ribs with turnip puree, and osso bucco in a parsley crust have helped build a strong clientele.

CAFÉ ON THE GREEN $$$$
Four Seasons Resort and Club
4150 North MacArthur Blvd., Irving
(972) 717-0700
www.fourseasons.com/dallas
Elegant dining in a setting noted for the Zen appeal of bamboo floors and a flowing, airy space is ideal for enjoying dishes from chef Katie Natale, who can wow with a peach-stuffed duck breast, burly lamb chops with mint coulis, pan-fried soft-shell crab with white asparagus and fresh-from-the-market goodies, such as purple-hull pea soup. Ask master sommelier James Tidwell to pair a perfect wine for you.

CRAFT $$$–$$$$

The W Hotel
2440 Victory Park Lane, Dallas
(214) 397-4111
www.craftrestaurant.com/craft_dallas_style
.html

A component menu from a New York landmark gives Dallasites a chance to mix and match their dinner courses. The menu offers roughly 50 items, which change almost daily with market offerings, which are split among first and main courses and side dishes in vegetable and starch categories. Roasted veal sweetbreads with fennel, dorade with littleneck clams, blue crab gratin, and braised sweet peas have been among the intriguing ideas.

FEARING'S $$$$

The Ritz-Carlton
2121 McKinney Ave., Dallas
(214) 922-4848
www.fearingsrestaurant.com

After a two-decade career at the Mansion on Turtle Creek, star chef Dean Fearing opened a place of his own at another prestigious address. In each of seven distinct dining venues under one roof, the popular southerner does much to please his ever-ardent fans, with pecan-crusted halibut, crab tacos, and—at brunch—stunningly good fried chicken.

THE MANSION ON TURTLE CREEK $$$$

2821 Turtle Creek Blvd., Dallas
(214) 559-2100
www.mansiononturtlecreek.com

True, the dress code is gone, but don't kid yourself—this is still a swell spot to dine. Now, the dining room has been toned down with contemporary chandeliers and paintings; there's a terrace hangout with fire pit for drinking; and the bar's rocking. The signature lobster tacos and tortilla soup remain, but the rest of the menu undergoes regular reworking to keep up with current food trends. You can always find good steak, fish, salads, and desserts.

NANA $$$$

2201 Stemmons Freeway, Dallas
(214) 761-7470
www.nanarestaurant.com

You'll enjoy a panoramic view of Dallas if you dine at this five-star restaurant on the 27th floor of the Hilton Anatole Hotel. Chef Anthony Bombaci tantalizes with such dishes as ahi tuna tartare with passion fruit and wasabi ice cream, a prize pick on the tasting menu at this elegant dining room. A stunning wine list and polished service make this a must-visit.

STEPHAN PYLES $$$$

1807 Ross Ave., Dallas
(214) 580-7000
www.stephanpyles.com

The beloved co-founder of Southwestern cuisine and creator of the legendary, defunct Star Canyon renovated a mid-century office building in the Arts District to much acclaim. Much praise goes to his sampler of ceviches, as well as prime picks from a shellfish bar, but you can never go wrong with his cardamom apple stuffed with pulled pork, steamed salmon over crab risotto, tuna escabeche, and the signature cowboy rib eye with red chile onion rings.

YORK STREET $$$–$$$$

6047 Lewis St. at Live Oak, Dallas
(214) 826-0968
www.yorkstreetdallas.com

This intimate establishment delineates the genius of chef-owner Sharon Hage, whose loving touch is seen in everything from the handpainted dinnerware and burnished pewter chairs to the organic meats flavored with freshly picked herbs. She changes the menu daily, but you can expect lovely things such as pan-seared rabbit, succulent Jamison lamb chops, fresh veggies from friends' gardens or the farmers market, along with special touches like complimentary dry sherry with almonds and olives, and post-dinner specialty teas.

Asian

ASIAN MINT $$
11617 North Central Expressway,
#135, Dallas
(214) 363-6655
www.asianmint.com
Can't decide if your palate is hungry for Thai or sushi? Head to Asian Mint, beloved for both. The curries are heavenly and devotees swear this is the best pad thai in town. Get a strong coffee to go with green tea ice-cream cake or with jasmine crème brûlée. And don't worry that the exterior looks off-putting; the interior is modern and soothing.

BISTRO B $
9780 Walnut St. at Audelia, Dallas
(214) 575-9885
Big, busy, and packed with young and old, this Vietnamese restaurant serves a fine pho with sliced rare steak, brisket and flank steak, and rice noodles, aromatic with subtle layerings of anise and coriander. The grilled pork over superfine vermicelli is a knockout with sliced green papaya on top and a boat alongside filled with mint, two kinds of basil, shredded carrot salad, cilantro, and crunchy fried onion.

FIVE SIXTY $$$-$$$$
300 Reunion Blvd. East, Dallas
(214) 741-5560
www.wolfgangpuck.com
High atop Reunion Tower, inside the rotating, sparkling ball overlooking downtown and the city beyond, Wolfgang's new pan-Asian effort proves to be sheer genius. Cool and sleek, the restaurant woos with beautiful sushi offerings and treatments in lamb, cod, and beef that hint of exotica. A well-chosen wine and sake list deserves a good look, too.

GREEN PAPAYA $$
3211 Oak Lawn Ave., Dallas
(214) 521-4811
www.greenpapayarestaurants.com

The namesake dish, a green papaya salad, offers a tart, clean treat for the palate at this modern Vietnamese favorite in Uptown. Noodle dishes prove pleasing, as do pho and other soups, and smooth, cool spring rolls.

NOBU $$$$
400 Crescent Court (Maple at McKinney Avenue), Dallas
(214) 252-7000
www.noburestaurants.com
The 10th installment in the Nobuyuki Matsuhisa–Robert De Niro international dining sensation made a big splash in Big D upon opening in the Crescent Court in 2005. Serene and utterly hip, this is the place to people-watch while nibbling sushi, sashimi, seared fish, and even steaks with South American treatments.

Barbecue

PEGGY SUE BBQ $-$$
6600 Snider Plaza, Dallas
(214) 987-9188
www.peggysuebbq.com
A favorite in the SMU area for more than a half-century, this cutie in Snider Plaza appeals to families. Smoked pork ribs and chicken are excellent, and the sides—like ranch beans and potato salad—are hard to beat. Don't even think of skipping the cobbler for dessert.

SAMMY'S BAR B QUE $-$$
2126 Leonard St., Dallas
(214) 880-9064
www.sammysbbq.com
Tucked away behind the Hotel ZaZa in Uptown, this comfortable, friendly cafe gives off a delicious aroma that you'll dream about weeks after experiencing. Try the brisket-sliced sausage combo platter, but leave room for the bodacious apple-crumb pie, too. If you want, sit outside on the breezy patio.

🔍 Close-up

The Variety of North Texas Cuisine

The irresistible appeal of Dallas–Fort Worth dining lies in its unmatched versatility: The North Texas duo may be down-home at heart, but together the pair can do high-falutin' with the best of them. While other cities would like to be all things to all people, the Big D–Cowtown megalopolis knows its strengths pretty well and plays to them with ease.

The couple's combined cultural history involves the foremost food groups of Texas—specifically Tex-Mex, chicken-fried steak, T-bones, and barbecue. The cattle-driving heritage always included Hispanic and Anglo cowboys and cooks, and their gastronomic heritage remains intact. And as the population of Mexican-Americans has skyrocketed here, so has the availability of taqueria eats and combination plates that rank as superior to nearly any other city's.

By the 1950s, DFW had proven its proficiency at giving Texas (and the world) what it wanted to eat: El Fenix, credited with creating the first-ever cheese enchilada and the combination plate, began in Dallas in 1918, and El Chico followed in 1940. The ballpark nachos were born just after the Texas Rangers came to Arlington Stadium in the early 1970s and a food-service executive decided to put chips, gooey cheese, and jalapeño slices together on the same plate. And we owe an incalculable debt to Mariano Martinez, who decided to put a margarita mix in an old Icee machine at his Mariano's Mexican Restaurant in Dallas's Old Town shopping center to create the first frozen margarita in 1971.

Fine food gained interest around the parts, too, when Helen Corbitt arrived at Neiman Marcus in the 1950s to put Dallas cuisine on the map with her launch of the still-beloved, elegant Zodiac Room. Before long, Ewald's and Arthur's became places to drink Old World wines and share chateaubriand in Dallas, while the Carriage House and Old Swiss House became such destinations in Fort Worth.

But Corbitt wouldn't be the only cuisine pioneer from Dallas. In the 1980s, chefs Dean Fearing and Stephan Pyles helped invent something called Southwestern cuisine by pairing flavors of Latin and Native America with classic culinary techniques. Today, Fearing's namesake restaurant at the Ritz-Carlton continues to wow, as does Pyles's at his self-named restaurant.

Inspired by Fearing and Pyles, chefs and diners across North Texas have spent the past 25 years embracing the arrival of influences that have endured. And thanks to the preponderance of Latin American people and foods, such formerly exotic cuisine has become part of our upscale dining vernacular—witness divine dishes such as sea bass crusted in crushed pepitas and pecans in a Key lime beurre blanc, and prime tenderloin carne asada with guajillo demi and lentil tamale.

Throughout Dallas and Fort Worth and the connecting suburbs, you'll find pockets of Asian populations and wonderful eateries, both of the hole-in-wall and beautiful, cool, and dark varieties. You don't have to look long to find excellent dishes, prepared with all authenticity, in Indian, Pakistani, Thai, and Vietnamese cuisines.

SONNY BRYAN'S "THE ORIGINAL" $
2202 Inwood Rd., Dallas
(214) 357-7120
www.sonnybryans.com
A cramped little smokehouse with nearly a century of experience, this is Dallas's favorite little barbecue shack. Get a chopped beef sandwich or a rack of pork ribs with an ice-cold longneck, but be sure to grab one of the warm sauce bottles, too. Then park yourself in one of the old school desks that serve as seating. Just be sure to arrive before mid-afternoon, when the food often runs out.

But we are loath to wander far from our roots. When you need a great burger, you can go for the giant, flat version served sizzling-hot from the well-seasoned grill at the iconic Jack's Burger House in Dallas, where trust-fund babies and construction workers sit cheek-to-jowl. Or head to Fort Worth's venerable Kincaid's Grocery, a tiny joint that turned eating a juicy, two-fisted burger into an art form more than 40 years ago.

Nobody goes long without a chicken-fried steak, which is served in loving abundance, alongside smothered pork chops and tender pork ribs, at Sweet Georgia Brown in Dallas's Oak Cliff neighborhood. In Cowtown, a destination for much of the same is Paris Coffee Shop, which has cured innumerable ills since the 1930s with its monster biscuits at breakfast, as well as extraordinary chicken-fried steak and chicken-and-dumplings at lunch.

And surely there's no place but downtown Fort Worth where can you walk five blocks in any direction and find a fabulous cut of prime beef. From the intersection of Main and Sixth—not far from the cattle-drive path cut through town by the legendary Chisholm Trail—you can be seated in front of a flawless steak in seconds at Del Frisco's, Ruth's Chris, Reata, or Grace.

Perhaps most telling about the finery found in handmade, downhome eats in Dallas and Fort Worth is the lavish praise from a somewhat unexpected source: In 1998, the James Beard Foundation bestowed its Regional Classics Award on Joe T. Garcia's Mexican Eats in Fort Worth, and in 2000, the same award went to Sonny Bryan's Smokehouse in Dallas. The restaurants have a combined 165 years experience in making Texans and their bellies mighty happy.

Best about zipping around to eat at various places in Dallas and Fort Worth is discovering (and rediscovering) those places that do lush food in the most basic settings. The Grape, which opened on Lower Greenville Avenue in the 1970s to begin a revival of a decaying neighborhood and to make French bistro dining accessible for regular people, remains a favorite among Dallas diners for its lovely mushroom soup, charcuterie plates, and sensational wine discoveries by the glass.

You can't find a funkier dog-eared joint than Jazz Café in Fort Worth's Cultural District, where owner Nick Kithas still whips up the best Greek salad, spanikopita, and feta-cheese omelet in town, between bursts on his trumpet when the jazz band shows up at Sunday brunch.

But it's the utterly humble environs of the Stockyards National Historic District on Fort Worth's north side that have served as the perfect launchpad for a cuisine whiz named Tim Love. At his Lonesome Dove Western Bistro, the owner-chef has won legions of dedicated fans—the line for the parking valet is about as long as a West Texas drought—and nabbed mountains of glowing reviews from national critics for fare that ranges from a grilled New Zealand red deer chop with truffled mac and cheese to coffee-crusted kangaroo tail.

Such palate thrills are plated nightly, just a few feet from the hotel where Butch and Sundance are said to have visited and the saloon where Cowtown's last gunfight took place nearly 120 years ago. Do they have anything like that in Houston?

Burgers

BURGER HOUSE $
6913 Hillcrest Ave., Dallas
(214) 361-0370
The late Jack Koustoubardis opened this Dallas institution in 1951. It's known for the incomparable Double Double Cheeseburger and zesty french fries generously sprinkled with Jack's "secret" seasoning salt (you can purchase some while you are there). Over the years, Burger House has expanded to multiple locations, but we still like the cramped original with its framed photographs of local sports heroes and covered patio.

GOFF'S HAMBURGERS $
6401 Hillcrest Ave., Dallas
(214) 520-9133
www.goffshamburgers.com

Relocated to tidy digs facing SMU, this institution changed hands but still offers the exceptional charcoal-grilled burgers that have been popular for more than 50 years. The hickory with cheese version is simply perfect, but regulars find it hard to pass up the chili cheeseburger. Fries are excellent, as are the apricot fried pies. Check out the old football photos on the walls.

SNUFFER'S RESTAURANT & BAR $$
3526 Greenville Ave., Dallas
(214)826-6850
www.snuffers.com

A well-worn saloon with at least three generations of dedicated fans, the original of this local chain makes an irresistible, thick burger topped with a variety of cheeses, as well as a fabulous basket of french fries smothered in cheese, jalapeños, and chopped bacon. Get a margarita on the side.

TWISTED ROOT BURGER $–$$
2615 Commerce St., Dallas
(214) 741-7668
www.twistedrootburgerco.com

A newer effort in struggling Deep Ellum, this hangout nabbed a Food Network appearance on *Diners, Drive-Ins and Dives*. A half-pound burger topped with creamy blue cheese and jalapeños gets high marks, as does a turkey burger topped with chipotle sauce, guacamole, and a thick slice of cheddar. Curly fries and homemade sweet potato chips are good, too. Get a bucket of "cold-ass" beer, while you're at it.

WINGFIELD'S BREAKFAST & BURGER $
2615 South Beckley Ave., Dallas
(214) 943-5214

Even the big-appetite folks who think they can eat everything in sight cannot finish one of the burgers at this South Dallas joint. It's enormous and every bit as good as it is huge. The patty's thick and the toppings are fresh, and the whole thing is super juicy, so much so that the bread typically falls apart. Crinkle-cut fries are the most popular, but you don't need 'em. There's no seating, so either take it home or eat in your car. There's often a line, so you're wise to call in your order.

French

FRENCH ROOM $$$$
Adolphus Hotel
1321 Commerce St., Dallas
(214) 742-8200
www.hoteladolphus.com

The grand dining room of the Adolphus Hotel in downtown Dallas is worthy of royalty with its rococo, cherub-strewn ceiling and menu of French creations. Sample the lump crabmeat cakes and the flourless hot chocolate cake. Service is sophisticated and unobtrusive. If you can't bear to leave once dinner is finished, while away the evening over cognac in the lounge adjacent to the restaurant.

L'ANCESTRAL $$$
4514 Travis Ave., Dallas
(214) 528-1081

Authentic and timeless, this mainstay has outlasted many a trendy place in the same Knox-Henderson neighborhood. It does so with flawless service and traditional dishes that include escargot, steak au poivre, Dover sole, and crème brûlée. This is a place to share with someone special or to celebrate an important occasion.

RISE NO 1 $$
5360 West Lovers Lane, Dallas
(214) 366-9900
www.risesouffle.com

All soufflés, all the time, may sound like a bit much. Au contraire—here in this little gem of a dining room in Inwood Village, it's perfection. Savory delights include the lobster or mushroom soufflés, while the chocolate dessert soufflé is nothing short of ethereal. Grilled steak and spinach salad are options, too. Lovely gift items from France are sold on-site, as well.

Home Cooking

BUBBA'S COOKS COUNTRY $
6617 Hillcrest St., Dallas
(214) 373-6527
www.babeschicken.com/bubbas-dallas
This converted 1927 Texaco station has been an exceptionally popular place since opening in 1981. And the fried chicken is sure good—hot, crunchy crust outside, juicy and plump inside. The two-piece (all white) dinner with a huge, yeasty roll, a side of smooth mashed potatoes with a thick, peppery gravy, and unadulterated pinto beans is a filling supper for less than 10 bucks.

CELEBRATION $$
4503 West Lovers Lane, Dallas
(214) 358-0612
www.celebrationrestaurant.com
Bring the kids and all your friends to this friendly ramble of rooms, where big plates of chicken-fried steak, pot roast, baked chicken, and meat loaf are served with family-style sides of mashed potatoes, salad, and more. The green-chile corn bread is downright addictive, so approach with caution. Just be sure to leave room for peach cobbler.

SOUTH DALLAS CAFÉ $
3126 Grand Ave., Dallas
(214) 428-8856
Soul food at this Fair Park–area haunt is as good as you'll find in Texas; though it may be out of the way, this restaurant is well worth finding. Kindly ladies on the serving line spoon up your choice of smothered pork chops, fried chicken, meat loaf, short ribs, fresh collard greens, bountiful sweet potatoes, hot-water corn bread, and darned fine cobbler.

Italian

ARCODORO/POMODORO $$$
2708 Routh St., Dallas
(214) 871-1924
www.arcodoro.com/dallas/default.htm
This contemporary Sardinian restaurant in Uptown combines two formerly separated (but sister) restaurants into a building resembling a village piazza, with a stucco exterior and a marble interior. Other attractions include secluded private dining areas, wood-burning ovens framed in Italian tile, and a romantic split-level patio for dining alfresco. The menu features exotic flavors such as berries, myrtle leaves, and calamari in squid ink. The thin-crusted pizzas are legendary.

CAMPISI'S RESTAURANT $$
5610 East Mockingbird Lane, Dallas
(214) 827-0355
www.campisis.com
The Campisi family first brought its thin-crust pizzas to Dallas in 1946 and these remain some of the city's favorites. Other goodies include baked lasagna and shrimp scampi. While there are newer locations of this outfit, the dated original is the best, due partly to its age factor. Leave time to check out the cool old black-and-white photos covering the walls; you'll see a celebrity or two hobnobbing in Big D. Trivia note: Jack Ruby dined here on the eve of the Kennedy assassination.

FIRESIDE PIES $$
2820 North Henderson St., Dallas
(214) 370-3916
www.firesidepies.com
This is pizza in a league of its own, thanks to hand-worked dough and expert baking in an oak-burning oven. Toppings include balsamic-roasted chicken, meatballs, smoked mozzarella, whipped ricotta, and Point Reyes blue cheese—and much more. There are grinders that provide at least two meals each, as well as robust salads. An enjoyable wine list includes some nice sangrias. Try for a seat on the patio in good weather. Other locations include stores in Dallas, Grapevine, and Fort Worth.

NONNA $$$
4115 Lomo Alto Dr., Dallas
(214) 521-1800
www.nonnadallas.com

A petite restaurant at the edge of Highland Park, this jewel can be loud when the house is full. Never mind that because the food's so good you can stand the rising decibel levels. Do start with the salumi plate, then lose yourself in the butternut squash soup with scallops, the white pizza topped with cherrystone clams, and the roasted pork loin with cannellini beans. The small but sensational wine list will appease even the pickiest wine snob.

Mexican/Tex-Mex

JAVIER'S $$$
4912 Cole Ave., Dallas
(214) 521-4211
www.javiers.net
Still a favorite after about 30 years, Javier's provides sophisticated Mexico City–style food. It's famous for the black bean soup and flavorful red snapper mojo de ajo. It's dimly lit, with a colonial Mexico ambience and smooth, congenial service. A cigar lounge serves a variety of port wines, tequilas, and cognacs.

MI COCINA $$$
77 Highland Park Village, Dallas
(214) 521-6426
www.mcrowd.com
Owner Mico Rodriguez turned his stylish interpretation of Tex-Mex favorites into a mini-empire, attracting happy addicts hooked on the formidable Lucy-changa, bacon-and-garlic-ridden salsa cha-cho, lovely shrimp tacos, and fabulous grilled meats served with a Latin stir-fry of brilliantly colored vegetables. Beware the delicious, mind-bending, tequila-rich frozen cocktails called the Mambo Taxi, Mambo Limo, and the Dilemma: they'll make you feel wittier and cuter than you really are. There are multiple locations in North Dallas, Mid-Cities, and Fort Worth.

PRIMO'S BAR & GRILL $$
3309 McKinney Ave., Dallas
(214) 220-0510
www.primosdallas.com

This Uptown favorite is where chefs love to hang out, grazing over platters of huevos rancheros, spinach quesadillas, grilled tacos, enchiladas suizas, and carne guisada. There's a lively Sunday brunch crowd, and the patio's fun in good weather.

Gas Station Tacos

Where do you find the best tacos in Dallas? At a gas station, of course. Possibly the best tacos in all of Dallas await inside a fancy truck stop and beer store called Fuel City. You place your orders at the taco-stand window at the northern end of the store, and whether you pull up at 3 a.m. or 3 p.m., there are devoted customers chowing down on tacos in their cars. You'll love the picadillo, the version of taco stuffed with ground beef mixed with bits of potato, a dab of garlic, and a lot of black pepper. It's tucked into a double layer of small white-corn tortillas and topped with chopped onion and cilantro. A wedge of Mexican lime comes on the side. The tiny container of green chile salsa is both superfluous and irresistible. (It goes just as well on the amazingly tender beef fajita taco, another good option.) Sitting in the shadows of downtown among strip clubs and liquor stores, Fuel City can't be considered a chic stop—but you'll be impressed (in mild weather) with the beautiful, bikini-clad chicas lounging beside the landscaped swimming pool next to the store's drive-through. They're just part of the scenery, and somehow it doesn't look like they've been eating tacos. Find Fuel City open 24 hours at 801 South Riverfront Blvd., Dallas, (214) 426-0011.

TACO DINER $$
3699 McKinney Ave., Dallas
(214) 521-3669
www.mcrowd.com/tacodiner
Exceptionally trendy and upbeat, this snappy hangout offers delightful dishes inspired by Mexico City and Oaxacan traditions. Do try fish tacos, guacamole-chicken salad, green enchiladas, and the sublime margaritas. There are other locations found in North Dallas.

VERACRUZ CAFÉ $$
408 North Bishop St., Dallas
(214) 948-4746
www.cafeveracruzdallas.com
Recently expanded, this destination in Oak Cliff's Bishop Arts District gets high marks for its moles, enchiladas, and the exceptional margaritas.

Seafood

DADDY JACK'S $$
1916 Greenville Ave., Dallas
(214) 826-4910
www.daddyjacks.org
Stuffed snapper is a great standby at this cozy, casual place on Lower Greenville that might remind you of a seaside village in New England. Be aware that the mussels in dreamy marinara sauce are hard to pass up and the crab cake is dependable, as well. Seasonal desserts are usually a treat, with the rhubarb pie as a leading example. The wine list is okay, as are beer choices.

DALLAS FISH MARKET $$$
1501 Main St., Dallas
(214) 744-3474
www.dallasfishmarket.com
You'll rarely find the fish served here at any other place in town, as this restaurant sources from some of the most exclusive providers on the planet. On a given day, depending on the season, you might find grilled, sushi-grade mako shark, as well as seared barracuda, sturgeon from the Columbia River, and the more common Prince Edward Island mussels. Landlubbers are pacified with bone-in rib eye steak and double-cut pork chop.

GO FISH $$$
5301 Alpha Rd., Dallas
(972) 980-1919
www.gofishoceanclub.com
Orzo with lobster and grilled mahi-mahi make the grade at this uber-contemporary lunch and dinner spot. If you love sushi, ask for the Rainbow Tower, and if you're a salad person, go for the Caesar topped with fried calamari. Among North Dallas fish options, this may be the best.

Steak

AL BIERNAT'S $$$$
4217 Oak Lawn Ave., Dallas
(214) 219-2201
www.albiernats.com
Here's the chic steak joint of choice for the Park Cities crowd and visiting celebrities. A New York–style energy presides, augmented by a polished staff who make regulars of everyone with seamless service. The bone-in rib eye, with an ideal balance of tender flesh and flavorful fat, is the prime pick, with the hearts of palm–arugula salad a perfect starter. Try a zin or cab from the 10,000-bottle wine collection.

BOB'S STEAK & CHOP HOUSE $$$$
4300 Lemmon Ave., Dallas
(214) 528-9446
www.bobs-steakandchop.com
Not the biggest, showiest beef palace in town, this mainstay in the meat market has the familiarity and coziness of a country club dining room. The staff keeps dinner at a nice pace and you want for nothing. Favorites include the Kansas City strip and the bone-in rib eye, both served with the signature glazed carrot and your choice of potatoes; go for the skillet potatoes with peppery gravy.

CAPITAL GRILLE $$$$
500 Crescent Court, Dallas
(214) 303-0500
www.thecapitalgrille.com
Although it's a chain, this steak place extends a warm welcome that makes even walk-in diners feel at home. The signature Delmonico, a thick,

porcini-crusted, bone-in rib eye, covers most of a dinner plate, and the kona coffee–crusted New York strip is equally impressive. For appetizers, you can't do better than the dish of pan-fried calamari and sweet-hot banana peppers.

CHARLIE PALMER AT
HOTEL JOULE $$$$
1530 Main St., Dallas
(214) 261-4600
www.charliepalmer.com
Off the lobby of a sexy little boutique hotel, this dining room brings out the very best of the renovated 1920s space it inhabits. Thanks to smart interpretations of celebrity chef Palmer's expert work, you'll enjoy fabulous beef in the form of wagyu flat iron steak, dry-aged New York strip, and even bison rib eye. There's excellent fish here, too, along with a most impressive wine list. Check out the retail wine shop, too.

DEL FRISCO'S DOUBLE
EAGLE STEAK $$$$
5251 Spring Valley Rd., Dallas
(972) 490-9000
www.delfriscos.com
Elegant beef executions include the New York strip, finished with aromatic butter, and the filet mignon atop blue-cheese mashed potatoes. A special finish is found in the many-layered, creamy lemon Doberge cake, a New Orleans touch from the managing partner, Dee Lincoln, who comes from the Crescent City. Start with crab cakes and be sure to try the gigantic, golden onion rings.

NICK & SAM'S $$$$
3008 Maple Ave., Dallas
(214) 871-7444
www.nick-sams.com
There are so many choices in steak at this lavish dinner place, your head spins a little. Try the silky filet mignon with a side of lobster macaroni and cheese, but don't ignore other offerings, such as tempura-fried crab claws and Asian-sauced baby lamb chops. Wine choices are abundant; ask the sommelier to find something that fits your price point.

PAPPAS BROS. STEAKHOUSE $$$$
10477 Lombardy Lane, Dallas
(214) 366-2000
www.pappasbros.com
The best of several dining rooms inside this large gathering place is the stone-and-wood edition that was once the cigar room. Sit by the fireplace and tuck into a marvelous filet with a fabulous bottle of cabernet. Good starters include the lobster bisque, and the cheesecake brings just the right end to the meal. The New York strip astounds, as does the rib eye. Excellent sides include the beautiful onion rings.

SILVER FOX $$$
3102 Oak Lawn Ave., Dallas
(214) 559-2442
www.silverfoxcafe.com
Modern, sleek, but yet still warm, this solid and sumptuous dining room in Uptown gives you comfort in the form of thoughtful service and exceptional flavor, starting with the New York strip au poivre. Broccoli au gratin is a fine side dish, as are the crisp sugar-snap peas. The dessert of choice is the bananas sautéed in cinnamon butter. The bar area makes for a nice place to sip a martini before your meal.

Vegetarian
COSMIC CAFÉ
2912 Oak Lawn Ave., Dallas
(214) 521-6157
www.cosmiccafedallas.com
This Indian-vegetarian restaurant doubles as a meditation space and coffeehouse. Unique to the Dallas restaurant scene, it holds yoga classes and Sufi poetry readings. Pakistani, Indian, and Southwestern U.S. influences are found in tomato soup with ginger, garlic, and basil, and in lentils rolled in flour tortillas with salad.

KALACHANDJI'S PALACE
AND RESTAURANT $-$$
5430 Gurley Ave., Dallas
(214) 823-1048
www.kalachandjis.com

A vegetarian delight housed in a Hare Krishna temple, this place seduces even carnivores with fresh, seasonal foods. There's an inexpensive Sunday feast and a weekly international specialty, such as Italian or Mexican, and even a vegetarian mock fish fry.

FORT WORTH

American Casual

BUFFET AT THE KIMBELL ART MUSEUM $$
3333 Camp Bowie Blvd., Fort Worth
(817) 332-8451
www.kimbellart.org
This lovely, light-filled space inside Louis Kahn's architectural masterpiece has become a favorite lunchtime meeting spot, even among people who don't always have time to wander through the museum's extraordinary collections. On mild days, you can sit beneath the wisteria on a small patio, but you bask in sunshine almost anywhere you perch here. Manager-chef Shelby Schafer turns out a splendid selection of salads, soups, quiche, sandwiches, and desserts each day; you pick up your choices in a self-service line, then find a table—if you're lucky enough to show up before or after the crowds. Typically a lunch-only spot, its evening dinners are special, too.

CAFÉ MODERN $$
3200 Darnell St., Fort Worth
(817) 840-2167
www.themodern.org
The brilliant architect Tadao Ando achieved an effort almost as impressive as creating a space for displaying some of the world's most important artworks. In designing the magnificent Modern Art Museum, he also produced a sanctuary in which some very artistic culinary works could be given proper presentation. Reaching out into a reflecting pool, the cafe's smooth lines and cool slate tones invoke a serene feel, and the food does its part to provide equal pleasure. Thanks to chef Dena Peterson, the cafe won praise in *Gourmet* magazine's best American restaurants feature. Vegetarians will like plentiful offerings,

including tomato-basil soup with pine nut–crusted mozzarella and eggplant napoleon, while carnivores can't resist the King Ranch chicken and Asian barbecued beef with udon noodles.

ELLERBE FINE FOODS $$$
1501 West Magnolia Ave., Fort Worth
(817) 926-3663
www.ellerbefinefoods.com
The menu changes almost daily, depending on what fresh finds chef Molly McCook discovers at the market and from her fish purveyor. Favorites have included bacon-wrapped trout stuffed with lemon and onion; creamy cauliflower soup with brie; sublime lamb chops; and hanger steak with crispy fries. Patio seating can be lovely. All wines sold on the wine list are offered at retail prices for taking home.

LILI'S BISTRO ON MAGNOLIA $$
1310 West Magnolia Ave., Fort Worth
(817) 877-0700
www.lilisbistro.com
Taking over space in a historic grocery building, owner-chef Vance Martin pleases a booming clientele with a menu that includes polenta fries, Asian crab cakes, beef tenderloin medallions, stuffed chicken, and sensational tabouli. The burger, available only at lunch, remains a best seller. A limited wine list suits most palates.

LUCILE'S $$
4700 Camp Bowie Blvd., Fort Worth
(817) 738-4761
The flatiron building sitting on a triangular piece of real estate dates from 1926, and your gaze can't help but be drawn to the charming yellow brick and the green glazed-tile roof. Most folks remember when it was a beloved dispensary of home cooking called Finley's Cafeteria, but Lucile's has become a neighborhood hangout in its own right. Every evening, there are regulars sipping martinis at the bar, and you can easily find someone who makes weekly pilgrimages for the chicken-fried steak, lobster bisque, or Greek salad. The crispy chicken–feta pizza, baked in a wood-burning oven, has become a staple, as

🔍 Close-up

Dinner and Drinks

Looking to treat yourself to an evening out and still keep to your budget? Eat in the bar. Most restaurateurs are happy to serve you there, where you can forage from appealing appetizer menus and share a few smallish, less expensive plates with a friend. Some savvy chefs understand the particular mood-and-food needs today and are providing a special menu just for the bar crowd. Happy grazing.

Dino's Steak and Claw House (342 Main St., Grapevine, 817-488-3100): Occupying a vintage bank building along the historic main drag, this romantic newcomer positions its black granite bar area front and center. Diners waiting on tables in the adjacent dining room are so pampered by the suave bartenders that they just want to stay put. Music wafts from the piano that sits between bar and dining room. Dino's signature is the Crab Cubes, square-shaped cakes that blend Maryland lump crab within a smooth crust, served on a narrow platter with Dijon honey sauce and a red-chile apple compote for dipping. Roasted eggplant tossed with a sesame-honey-mint dressing makes for a surprisingly good salad, and grilled Texan quail in a treatment of porcini mushrooms and sherry is the perfect complement. Appetizers are $6.95 to $11.95.

Five Sixty by Wolfgang Puck (300 Reunion Blvd., Dallas, 214-741-5560; www.wolfgangpuck .com): Shimmery and elegant, the new occupant high above downtown Dallas in the big twinkly ball topping Reunion Tower lives up to expectations. Across a floor of dark, smooth river rocks from the sushi bar, the long, silver-and-ivory lounge features a glass-topped bar with round armchairs adjacent to a seating area with low cocktail tables. All, of course, offer the magnificent, rotating view of Big D and environs. The sushi bar produces nigiri and sashimi selections, with specialties including big eye tuna, hamachi, sea scallops, and black tiger shrimp, and there are dragon, rainbow, and other rolls, as well. Early favorites among appetizer dishes are the tai snapper sashimi with seaweed salad in a sesame-lemon dressing, as well as the robata grill's Maine lobster with Thai basil–yuzu chile pesto. Appetizers are $7 to $25.

Grace (777 Main St., Fort Worth, 817-877-3388; www.gracefortworth.com): Effecting a mid-century look that borrows sensibilities from the Four Seasons in New York, this modern

well. Ask for a table alongside the windows at the apex end of the room, where you have a view of the boulevard and the busy clientele, too.

OLENJACK'S GRILLE $$
770 Rd. to Six Flags East, Suite 100, Arlington
(817) 226-2600
www.olenjacksgrille.com
Chef Brian Olenjack meets the need in Six Flags-land for good, non-chain food in a handsome setting. Terrific specialties include fried antelope ribs, shrimp and grits, pulled chicken ravioli, and roasted duck risotto. Sunday brunch is popular, as are quick dinners before Dallas Cowboys football or Texas Rangers baseball games at nearby stadiums.

American Upscale

BONNELL'S FINE TEXAS CUISINE $$$$
4259 Bryant Irvin Rd., Fort Worth
(817) 738-5489
www.bonnellstexas.com
Owner-chef Jon Bonnell sets the bar high by sourcing a stunning number of local and regional ingredients for his pro-Texas menu. Among specialties are his elk tacos, lamb chops, pecan-crusted Texas redfish, and green chile–cheddar grits. Service is usually smart and attentive, and there's a nice bar area for just sipping and nibbling. A good wine cellar is on-site, too.

American restaurant's cocktail lounge—with its big windows and sleek walnut-and-granite interior—has clearly become a town favorite in just a couple of months. There's almost always a crowd at the L-shaped bar and at little tables inside and on the long, narrow patio alongside a downtown sidewalk. Good for sharing, the artisan cheese platter presents a trio of cured meats (think duck prosciutto and Berkshire pork) with a trio of American cheeses (usually something creamy and something hard); and the addictive little croquettes of creamy, roasted eggplant with Parmesan inside a warm, crunchy crust, with a blue cheese dressing for dipping. Good for soaking up the alcohol, the fish and chips offers halibut inside golden jackets, and sliders consist of round rolls enclosing shredded, tender short rib meat topped with caramelized red onions. Bar menu items are $6 to $16.

Neighborhood Services (5027 West Lovers Lane, Dallas, 214-350-5027, www.neighborhood servicesdallas.com): This white-hot hangout a stone's throw from the Inwood Theater nails the corner bistro idea, offering plentiful, comforting food at easy-going prices. The look is modern tavern, with blonde woods and heavy but comfortable furniture. There's a long bar with stools, as well as booth seating in the bar area. Hearth-baked flatbread is another word for pizza, and it's splendid. The one topped with house-made fennel sausage and ricotta, along with cippolini onions, is unforgettable. Ricotta shows up again in lobster fritters, served with a classic cocktail sauce, and pan-roasted blue mussels flecked with Spanish cured chorizo come with a loaf of crusty bread. Starters range from $8 to $14.

The Wine Thief (1330 Houston St. at the Omni Hotel, Fort Worth, 817-350-4100, www.bobs-steakandchop.com): Dark and cozy, the wine bar adjacent to the new Bob's Steak and Chop House inside the gorgeous new Omni Fort Worth Hotel removes you from the busy restaurant hubbub—if not entirely from the bustling hotel lobby din. Nevertheless, candlelight and booth seating appeal to couples and foursomes. The tenderloin crostini suits a carnivore perfectly, with thick slices of cool, medium-rare prime beef atop buttery, toasted baguette slices. Smoked salmon provides a classic taste, and the thick, golden onion ring bangles have become a Bob's signature for a good reason. Get the primi chili if you require something warm and hearty. Appetizers are $8.95 to $14.95.

CAFÉ ASPEN $$$
6103 Camp Bowie Blvd., Fort Worth
(817) 738-0838
cafeaspen.com

Divided by fabric-draped partitions, this quiet, candle-lighted spot is luxurious but not fussy, and the attentive, able staff pampers business types and coddles couples. The old guard loves this charming, elegant dining spot, which lavishes the palates with creatively prepared tuna, salmon, beef tenderloin, veal chop, and rack of lamb with such New American treatments ranging from berry-wine sauces to chile or nut crusts and vegetable salsas. Generations of diners go weekly for the spinach with bacon, mushrooms, red onion, apple, and parmesan with honey mustard. The don't-miss desserts include lemon coconut cake and bourbon-buttermilk fudge cake. In back, there's a hopping patio where you can sip martinis and nibble on lighter meals.

GRACE $$$$
777 Main St., Fort Worth
(817) 877-3388
www.gracefortworth.com

Arrive early to enjoy the Wine Me, Dine Me menu, a four-course deal with wine pairings for $40. Starters typically include choices such as beef bruschetta with heirloom tomato and avocado, followed by an asparagus soup and a main

(Q) Close-up

Frozen Custard

Frozen custard, delightfully rich and creamy, is catching on in North Texas. The dessert, which contains more eggs and less air than ice cream, originated at Coney Island. Here's where to find it:

Curly's Frozen Custard
4017 Camp Bowie, Fort Worth
(817) 763-8700
www.curlysfrozencustard.com
This little shop with just a couple of tables outside opened in 2002, using a proprietary blend of Bourbon and Indonesian vanilla to great effect. Custard comes in vanilla, sugar-free vanilla, lemon, chocolate, and a flavor of the month. Besides cones, Curley's serves sundaes, and concretes—custard with all sorts of yummy goodness blended in, like pecans, caramel, almonds, hot fudge—you get the idea.

Culver's Frozen Custard
1301 South Central Expressway, McKinney
(972) 548-7500
2709 Flower Mound Rd., Flower Mound
(972) 355-3787
www.culvers.com
A slightly smaller custard menu, but also serves more extensive meals, including pot roast, shrimp, and North Atlantic cod.

Freddy's Frozen Custard and Steakburger
3040 Justin Rd., Highland Village
(972) 317-3600
2820 TX 121
Euless, Texas
(817) 685-8807

Concretes, sundaes, cones, shakes, malts, carryout cartons. A fresh strawberry mix-in is especially nice here.

Sheridan's Frozen Custard
7428 Denton Highway
Watauga, Texas
(817) 514-7437
www.sheridansfrozencustard.com
A chain with headquarters in Kansas, Sheridan's has vanilla and chocolate custard scooped into cones and sundaes, blended into lattes and frappes, mixed into concretes, layered into pies, and packed into quarts and pints to take home.

Woolley's Frozen Custard
7630 North Beach St., #166, Fort Worth
(817) 503-9918
124 Grapevine Highway, Suite F, Hurst
(817) 428-4464
www.woolleysfrozencustard.com
Woolley's serves vanilla and chocolate in the usual variations, plus a Dublin shake blended with Dublin Dr Pepper syrup. (Dublin Dr Pepper is made at the original Dr Pepper plant in Dublin, Texas, using cane sugar rather than corn syrup.)

---

course choice such as a spring-onion quiche with bacon, Gruyere, and frisée, finished with something like banana pudding with Nilla Wafers. Or perch at the bar with a glass of wine and a plate of grilled flatbread topped with jumbo shrimp, smoked tomato jam, and basil. The lemon tart with almond crust provides a sublime finish.

MICHAELS RESTAURANT & ANCHO CHILE BAR $$$
3413 West Seventh St., Fort Worth
(817) 877-3413
www.michaelscuisine.com
Contemporary ranch cuisine means signature pizzas topped with ancho chicken, plates of

jalapeño shrimp, or dinners pairing lamb chop with goat cheese and raspberry chipotle sauce. The dining room is as artful and chic as neighboring galleries, while the adjoining bar is dark, cozy, and filled with well-heeled, martini-sipping regulars.

Asian

HUI CHUAN $$
6100 Camp Bowie Blvd., Fort Worth
(817) 989-8886
www.huichuansushi.com

Tucked into a serene spot next to Haltom's Jewelers in the 50-year-old Ridglea Village, the little Asian jewel box was the first to bring sushi to the middle section of the boulevard. You can pull into the sushi bar or hop on a stool at one of the tall two-tops; either way, you're likely to make friends before your meal is over. The usual rolls (spider, Philadelphia, rainbow, etc.) are offered, as is every imaginable nigiri and hand roll. But look for specials on the blackboard, or just give yourself over to the unusual, such as grilled salmon cheek or oyster shooters. Tapas offerings include small plates bearing goodies like baked green mussels with spicy mayo dressing, fried soft shell crab with ponzu sauce, and sautéed asparagus with onion, tomato, and mushroom. A good sake list is available, as is a wine list with nice finds.

PIRANHA KILLER SUSHI $$$
335 West Third St. in Sundance Square, Fort Worth
(817) 348-0200
www.piranhakillersushi.com

Every roll imaginable decorates this lively menu, but it's the salads that attract the most attention. Choice picks include the spicy tuna salad with avocado, tomato, and citrus chile; Caribbean tuna tartare; and sashimi salad with tuna, conch, white tuna, and veggies. Fancy martini choices fill a long bar menu, and the bar area is nice for catching up with friends. (There are two Arlington locations, too.)

SZECHUAN $$
5712 Locke Ave., Fort Worth
(817) 738-7300

An institution in its own right, this anchor in the Locke Block near the boulevard's intersection with Horne Street has at least three generations of patrons who can recite the menu by heart. Decorated with contemporary art, it's a comfortable place even if you're a newcomer, thanks to a menu with plentiful Chinese offerings and a staff that can help you find your way. Among more interesting specialties are the shrimp with honey-coated pecans, whole Peking duck, and the spicy lobster with black bean sauce. When you just want some comfort but in a special package, go for the Bird's Nest, combining chicken and shrimp with veggies in a potato basket. The hot and sour soup is likely the best in town.

TOKYO CAFÉ $$
5121 Pershing Ave., Fort Worth
(817) 737-8568
www.thetokyocafe.com

A youthful clientele keeps the tempo upbeat in the evenings, when you're likely to find couples and groups of friends at tables and single diners reading a novel while munching on rolls at the sushi bar. Traditional Japanese decor—paper lanterns, bamboo screens—fills the two cozy rooms, where you can sip Ichiban, sake, or white wine while mulling over choices. Start with the salmon crudo, a long plate decorated with thin, velvety slices of salmon drizzled with cilantro and chile oils, scattered with cracked black pepper and topped with sprigs of microherbs. A recent hit from the blackboard was the Stop Dropping Roll, combining smooth albacore, crunchy fresh jalapeño, creamy avocado, and spicy crab inside the sticky rice, with tobikko, or bright red flying fish roe, with a pleasing saltiness and a crunchy texture. Fried gyoza and pumpkin soup are among non-fish options.

THAI TINA'S $$
600 Commerce St., Fort Worth
(817) 332-0088
www.thaitinas.com

Recently moved from a run-down spot amidst auto body shops to sleek new digs off the Embassy Suites lobby downtown, this charming bistro serves possibly the best Thai in North Texas. The beef salad with mint and basil can't be beat, nor can the spring roll salad with pork. The chicken with red curry and vegetables may be the best-selling dish of all. If there's a drawback, it's a spotty wine list. Look for specialty martinis and appetizer plates in the bar at happy hour.

TU HAI RESTAURANT $
3909 East Belknap St., Haltom City
(817) 834-6473
Everyone's favorite Vietnamese restaurant won't win any beauty contests, but that's fine. Service is friendly in the small, utilitarian cafe in a drab shopping center, and the food couldn't be better. Favorites, in addition to traditional pho (soup with sliced steak and crunchy vegetables), are the Saigon pancake, the vermicelli topped with grilled pork and eggroll, and the chicken lemongrass.

Barbecue

ANGELO'S BARBECUE $–$$
2533 White Settlement Rd., Fort Worth
(817) 332-0357
www.angelosbbq.com
The oldest and most famous barbecue joint in town, Angelo's wins high praise for smoked beef brisket and pork ribs. Do try sides of potato salad and coleslaw, too. The giant schooners of ice-cold beer are mightily refreshing.

HARD EIGHT BBQ $$
688 Freeport Parkway in Coppell
(972) 471-5462
www.hardeightbbq.com
A cavernous place near DFW Airport, this is one of the Hill Country–style joints where you visit the massive smoke pits out front to choose the meats you'll eat. Picks include pork ribs, beef brisket, pork shoulder, sausage, and steak, and they're all good. Sides range from potatoes to salad, but you'll want to leave room for peach cobbler.

RAILHEAD SMOKEHOUSE $$
2900 Montgomery St., Fort Worth
(817) 738-9808
www.railheadonline.com
The debate on what's better—pork ribs or beef brisket—is a lost cause at the city's most popular barbecue joint, where you're best advised to get a plate combining both. These hickory-smoked vittles, as well as the smoked turkey breast and chicken quarters, go beautifully with ice-crusted mugs of beer and servings of homemade potato salad and beans. Don't plan a quick trip to this West Side favorite, because it's packed to the rafters, and parking spaces are a block away on busier nights. There's a drive-through, however, that works well if you're just picking up a pound of brisket and a pound of ribs to take home.

Burgers

DUTCH'S BURGERS & BEER $$
3009 South University Dr., Fort Worth
(817) 927-5522
www.dutchshamburgers.com
A busy hangout across the street from TCU, this family-friendly burger spot won a top-10 ranking in *Texas Monthly*'s top 50 burgers story in 2009. All-natural beef goes into the monster patties, served atop sensational bakery buns and topped with anything from blue cheese with bacon to chili and cheese. The grilled chicken sandwich covered in freshly roasted green chile is downright wonderful, too, as is the Greek salad.

FRED'S TEXAS CAFÉ $$
915 Currie St. in Fort Worth
(817) 332-0083
www.fredstexascafe.com
A dive joint of the first order, Fred's rose to national fame with an appearance on Food Network's *Diners, Drive-Ins and Dives* in 2009. The popular choice is the Diablo burger, incorporating chipotle chiles and topped with spicy mustard. Fred's french fries are among the best on the planet, while the portobello tacos have won fans among vegetarians, too. Patio dining is a blast in nice weather, especially when live music is on tap.

Burger Bonanza

The Kincaid's burger legend began when this corner grocery shop's butcher began in 1966 to cook up burgers from the surplus choice ground beef he had on hand each day to feed neighborhood folks. A decade later, people would read stories in national publications about Kincaid's burgers and join the throngs eating them while standing alongside the old wooden grocery shelves that were filled with canned soup and bags of flour. By the 1980s, national publications declared this the best burger anyplace, yet the little-town flavor forever remains in the sandwich and the service. You can still stand up with your elbows propped upon the grocery shelves, but you'd probably rather sit down at one of the picnic tables installed up front to eat one of these giant, juicy sandwiches, still cooked on the flat grill, wrapped in white tissue paper and served in a little paper bag. Find the original at 4901 Camp Bowie Blvd. in Fort Worth, (817) 732-2881, www.kincaidsham burgers.com.

KINCAID'S $
4901 Camp Bowie Blvd., Fort Worth
(817) 732-2881
www.kincaidshamburgers.com
A Cowtown institution of the first order, this 70-year-old corner grocery on the venerable West Side has been publicized around the world for its astounding burgers. The half-pounders are hand-formed from freshly ground beef and served sizzling hot and drippy inside warm buns. Grab an order of pimento cheese–stuffed jalapeños and crinkle-cut fries, too, then eat the tra-

ditional way, standing up with elbows propped atop the wooden grocery shelves, or sitting at picnic tables in front.

LOVE SHACK $$
110 East Exchange, Fort Worth
(817) 740-8812
817 Matisse St., Fort Worth
(817) 348-9655
www.shakeyourloveshack.com
Celebrity chef Tim Love's claim to burger fame is his Dirty Love Burger, a custom grind of prime steak and brisket that he tops with cheeses and a fried quail egg. It's a magnificent, delicious mess, perfect with a side of crinkle-cut fries and a butterscotch milk shake. At the Matisse location, you can order all kinds of fun appetizers, too, as well as a cucumber-jalapeño margarita. Live music at both shops.

Deli

CARSHON'S DELICATESSEN $–$$
3133 Cleburne Rd., Fort Worth
(817) 923-1907
www.carshonsdeli.com
Fort Worth's oldest deli in continuous business, this was also for many years the only Kosher-style kitchen operation in town. Not far from Texas Christian University, this south-side, no-frills spot has a following addicted to the Rachel, concoction of corned beef and turkey with melted Swiss, coleslaw, and Russian dressing, grilled on buttery rye. Other faves include French toast stuffed with bananas, as well as the chicken noodle soup and chopped liver on rye. Under no circumstances should you skip the chocolate or butterscotch pie.

YOGI'S DELI & GRILL $–$$
4855 Bryant Irvin Rd., Fort Worth
(817) 292-9665
2710 South Hulen St., Fort Worth
(817) 921-4500
Rare is the eating place where you'll find Kosher specialties and Tex-Mex treasures on the same menu, but it works at this favorite breakfast-lunch spot. Fried matzo with eggs, onion, and salami is

Close-up

The Outlaw Chef

Terry Chandler, owner of Fred's Texas Café in Fort Worth, is definitely ready for his close-up. Hollywood came calling in early 2009, and it was high time. Chandler, whose tongue-in-cheek nickname is "the Outlaw Chef," owns the Fort Worth landmark cafe, recently featured on the Food Network program called *Diners, Drive-Ins and Dives*. The food television folks couldn't have picked a better place, as Fred's may well be the most beloved of all Cowtown's divey diners.

Chandler was not quite a teenager when his folks founded the little watering hole with solid, stick-to-your-ribs food some 30 years ago, naming it for the family dog, Fred. Today the little ramshackle spot sits tucked away in what was for many decades a relatively quiet industrial area off Seventh Street but is now blossoming into a white-hot quarter of boutiques, fancy restaurants, and upscale condos, serving to bridge the short distance between the hopping downtown and the booming Cultural District. Most remarkable about Fred's is that as this momentous transformation takes place all around it, the low-key cafe remains a comfy hangout with very cold beer, ball games on TV, a particularly carefree attitude, and an exceptional menu that includes goodies such as smoked chicken tacos, New Mexico–style green chili, calf fries with chipotle gravy, and brunch migas with ranchero sauce.

For years, its regulars knew it as the place to take the date you wanted to test: If he or she could warm up to the getting-real spirit of Fred's, you'd found a keeper. There were devotees who were downright worried when a fire—probably caused by a tossed cigarette—prompted a remodeling of the old place a couple of years ago. The loyal clientele fretted that Fred's might lose some of its signature run-down character, but Chandler was quick to caution, "It's still Fred's, but with a face-lift."

Sure enough, the cafe's famously eccentric essence prevails, but there are signs that Fred's—which Chandler now co-owns with wife, Jennifer—has adopted a smidge of establishment practices: There's actually a printed menu these days, rather than a mere recitation of a couple things the server felt like telling you; you can now order wine, not just beer, with a full liquor license in the works; credit cards are finally accepted; and there's no smoking indoors.

Inside, your seating choices remain the sparkly gold-vinyl booths and a handful of bar stools, but the back wall is now covered with a cowboy mural, which is a nod to Chandler's outside work. Just last summer he worked for five weeks as the official chuck-wagon chef at the legendary 6666 Ranch at Guthrie, where he fed 30 cowboys two meals daily.

During the ranch gig, Chandler's work started at 2 a.m., precisely the time when some folks are leaving Fred's for the night. And while the jobs wouldn't seem to have an obvious link, Chandler has no trouble showing how easily they connect. It's all in the food, and the passion behind it.

Chandler loves to share stories about spending time with a grandpa who was part Cherokee, a grandma who grew up in West Texas ranch country, and a great-uncle who was a West Texas chuck-wagon cook of renown and who would whip up vittles at get-togethers at the family

Bar-Z Ranch on the Panhandle's cap rock. As a boy, Chandler was hooked on this cowboy life. Back in Fort Worth, he washed dishes and learned to cook at Fred's, all the while busting broncs in local rodeos. During his Marine Corps stint, Chandler fell in love with street food in far-flung places around the world, then went on to work as a gypsy chef at places like a seafood restaurant on a North Carolina beach and a guest ranch in Southern Colorado.

Over the years, Chandler has increasingly combined classic cooking techniques he learned from fellow chefs with his own chuck-wagon experience. Adding to his distinctive appeal, Chandler dresses in trail-era costume, with his signature knee-high boots complementing the long braid hanging down his back, whether he's working at Fred's or catering a party from his chuck wagon.

"I make the food I'm doing on my wagon translate to Fred's, and the spirit is the same," Chandler says. "It's all about want-to. Cowboys and chuck-wagon cooks—neither one make good money. It's all about the love for the job."

When Chandler became bored with simply flipping the mighty fine burgers at Fred's, he began to expand the menu. He launched Hot Night on Friday evenings, making specials like New Mexico–style lamb green chile, rib eye steaks in chipotle brown butter, and shrimp tacos with mango-habañero salsa. On Saturday night he might offer an order of butter-seared quail with a chile de arbol–red wine reduction or buffalo tenderloin with his fire-roasted tomatillo sauce. From his smoker, you get smoked chicken tacos, while the fryer produces some of the best buttermilk-battered chicken-fried steak you've ever tasted, and it's always good with green chile hominy on the side.

Among newer kitchen revelations has been the Sunday brunch debut, a remarkably simple but satisfying experience. This isn't the place to find granola, yogurt, and fruit; as per usual, Fred's brunch is pure Texas goodness. Tops is the plate of quail with eggs your way, in which the grilled, meaty birds get even better with just a spoonful of rich, roasted tomato salsa, spiked with fresh jalapeño. Somewhat lighter, the brunch migas features eggs scrambled with corn-tortilla strips with a side of refried beans, a joy with an 18-ounce mimosa on the side.

Yet, in spite of the gussied-up chuck-wagon offerings, Fred's burgers remain the most popular menu item. These are made with premium Texas-raised ground beef, hand-formed, seasoned with a little salt and pepper, and cooked to order on a hot, flat-top griddle. If you're made of tough stuff, the one to order is the Diablo burger, in which Chandler packs bits of his smoked jalapeños into the patty and tops it with spicy mustard. For an extra kick, add a few drops of the "rooster sauce," the Asian chile condiment sitting next to the bottle of ketchup on your table. This pairs perfectly with the divine fries, hand-cut into long strips, skin-on, from Idaho russets.

A few minor changes lie ahead at Fred's. The kitchen, which was built to feed a crowd of 40 people at a time, strains to turn out food for more than 200 on a busy evening, and Chandler's seven cooks struggle to find working space, so he's planning to enlarge it somewhat. The patio has been enclosed for year-round seating, too. But nobody should worry. It's still Fred's, just with improved packaging. And right in time for a shot at fame. Find Fred's Texas Café at 915 Currie St., Fort Worth; (817) 332-0083.

as winning as the giant platters of huevos rancheros and the beef gorditas. Expect big crowds at weekend breakfast and weekday lunch.

French/European

BISTRO LOUISE $$$
2900 South Hulen St., #40, Fort Worth
(817) 922-9244
www.bistrolouise.com

A sumptuous study in New Mediterranean pleasures, this flow of blue-green dining rooms in a shopping center southwest of downtown presents innovative works inspired by the owner-chef's frequent trips to Provence and Tuscany. Stylishly garbed and meticulously coiffed patrons tuck into gorgeous plates of seafood and game, pastas, and roasted vegetables, and enjoy popular selections, as well as great new finds, from a lengthy wine list.

**CACHAREL RESTAURANT &
GRAND BALLROOM** $$$
2221 East Lamar Blvd., Arlington
(817) 640-9981
www.cacharel.net

A sophisticated dining room atop an office building in North Arlington never disappoints because there's such a consistent treatment in gems such as escargots with mushrooms, grapes and pecans in a cream sauce, and sautéed lamb noisettes in a shallot-tarragon sauce with a wild mushroom risotto. The prix-fixe menu changes daily but there is always a large selection of steaks, fresh fish, and fowl. The dessert and wine lists deserve praise, too.

SAINT-EMILION RESTAURANT $$$
3617 West Seventh St., Fort Worth
(817) 737-2781
saint-emilionrestaurant.com

Long a favorite among the West Side carriage trade, this enclave of delights from the French countryside makes you feel as though you've awakened inside a dining room in the Loire Valley. Upscale yet comfortable, Saint-Emilion is named for the owner's home and offers a fixed-price, multi-course meal of creatively wrought salads, fresh seafood, wild game, chops, fresh vegetables, and lovely desserts. The gracious staff can make wise recommendations from a wine list laden with thoughtfully chosen French finds.

TASTE OF EUROPE $
1901 West Pioneer Parkway, Arlington
(817) 275-5530
www.tasteofeuropetx.com

Just one spoonful into the cup of lush borscht, a purplish-red beet soup filled with bits of crunchy cabbage, alongside a loaf of hot, homemade bread, and you'll be sold on this dining room from Belarus. The nondescript exterior belies the warmth found within, from the friendly staff to the gorgeous gifts—particularly the nesting dolls, scarves, and teapots—from Eastern Europe. Salads include those made from roasted eggplant and red bell peppers, and worthwhile entrees range from hot meat dumplings to lamb pilaf, and warm, fruit-filled strudels make a fine dessert.

Greek/Middle Eastern

**HEDARY'S MEDITERRANEAN
RESTAURANT** $$–$$$
6323 Camp Bowie Blvd., Fort Worth
(817) 731-6961
www.hedarys.com

Cowtown's first Middle Eastern restaurant has no can opener or microwave on the premises, so your food is incredibly fresh. Owned by a first-generation Lebanese family and its children, Hedary's is much loved for its maza, the multiple dishes of various salads such as tabbuli, labni, and hummus, as well as for its lamb kibbi, sirloin kafta, stuffed grape leaves, and the phenomenal baked lemony chicken. Finish with the extraordinary qahwi, a tiny cup of dark, aromatic coffee, and the rice pudding, fragrant with rose water.

Lebanon Comes to Cowtown

Hedary's, which calls itself a Mediterranean restaurant, is actually Lebanese. Folks in Fort Worth with a long memory recall when, some 30 years ago, the Hedary family introduced us to Lebanese "pizza." Generations of the family have worked in their kitchens and dining rooms since the days when they hung their first sign on their original tiny White Settlement Road cafe, and we've all but forgotten the charm of discovering that the Hedarys initially thought "pizza" meant restaurant. The Ridglea shop has been a fixture since before many Camp Bowie dining patrons were born, but devotees have never tired of the honest flavors coming from the fresh dishes (still not a can opener or freezer in the place). Find Hedary's at 6323 Camp Bowie Blvd. in Fort Worth, (817) 731-6961, www.hedarys.com.

JAZZ CAFÉ $–$$
2504 Montgomery St., Fort Worth
(817) 737-0043

A funky dive of the first order, this standby in the Cultural District does a great gyro sandwich, as well as an excellent turkey-avocado sandwich. The Greek salad has no match in town, and the black bean soup is exceptional as well. On Saturday and Sunday, the breakfast dishes of choice are the SOB eggs (scrambled with tortillas, with black beans on the side) and the feta omelet with biscuits. Live jazz music plays on Sunday morning.

Home Cooking

BABE'S CHICKEN DINNER HOUSE $$
104 North Oak St., Roanoke
(817) 491-2900
www.babeschicken.com

The line forms as early as 4:30 p.m. for the evening meals at this monument to home cooking. Tucked within a wonderful, 1908 rock building on the historic main road through tiny Roanoke, Babe's comforts your palate with platters of freshly fried, juicy chicken or meaty chicken-fried steaks. Served family style, dinners come with mashed potatoes, corn, green salad, and fluffy buttermilk biscuits.

BUTTONS RESTAURANT $$–$$$
4701 West Freeway, Fort Worth
(817) 735-4900
www.buttonsrestaurant.com

Chef Keith Hicks is one groovin' dude, turning out fancy versions of soul food favorites while '70s hits (Al Green is pretty hot here) play on the stereo. Chicken and waffles, a big Harlem favorite, are a hit, as is the fried green tomato appetizer, topped with a fried egg. A martini menu is popular, too.

DREW'S PLACE $
5701 Curzon Ave., Fort Worth
(817) 735-4408
www.drewssoulfood.com

The long lines streaming out the door at high noon tell you you've come to the right place for a fine dose of soul food. Then you catch a whiff of the home cooking wafting from the kitchen, and there's no way any crowd could discourage you from staying. A fixture at the edge of the Como neighborhood, Drew's is a bright, cheery family operation where everybody is made to feel as though they're sitting at the kitchen table with loved ones. The biggest trouble you'll have here is deciding between the smothered pork chops, fried chicken, meat loaf, and catfish.

DIXIE HOUSE CAFÉ $
515 Houston St., Fort Worth
(817) 347-9333
www.dixiehousecafe.com

In the morning you can feast on breakfast tacos, veggie omelets, and eggs with pork chops, as well as enormous, gooey cinnamon rolls. At lunch and dinner, there's chicken-fried steak, pot roast, meat loaf, and baked chicken, plus the Dixie House's famous desserts. (Check the Web site for four other area locations.)

PARIS COFFEE SHOP $
704 West Magnolia Ave., Fort Worth
(817) 335-2041
www.pariscoffeeshop.net

Go early for a lunch at this corner cafe, one of the last places in town where a great plate of old-fashioned home cooking is found for five or six bucks. Choose from standards like baked chicken, meat loaf, chicken-fried steak, or chopped steak, and leave room for pie. Breakfast is a huge draw, thanks to some of the biggest and best biscuits in town.

Italian

AVENTINO RISTORANTE $$$
3206 Winthrop Ave., Fort Worth
(817) 731-0711
www.aventino.us

Gorgeous and serene, this little trattoria evokes the mood of a Greenwich Village dining room. Beef carpaccio with arugula and shaved Parmesan is divine, as is the short rib lasagna. Some regulars like to go perch on stools at the bar to sip cocktails and nosh on appetizers.

NONNA TATA $$
1400 West Magnolia Ave., Fort Worth
(817) 332-0250

A teensy bistro in historic Fairmount will knock your lights out with authentic dishes from the old country. Handmade pastas will delight, as do lighter dishes of arugula salad and sautéed chicken. This is a BYOB operation, so be sure to schlep a good bottle of wine along.

LA PIAZZA $$$$
600 South University Dr., #601, Fort Worth
(817) 334-0000
www.lapiazzafw.com

Chic and tres exclusive, this house of haute Italian cuisine is known as much for its stylishness as its lovely food. Beautiful presentations and delicate flavors in servings of fish, meats, fowl, and pastas are what keep the prosperous, fashionable clientele coming back with great regularity. A plush interior, bathed in subtle light, a fine—if pricey—wine list, and a knowledgeable staff have kept La Piazza at the top of most lists for well over a decade.

PIOLA ITALIAN RESTAURANT
AND GARDEN $$
3700 Mattison Ave., Fort Worth
(817) 989-0007

Tucked away in the Monticello neighborhood, this delightful keeper in a lovely little cottage comes from Bobby Albanese of Ruffino's. Good picks include Grandma's lasagna, bruschetta with goat cheese and tapenade, and baby portobellos stuffed with shrimp.

SARDINES RISTORANTE ITALIANO $$
509 University Dr., Fort Worth
(817) 332-9937
www.sardinesftworth.com

This dark and intimate favorite in the Cultural District is beloved for heavily garlicked pasta plates, grilled fish and chops, good Italian wines and beers, and live jazz nightly. Shoot-from-the-hip service is often entertaining, and pleasant porch dining is great after the museums or the theater.

Mexican/Tex-Mex

BENITO'S $$
1450 West Magnolia Ave., Fort Worth
(817) 332-8633

This friendly duo of dining rooms is where savvy diners go for a fix of food from Mexico's interior. Specialties include chiles rellenos stuffed with Oaxacan cheese, the Yucatecan-style tamale steamed inside a plantain leaf, and pork tips

Favorite DFW Dishes

Lobster taco (even better than the famous tortilla soup) at the Mansion on Turtle Creek, one of the signature dishes that launched Southwestern cuisine founder Dean Fearing (even if he's now at the Ritz-Carlton). 2821 Turtle Creek Blvd., Dallas, (214) 559-2100.

Mushroom soup with crusty French bread, the signature at The Grape, which also serves a lovely glass of wine from South Africa, New Zealand, or Texas. 2808 Greenville Ave., Dallas, (214) 828-1981.

Popovers with strawberry butter at the Zodiac Room inside Neiman Marcus, made by the same recipe Helen Corbitt developed in the 1950s and still best alongside her mandarin orange soufflé and chicken salad. 1618 Main St., Sixth Floor, Dallas, (214) 891-1210.

Bittersweet chocolate semifreddo at York Street, the sparkling jewel belonging to chef Sharon Hage, whose talent for constantly adapting her menu to new offerings at the market is legendary. 6047 Lewis St., Dallas, (214) 826-0968.

Pizza at Fireside Pies, topped with chicken-fennel sausage, roasted garlic, and assorted cheeses from the nearby Mozzarella Company, best eaten on the patio with a cool glass of sangria. 2820 North Henderson Ave., Dallas, (214) 370-3916.

Juicy, crumbly cheeseburger with crinkle-cut fries at Kincaid's Grocery, where you can still eat standing up along the grocery counters or at picnic tables. 4901 Camp Bowie Blvd., Fort Worth, (817) 732-2881.

Grilled New Zealand red deer chop with truffled macaroni and cheese and fried artichoke in a historic building within the fabled Stockyards, at Lonesome Dove Western Bistro, 2406 North Main St., Fort Worth, (817) 740-8810.

Chicken-fried steak with well-peppered cream gravy and fluffy homemade yeast rolls at the vintage Paris Coffee Shop, 700 West Magnolia Ave., Fort Worth, (817) 335-2041.

Chicken enchiladas topped with a tomatillo–green chile sauce at El Asadero, where the fiery jalapeño salsa should come with a fire-hazard warning. 1535 North Main St., Fort Worth, (817) 626-3399.

Roasted sable fish with three-beet escabeche at Lanny's Alta Cocina Mexicana, where nouvelle Mexican cuisine gets a French twist. 3405 West Seventh St., Fort Worth, (817) 850-9996.

sautéed with calabacitas, or a stew of squash and tomato. Dishes with Tex-Mex leanings are offered, too, such as enchiladas in sour cream sauce and chalupas smothered in cheeses and beef. Breakfast is offered all the time, which is popular with the after-bar crowds that stream in on weekends. Good margaritas and a selection of Mexican beers add to the appeal.

EL ASADERO MEXICAN STEAK HOUSE $
1535 North Main St., Fort Worth
(817) 626-3399
www.elasadero.com
Some of the hottest salsa in creation will burn an everlasting memory of this wonderful little dive into your brain. Once you've had the green enchiladas packed with chicken and topped with tangy tomatillo sauce and gooey white cheese, you'll plot your next return. Cold Carta Blanca and Dos Equis beers, along with the especially friendly staff, are crowd-pleasing.

ESPERANZA'S BAKERY & CAFÉ $
2122 North Main St., Fort Worth
(817) 616-5770
1601 Park Place Ave., Fort Worth
(817) 332-3848
www.joets.com
Yes, people love the enchiladas here, but if you see what the Spanish-speaking patrons are eating, you'll find Mexican soul food is the real specialty. Try the guisado de res, tender stewed beef tips in a robust chile verde sauce with rice and beans, or for pure comfort, the caldo de res, a bowl of soup including big beef chunks with a pile of fresh vegetables, such as cabbage, potato, carrots, and corn. Breakfasts are enormously popular here, too.

GLORIA'S $$
3901 Arlington Highlands Blvd.,
Arlington
(817) 701-2981
www.gloriasrestaurants.com
Only if you've been hiding under a rock would you not know about this popular "Salva-Mex" operation, a local mini-chain grown from a homey spot in Dallas's Oak Cliff neighborhood. Sunny and

casual-chic, Gloria's is the place to find a small traditional Salvadoran menu within an expansive, modern Mexican spread. It's a lively spot where families and grown-ups find common ground. Go at brunch for an omelet filled with fajita beef or chicken with black beans and pico de gallo on the side, or for eggs scrambled with Argentinian sausage and three eggs any style with flank steak. Locations also in Colleyville, Fort Worth, Frisco, Dallas, Garland, and Rockwall.

JOE T GARCIA'S MEXICAN
RESTAURANT $$
2201 North Commerce St., Fort Worth
(817) 626-4356
www.joets.com
Quite possibly the most famous restaurant in Texas, this 1930s landmark has grown from a tiny house to a magnificent spread of bloom-framed gardens. The main menu offers plated dinners of enchiladas and tacos or chicken and beef fajitas, but you can order off the menu, opting for tortilla soup and fajita-topped salads. The margaritas tend to be lethal but are always delicious. Lines can be long at peak lunch and dinner hours.

LANNY'S ALTA COCINA MEXICANA $$$$
3405 West Seventh St., Fort Worth
(817) 850-9996
www.lannyskitchen.com
The great-grandson of Joe T. Garcia has made a name for himself with elevated Mexican cuisine. The style and sensibility will remind you nothing of Tex-Mex but will transport you to the swankiest of all Mexico City restaurants. Among beautiful efforts are lobster ravioli, carne asada in a cabernet reduction, and the most elegant desserts the mind can conceive. An inspired wine list is offered, too.

LA PLAYA MAYA $$
6209 Sunset Dr., Fort Worth
(817) 738-3329
www.laplayamaya.com
Settle in first for a cold Bohemia or an "uptown" margarita made with Herradura, then get down to the business of carne asada or sautéed shrimp

with an herb-garlic sauce. Lunch specials are numerous and include far more than the usual—such as fried whole catfish with fries, shrimp in ranchero sauce, and the cowboy enchilada, a flour tortilla stuffed with fajita beef or chicken and topped with queso. Sweet endings include coconut ice cream with Kahlua and traditional flan.

Pizza

BRIX PIZZA & WINE BAR   **$$**
2747 South Hulen, Fort Worth
(817) 924-2749
www.brixpizzeria.com
You'll want to linger a while over plates of bruschetta and inventive salads, but just be sure to leave room for divine pizza from the wood-burning oven. Toppings include everything from Italian sausage and ricotta cheese to mushrooms, spinach, and jalapeños.

COAL VINES PIZZA SOUTHLAKE   **$$**
1251 East Southlake Blvd., Southlake
(817) 310-0850
www.coalvines.com
A fashionable pizza bistro exudes sidewalk cafe charm, thanks to a breezy patio. Brunch is fun, thanks to a crisp pizza topped with spinach, pancetta, and over-easy eggs, especially with a lovely Greek salad as an appetizer.

ROCCO'S WOOD FIRED PIZZA   **$$**
5716 Locke Ave., Fort Worth
(817) 731-4466
www.roccosfortworth.com
From a wood-burning oven comes sensational pizza, topped with all sorts of goodies from sliced meatballs, smoked shrimp, and ground sirloin to fresh spinach and black truffles. Nice salads and desserts are on the menu, too. Note: This is a take-out place only.

Seafood

EDDIE V'S PRIME SEAFOOD   **$$$$**
3120 West Seventh St., Fort Worth
(817) 336-8000
www.eddiev.com

Prime seafood means a bounty of fresh-caught goods from Hawaii, the East Coast, and waters in between. Roughly 75 percent of the menu is fish, but there are gorgeous steaks from Allen Bros. available, too. The bar has an ample list of exceptional appetizers, from cashew-crusted calamari to tuna tartare. Early in the evening, find drink and snack specials. Live music nightly in the lounge.

Eddie V's

If you're fishing for good seafood dining, you can't overlook Eddie V's Prime Seafood in Fort Worth, a restaurant bringing fish to landlocked North Texas like nobody has dared before. In spring, seasonal bivalves to try from the raw bar are the big, meaty Salt Ponds, the prized oysters from Point Judith Pond, Rhode Island. Favorite sashimi offerings are often goodies such as those made from Opakapaka, Hapu'Upu'U, Hamachi, and Tasmanian salmon, all caught along Hawaii's coast. Look also for temptations like black cod baked in parchment paper with a tomato fennel broth, haricots verts, heirloom tomatoes, and basil; and seared black grouper with a sweet corn puree and sun-dried tomato relish. It's located at 3100 West Seventh St., Fort Worth, 817-336-8000, www.eddiev.com.

FLYING FISH   **$–$$**
2913 Montgomery St., Fort Worth
(817) 989-2277
www.flyingfishinthe.net
Restaurateur Shannon Wynne brings his favorite Caddo Lake fish-shack experiences to this cheery hangout, cluttered with lake retreat memorabilia.

Fried platters abound, but the barbecued shrimp po'boys, grilled tilapia tacos, and snapper Veracruz are best.

J&J OYSTER BAR $$
612 North University Dr., Fort Worth
(817) 335-2756
www.jjbluesbar.com
Iced trays of Gulf oysters, platters of steaming crawfish, piles of fresh, you-peel-'em shrimp, baskets of fried clam strips, jalapeño hush puppies, and frosty mugs of beer—what more could you want? Cheap, super-casual seafood dining at its best comes with quick, friendly service and a great patio.

PIERRE'S MARDI GRAS $
2816 South Cooper St., Arlington
(817) 557-9990
www.pierresmardigras.com
A post-Katrina story with a happy ending, this Cajun eatery brings you the best of the Crescent City without the long drive or Bourbon Street hangover. Your options are numerous, from a po'boy piled with fried shrimp, oysters, barbecued shrimp, sausage, or roast beef to red beans and rice with sausage or seafood gumbo. Leave room for bread pudding.

Steaks

BOB'S STEAK & CHOP HOUSE $$$$
1300 Houston St., Fort Worth
(817) 350-4100
www.bobs-steakandchop.com
Shrimp remoulade and crab cakes are the star starters, with the bone-in rib eye and Kansas City strip favored among the prime steak options. The best sides are the skillet potatoes with green peppercorn sauce and the massive glazed carrot.

CATTLEMEN'S STEAKHOUSE $$–$$$
2458 North Main St., Fort Worth
(817) 624-3945
www.cattlemenssteakhouse.com
Since 1947, this mainstay in the Stockyards National Historic District has welcomed as many dyed-in-the-wool cowboys and international tourists as the weekly rodeo that takes place a few doors away in Cowtown Coliseum. Campy without intending to be, the saloon and dining rooms whisk you back to an era long, long past, as witnessed by the grainy photos of championship cattle from decades of stock show competition. Order the signature "Heart O' Texas Rib Eye," a nicely marbled slab, and watch the grizzled grill man fire that baby over the open fire serving as the focal point in the main dining room.

DEL FRISCO'S STEAKHOUSE $$$$
812 Main St., Fort Worth
(817) 877-3999
www.delfriscos.com

Boot Tops at Bob's

Its signature côte de bouef and Kansas City strip may be identical to those served at the other locations in the Dallas-based chain, but the Fort Worth Bob's Steak and Chop House bears an exclusive—if rather unexpected—Cowtown imprint. As you enter the sleek restaurant from the bustling Omni Hotel lobby, note the fancy doorstops: Beautiful brown leather boot tops with intricate tooling and stitching have been transformed into wine bottle sleeves by renowned boot maker M.L. Leddy's in the Fort Worth Stockyards; Bob's weights them with rocks for this decor function. Sold next door at the hotel's Kimbell Museum Gift Shop, the clever creation can also be a wine gift tote, vase, or handbag. It's $80 at the shop, open from 7 a.m. till 9 p.m. daily, (817) 350-4109. The restaurant is at 1300 Houston St., Fort Worth, 817-350-4100, www.bobs-steakandchop.com.

 **Close-up**

Sunday Brunch

By the time Sunday rolls around, you're ready to celebrate surviving another week. Quick, before another round of carpool, soccer practice, and computer crashes, grab some prized companions and go toast a day of freedom from stress. It's called Sunday brunch, and it's the only civilized way to get your week going in the right direction. To help you along, we checked out new arrivals on the brunch scene. Here are the best in Dallas–Fort Worth.

Gloria's (3901 Arlington Highlands Blvd., Arlington; 817-701-2981; www.gloriasrestaurants .com; locations also in Colleyville, Fort Worth, Frisco, Dallas, Garland, and Rockwall): This popular "Salva-Mex" operation, a local mini-chain grown from a homey spot in Dallas's Oak Cliff neighborhood, is sunny and casual-chic. You'll find a small traditional Salvadoran menu within an expansive, modern Mexican spread. It's a lively spot where families and grown-ups find common ground. There's an omelet filled with fajita beef or chicken with black beans and pico de gallo on the side; eggs scrambled with Argentinian sausage and three eggs any style with flank steak. A good hangover buster is the Mexican favorite, chilaquiles, with a Michelada—that's beer over ice with a dash of hot sauce and plenty of lime—on the side.

Mac's on 7th (2600 West Seventh St., Fort Worth; 817-332-6227; www.macsteak.com): New in Montgomery Plaza, this outpost of a 20-year veteran in Arlington's restaurant scene brings contemporary American dining to the burgeoning Seventh Street Corridor. The menu's much like the one at the Colleyville Mac's, big on steaks and fish. Our brunch visit found tables and booths in the sleek, bright interior bustling with families—and grown-ups in need of a bloody Mary. If you crave stick-to-your-ribs food, order the chicken-fried steak with scrambled eggs, complete with biscuits and gravy—and worry about your waistline tomorrow. Slightly lighter is the Eggs Point St. George, a variation on Benedict, with poached eggs topping a bed of lump white crabmeat atop English muffins, beneath a Hollandaise blanket; the blessing here is that you can get a half-order. Best of the lot is the fluffy omelet packed with spinach, sautéed mushrooms, bacon, green onion, and Jack cheese, and if you want to sub sliced tomatoes for the hash browns (these are pretty darn good, so think carefully), it's a-okay. A small buffet station serves various fruit options.

Lambert's (2731 White Settlement Rd., Fort Worth, 817-882-1161; www.lambertsfortworth .com): The Sunday spread is a crowd-pleaser for those wanting to drink and gorge as well as those looking for lean, clean choices, too. As at lunch and dinner, the setting is rancho-moderne, so you're fine in boots and jeans or any old outfit. Choice nibbles from the short buffet line—replenished by the kitchen staff frequently, so nothing sits long—are the eggs migas with fresh salsa, crispy smoked bacon, lush salmon smoked on site, a platter of freshly cut fruit with berries, fluffy green salad, and a carving station with smoked prime rib and pork roast (get the velvety mustard sauce). From the menu, you can choose items such as buttermilk biscuits with creamy sausage gravy and a sinful plate of brioche French toast with whipped cream and maple syrup. Oh, and exceptional eggs Benny, thanks to perfect hollandaise.

Vidalias (200 Main St., Fort Worth; 817-210-2222; www.marriott.com): Inside the Renaissance Worthington, in the space formerly occupied by the Chisholm Club and Sam & Harry's, an upscale Southern-style restaurant gives down-home food a special touch. Most diners tend to be hotel guests, but the weekend splurge brings plenty of locals with families in tow. Here's where you'll find shades of that favorite of Fort Worth buffets, the big Sunday 'do that was once served upstairs on the hotel's famous bridge. Prized picks from the cold line include smoked salmon, a vast selection of cheeses, plenty of fresh fruit and salads, sushi, and shrimp on ice. The hot side includes eggs, bacon, sausage, pancakes, made-to-order omelets, carved meats, fresh fish, and lots of pastries and desserts.

Dallas-Area Dining Stats

- Dallas has one five-diamond restaurant, seven four-star restaurants, and 10 four-diamond restaurants.
- According to the Texas Restaurant Association, the Dallas area has more than 7,000 restaurants to enjoy.
- In 2009, three of Dallas's celebrity chefs opened new restaurants: Kent Rathbun, Rathbun's Blue Plate Kitchen; Wolfgang Puck, Five Sixty by Wolfgang Puck; and Stephan Pyles, Samar.
- Zagat Survey ranked The French Room at the Adolphus the No. 1 restaurant in the U.S. (2006), as it wrote "there aren't enough superlatives" to describe it.
- Fearing's, Chef Dean Fearing's namesake restaurant in the Ritz-Carlton, Dallas, was named "Best New Restaurant" and "Restaurant of the Year" by *Esquire* magazine (2007).
- The Mansion Restaurant, at the Rosewood Mansion on Turtle Creek, was ranked among the "Best New Restaurants in 2008" by *Esquire* magazine.
- Several nationally ranked steak and chop houses can be found in the Dallas area, including Bob's Steak & Chop House, which is currently ranked No. 3 according to the USDA Prime Steakhouses chart.
- Dallas Fish Market was ranked among the Top 10 seafood restaurants for 2008 by *Bon Appetit* magazine.
- The frozen margarita machine was invented in Dallas.

(Source: Greater Dallas Restaurant Association)

A magnificent wave of butter essence floats upward from the exquisite filet, nearly 2 inches thick and redolent with salt-and-pepper spice blend. Even more brilliant, the New York strip induces a serious swoon with its thin-crust char surrounding a smooth, juicy interior. Few things—save perhaps the giant, golden bangles of fried onion rings—can top the signature crab cake appetizer, a toothsome bundle of crabmeat pieces studded with pimento that you swab with a sumptuous lobster creole sauce.

GRADY'S $$$–$$$$
2443 Forest Park Blvd., Fort Worth
(817) 922-9980
www.gradysrestaurant.com

The town's favorite cowboy cook, Grady Spears, whips up a mean chicken-fried steak with cream gravy, as well as a very nice beef tenderloin with cabernet reduction. Pecan-crusted salmon sells well, too, as does the pork chop. Great sides include cheesy grits and spinach salad. For dessert, try the white chocolate bundt cake.

JR'S STEAKHOUSE $$$–$$$$
5400 Highway 121, Colleyville
(817) 355-1414
www.jrsfinedining.com

Ask for the plump, lush rib eye to be cooked with an outer char to get proper balance for the melted cook's butter on top and the heavy garlic-herbed mashers beneath. For sensory overload, order the pepper-crusted filet, a 3-inch-thick wonder glazed with a brandy demi. Expect to find a mix of dinner dates and business types.

LAMBERT'S $$$$
2731 White Settlement Rd., Fort Worth
(817) 882-1161
www.lambertsfortworth.com
In a setting that's rather modern ranch, choice chow is the pan-roasted chicken, halibut with sautéed spinach, or a T-bone topped with red chile enchiladas. The best dessert is the coconut cream pie, hands-down. If you like, you can just sit in the bar and snack on ceviche and fried calamari, with a handmade margarita on the side.

LONESOME DOVE WESTERN BISTRO $$$$
2406 North Main St., Fort Worth
(817) 740-8810
www.lonesomedovebistro.com
Celebrity chef of Iron Chef fame Tim Love brought style and sophistication to Stockyards dining with his western bistro. The menu typically offers grilled quail quesadilla with goat cheese and black bean puree, buffalo burger on sourdough, barbecued duck spring rolls, braised lamb shank with sautéed spinach, and red corn-crusted halibut with cilantro-orange butter. It's

a smart place to take dates and clients before a concert at Billy Bob's.

REATA RESTAURANT $$$
310 Houston St., Fort Worth
(817) 336-1009
www.reata.net
From tenderloin tamales to steak with enchiladas to field greens with goat cheese and candied pecans, this is the destination for creatively sauced and generously plated giddyup goodies. Decorated in the style of the *Giant* movie ranch for which it's named, this place is a huge hit with business folks, Lone Star visitors, and locals out for a good time.

Vegetarian

SPIRAL DINER $–$$
1314 West Magnolia Ave., Fort Worth
(817) 332-8834
www.spiraldiner.com
Fort Worth's only vegan restaurant has won numerous national awards for an inventive, winning menu. Among goodies are meatless tacos, enchiladas, chili, sandwiches, and much more, all of which sworn carnivores enjoy. Breakfast is a big hit, too, and there's a great list of organic beers available.

NIGHTLIFE

Not too long ago, Friday and Saturday were the big party nights around Dallas and Fort Worth. Then Thursday became a popular going-out night. Of course, who doesn't want to celebrate hump day on Wednesday? Then there's half-price this and that on Tuesday night, and Monday night's always good for football or other games. And Sunday, well, you just want to bid the weekend farewell. This is likely the kind of thinking that's made every evening good for going out on the town.

From good little cocktail bars to chic dance spots to down-home country-music clubs to movie theaters and comedy clubs, there's plenty to do when the sun goes down. Don't be surprised if beer and wine are all that's offered; some Texas bars don't sell mixed drinks. Unless otherwise noted, dress is casual at area nightspots.

A few rules to keep in mind: if there's live music, a cover charge is likely in place; and the Texas Alcoholic Beverage Commission (TABC) says bars must close—or at least stop serving alcohol—at 2 a.m. And if clean air is a plus in your book, prepare to smile—Dallas has a smoking ban in effect for all restaurants and bars, and Fort Worth can't be far behind.

DALLAS

Bars

ADAIR'S SALOON
2624 Commerce St., Dallas
(214) 939-9900
www.adairssaloon.com
A beloved hole-in-the-wall, this rowdy joint is known as the place to take your date to see if he or she is a keeper or a priss who should be dumped. Oldies play on the jukebox, video and shuffleboard provide entertainment, and the occasional live band shows up to play. The beer's cold and the burgers are excellent.

ANGRY DOG
2726 Commerce St., Dallas
(214) 741-4406
angrydog.com
An institution in Deep Ellum, this joint has a long wooden bar that begs your bellying up. Drink a cocktail or choose from among 100 bottled or 20-plus tap beers. Hot dogs are the signature snack.

THE GINGER MAN
2718 Boll St., Dallas
(214) 754-8771
www.gingermanpub.com
Beer is the name of the game at this pub in the Quadrangle/Uptown district, with 74 on tap and 110 in bottles, domestic and imported. A cute old cottage provides the cozy setting, with lots of seating areas, bar stools, and a beer garden out back. There's a lounge upstairs, as well. A jukebox provides the tunes, but there are live cover bands on Saturday. Buy the beer special on Tuesday and keep the logo glass.

HUMPERDINK'S
6050 Greenville Ave., Dallas
(214) 368-1203
www.humperdinks.com
This is the original location of a place begun in the 1970s (others are found in Addison, North Dallas, Arlington, and Richardson) now known for the 100-ounce "tower" of beer. House brews include Raspberry Blonde and Honeypot Lager, and you can purchase take-home kegs for your own party. Though it's not marketed as a sports

bar, you can always find games on the big screens and multiple TVs scattered around the various rooms. Burgers and other American edibles are on the menu.

KNOX STREET PUB
4447 McKinney Ave., Dallas
(214) 528-5100
www.knoxstreetpub.com
A mainstay in the busy Knox/Henderson area, this place tends to attract younger patrons with its big beer selection. There's a full bar, too, as well as a DJ spinning tunes until closing time on weekends. The valet parking is complimentary.

LEE HARVEY'S
1807 Gould St., Dallas
(214) 428-1555
www.leeharveys.com
Often rated "best bar" by local publications, this bar inside an old house has a loyal clientele who enjoy happy hour all day, Sunday through Tuesday. There's a large yard with picnic tables outside, perfect for sipping drinks and noshing on award-winning onion rings. The bonus is the bar cat named Bacon who penned the bar's recipe book; proceeds from the book sales benefit the Dallas SPCA. You can bring your dog on Sunday afternoon, and the bar provides water bowls.

THE QUARTER BAR
3301 McKinney Ave., Dallas
(214) 754-4940
On the brick portion of McKinney in an early 20th-century building, connected to the bakery/cafe Breadwinner's, this popular destination for younger singles is always packed on weekend nights. Drinks are reasonably prices and the jukebox music is loud. Sit on lounges and couches or be ready to stand and mingle. A rooftop patio is refreshing. Valet parking.

REPUBLIC
2922 North Hall St., Dallas
(214) 740-1111
www.republicdallas.com

525 Meadow Creek Dr., Irving
(972) 580-7906
www.republiclascolinas.com
The original location in Uptown has been voted "Best Place to Be Seen" by *D Magazine* readers, and it's known as a place frequented by Dallas Cowboys players. This is a place for top-shelf cocktails made with Grey Goose and Cabo Wabo, as well as handmade frozen mojitos and cosmopolitans using fresh fruit. Look for a crowded patio, plasma TVs, and plush leather couches.

TIME OUT TAVERN
5101 West Lovers Lane, Dallas
(214) 956-9552
Regulars know this as TOT, a basic, somewhat divey bar popular for its picnic tables, shuffleboard, pool, graffiti, beer signs, and ticket stubs tacked to the walls. Happy hour beer prices are tasty.

Comedy Clubs
ADDISON IMPROV
4980 Belt Line Rd., Addison
(972) 404-8501
Headliners have included national names like John Witherspoon, Hal Sparks, and Mike Epps. This is also a place for Comedy Defensive Driving, a great place for your traffic offense penance. A full dinner menu is offered.

BACKDOOR COMEDY
Doubletree Hotel
8250 North Central Expressway, Dallas
(214) 328-4444
www.backdoorcomedy.com
Comics playing here have appeared on Comedy Central and BET, and regulars have included Paul Varghese of NBC's *Last Comic Standing*, with special appearances from the likes of David Spade and Bill Engvall. Open-mic night is Thursday and Saturday. Ask about stand-up workshops.

Concert Bar Venues
THE GRANADA THEATER
3524 Greenville Ave., Dallas
(214) 824-9933
www.granadatheater.com

A vintage movie theater turned music venue, this one never fails to please. A full bar is offered.

HOUSE OF BLUES
2200 North Lamar St., Dallas
(214) 978-BLUE
www.houseofblues.com/venues/clubvenues/dallas
One of the locations in a nationwide chain, this edition is found downtown in the Brewery district. Big names performing on the stage to date include Usher, Snoop Dogg, Katy Perry, and B. B. King. An enormous venue with a separate restaurant, it's definitely a destination. Sunday Gospel Brunch is very popular.

SONS OF HERMANN HALL
3414 Elm St. at Exposition Ave., Dallas
(214) 747-4422
sonsofhermann.com
In a fraternal club venue founded in 1890, this saloon brings in exceptional music groups perfect for sipping and dancing crowds. Swing dance night is Wednesday and includes an hour of lessons, Thursday is acoustic music night and weekends brings live acts from around Texas and the nation. You can play billiards here, too. Note that it's a cash-only outfit.

Country Music Clubs

COWBOY'S RED RIVER
10310 Technology Blvd., Dallas
(214) 352-1796
www.cowboysdancehall.com
When they were up-and-coming acts, Neal McCoy and Tracey Byrd played this honky-tonk, where the house band called Runnin' Behind plays most nights. You can shoot pool, take free dance lessons on Wednesday and Friday, and order drinks from a full bar.

GILLEY'S
1135 South Lamar St., Dallas
(214) 421-2021
www.gilleysdallas.com
A descendant of the Houston-area honky-tonk featured in John Travolta's *Urban Cowboy*, this giant dance club hosts local acts as well as marquee names like Dwight Yoakum. There are large and small dance floors, with free dance lessons at 6 p.m. on Saturday. You can ride a mechanical bull, shoot some pool, and enjoy cocktails from a full bar.

WEEKENDS CRAZY HORSE SALOON
600 Cooke Dr., Rowlett
(972) 475-6438
At Harbor Bay Marina on Lake Ray Hubbard, this country bar is a friendly corner of Texas with no cover charge. Pool tables are offered, and there's karaoke on Thursday. Live music is on tap Friday and Saturday, and there's a late-night taco bar Thursday through Saturday. Expect to find sports showing on several TVs.

Dance Bars

AURA
2912 McKinney Ave., Dallas
(214) 220-2872
www.aurauptowndallas.com
There's usually a wait outside on weekends at this popular, newer nightspot, which offers VIP tables and bottle service starting at $300. Very modern in styling, this has been a hit with pro basketballers and Paris Hilton, among others. DJs spin hip-hop and electro dance stuff.

GHOSTBAR
2440 Victory Park Lane, Dallas
(214) 720-9919
From the same group that produced the popular Rain nightclub at the Palms Las Vegas comes this glowing-blue bar perched high atop the W in Victory Plaza. The crowd tends to be 20-something women and men in their 30s and 40s, and it's a popular scene for bachelorette parties. You can book a table ahead and pay for bottle service, and it will cost you. Don't be surprised to find a guest DJ from New York or L.A. There's no cover on Tuesday through Thursday and women (without dates) come in free on Friday and Saturday. A dress code is in effect, meaning no flip-flops, shorts, athletic wear, tennis shoes, or ball caps.

LOTUS BAR
2900 McKinney Ave., Dallas
(214) 468-0300
lotusbar.com

A Zen tone is achieved with waterfalls, neutral color palette, low lighting, and oversized sofas at this lounge and dance club. Backspin Fridays mean the DJs play '80s and '90s music, and there's the customary bottle and VIP table service here. Britney Spears dropped by when she was making a Dallas stop on her tour.

ZUBAR
2012 Greenville Ave., Dallas
(214) 887-0071
thezubar.com

Rather New York in tone and looks, this posh place is done in red, copper, and dark wood, and the clientele is well dressed. Local art hangs on the walls, overstuffed couches and large booths accommodate groups of friends, and visiting DJs spin good dance tunes.

Live Music Bars

BALCONY CLUB
1825 Abrams Parkway, Dallas
(214) 826-8104

Sitting above the famous old Lakewood Theater, here's a venue known for live jazz. Musicians love to hang out here, where outdoor patio seating and indoor booths make for an intimate experience. Specialty martinis are good for sipping.

BARLEY HOUSE
5612 Yale Blvd., Dallas
(214) 824-0306
www.barleyhouse.com

Local bands play this SMU-area favorite, where food includes a long list of fried goodies. On Wednesday, beer and drinks are discounted.

LAKEWOOD BAR & GRILL
6430 Gaston Ave., Dallas
(214) 826-3888
www.lbgdallas.com

A neighborhood favorite for decades, this laid-back joint features live cover bands, pool tables, sports on TV, good burgers, and a cool cocktail.

POOR DAVID'S PUB
1313 South Lamar St., Dallas
(214) 565-1295
www.poordavidspub.com

A dive bar with a huge following, this hangout calls itself "listener friendly," urging you to pay attention to the music playing onstage. Over the years, acts like Lyle Lovett and Robert Earl Keen and the Dixie Chicks have played here. Seating on the patio, too.

Movie Theaters

All over Dallas County, you'll find the usual multiplexes from AMC, Rave, Hollywood, and all the usual suspects. Here are a few special theaters, noted for bringing indie flicks to town.

ANGELIKA FILM CENTER
5321 East Mockingbird Lane, Dallas
(214) 841-4713
www.angelikafilmcenter.com

An anchor in Mockingbird Station, this ultra-contemporary theater has a cafe/bar off the lobby and even offers cry-baby matinee features, allowing you to bring your infant to early showings.

INWOOD THEATER
5458 West Lovers Lane
(214) 764-9106
www.landmarktheatres.com/Market/Dallas/InwoodTheatre.htm

A vintage movie palace, this one has been reconfigured to offer three screens and is beautifully restored. You can gets drinks from a bar and sit in comfy LoveSac chairs and couches, or you can go have a cocktail in the Inwood Lounge, off the lobby, before or after your showing.

MAGNOLIA
3699 McKinney Ave., Dallas
(214) 764-9106
www.magpictures.com

That's Entertainment!

Many movies and TV shows have been filmed in the Dallas–Fort Worth area, including the following:

The Big Show, 1936, Dallas

Girl in Room 20, 1946, Dallas

Juke Joint, 1947, Dallas

The Giant Gila Monster, 1959, Dallas

State Fair, 1962, Dallas

Bonnie & Clyde, 1967, Dallas and area

Benji, 1973, McKinney

Logan's Run, 1975, Dallas and Fort Worth

Semi-Tough, 1977, Dallas

Dallas, 1978–1990, Dallas

Dallas Cowboys Cheerleaders, 1978, Dallas

The 36 Most Beautiful Girls in Texas, 1978, Fort Worth

The Acorn People, 1980, Dallas

The Oldest Living Graduate, 1980, Dallas

Tender Mercies, 1981, Waxahachie

Silkwood, 1982, Dallas

Places in the Heart, 1983, Waxahachie

The Trip to Bountiful, 1985, Dallas, Waxahachie, and area

Over the Top, 1987, Fort Worth

Baja Oklahoma, 1987, Fort Worth

Born on the Fourth of July, 1988, Dallas and area

Daddy's Dyin, Who's Got the Will?, 1989, Dallas and area

Problem Child, 1989, Dallas

The Covenant, 1990, Dallas

JFK, 1991, Dallas and area

Necessary Roughness, 1991, Denton

Leap of Faith, 1992, Irving

Pure Country, 1992, Fort Worth and area

Walker, Texas Ranger, 1992–2005, Dallas, Fort Worth, and area

Barney & Friends, 1992–present, Dallas

Wishbone, 1995–1998, Dallas

Bottle Rocket, 1994, Dallas and area

The Apostle, 1997, Dallas area

Any Given Sunday, 1999, Irving

Dr T and the Women, 2000, Dallas area

The Rookie, 2002, Arlington

A destination within the West Village, this five-screen theater specializes in foreign films not showing elsewhere. There's comfortable seating and an adjacent bar. Parking is plentiful in the garage immediately north of the theater.

STUDIO MOVIE GRILLE
5405 Beltline Rd., Addison
(972) 991-6684

1600 South Stemmons Freeway, Lewisville
(469) 549-2845

4721 West Park Blvd., Plano
(972) 964-3789

11170 North Central Expressway, Dallas
(214) 361-2966

A growing chain in the area, this theater concept offers comfortable seating with tables and full restaurant service. You can eat quesadillas, salads, and burgers at your seat, along with adult beverages, while watching first-run films.

Piano Bars

FRUIA'S TRE AMICI
18020 Dallas Parkway, Dallas
(972) 250-4400

Pianist W. T. Greer plays in the bar, Tuesday through Saturday evening. Favorites include show tunes. Sip a scotch before a steak dinner or a cognac afterward, mellowing out with the music.

LIBRARY
Warwick Melrose
3015 Oak Lawn Ave., Dallas
(214) 521-5151
www.warwickmelrose.com

Dallas's favorite place to sip a Manhattan and listen to live music from a baby grand has been in this sumptuous, cozy bar off the historic hotel's lobby. A wonderful place to go with a date, the setting of stocked bookshelves and candlelight tends to draw a crowd 40 and older. Drink specials are common.

MANSION ON TURTLE CREEK
3411 Gillespie St., Dallas
(214) 559-2100, (888) 767-3966
www.mansiononturtlecreek.com

The bar at this landmark offers live music from a grand piano Wednesday through Saturday. You can nab a seat at the bar or take one of the many two-tops. There's seating by a fireplace, too, and lots of candlelight. Decor speaks of very old money. Ask for one of the specialty cocktails.

Pubs

IDLE RICH PUB
2614 McKinney Ave., Dallas
(214) 965-9926
www.idlerichpub.com

An Uptown hangout on the McKinney Avenue trolley line, this casual bar has indoor seating and a patio for people-watching. A big tent comes out for the two-day St. Pat's party and British billiards is the game of choice, year-round. An Amstel Light commercial was filmed here recently, but there's much more than brew—find 60 single malts on the menu.

TRINITY HALL
5321 East Mockingbird Lane, Dallas
(214) 887-3600

A lovely Irish bar patterned after a Dublin original, this Mockingbird Station jewel serves authentic pub food and offers more than 145 brands of beer. On Tasting Tuesday, pay $25 for a two-hour tasting of selected beers, wines, and whiskeys. Live music is frequently offered.

Sports Bars

AUSTIN AVENUE GRILL AND SPORTS BAR
935 West Parker Rd., Plano
(972) 422-8003
www.austinavenue.com

A family-friendly sports bar, this place has a video arcade for younger patrons. The grown-ups will dig the 32 TVs, nine big screens, and three projection screens, as well as happy hours at almost all hours. There are dart boards and pool tables, too, with league play available. If you're a transplant, check out the Redskins, Steelers, and Eagles fan clubs meeting here.

THE BOARDROOM
2990 Olive St., Dallas
(214) 740-0555
www.dolcegroup.com/theboardroom
A high-end version of the sports hangout, this one doubles as a martini bar, fitting in well with the sleek environs of Victory Park. Seating is in booths and at the bar, all wrapped in a focused modern design. This one's for the professional who wants a nice cocktail while watching a ball game. On Monday, if there's not an important game, you can catch a Dinner & Movie special. Valet parking is almost your only choice here.

FRANKIE'S
3227 McKinney Ave., Dallas
(214) 999-8932
www.frankiesbar.com
Whatever game you're itching to watch is likely on one of the 26 plasma TVs or on the two projection screens. As much as people come for sports, they come also for the good food, which includes steaks, salads, and weekend brunch. Happy hour is huge here, and there's free pizza on Tuesday evening.

Wine Bars

CORK
3636 McKinney Ave., Dallas
(214) 379-7031
www.corkwines.com
A modernistic, airy retail wine shop on the edge of Uptown's West Village has wine tasting/learning opportunities unlike anyplace else. Staffers guide you through the tasting process, which you can share with fellow tasters. You get help also from interactive tasting stations, helping you decide which wines you want to take home from the retail operation.

CRUSH
3205 Knox St., Dallas
(214) 252-9463
www.crushwinesdallas.com

This intimate wine bar within a wine shop offers 5-ounce pours of 15 to 20 bottles of wine from a list that changes daily. It's a good way to taste a variety of wines and figure out where your interests lie. Cheese and meat nibbles are available, too.

TIMES TEN CELLARS
6324 Prospect Ave., Dallas
(214) 824-9463
www.timestencellars.com
The Dallas tasting room of a West Texas winery loves to have fun. Frequent events have included serving wood-fired pizzas on Wednesday evenings, hosting live jazz groups on Sunday afternoons, and staging all manner of tasting events throughout the week. At any time, you can pop by to try the various pours and buy some to take home. Discounts are offered on cases.

FORT WORTH

Bars

BOOGER RED'S
109 East Exchange St., Fort Worth
(817) 624-1246
www.h3ranch.com/booger
Attached to the Stockyards Hotel, this favorite with tourists offers saddles as bar stools and a wealth of cowboy decor. The especially popular Buffalo Butt Beer is served in its own iced bucket, but the bar is known for a good tequila selection.

FLYING SAUCER
111 East 4th St., Fort Worth
(817) 336-7470
www.beerknurd.com
The original in a growing but groovy chain, this beer bar serves more than 100 brews on tap and 150 in the bottle, with choices from around the world. Find it in a charming building downtown, with thousands of plates covering the walls. Food includes pizza, sausages, and sandwiches, and there's frequently live music on the patio.

THE GINGER MAN
3716 Camp Bowie Blvd., Fort Worth
(817) 886-2327
ftworth.gingermanpub.com
A renovated cottage in the Cultural District holds a swell little beer joint serving 67 draft beers and more than 100 bottle choices. A fabulous patio sits in front, and there are two dart boards and cozy seating areas inside. On Monday, it's $3 Texas drafts by the pint, Tuesday you can keep the glass with your pint purchase, Wednesday offers a $3.50 special, and Thursday is trivia night.

LIBRARY
611 Houston St., Fort Worth
(817) 885-8201
www.librarybars.com
Bar hoppers like this downtown mainstay for after-work sipping and the daily specials, which range from $1.50 domestic drafts and well drinks early in the week to $3 Long Island iced teas on weekends. People like the hangout vibe with kickin' music in the background.

SNOOKIE'S BAR & GRILL
2755 South Hulen St., Fort Worth
(817) 207-0788
www.snookiesbar.com
Happy hour happens daily at this popular grill, where the bar scene takes over in the evening. Wednesday brings the karaoke crowd, and it's a fun place to watch a game pretty much any day of the week.

TEN MARTINI BAR & LOUNGE
835 Foch St., Fort Worth
(817) 850-9900
Regulars liken this unto the *Sex & the City*–style bars, where martinis are quaffed by well turned-out patrons. This is part of the booming West 7th development, catering to a growing crowd of chic folks not interested in the cowboy bar scene.

Brew Pubs
THE COVEY
3010 South Hulen St., Fort Worth
(817) 731-7933
www.thecovey.com
Locally owned, this restaurant features an on-site brewmaster, crafting a number of handmade beers. The best option is to order a flight of beers, allowing you to taste each of the products from lightest to darkest, influenced by brewmasters from Washington State to Bavaria. The staff can help you pair each with a particular appetizer, as well. There's a full bar, too, if you're into cocktails or wine.

Comedy Clubs
FOUR DAY WEEKEND
312 Houston St., Fort Worth
(817) 226-4329
www.fourdayweekend.com
A nightclub with an in-residence comedy troupe has been the delight of Sundance Square for nearly eight years. It's improv at its best, with two showtimes on Friday and Saturday evenings. A bar area welcomes you for a pre-show nip.

HYENA'S COMEDY NIGHT CLUB
605 Houston St., Fort Worth
(817) 877-5233
www.hyenascomedynightclub.com/ft-worth
A popular club for stand-up routines, this night-spot offers two shows each on Friday and Saturday night. A comedy defensive driving school is offered on-site, too.

Concert Venues
BASS PERFORMANCE HALL
525 Commerce St., Fort Worth
(817) 212-4200, (877) 212-4280
www.basshall.com
While this astounding hall hosts everything from the Fort Worth Opera to the world-renowned Van Cliburn Piano Competition, it's also a venue for such visiting musical acts as Lyle Lovett, Steve Winwood, and Julio Iglesias.

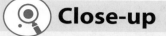

Close-up

Let's Go Honky-Tonkin'

If you're visiting Texas, you haven't experienced the Lone Star State's old-fashioned heritage if you haven't gone out to a honky-tonk to do some boot-scootin'. Even if you don't want to dance, you owe it to yourself to see the country-western lifestyle in action. Here are the two most famous places to do just that.

Billy Bob's Texas, long known as the "World's Largest Honky-Tonk," is a Fort Worth Stockyards landmark and covers just about seven acres. Major music stars play there, from Willie Nelson and George Jones to Pat Green and Travis Tritt, sometimes to crowds of up to 6,000 people. There's music every night, as well as live bull riding, dancing, food and drink, shopping, and games.

It was opened in 1981 by business partners Billy Bob Barnett, a former pro football player, and Spencer Taylor, a nightclub owner and former car salesman. They renovated an empty former department store that had been a cattle barn when constructed in 1910. Willie, Waylon, and friends were the earliest entertainers there, but Billy Bob's fell on hard times in the late 1980s and closed briefly. Local developer Holt Hickman and former councilman Steve Murrin got the club open again, and Billy Bob's has been going strong since 1989. Over the years, you've seen it as a location in such TV shows as *Walker, Texas Ranger*, starring Chuck Norris, and movies like *Over the Top* (1987) starring Sylvester Stallone; *Baja Oklahoma* (1988) starring Lesley Ann Warren, Peter Coyote, and Willie Nelson; *Necessary Roughness* (1991); and George Strait's *Pure Country* (1992). Billy Bob's has been recognized as Club of the Year by the Academy of Country Music several times.

About a half-hour east in Dallas, **Gilley's** is a resurrected version of what was once the world's largest honky-tonk. The original Gilley's was a famous cowboys' nightclub outside of Houston, in Pasadena, from 1970 until 1990. Named for co-owner Mickey Gilley, who was a Louisiana native, a musician, and a cousin of Jerry Lee Lewis, it was labeled "a den of sin" by another cousin, TV evangelist Jimmy Swaggart. Gilley's was a massive success, bringing in droves of locals and tourists daily, and you could see acts like Loretta Lynn, Ernest Tubb, Emmylou Harris, and Roseanne Cash, among many others, playing there. If you didn't go to Gilley's, you could listen to it, as *Live at Gilley's* was a weekly radio broadcast to 500 stations across the nation and around the world on Armed Forces Radio. In 1979, John Travolta and Debra Winger starred in the movie *Urban Cowboy*, filmed at Gilley's.

The club suffered serious legal and business problems and closed in 1989, then burned to the ground in 1990. Mickey Gilley opened the Dallas Gilley's in 2003, and it's a big dancin'-and-drinkin' joint a few quick blocks south of downtown and the convention center. Used mostly for special events, the 65,000-square-foot complex still has plenty of dance floor space and the renowned mechanical bull. You can find live music there on Friday and Saturday nights. For details on the clubs, visit billybobstexas.com and gilleysdallas.com.

BILLY BOB'S TEXAS

2520 Rodeo Plaza, Fort Worth

(817) 624-7117

billybobstexas.com

Possibly the most famous honky-tonk in the world, it's also the world's largest and a place to find first-rate acts like Willie Nelson, Pat Green, George Jones, and other country music stars. Inside, 127,000 square feet of space with a massive dance floor, 32 individual bars, live professional bull riding, souvenir and clothing shops, and a couple of food stands. There's no mechanical bull, but there is a fake bull on which to have your photo taken.

Country Music Clubs

PEARL'S DANCEHALL & SALOON
302 West Exchange Ave., Fort Worth
(817) 624-2800
www.pearlsdancehall.com
Western Swing is the music and dance specialty inside this two-story, redbrick building dating from 1928. Note the long copper bar with the ornate mahogany back and the tin ceiling. Wednesday night offers $1 top-shelf margaritas for the ladies, and there's happy hour early Wednesday and Thursday evening, too. Interestingly, the name comes from a bordello opened many years ago by Buffalo Bill Cody, who spent time in town with his Wild West Show.

RODEO EXCHANGE
221 West Exchange Ave., Fort Worth
(817) 626-0181
www.rodeoex.com
Show up on Tuesday evening for free dance lessons or sign up for an eight-week course at this favorite in the Stockyards. On Saturday, happy hour lasts until 9 p.m., and there's live music Friday and Saturday night. A pool tournament happens every Thursday evening.

WHITE ELEPHANT
106 East Exchange Ave., Fort Worth
(817) 624-8273
www.whiteelephantsaloon.com
Almost as old as Fort Worth itself, this landmark in the Stockyards district has been hailed as among the best bars in America by *Esquire* magazine and has been used on location for filming *Walker, Texas Ranger*. Live music features good local talent nightly, and there's always good people-watching. Burgers from the adjacent Love Shack are exceptional.

Live Music Bars

THE AARDVARK
2905 West Berry St., Fort Worth
(817) 926-7814
www.the-aardvark.com

A fave with the TCU student population, this creaky old club hosts talent that hasn't hit the big time quite yet. Amaretto sours are the house specialty, and there's food to soak up the liquids, too.

8.0
111 East 3rd St., Fort Worth
(817) 336-0880
www.eightobar.com
Sit on the patio beneath the trees and listen to live music, offered Wednesday through Saturday at this popular Sundance Square restaurant and bar. DJs spin the tunes when there's nobody on stage.

FRED'S TEXAS CAFÉ
915 Currie St., Fort Worth
(817) 332-0083
www.fredstexascafe.com
Every night and on Sunday afternoon, there's a different local band playing on the patio at Fred's. This beloved dive in the Cultural District simply doesn't quit, even as flashy modern development pops up around it. Happy hour is ongoing anytime it's raining, and there are happy hour specials in dry weather at various hours, depending on the day in question. Patio seating is a commodity, so try to arrive earlier rather than later. And do have a Fredburger with killer fries.

J & J BLUES BAR
937 Woodward St., Fort Worth
(817) 870-2337
www.jjbluesbar.com
The place to hear the blues in Fort Worth, this near-downtown venue has hosted Bugs Henderson, Koko Taylor, James Cotton, and others in its 20 years of business. Sunday is jam night.

J. GILLIGANS
400 East Abram, Arlington
(817) 274-8561, (817) 860-0110
www.jgilligans.com
An Irish-themed bar in downtown Arlington offers local live music every weekend. This University of Texas at Arlington hangout serves a good burger.

SCAT JAZZ LOUNGE
111 West Fourth St., Fort Worth
(817) 870-9100
www.scatjazzlounge.com
A newish cabaret-style jazz club operates on the basement level of the historic Woolworth Building just off Sundance Square. Modeled after the old jazz clubs of New York, this is a charming place to sip a gin and tonic and chill to the tunes in a pretty setting with rich red curtains and smooth deco styling.

Dance Clubs

BAR 9
900 Houston St., Fort Worth
(817) 336-2253
The laid-back but trendy setting appeals to a youngish, mostly professional crowd. Hang out on couches or dance the night away with DJs providing the thumping tunes. There are two floors here, along with a large marble bar and bottle service.

CITY STREETS
425 Commerce St., Fort Worth
(817) 335-5400
www.citystreetsfortworth.com
There are multiple dance floors inside, and each day brings a different special. Sometimes the come-ons can be cheesy (bikini contests! No cover for college students!), but there's usually a buzz about in the various rooms, such as Indigo, a nautical-themed dance club; Racks 'n Balls, with pool tables and dart boards; Cages, where go-go dancers shake it to hip-hop tunes in metal cages; and Tabu Lounge, with karaoke fun.

EMBARGO
210 East Eighth St., Fort Worth
(817) 870-9750
Styled after a Havana nightclub, this downtown darling wows its regulars and newcomers alike with live music or DJ spins most nights and salsa lessons on Thursday. The entertaining bartenders and handmade mojitos are easily the best to be found in town, and later in the evening, there's

a taco truck outside to give you sustenance for more dancing.

GLORIA'S
2600 West Seventh St., Fort Worth
(817) 332-8800
gloriasrestaurant.com
Technically this Montgomery Plaza delight is a Salvadoran-Mexican restaurant, but there's a live band onstage on Saturday evening and salsa lessons are available.

Movie Theaters

All over Tarrant County, you'll find the usual multiplexes from AMC, Rave, Hollywood, and all the usual suspects. Here are a few special theaters offering a little something extra.

MOVIE TAVERN AT HULEN
4920 South Hulen St., Fort Worth
(817) 546-7090, (817) 546-7091
www.movietavern.com
With 11 screens, this theater behind Hulen Mall puts you in comfortable, high-back chairs and pampers you with table service for food and drink. Other locations include 2404 Airport Freeway, Bedford, (817) 563-SHOW and (817) 358-9602; and 6801 Ridgmar Meadow Rd. in Fort Worth, (817) 989-7470, (817) 377-9801.

STUDIO MOVIE GRILL
255 Merchants Row, Arlington
(817) 466-4440
www.studiomoviegrill.com
You can have cocktails, pizza, burgers, quesadillas, and brownie sundaes at your seat. The staff will drop off your bill about 40 minutes before the movie ends.

Piano Bars

EDDIE V'S LOUNGE
3120 West Seventh St., Fort Worth
(817) 336-8000
www.eddiev.com
Attached to the super-swanky seafood restaurant in Museum Place, this lovely cocktail lounge

features a piano and sometimes a trio nightly. It's mood music, from sultry jazz favorites to Sinatra. Happy hour is early each evening, with drink and appetizer specials.

PETE'S DUELING PIANO BAR
621 Houston St., Fort Worth
(817) 335-7383
www.petesduelingpianobar.com
Modeled after the original in Austin, this dueling piano bar offers a sing-along, drink-along party each night, starting at 8 p.m. Four piano players rotate in pairs on two baby grands to play hits from all eras, with Elvis, ZZ Top, Bon Jovi, Pat Green, Willie Nelson, Elton John, Frank Sinatra, and the Beatles among favorites.

Pubs

BAKER STREET PUB & GRILL
6333 Camp Bowie Blvd., Fort Worth
(817) 377-9772
www.sherlockspubco.com
This is about as authentically British as Bennigan's is Irish, but it's monstrously popular, nevertheless. Happy hour lasts all day Sunday, and there are specials throughout the week, too. It's a Coors Light crowd, edging more toward young than middle-aged. Sidewalk cafe seating is nice in pretty weather.

FINN MACCOOL'S PUB
1700 Eighth Ave., Fort Worth
(817) 923-2121
On the edge of the Fairmont Place, Ryan Place, and Berkeley neighborhoods, this watering hole with pool tables occupies an old shotgun space in the Medical District. You can throw darts and eat a pizza here, too.

POAG MAHONE'S IRISH PUB
2710 West Seventh St., Fort Worth
(817) 332-9544
Throw darts, shoot pool, drink, and make friends at this hangout, one of several along the Seventh Street corridor.

Sports Bars

BOOMERJACK'S GRILL
2600 West Seventh St., Fort Worth
(817) 810-2666
www.boomerjack.com
Watch a game on more than a dozen TVs, eat a burger, and listen to live music. The patio seating in the middle of Montgomery Plaza is a great place to catch a breeze and people-watch. Appetizer buffet at happy hour, too.

BUFFALO BROS.
3015 South University Dr., Fort Worth
(817) 386-9601
www.buffalobrostx.com
Across the street from TCU, this little hangout is a good stop for pizza, wings, and beer after the game or anytime you want to see any game on the air. Happy hour every afternoon.

FOX & HOUND ENGLISH PUB & GRILLE
6051 Southwest Loop 820, Fort Worth
(817) 423-3600
603 Houston St., Fort Worth
(817) 338-9200
www.tentcorp.com
Almost as truly English as Steak & Ale was in its heyday, this gathering place brings in big crowds for ball games on TV. Plenty of domestic and imported beer varieties and drink specials keep patrons happy, and there's the usual menu of nachos and burgers to soak up the suds.

NO FRILLS GRILL & SPORTS BAR
1550 Eastchase Parkway, Fort Worth
(817) 274-5433
www.nofrillsgrill.com/ftworth
4914 Little Rd., Arlington
(817) 478-1766
www.nofrillsgrill.com/arlington
Ready for some football? It's showing here on 45 televisions. There's also NTN Trivia, pool tables, darts, and shuffleboard with lots of neon beer signs and a 50-item menu.

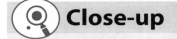

Close-up

Downtown Fort Worth

Downtown Fort Worth is the envy of many American cities. Even Dallas's officials have made the trip 35 miles west to see what Fort Worth is doing so right. One of its great joys, for example, is its vibrant, walkable quality, with ample free parking—almost unheard of in a city this size.

Sundance Square has parking lots smack in the middle of the action, free on weekends and after 5 p.m. weekdays, unlike many of the downtown areas revitalized in the 1980s and early '90s.

Perhaps the very ground here was made for gathering: Fort Worth was a major stop on the Chisholm Trail in the late 1800s, when tired, thirsty cowboys shook off the trail dust at saloons and dance halls. They had to deal with outlaws, like the Sundance Kid, for whom the square was named. But today's downtown patrolled by police on both horseback and bicycles is pretty much a bad-guy-free zone. In fact, in 2008 the city was the sixth-safest in the country compared to 39 other major cities in terms of violent crime per capita, according to the Fort Worth Police Department.

So, strolling day or night is not a problem. A typical night out could include dinner at one of the restaurants, a movie or a concert, and drinks and dancing afterward, all within walking distance. Or, plan an afternoon of snacking and shopping.

While parking is usually not a problem, keep an eye out for one-way streets; they can be a little confusing at first. And don't worry about asking people for directions. In laid-back Cowtown, people are friendly and generally happy to help. You won't find the rudeness that can be prevalent in the heart of cities elsewhere.

Most people get a kick out of the Wild, Wild West topiaries you'll see as you walk through downtown, sometimes wrapped in burlap against chilly weather.

Downtown also has its share of historical buildings, most dating from the turn of the 20th century. You can't fail to notice the Jett Building, constructed in 1907—it's the one with the big longhorns painted on its side. The Chisholm Trail Mural on the building's southern side was painted in the 1980s to remember the Fort Worth part of the cattle drives from 1887 to 1875.

Dinner can be nouveau cowboy at Reata, 310 Houston St. (817-336-1009, www.reata.com); high-end steak at Del Frisco's Steakhouse, 812 Main St. (817-877-3999, www.delfriscos.com); or as casual as you like with Tex-Mex, chains, burgers, pizza, and sushi all part of the mix.

Wine Bars

FARPOINTE CELLAR AND WINE BISTRO
721 East Southlake Blvd., Southlake
(817) 416-7500
www.farpointecellar.com

In the bar next to the wine shop, you'll find lots of fellow wine fans checking out new discoveries from around the world. Weekend tastings help you figure out what wine you'll probably like next.

INTO THE GLASS
322 South Main St., Fort Worth
(817) 442-1969
www.intotheglass.com

Right on the main drag in Grapevine's Historic District, this adorable cafe specializes in boutique wines that you're not going to see on every wine list. It's a lighthearted place to learn about wines and hang out with friends. There's food menu that tends toward lighter items, and you can get beer and mixed drinks, too. Check out the live music on weekend evenings.

Pick your first-run movie at the AMC Palace 9 Theater, 220 East Third St. (showtimes, 888-AMC-4FUN; guest services, 817-336-0431, www.amctheatres.com). Or plan in advance to take in a show at Bass Performance Hall, 525 Commerce St., (817) 212-4325, www.basshall .com), where you could see anything from *Madame Butterfly* to Lyle Lovett.

Afterward, hit a nightspot with DJs pumping out infectious dance music, or a live band—take your pick. At 8.0 Restaurant and Bar, 111 East 3rd St. (817-336-0880, www.eightobar. com), the youngish crowd likes to see and be seen out on the patio where the band plays. Try karaoke or dance to pop and Top 40 hits at City Streets, 425 Commerce St. (817-335-5400, www.citystreetsfortworth.com); or request your favorites at Pete's Dueling Piano Bar, 621 Houston St. (817-335-7383, www.petesduelingpianobar.com). If you're a beer connoisseur, the Flying Saucer, 111 East Fourth St., (817) 336-7470, www.beerknurd.com, has everything from exotic Brazilian brews to American favorites, with a band often playing on the patio.

If daytime shopping is more your style, you can easily park and walk to boutiques brimming with Texas-style fashion and jewelry, browse books, hit a gallery, or take a seat on a bench and people-watch.

First, eyeball some fancy duds at Leddy's Ranch at Sundance, 410 Houston St. (817-336-0800, www.leddys.com). Amble on down Houston Street, and stop in at Retro Cowboy, 406 Houston St., (817) 338-1194; Milan Gallery, 505 Houston St., (817) 338-4278, www.milan-gallery.com; or Pappagallo Classiques, 408 Houston St., (817) 698-8100, www.pappagallo-classiques.com.

It's probably time by now for chocolate (when isn't it?) so cut over to Fourth Street and get a bag of truffles at Schakolad, 106 East Fourth St. (817-870-2400, www.schakolad.com).

Then, for stunning turquoise jewelry to go with your new outfit, try Barse, 501 Main St., (817) 820-0404, www.barse.com. Also along Main Street, pick up a gift for your friends back home at Vessels, 310 Main St., (817) 882-8743, www.giftvessels.com. Earth Bones, 308 Main St., (817) 332-2662, is a good place to find a profound or funny greeting card.

Also stop in at Sid Richardson Museum, 309 Main St. (817) 332-6554, www.sidrichardson museum.org, to gaze at 40 paintings by the Picassos of Western art: Frederic Remington, Charles Russell, and others.

Finally, grab a cup of coffee and sink into a comfy chair, or browse the Texas section at the big Barnes & Noble, 401 Commerce St., (817) 332-7178, www.barnesandnoble.com.

Of course, there's still more to see and do downtown. For further exploration, check out www.fortworth.com, the convention and visitors bureau's Web site.

LA BUENA VIDA
416 East College St., Grapevine
(817) 481-9463
www.labuenavida.com

A winery in Grapevine's historic quarter offers a tasting room and lovely patio, giving you a place to sip wines from Texas and the world. On weekends, there's live music, too. Graze on appetizers, shop for wine accessories, and meet other people doing the same.

WINE STYLES
2600 West Seventh St., Fort Worth
(817) 332-9463
www.winestyles.net/montgomeryplaza

A combination wine shop and wine bar in Montgomery Plaza brings in a crowd when live music is offered on Friday night. Buy a bottle to enjoy at one of the cafe tables at retail with no corkage fee. Join the wine club and get two new wines monthly with membership, as well as 10 percent off other wine buys.

THE WINE THIEF
1300 Houston St., Fort Worth
(817) 535-6664
www.omnihotels.com
Right off the lobby at the fancy new Omni downtown, this quiet, dark wine bar offers a number of wine flights. If you like Spanish sparkling wines or big California cabs, they have a flight for you. Pair these with plates of cheese, smoked salmon, beef tenderloin on crostini, or petite lamb chops.

WINSLOW'S WINE CAFE
4101 Camp Bowie Blvd., Fort Worth
(817) 546-6843
www.winslowswinecafe.com
Fashioned from a 1920s service station, this charmer in the Cultural District mixes a cafe, wine shop, and gathering spot into one. More than 100 wines are typically available, with choices pairing nicely with goodies from the wood-burning oven. Seating on the patio in nice weather is the best.

ZAMBRANO WINE CELLARS
910 Houston St., Fort Worth
(817) 850-9463
www.zambranowines.com
A warm, cozy wine bar in downtown Fort Worth gives people a place to simply unwind over wine. Patrons peruse a wine menu detailing some 200 wine selections, with emphasis on California's appellations and smart picks from South America, Australia, and South Africa, too. Prices you'll see on the list will be discounted 50 percent if you're buying bottles to take home. Special offerings are available when visiting winemakers come to town, as well.

SHOPPING

Shopping is practically an art form in Dallas, regardless of your budget and taste. Or, lacking either, just window-shopping in some parts of the city is a blast. Increasingly compared to New York and reportedly containing more retail space, the scene here has been more than a century in the making and is still evolving constantly, as both fresh and established retailers reclaim parts of the city. Western wear, retro furnishings, designer boutiques, art galleries—it's all here.

The legacy began in 1907 when the first Neiman Marcus store opened, and developed a reputation for high quality and prices to match. The excitement of getting a box bearing the Neiman's logo became akin to finding a blue Tiffany's box under the tree. Then came the Neiman's Christmas catalog, an annual news event as Neiman's included over-the-top fantasy gifts like limited edition BMWs. Neiman's put Dallas on the international shopping map, and the high-end, pricey reputation stuck. The shopping was here, and the oil money paid the bill. High-end retailers and designers are still coming: In the newly developed Victory Park area near American Airlines Center, for example, you can pick up a bespoke men's suit for as much as $30,000 at Duncan Quinn.

Some of the freshest, most exciting shopping is in art and interiors in the Design District on or near Dragon Street. The Design District has always been filled with custom and antique shops, most of which sold "to the trade," leaving out the majority of consumers. Today those shops have opened to the public, and art galleries are flooding the Dragon Street area, fleeing high Uptown rents. The result is a developing gallery scene that's been compared to Chelsea or SoHo.

In Fort Worth shopping is less of an obsession, but Cowtown is no slacker in that department. Upscale and casual western wear downtown, interesting boutiques along Camp Bowie, a Neiman's of its own on the west side of the city, and pockets of sophisticated shops and interesting eateries in the Park Hill area near Texas Christian University make Fort Worth shopping both eclectic and easygoing.

DALLAS AREA

Antiques and Fine Art

ADELE HUNT'S EUROPEAN COLLECTIBLES
1007 Slocum St., Dallas
(214) 651-7542
adelehunt.com
Another favorite on Antique Row, Adele has handpicked English antiques from the 18th and 19th centuries, along with antique books in French, English, and Swedish.

ALTERNATIVE FURNISHINGS
100 East Louisiana St., McKinney
(972) 547-0721
alternative-furnishings.com
Located on the charming square in downtown McKinney, a half-hour's drive north of Dallas, this is where you go to find wooden doors that look like historical artifacts, iron wall hangings, pieces from India, and architectural pieces from around the world. New arrivals appear in the store weekly.

Close-up

The Galleria Dallas

There can be no serious debate over where to begin and end your shopping during any season of excessive spending. Just one look at the landmark mall that is the Galleria Dallas, and you know it's Dallas's most spectacular place of over-the-top retail joys.

Opened in 1982, Dallas's grande dame of shopping pleasures was inspired by the Galleria Vittorio Emanuele, the glass-domed shopping street in Milan. Soaring skylights and arches, ivory-hued Egyption limestone, and white Australian eucalyptus surfaces provide an elegant backdrop for sensational decor, which changes with the seasons.

The Galleria is at its most magnificent during the holidays, naturally. Trunk shows are plentiful, but even if you just want to gawk, you shouldn't miss the 95-foot-high Christmas tree, said to be the tallest indoor version anywhere. Shooting high into the Galleria's four-story atrium from the centrally situated ice rink, the tree springs to life five times a day with its Illumination Celebration, in which 225,000 twinkling lights perform a computer-choreographed dance to a recorded symphonic presentation.

Each Saturday between Thanksgiving and Christmas, you can see a late-afternoon ice show starring Missile Toes, the Galleria's skating Santa Claus, whose acrobatic stunts include pyrotechnics firing from his blades. Following Missile Toes's performance, you'll see the Grand Tree Lighting Ceremony, followed by a skating show.

Bring the kids to share their wish lists with Santa in his village, near Saks Fifth Avenue on Level 2, daily through Christmas Eve. If they still have energy to burn, take them to the Galleria's Play Place, a jungle-themed recreation space for the smallest guests. But plan on leaving your parking anxieties at home: Pulling up to the Galleria, look for the parking directors in red Santa hats and suits whose goal is to direct you to one of roughly 10,000 parking spaces.

Shopping devotees will want to pay close attention to the special offerings among the 200-plus stores filling 1.9 million square feet. Newer additions include the American Girl Boutique and Bistro, the first to arrive in Texas, along with Lone Star editions of Kate Spade and Samsonite Black Label stores.

Specialty stores also include lululemon athletica, where workout wear follows cool yoga styling, and Pumpkin Patch, a hot kids' clothing store from New Zealand. Thomas Pink, the Jermyn Street, London shop for men and women, and Karen Millen, a fashion-forward boutique for women, chose the Galleria Dallas for their first Texas locations.

Tiffany & Co., Cartier, and Bailey, Banks & Biddle lead the list of super-bling shops, but don't overlook whimsical pretties from Baccarat and the trendsetting creations at Ylang-23, a Dallas original. But for the true collector, you must head to the Old World, where unusual finds have included an Edward Marshall Boehm limited edition porcelain called "Dance of the Proud Peacock," priced at about $15,000.

Eat on the run if you must—there's Corner Bakery and La Madeleine—but you probably owe it to yourself to meet your girlfriends for martinis or your loved one for dinner at Grill on the Alley, where your elegant dinner of braised short ribs or filet mignon with bordelaise sauce takes on a Beverly Hills tone.

You can always make a weekend of your shopping exploits, putting your feet up between spending sprees at the lovely, smoke-free Westin Galleria. The hotel provides limousine service if you want to eat elsewhere while staying there, and there's a running map if you need to get in a jog. Why not enjoy the style for which the Galleria is known?

For details, visit www.galleriadallas.com.

BANKS FINE ART
1231 Dragon St., Dallas
(214) 352-1811
banksfineart.com
A formal, elegant, and large gallery with soaring ceilings, this one exhibits and sells more than 900 traditional and impressionist oil paintings by American and European artists of the 19th century, as well as art by modern-day oil painters. Co-owner Bob Banks has done appraisals for *The Antiques Roadshow*.

CHRISTOPHER H. MARTIN GALLERY
1933 Cedar Springs Rd., Dallas
(214) 880-9667
christopherhmartin.com
Abstract art, typically on canvas and in prints, would be at home in a New York loft. Artist Martin is of national renown; look here for his "Kidz Creations," painted with children in hospitals, special-needs schools, and various cause events. He has a second showroom at 2412 Victory Park Lane, (214) 880-1770.

DAVID DIKE FINE ART
2613 Fairmount, Dallas
(214) 720-4044
daviddike.com
A good place to find regional art, this gallery specializes in 19th-century and early 20th-century European and American oil paintings, with emphasis on Texas painters. There's an annual Texas art auction here each year.

JOEL COONER GALLERY
1601 Dragon St., Dallas
(214) 747-3603
www.joelcooner.com
Cooner roams the world to find authentic artifacts and art from Africa, Asia, and the Pacific, as well as pre-Columbian pieces from the New World. Masks, shields, weapons, gourds, and more fill a gallery with large windows allowing plenty of light.

PHOTOGRAPHS DO NOT BEND
1202 Dragon St., Suite 103, Dallas
(214) 969-1852
www.pdnbgallery.com
Photographic art from the early 20th century to the present covers a variety of styles, from the work of 1930s photographer Nikolas Murray and his fellow artist Frida Kahlo to Michael O'Brien's noted shots of the 1980s and 1990s of ZZ Top and Willie Nelson, among many other Texans.

THE PITTET COMPANY
1215 Slocum St., Dallas
(214) 748-8999
pittetarch.com
One in a cluster of sought-after businesses in the Slocum Street Antique and Design Association in the Dallas Design District, this architecturals warehouse is among 40 showrooms beloved by professional and amateur designers. Look here and in neighboring businesses for 17th-, 18th-, and 19th-century goods, including furniture, paintings, and accessories.

RIDDELL RARE MAPS & FINE PRINTS
2611 Fairmount St., Dallas
(214) 953-0601
antiquemapshop.com
A cornerstone in the Uptown antiques area, this unusual shop stocks maps of various parts of the world, along with historical sketches and prints, some of which are surprisingly affordable.

THE WHIMSEY SHOPPE
2923 North Henderson, Dallas
(214) 824-6300
thewhimseyshoppe.com
A favorite in the Knox-Henderson area, this is your destination for French antiques from the 18th, 19th, and early 20th centuries. Armoires, grand dining tables, and other big furniture pieces are the specialty. The owners make regular buying trips to France.

Bookstores

BARNES & NOBLE
Lincoln Park, 7700 West Northwest Highway, (214) 739-1124
616 Preston Royal Shopping Center, (214) 363-0924
Prestonwood Center, 5301 Beltline Rd., Suite 118, (972) 980-0853
3634 Irving Mall, (972) 257-8320
MacArthur Park at Las Colinas, 7615 North MacArthur Blvd., (972) 501-0430
2201 Preston Rd., (972) 612-0999
Creekwalk Village, 801 West Fifteenth St., Suite E, (972) 422-3372
www.barnesandnoble.com
Barnes & Noble, typically with Starbucks shops inside and a vast inventory of books, music, and DVDs, has numerous Dallas County locations, including those listed above.

BORDERS
3600 McKinney Ave., (214) 219-0512
5500 Greenville Ave., (214) 739-1166
10720 Preston Rd., Suite 1018, (214) 363-1977
2709 North Mesquite Dr., (972) 279-5203
1601 Preston Rd., Suite J, Plano, (972) 713-9857
www.borders.com
Borders stores often include a Seattle's Best Coffee. There are multiple Dallas County locations including those listed here.

HALF-PRICE BOOKS
5803 East Northwest Hwy, (214) 379-8000
13388 Preston Rd., (972) 701-8055
3221 Preston Rd., (972) 668-3477
3401 West Airport Freeway, (972) 659-0634
2100 Alamo Rd., (972) 234-4286
www.halfpricebooks.com
Half-Price Books grew from a most humble shop in a converted Laundromat to a highly respected regional chain selling all manner of new and used books, movies, music, and video games. They'll buy almost anything used in print or recordings, too, and they give discounts to teachers and librarians.

LEGACY BOOKS
7300 Plano Parkway, Plano
(972) 398-9888
www.legacybooksonline.com
Located in The Shops at Legacy, this one claims to be the largest independent bookstore in the nation, and it could be at 24,000 square feet and 110,000 titles. It's a place you want to spend time enjoying, with light wood floors, clean, modern lines, and reading areas in the three-story space. A fabulous demo kitchen lets visiting chefs prepare food during cookbook promotions. The cafe serves beer and wine, along with coffee.

Boutiques and Gift Shops

THE BLUES JEAN BAR
6810 Snider Plaza, Dallas
(214) 368-5326
thebluesjeanbar.com
Found near the SMU campus, this destination for jeans offers more than 20 brands for both men and women in a setting fashioned after a pub.

COTTON ISLAND
1900 Preston Rd., #258, Plano
(972) 769-1085
6601 Hillcrest Blvd., Dallas
(214) 373-1085
www.cottonisland.com
Aimed at fashionable, youthful shoppers, this boutique offers designs by Free People, Ella Moss, J Brand, Citizens of Humanity, Juicy Couture, and Sperry.

FORTY FIVE TEN
4510 Mckinney Ave., Dallas
(214) 559-4510
www.fortyfiveten.com
If you need something ultra-chic in men's or women's clothing, accessories, jewelry, fragrances, home scents, and decor, this is it. Designers featured include Alberta Ferretti, Alexander McQueen, Moschino, Givenchy, Tim Hamilton, and Tom Ford. There's a charming cafe in the rear for lunch, too.

MARNIE ROCKS
8413 Preston Center Plaza Dr., Dallas
(214) 369-1200
marnierocks.com
Fabulous beaded jewelry and pendants on gold chains from this shop show up on celebs. Creations with your birthstones, zodiac signs, and initials are among items available, and there are handbags and clutches, too.

TALULAH BELLE
2011 Abrams Rd., Dallas
(214) 821-1927
http://talulahbelle.com
This feminine store sells gifts, pet products, and bath and body goodies, and it's the perfect place for finding an unusual gift for a friend. Among favorite items are custom-painted photo boxes by Sugar Boo Designs, and My Hand Company's body products.

TART PASTRY BOUTIQUE AND STUDIO
5219 West Lovers Lane, Dallas
(469) 335-8919
7140 Bishop Rd., Plano
(972) 673-0446
tartbakerydallas.com
Boutique cakes and cupcakes come from the team of a chef and a graphic designer, so the baked goods are as beautiful and brilliantly conceived as they are delicious. There's even a cupcake bar for you to select frostings and toppings yourself.

UPTOWN COUNTRY HOME
3419 Milton Ave., Dallas
(877) 232-2042
www.uptowncountryhome.net
It's shabby-chic heaven at this little find near SMU. Small pieces include sconces and mailboxes; bigger ones are china cabinets, chairs, and tables. Odds and ends include pajamas and candles.

Clothing, Kids
BEBE GRAND
2013 Abrams Parkway, Dallas
(214) 887-9224

Exceptionally fine layette items, bedding, furniture, clothing, toys, and other baby goods raise the bar for this genre.

KIDBIZ
8408 Preston Center Plaza, Dallas
(866) 877-7734
Trendy kidswear includes Polo by Ralph Lauren, Seven jeans, and Juicy Couture. Order online, too.

SAFARI KIDS
5960 West Parker Rd., Plano
(972) 473-3336
Cool kids' clothes range from playwear to dressy togs. Nice accessories for new babies, too.

TEN MONKEYS
5600 West Lovers Lane, Dallas
(214) 350-2888
tenmonkeys.net
Found in Inwood Village, this colorful spot comes complete with faux palm trees to give tropical flavor. Cute clothes for small fries are just the half of it; they host birthday parties, too.

Clothing, Men's
CIRCA 2000
5800 Legacy Dr., Plano
(972) 673-0920
www.circa2000mens.com
Jack Victor and Jhane Barnes are among popular designers in men's suits represented here, and casual attire comes from Tommy Bahama, St. Croix, and Saltaire. Tailors here will make house calls, too.

H.D.'S CLOTHING COMPANY
3018 Greenville Ave., Dallas
(214) 821-5255
www.hdsclothing.com
Edgy best describes the casual duds here, imported from Paris, Milan, and London. Diesel is among brands in skinny men's jeans. Women's styles are found here, too.

MALLASADI MEN'S BOUTIQUE
5100 Belt Line Rd. #610, Dallas
(972) 404-4045
Noted for its fashion savvy by *Esquire* magazine, this is an elegant store stocked with designer dress shirts, pants, sports coats, and casual wear from Europe, along with fashionable belts and accessories.

Q SHIRTMAKERS
3699 McKinney Ave., Dallas
(214) 780-9888
85 Highland Park Village, Dallas
(214) 780-0555
www.qcustomclothier.com
Dress shirts, suits, and trousers are made to your style and preference, using only top-notch fabrics like cashmere, wool, cotton, and others.

Clothing, Women's
MELANIE GAYLE
6818 Snider Plaza, Dallas
(214) 369-17007
401 Legacy Dr., Plano
(469) 467-9121
www.melaniegayle.com
Fantastic party dresses from designers like Ali Ro, Soshanna, and Tricia Fix and denim from Alley Row and others complete the trendy girl look. More affordable than some stores.

STANLEY KORSHAK
500 Crescent Court, Dallas
(214) 871-3600
stanleykorshak.com
Smallish version of a very up-market department store, this landmark sits within the Crescent Court, itself resembling a French château. Glam gowns, casual clothing, fine jewelry, couture wedding wear, cosmetics, and accessories bring in shoppers, as do trunk shows.

Flea Markets
FIRST MONDAY TRADE DAYS
800 Flea Market Rd., Canton
(903) 567-6556
www.firstmondaycanton.com

Found in the town of Canton, about an hour east of Dallas, this decades-old flea market is one of the largest in the south and easily the most popular in the state. Spread over 100 acres between Farm Road 859 and Texas Highway 19, this is the destination for hundreds of thousands of visitors annually. You can find anything and everything, new and used, at this popular gathering spot on the weekend prior to the first Monday of each month. Traffic is lighter in January, February, March, July, and August and heaviest in April, May, June, October, November, and December. To get there, take exit 526 off I-20, near Tyler. Parking is $4.

Home Furnishings
THE ARRANGEMENT
13710 Dallas Parkway, Suite C, Dallas
(214) 748-4540
www.thearrangement.com
To get the upscale Texas look at home, try this store on for size. The tagline, "Best of the New West" says it all about the living, bedroom, dining room, and total home accessory selection. There's everything from art to upholstery, too.

WEIR'S FURNITURE VILLAGE
3219 Knox St., Dallas
(214) 528-0321
5801 Preston Rd., Plano
(972) 403-7878
www.weirsfurniture.com
The signature furniture store in Dallas since 1948, Weir's is your destination for classic, traditional, tasteful pieces for every room in the house. Everything from small to large items, including artwork and patio furniture, is stocked here.

Imports and Handcrafts
BIG MANGO TRADING COMPANY
1130 Industrial Blvd., Dallas
(214) 752-4755
www.bigmangotrading.com
Found on the outskirts of the Design District, this fabulous warehouse stocks treasures from Asia,

particularly in the Bali and Java areas. You can fill your home, patio, or tabletops with the goods found here.

LA MARIPOSA IMPORTS
2813 North Henderson Ave., Dallas
(877) 826-0069
www.lamariposaimports.com
Here's the total store if you're in search of folk art, clothing, fiesta supplies, and such from Mexico and South and Central America. More than a few weddings have been outfitted by this wonderful store.

Malls and Shopping Areas

GALLERIA DALLAS
13350 Dallas Parkway, Dallas
(972) 702-7100
www.galleriadallas.com
A grand name in Texas shopping, this mall is as much about fashion as it is family entertainment. Stores run the range from J. Crew, BCBG, Dallas Cowboys Pro Shop, and Old Navy to Tiffany & Co., American Girl, Nordstrom, Saks Fifth Avenue, and Macy's. There's an ice-skating ring with spectacular shows during the winter holidays, along with play areas and other diversions, including movie theaters and loads of dining, such as Grand Lux Café, Oceanaire, and La Madeleine. The Westin Hotel is attached.

HIGHLAND PARK VILLAGE
47 Highland Park Village, Dallas
(214) 559-2740
hpvillage.com
A National Historic landmark and one of the first American shopping centers, this 1931 jewel bears Mediterranean-inspired architecture and functions as a centerpiece for the vaunted community of the same name. Found at Preston Road and Mockingbird Lane, this is home to Chanel, Jimmy Choo, Hermès, Harry Winston, and dozens of other fashion names, as well as homegrown retailers like Calame Jewelers and Cooter's Village Camera. There's a small movie complex on one corner of the center, a Tom Thumb grocery store, and a handful of restaurants, including Mi Cocina, Who's Who Burgers, Café Pacific, and Patrizio.

NORTHPARK CENTER
8687 North Central Expressway, Dallas
(214) 361-6345
northparkcenter.com
Considered among the finer shopping centers in North America, this elegant entry defies all mall stereotypes. Yes, you'll find Gap, Victoria's Secret, and Macy's here, but there's also a wealth of high-end stores like Neiman Marcus, Barney's, and Nordstrom, along with boutiques from top-rate designers like CH Carolina Herrera, Herve Leger, Versace, and Salvatore Ferragamo, to name a few. It's like Rodeo Drive, but indoors, and it's home to some of the best modern sculpture in Texas, too. It's best to consult a map to find your way around. In addition to 235 stores, there's an AMC movie complex and plenty of great restaurants, such as La Duni (for Latin cuisine), Cibus (Italian), and McCormick & Schmick (seafood). Parking is plentiful and valet parking is available. "Fashion at the Park," held in fall and spring, is a primo Dallas event bringing New York and Paris runway style to Dallas, with a 20,000-square-foot tent, complete with a catwalk, bar, and DJ. Designers like Nicole Miller, Roberto Cavalli, and others make appearances.

THE PLAZA AT PRESTON CENTER
8311 Preston Center Plaza Dr., Dallas
(469) 232-0000
theplazaatprestoncenter.com
Located between the Dallas North Tollway and Central Expressway off Preston Road at Northwest Highway, this cluster of high-end retail is home to Orvis, Bachendorf's (fine jewelry), Marnie Rocks (fashion jewelry), Lucky Dog Barkery, a florist, travel agency, grocery, and other neighborhood favorites. Popular restaurants include Mi Cocina, Houston's, and R+D.

THE SHOPS AT LEGACY
7200 Bishop Rd., Plano
(214) 473-9700
shopsatlegacy.com
The Schakolad Chocolate Factory, Legacy Books, and Culinary Connections are among specialty stores in this lovely center that breaks the cookie-cutter mold. Look for a dance studio, tailor, and plentiful dining.

WEST VILLAGE
3699 McKinney Ave., Dallas
(214) 219-1144
westvil.com
Situated at the corner of McKinney Avenue and Lemmon Avenue in Uptown, the West Village (not connected with the Highland Park Village) brings lots of shopping, indie movies, and dining to the young, vibrant district of condo dwellers. Shop at Banana Republic, Tommy Bahama, and Lucky Jeans, along with Cowboy Cool and Cork, the latter a great wine store. Good eats are had at The Village Burger Bar and Taco Diner. Social House is a popular gastropub, too.

Music Stores

BILL'S RECORDS
1317 South Lamar St., Dallas
(214) 421-1500
www.billsrecords.com
A legend simply for having survived as an indie for more than 20 years, this south-of-downtown destination is your place for a great selection of CDs, vinyl, T-shirts, artwork, collectibles, and a lot more. Plus, there are free music performances on weekends.

Specialty Foods

CENTRAL MARKET
5750 East Lovers Lane, Dallas
(214) 234-7000
320 Coit Rd., Plano
(469) 241-8300
www.centralmarket.com
From the San Antonio–based H.E.B. family-owned grocery chain, this upscale food and wine store revolutionized grocery shopping in Texas. If you want 15 kinds of apples, this produce department will thrill you. Any kind of meat and fish that can be found and eaten is marketed here. The wine department staff will locate nearly any vintage you can name. The ready-made foods area stocks gourmet-to-go meals in abundance, from sushi to barbecue to pizza. Healthy-living departments furnish all types of vitamins, supplements, and skin-care products, too. Stores offer a full calendar of cooking classes; check Web site for current schedules.

DALLAS FARMERS MARKET
1010 South Pearl Expressway, Dallas
(214) 939-2808
www.dallasfarmersmarket.org
Look in the southeast corner of downtown Dallas at the corner of Harwood and Marilla streets for the sea of covered stalls, manned by regional farmers who bring in a bounty of produce for sale daily. There is a huge flower and garden market, too, with excellent prices, as well as a number of vendors selling ready-made food items, spices, bakery products, jams, and jellies, too. Cooking classes and other events—frequently helmed by local celebrity chefs—are often offered in a very nice community classroom in the market's central building. Cafes are on-site, as well.

FIESTA MART
611 West Jefferson, (214) 944-3300
9727 Webb Chapel, (214) 353-7650
3030 South Lancaster, (214) 302-4000
5334 Ross Ave., (214) 887-3000
975 East Irving Blvd., Irving, (972) 554-2574
2940 South First St., Garland, (972) 271-9060
8060 Spring Valley Rd., (972) 783-8255
1200 East Parker Rd., Plano, (972) 881-3211
www.fiestamart.com
The Houston-based chain specializing in Latin American groceries and related food goods offers excellent pricing on items that are hard to find otherwise. There are many other locations in addition to those listed here.

JIMMY'S FOOD STORE
4901 Bryan St., Dallas
(214) 823-6180
www.jimmysfoodstore.com
Near downtown in East Dallas, this Italian specialty store sells an astounding number of pastas (frozen and packaged), meats, cheeses, breads, wines, and much more. The sandwiches made to order daily will spoil you forever. Hit the espresso bar for a pick-me-up.

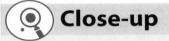

Close-up

Whole Foods Now

Shopping for organic and natural foods at an earth-conscious store has sure changed since this became popular three decades ago at a small and humble store down in Austin. Today, when you go to Whole Foods Market, it's hard to find any traces of that hippie-dippy co-op tableau, filled with folks you were sure lived in communes.

Now when you go in search of hormone-free steaks, wild salmon, organic herbs, and artisan breads at the beautiful stores in the Dallas area—particularly those on Forest Lane and the dynamic new flagship store on Park Lane in Dallas—you get free concierge shopping service while you go upstairs for a 50-minute treatment inside the company's full-service spa. That's the modern Whole Foods Market, where the grocery-shopping environment appeals to the food purist who wants ample servings of luxury and service on the side.

But beyond the niceties in what's become the world's largest natural and organic foods retailer, you find the principles remain the same as at its genesis in 1980: WFM is committed to sustainable agriculture, with strict quality standards. If you want to know what food and body products are good for you and are made in ways that are safer for the environment, this is where you shop.

While a recent *New York Times* story reported that some hard-core shoppers devoted to a "smaller carbon footprint" and supporting the smallest farmers have gone to alternative shopping sources, it's obvious that WFM made mainstream moves like building gorgeous, 60,000-square-foot-plus supermarkets to compete for a bigger piece of the audience that now cares about natural products.

Of the more than 270 stores in North America and Great Britain, seven are in North Texas, with locations in Arlington; in Dallas at Forest Lane, Park Lane, Highland Park, and Greenville Avenue; and in Plano and Richardson. Another will open in the fall of 2010 in Fairview, just north of Allen, and another is expected in 2011 in Fort Worth. In case you wondered what you can gain by doing business at one of these, here's a list of five benefits.

You're supporting a Texas-based company that in September 2009 bought 776 million kilowatt-hours of RECs from West Texas wind farms, which equals 100 percent of the company's electricity use in all its North American locations. The investment helps bring new power to the Texas grid, too.

WFM did away with plastic bags in 2008. If you bring in your own shopping bag, you get a 5-cent refund per shopping bag you bring.

The company employs people it calls "foragers," whose job is to find local farmers, cheese-makers, and so on, and that also helps keep fuel emissions down. In addition, the company has begun offering "microloans" to help small farmers and producers. A tour of the Dallas–Fort Worth store reveals salad dressings, grilling sauces, fresh queso and salsa, and several cheeses from producers within 30 to 100 miles of Dallas–Fort Worth.

WFM offers on its Web site a podcast cooking show called *Secret Ingredient*, in which each weekly offering teaches you how to make something new. These five-minute videos may show you how to create a new dish with familiar ingredients, such as a spicy brunch item called Eggs in Purgatory, or how to use a novel product, such as black truffle oil in razor clam chowder. In stores, there are tours for individuals and groups that teach you what new ingredients are stocked and how they're used, and there are tours with registered dieticians that address special health concerns, such as gluten intolerance.

The company's expressed core values include community support. On one day each quarter, the stores give 5 percent of total sales to a local charity, such as the Safe Haven, Cook Children's Hospital, or Boys and Girls Club of Arlington. Charities like those also receive 5 percent of total profits from the stores at year's end.

More details are found at www.wholefoodsmarket.com.

WHOLE FOODS

4100 Lomo Alto Dr., (214) 520-7993
2118 Abrams Rd., (214) 824-1744
11700 Preston Rd., (214) 361-8887
60 Dal Rich Village, (972) 699-8075
2201 Preston Rd., Plano, (972) 612-6729
www.wholefoodsmarket.com

The Austin-based chain known for organic, natural foods and related products has several Dallas-area locations. The most elaborate store is the one at Preston-Forest, with a full spa on the upper level and a personal shopping service available. Check with individual stores for special events, classes and free tours.

Sporting Goods

LUKE'S LOCKER

3607 Oak Lawn Ave., Dallas
(214) 528-1290
www.lukeslocker.com

The ultimate store for runners and walking enthusiasts, Luke's sponsors a number of races and running clinics and groups.

MOUNTAIN HIDEOUT

5643 West Lovers Lane, Dallas
(214) 350-8181
www.mountainhideout.com

The best in outdoors footwear and eyewear are in stock. Lines represented include North Face, Ugg, Patagonia, Eagle Creek, Reef, and Asolo.

REI

4515 LBJ Freeway, Dallas
(972) 490-5989
2424 Preston Rd., Plano
(972) 985-2241

Renowned for outdoors wear and gear, this store offers plentiful opportunity for getting happily lost.

Thrift Stores/Resale Shops

DOLLY PYTHON

1916 Haskell Ave., Dallas
(214) 887-3434

Just east of downtown, this vintage clothing shop includes clothing, books, accessories, and the odd piece of art in its inventory. Much of the stock comes from estate sales.

LABELS DESIGNER CONSIGNMENT BOUTIQUE

18208 Preston Rd., Dallas
(972) 867-3366
www.labelsdcb.net

You can find Jimmy Choo, Chanel, Louis Vuitton, and other designer duds at this consignment shop, where sales reps are called sales therapists.

Western Wear

COWBOY COOL

3699 McKinney Ave., Dallas
(214) 521-4500
www.cowboycool.com

A favorite boutique in the West Village, this caters not to the authentic or drugstore cowboy but the stylized cowboy or cowgirl. This is western wear with attitude and meant for the fashionista who wants to get noticed.

PINK'S WESTERN WEAR

2475 North Stemmons Freeway, Dallas
(214) 634-2668
www.pinkswesternwear.com

Here's a no-nonsense place for authentic giddy-up gear. Pink's, with more than 35 years in the business, stocks hats, belts, jeans, boots, outerwear, shirts, jewelry, moccasins, and purses, with brands like Lucchese, Old Gringo, Ariat, Corral, Double H, Wrangler, and Cinch. Other locations are at 13420 Preston Rd., Dallas, (972) 392-7465, and 8998 Preston Rd., Frisco, (469) 633-9675.

FORT WORTH

Antiques and Fine Art

CROSS-EYED MOOSE

2340 North Main St., Fort Worth
(817) 624-4311
www.crosseyedmoose.net

This Stockyards site is where you go for the more unusual finds, particularly in cowboy and western furniture, lighting, collectibles, and vintage western wear.

DOW ART GALLERIES
3330 Camp Bowie Blvd., Fort Worth
(817) 332-3437
www.dowart.com
Not a bit showy on the outside, this is a place known for Fort Worth's finest artwork and restorations. Right in the Cultural District, it's been in business since 1935 and has made a name for working on family heirlooms and fine paintings. Collectors from around the world stop here especially for paintings from early Fort Worth, Taos, and Texas. Custom framing is a big deal, too.

EDMUND CRAIG GALLERY
3550 West Seventh St., Fort Worth
(817) 732-6663
www.edmundcraiggallery.com
Among the younger galleries in town, this one serves the collector with eclectic taste. Original works by artists from the region and nation are showcased, and works include even those in the realm of jewelry.

GALERIE KORNYE WEST
1601 Clover Lane, Fort Worth
(817) 763-5227
www.kornyewest.com
Friendly and yet intimate, this gallery presents original masterworks in the academic and impressionist styles from antique works to works by living artists. There's a wide variety of representational art embracing the academic and impressionistic artistic styles, particularly those living artists working in American representational art.

K. FLORIES ANTIQUES
3915 Camp Bowie Blvd., Fort Worth
(817) 763-5380
There's a full line of high-end antiques here, with paintings, rugs, and silver, too. Buying and selling at estate sales is a specialty.

MILAN GALLERY
505 Houston St., Fort Worth
(817) 338-4278
www.milangallery.com
The downtown destination gallery showcases more than 400 pieces of original artwork from national and international artists working in oils, acrylics, watercolors, mixed media, and sculptures, among others, on three floors.

MONTGOMERY ST. ANTIQUE MALL
2601 Montgomery St., Fort Worth
(817) 735-9685
You can find nearly anything at Fort Worth's largest antiques mall, with 240 booths to browse. Allow extra time so you can have lunch in the Secret Garden Tea Room.

PEASE-COBB ANTIQUES
3923 Camp Bowie Blvd., Fort Worth
(817) 763-5108
www.pease-cobbantiques.com
For more than 20 years, this outfit has bought, sold, and appraised high-quality antique pieces. Estate liquidations are a specialty, as is insurance and other appraisal work.

STUDIO SABKA FINE ART GALLERY
3411 West Seventh St., Fort Worth
(817) 870-0003
www.studiosabkaartgallery.com
Original, recreation, print, and custom works are featured in the media of murals, mosaics, still lifes, portraits, scenery, and caricatures. Appraisals and art lessons are offered, too.

WILLIAM CAMPBELL CONTEMPORARY ART & GALLERY
4935 Byers Ave., Fort Worth
(817) 737-9571
www.williamcampbellcontemporaryart.com
Now into a fourth decade, William Campbell is a name associated with the best in contemporary art from around the region, nation, and world. Art appraisal and brokerage services are available, too.

Bookstores

BARNES & NOBLE

University Park Village, 1612 South University Dr., (817) 335-2791
Hulen Shopping Center, 4801 Overton Ridge Blvd., (817) 346-2368
Sundance Square, 401 Commerce St., (817) 332-7178
Shops at North East Mall, 861 NE Mall Blvd., Hurst, (817) 284-1244
3881 South Cooper St., Arlington, (817) 472-7559
934 East Copeland Rd., Arlington, (817) 277-5184
1430 Plaza Place, Southlake, (817) 442-0207
www.barnesandnoble.com.

Barnes & Noble, typically with Starbucks shops inside and a vast inventory of books, music and DVDs, has numerous Tarrant County locations.

BOOK RACK

2304 West Park Row Dr., Pantego
(817) 274-1717
www.thebookrack.com

Found in the Arlington area, this is a store buying and selling used books.

BORDERS

4601 West Freeway, (817) 737-0444
1131 North Burleson Blvd., (817) 447-8660
4000 Arlington Highlands Blvd., (817) 557-4831
5615 Colleyville Blvd., (817) 503-8092
www.borders.com

Borders stores often include a Seattle's Best Coffee. There are several Tarrant County locations.

CONNECTIONS BOOK STORE

2428 Forest Park Blvd., Fort Worth
(817) 923-2320

Found near TCU and the lovely Berkeley neighborhood, this small, eclectic bookstore has editions on topics from addiction to zinnias, along with a nice collection of children's books.

HALF-PRICE BOOKS

5417 South Hulen St., Fort Worth
(817) 294-1166
475 Sherry Lane, Fort Worth
(817) 732-4111
www.halfpricebooks.com

Half-Price grew from a most humble shop in a converted laundromat in Dallas to a highly respected regional chain selling all manner of new and used books, movies, music, and video games. They'll buy almost anything used in print or recordings, too, and they give discounts to teachers and librarians.

TCU BOOKSTORE

2950 West Berry St., Fort Worth
(817) 257-7844
tcu.bncollege.com

Whether you're a student at Texas Christian University doesn't matter; this two-story store carries much more than textbooks. There's a wide variety of reading, as well as TCU merchandise, a Clinique makeup counter, home decor, and more. There's even a cafe that serves coffee, tea, and food such as sandwiches, salads, and pastries.

Boutiques and Gift Shops

DOMAIN XCIV

3109 Seventh St., Fort Worth
(817) 336-1994
www.domainxciv.com

A designer's dream come true, this is a treasure chest of fine home furnishings right in the Cultural District. You'll find a mix of European antiques, Peacock Alley luxury bedding, imported bath products from Côté Bastide and Lady Primrose's; dinnerware from Provincial; and custom work in dried floral arrangements.

MILAGROS FRAMES & GIFTS

851 Foch St., Fort Worth
(817) 332-1818
www.milagrosframesandgifts.com

Taking its name from the small charm found all over Mexico and other Latin American countries, the word means miracles and can be a small reminder of a person, event, or pet or can serve as a good luck charm or unique ornament. These are sold at Milagros, as is an upscale mix of distinctive gifts and home accents. And for custom framing, you can make appointments.

P.S. THE LETTER
5136 Camp Bowie Blvd., Fort Worth
(817) 731-2032
www.pstheletter.com
The ultimate in personal service is what keeps the clientele loyal at this shop specializing in personalized stationery for weddings, parties, and social occasions. There's also a wide selection of china, silver, crystal, and gift items for birthdays, babies, and pets.

RUBY
1540 South University Dr., Fort Worth
(817) 332-7829
www.shopruby.com
Located in University Park Village, this is a great place to run in and grab the perfect gift or accessory. Look for headbands, purses, wallets, shoes (including Reef flip-flops), jewelry, and watches.

SPOILED PINK
4824 Camp Bowie Blvd., Fort Worth
(817) 737-7465
www.spoiledpink.com
A former model in Chicago, New York, and Germany, Amy Churchill opened a shop offering the best styles of the fashion season in a range of prices that would be good for most everyone's budget. Crazysticks fragrances to Betsey Johnson clothing designs, there's a wide range of goodies in the way of scarves, purses, bath and beauty products, dresses, jewelry, shoes, and clothes for men and for women, as well as other select items.

UNCOMMON ANGLES
2600 West Seventh St., Fort Worth
(817) 335-9933
www.uncommonanglestx.com
A gallery of beautiful, handcrafted items from more than 200 artisans specializing in unusual art, this cool store makes a trip to Montgomery

Plaza necessary for anyone decorating a home in a contemporary style. Among collectibles are handblown glass pieces, functional and sculptural ceramics, wooden boxes, kaleidoscopes, paintings and sculptural wall art, clocks, accent furniture, and a large collection of jewelry.

Clothing, Kids
ANIMAL CRACKERS
6100 Colleyville Blvd., Colleyville
(817) 416-6246
www.animalcrackers.com
An edgy, contemporary shop infusing kids' clothes with a touch of glamour, this is the shop for a leopard print outfit or something studded with crystals. Flowers by Zoe, Queen Christine, and the Les Tout Petits lines are popular.

BABY BLISS
1243 Main St., Southlake Town Square
(817) 251-6600
If you're over the boring high chairs and strollers and clothes that look like all the rest, this is the shop you need. There's lots of Dwell Baby bedding, toys, bibs, and wall art, along with high chairs and strollers from Orbit, Bugaboo, and Bloom. Eco-friendly options include the Sage Creek Organics line of clothing made of organic cotton, with no dangerous chemicals or dyes, and Green Toys, which are made from recycled milk jugs.

JOLI PETITE BABY BOUTIQUE
251 Town Center Lane, Keller
(817) 741-6787
jolibebeboutiquellc.com
There's a design team that will make house calls to design your nursery, and custom baby bedding means you choose fabric and design and it's made to fit your crib. There's nursery furniture, including traditional and round cribs and cradles, too. Custom projects also include diaper stackers, toy bags, changing pad covers, window treatments, and more. Lines represented include Medela, Bratt Décor, Robeez, Kissy Kissy, 2 Red Hen, Bunnies by the Bay, and Caden Lane. Clothing and other accessories are sold, too.

ZOE & JACK
5137 Birchman Ave., Fort Worth
(817) 989-2200
www.zoeandjack.com
For sweet and swanky children's togs, nursery items, and cool gifts, this store in a renovated Arlington Heights bungalow sells Baby Soy products, the Pasadena-based brand that creates onesies, cardigans, tees, pants, bibs, blankets, hats, and socks from organic soy fiber. There's also a nursery design center, complete with hundreds of fabric swatches to start the process.

Clothing, Men's

DEAN-KINGSTON
821 Foch St., Fort Worth
(817) 698-8323
www.dean-kingston.com
In the blossoming Cultural District/Seventh Street corridor, this boutique sets itself apart first with the turquoise '64 Cadillac perched on the rooftop. Tricked out with art, sculpture, and industrial urbanity, Dean-Kingston brings New York and L.A. fashion sense to town, with men's and women's clothing from Pure Bohemian, Walter, Martiniwear, and Jon Sonen. Sip wine while you shop.

THE FASHION LOUNGE
3901 Arlington Highlands Blvd., Arlington
(888) 314-8319
www.thefashionlounge.com
Men and women are served at this contemporary shop, where brands include Abi Ferrin, Sky, Hale Bob, Ed Hardy, Paco, Smet, William Rast, and Blackburn.

Clothing, Women's

A HOOPER
4601 West Freeway at Hulen Street, Fort Worth
(817) 348-9911
Bright and cool, this intimate boutique features streamlined fashion for sophisticated shoppers who have money to spend and a strong sense of personal style.

DIRTY LAUNDRY
3007 South University Dr., Fort Worth
(817) 924-0445
Cute, fun, flirty fashions are best suited to the youthful woman.

HEAD OVER HEELS
5122 Camp Bowie Blvd., Fort Worth
(817) 738-0811
www.headoverheelsshoes.com
This clever shoe shop brings brands like Claudia Cuiti, Elaine Turner, Juicy Couture, Kate Spade, Pucci, Rafe, Sam Edelman, and Tory Burch to town. For handbags, expect designs from Elaine Turner Collections and Rafe Handbags.

SHOE GYPSY
2966 Park Hill Dr., Fort Worth
(817) 927-7700
www.shoegypsy.com
Catering to men and women alike, this shop seeks out rare, hard-to-find foot fashions. You'll shop in comfort, sitting on a comfy retro sofa or airport-style seating. Men's shoe brands include Ben Sherman, Converse, Creative Recreation, Gola, J Shoes, PF Flyer, Puma, and TOMS. Women's are BC, Dolce Vita, Gola, Lacoste, Naughty Monkey, PF Flyer, Pink Studio, PUMA, Rocket Dog, Seychelles, Simple, Sugar, TOMS, and UGG.

Flea Markets

FIRST MONDAY IN WEATHERFORD
119 Palo Pinto St., Weatherford
(817) 598-4124
www.ci.weatherford.tx.us
First Monday Trade Days is an old, friendly open-air market held on the weekend prior to the first Monday of each month. More than 500 vendor spaces are occupied by dealers in gifts, crafts, antiques, junk, and food. Farmers, ranchers, and merchants from the area gather on the square with items to sell. More than 6,000 visitors come to town each month for the fun and trading.

WEEKEND FLEA MARKET AT WILL ROGERS
3401 West Lancaster Ave., Fort Worth
(817) 473-0505
Almost every Saturday and Sunday, the livestock barns at Will Rogers Memorial Center in the Cultural District are filled with vendors selling antiques, collectibles, lots of western and Indian jewelry, and art and collectibles, both new and used.

Home Furnishings
BRUMBAUGH'S LEATHER GALLERY
11651 Camp Bowie West Blvd., Fort Worth
(817) 244-6484
www.brumbaughs.com
If you're working on Texas styling for your house, you shouldn't skip a visit to this 50,000-square-foot showplace. There's vintage western, cowgirl chic, and everything between for the entire home.

DESIGN & GRACE
419 South Main St., Grapevine
(817) 421-9518
www.designandgrace.com
For cooking and entertaining, this is a necessary place. Magnificent finds from Italy, Germany, Denmark, France, and Austria are here, making everything from a coffee gathering to a grand dinner party a pleasure to host. Every imaginable kitchen gadget is stocked here, and there are serving pieces you'd expect to find in shops in New York or San Francisco.

DH COLLECTION
3320 West Seventh St., Fort Worth
(817) 877-1994
www.dhcollection.com
This is a destination for fashion for your home, starting with fabulous Italian bed linens and linens from Nancy Koltes and Ann Gish. Furniture is by Precedent, Robin Bruce, Rowe, and Oly Studio. Home decor goods include shelving and clocks, candles, towels, and bath products.

RIOS INTERIORS
2465 North Main St., Fort Worth
(817) 626-8600
www.riosinteriors.com

First Monday Flea Markets

A major Texas flea market can be a little intimidating. The huge First Monday Canton Trade Days in Canton, east of Dallas, for example, has more than 3,000 vendors spread over 100 acres. A few things to keep in mind:

- Like most flea markets everywhere, arriving early is important for getting some of the best merchandise, especially antique furniture in good condition. Dealers wait for the markets to open and snap up good items fast.
- You'll probably be walking on dirt, and doing it for a long time, so wear comfortable shoes, and bring water to drink, especially in summer. Most flea markets have some sort of food court, but it's smart to bring snacks.
- If you're planning to really spend the bucks, bring a wagon or cart of some kind to haul things around in. Or, ask vendors if they'll hang on to your purchases and pick them up on the way back to the car.
- Bargain. You are not expected to pay full price.

For a rustic or hacienda style, you'll want to visit this northside favorite near the famous Stockyards. Custom creations in leather, wrought iron, and weathered board are among furniture pieces in a vast showroom. Look here for beds, lamps, armoires and cabinets, desks, chairs and ottomans, dining chairs, dining tables, cocktail tables, and sofas and loveseats, as well as locally crafted artworks.

Imports and Handcrafts

EL SOL MEXICAN IMPORTS
6008 Denton Highway, Wautaga
(817) 656-1046
www.elsolimports.com
High-quality wrought-iron designs, pottery, indoor/outdoor furnishings, beds, bureaus, coffee tables, end tables, mirrors, sconces, chandeliers, towel racks, and wine racks are among goods imported from Mexico. Ask about custom finishes on furniture.

PLAZA DEL SOL IMPORTS
2816 West Seventh St., Fort Worth
(817) 336-7460
Wall decor, especially pewter crosses, are plentiful here, as is glassware, Talavera pottery, and other tablewares from Mexico.

TERRA COTTA MULE
6711 Camp Bowie Blvd., Fort Worth
(817) 732-4200
In addition to Mexican imports, you can find home decor from the southwestern U.S., India, and Africa.

Malls and Shopping Areas

ARLINGTON HIGHLANDS
4000 Retail Connection Way, Arlington
(214) 572-0777
www.arlingtonhighlands.com
Newest among shopping entities in Tarrant County, this open-air complex that's fashioned to look like an old town square is home to Ann Taylor Loft, Francesca's, James Avery, Jos A. Bank, Sunglass Hut, Ulta Cosmetics, White House Black Market, World Market, and WineStyles, along with more than a dozen places to eat and sip, such as Which Wich Superior Sandwiches, The Melting Pot, The Keg Steakhouse & Bar, Red Robin Gourmet Burger & Spirits, Potbelly Sandwich Works, Piranha Killer Sushi, Gloria's, P.F. Changs, Mimi's Café, McAlister's Deli, Kincaid's, Freebirds, Chuy's, and Dave & Busters. Entertainment is found at Studio Movie Grill, the Little Gym, Improv Comedy Club, and Splitsville, an upscale bowling alley.

HULEN MALL
4800 South Hulen St., Fort Worth
(817) 294-1200
www.hulenmall.com
Anchors at this south-side mall are Dillard's, Sears, and Macy's, with other shops including Abercrombie & Fitch, The Body Shop, Brighton Collectibles, Caché, Charlotte Russe, Coach, Express, The Disney Store, Forever 21, Gap, Gymboree, Limited, StrideRite, and Victoria's Secret. There's a Movie Tavern here, a kids' play area, and several fast-food options.

MONTGOMERY PLAZA
2600 West Seventh St., Fort Worth
(817) 348-9260
A brilliant renovation to a historic Montgomery Ward building—one of the biggest in the nation—gave the Cultural District a chic place for shopping and dining, with loft apartments on the upper floors. Among eating spots is Boomerjack's Grill, Mac's on 7th, Pei Wei, and Gloria's Mexican/Salvadoran restaurant; you can shop at Merle Norman, Dolce Vita, Uncommon Angles, Lash Lounge, Luke's Locker, and Wolf Camera.

NORTH EAST MALL
1101 Melbourne Rd., Hurst
(817) 284-3427
www.simon.com/mall/mall_info
.aspx?ID=220
Nordstrom is the sexiest of the department store lineup, which also includes Dillard's, Macy's, JCPenney, Dick's Sporting Goods, and Sears. Specialty stores include Coach, Abercrombie & Fitch, Eddie Bauer, Banana Republic, Godiva Chocolatier, Eddie Bauer, Brighton Collectibles, Tony & Guy, Chico's, Gap, Hollister, Brookstone, and Sephora. There's an 18-screen Rave Motion Pictures theater, too, as well as sit-down dining sites Carrabba's Italian Grill and R.J. Gator's Hometown Grill & Bar. A kids soft play area keeps little ones happy.

PARKS AT ARLINGTON MALL
3811 South Cooper St., Arlington
(817) 467-0200
www.theparksatarlington.com

At the center of this complex, a menagerie-themed carousel provides a bit of diversion, and it's just $2 a ride. In addition, there's an NHL-size ice arena for skating ($6 plus skate rentals), an 18-screen AMC movie theater, and a kids' soft play area with characters from the Golden Books stories. More than 180 specialty stores include Coach, Bare Escentuals, Banana Republic, Aeropostale, Hollister, Origins, Build-A-Bear Workshop, Caché, AGX, Starbucks, Anchor Blue, G by Guess, Barnes & Noble Booksellers, DSW, Lifeway Christian Store, Forever 21, and Dick's Sporting Goods, along with Dillard's, Macy's, Sears, and JCPenney. There's a Cheesecake Factory and a 900-seat food court.

RIDGMAR MALL
1888 Green Oaks Rd., Fort Worth
(817) 731-0856
www.ridgmar.com
Among more than 125 shops, eateries, and department stores at this favorite on Fort Worth's west side is the city's only Neiman Marcus, along with locations of Macy's, Sears, Dillard's, and JCPenney stores. Other stores include Ann Taylor, f.y.e., Forever 21, Old Navy, Origins, New York & Company, The Children's Place, and Victoria's Secret. For dining, your sit-down options are Chili's and the lovely Zodiac in Neiman Marcus. There's a 13-screen Rave Movie Theatre, too, and a toddlers' play area.

SOUTHLAKE TOWN SQUARE
1256 Main St., Southlake
(817) 912-0252
www.southlaketownsquare.com
FR 1709 slices through the middle of Southlake and offers a re-created town square with the best shopping in this part of the county. Definitely on the fancy end of the spectrum, this one is home to Ann Taylor, Anthropologie, Apple, Baby Bliss, Banana Republic, Barnes & Noble, bebe, Caché, Coach, The Container Store, dELiA'S, Gap, J. Crew, James Avery, Nine West, Papyrus, Pottery Barn, L'Occitane, Wine Styles, Williams-Sonoma, Owl's Nest Toy Shop, White House Black Market, Francesca's, Aveda Concept Spa, European Day Spa, Terrace Retreat Med Spa, Terrace Retreat Salon and Spa, The Boardroom

Salon for Men, Larry North Fitness, and Nexgym. Dining and entertainment includes Blue Mesa Café, Brio Tuscan Grille, Café de Soleil, Café Express, Campania Pizza & More, Cheesecake Factory, Corner Bakery, Mi Cocina, Pei Wei, Taco Diner, Which Wich, and the Harkins Movie Theaters. There's a Hilton Dallas/Southlake Town Square here, too.

SUNDANCE SQUARE
Downtown Fort Worth
www.sundancesquare.com/shopping
Smack in the middle of downtown, there's an eclectic mix of gifts, home furnishings, jewelry, and accessories stores, including Barnes & Noble, Barse Sterling Silver, Earth Bones, Flowers To Go, Haltom's Jewelers, Jos A. Bank, Leddy's Ranch at Sundance, Milan Gallery, Pappagallo Classiques, Parfumerie Marie Antoinette and Spa, Retro Cowboy, Schakolad Chocolate Factory, Sid Richardson Museum, Texas Rangers Team Shop, Thomas Kinkade Gallery, and Vessels.

UNIVERSITY PARK VILLAGE
1612 South University Dr., Fort Worth
(817) 332-5700
www.universityparkvillage.com
An attractive, redbrick, open-air center offers more than 30 stores, including Ann Taylor, Apple Store, Chico's, Luke's Locker, Yves Delorme, Banana Republic, Barnes & Noble, Nine West, Pottery Barn, Starbucks, and Williams-Sonoma, plus a variety of handpicked local favorites, like Ruby and Francesca's Collections. Dining includes Blue Mesa Grill, Chili's Bar & Grill, La Piazza, McKinley's Bakery, and Starbucks.

Music Stores

CD WAREHOUSE
6242 Rufe Snow Dr., (817) 428-6641
1112 North Collins St. #A, Arlington, (817) 469-1048
4800 South Hulen St., (817) 361-8787
www.cdwarehouse.com
CD Warehouse is a leading outlet for new and used CDs and DVDs.

ERNEST TUBB RECORD SHOP
140 East Exchange Ave., Fort Worth
(817) 624-8449
www.etrecordshop.com
Founded by the legendary country music crooner, this well-loved shop stocks the best in good, old music from Gene Autry, Lefty Frizzell, Jerry Lee Lewis, and Bob Wills, as well as records, tapes, CDs, videos, and memorabilia of country music past and present, along with bluegrass and gospel tunes, too.

RIDGLEA MUSIC
3345 Winthrop Ave., Fort Worth
(817) 731-1831
www.ridgleamusic.com
A fixture in Fort Worth for more than a half-century, this shop offers private music lessons and exceptional instruments, including guitars, amplifiers, public-address systems, drums, and band and orchestral instruments. There's a good service department for guitars and band and orchestra instruments.

Outlet Shopping

GRAPEVINE MILLS
3000 Grapevine Mills Parkway, Grapevine
(872) 724-4900
www.grapevinemills.com
Found just two miles north of DFW Airport, this behemoth shopping center offers 1.6 million square feet of shopping and entertainment. More than 180 stores include discounted goods at names like Abercrombie & Fitch, Victoria's Secret, Forever 21, Old Navy, Group USA, Oakley Vault, Ann Taylor Loft, Coach House Gifts, NIKE outlet, The Disney Store, JCPenney, Marshalls, Neiman Marcus Last Call Clearance Center, Saks Fifth Avenue Off 5th, Banana Republic, and J. Crew. There's a 30-screen movie theater showing first-run films, and there's a lot to eat at Rainforest Café, Corner Bakery Café, Starbucks, Steak n Shake, Cozymel's, and Chili's Too, among numerous restaurants.

JUSTIN BOOT OUTLET
717 West Vickery Blvd., Fort Worth
(817) 654-3103
www.justinboots.com
Based in Fort Worth, the world-renowned Justin Boot Company sells seconds and overstocks at its outlet on the south side of downtown. Classic lace-up ropers, steel-toed work boots, and casual chukkas, along with belts and other accessories, are sold at discounts.

Specialty Foods

ARTISAN BAKING CO.
4900 White Settlement Rd., Fort Worth
(817) 821-3124
www.artisan-baking-company.com
Artisan Baking Company sells excellent, hand-made breads baked by a small family on a daily basis. Organic ingredients are typical, as is the use of European-style, high-fat butter, unbleached and whole grain flours, whole milk and heavy cream, fresh eggs, and garlic from Gilroy, California. The fruits, veggies, and herbs found in the breads come from fellow vendors at the Cowtown Farmers Market. Scones, cookies, granola, biscotti, and breakfast pastries are among daily offerings. Store shelves are stocked also with Wildflower Soaps and Aduro Bean Coffee, local businesses.

CENTRAL MARKET
4651 West Freeway, Fort Worth
(817) 377-9307
1425 East Southlake Blvd., Southlake
(817) 310-5600
www.centralmarket.com
From the San Antonio–based H.E.B. family-owned grocery chain, this upscale food and wine store revolutionized grocery shopping in Texas. If you want 15 kinds of apples, this produce department will thrill you. Any kind of meat and fish that can be found and eaten is marketed here, as are 700 kinds of cheeses. The wine department staff will locate nearly any vintage you can name. The

ready-made foods area stocks gourmet-to-go meals in abundance, from sushi to barbecue to pizza. Healthy-living departments furnish all types of vitamins, supplements, and skin-care products, too. Stores offer a full calendar of cooking classes; check Web site for current schedules.

COWTOWN FARMERS MARKET
3821 Southwest Blvd., Fort Worth
(817) 462-1426
www.cowtownfarmersmarket.com
Found on the west side of the Highway 377/183 traffic circle in southwest Fort Worth, in front of the Texas Outdoors Store, this market operates every Saturday, year-round from 8 a.m. until the vendors sell out of products. On Wednesday in summer, there's often a morning market, too. It's the only market in town wherein all goods sold are either grown, raised, or produced within 150 miles of town. Aside from fruits, vegetables, and herbs, vendors also sell baked goods, coffee, dog treats, flowers, goat cheese, honey, jelly, meat, soap, tamales, and salsa.

FIESTA MART
245 Northeast 28th St., (817) 625-3500
1300 East Pioneer Parkway, Arlington, (817) 804-7800
2700 8th Ave., (817) 920-1900
421 West Bolt St., (817) 920-1930
7809 Camp Bowie West, (817) 696-9631
4245 East Berry St., (817) 531-1067
www.fiestamart.com
The Houston-based chain specializing in Latin American groceries and related food goods offers excellent pricing on items that are hard to find otherwise.

GEORGE'S IMPORTED FOODS
4424 White Settlement Rd., Fort Worth
(817) 737-0414
A small family-run store near the Monticello neighborhood, this 1951 institution sells Greek and other Mediterranean products. At lunch, you can get a good turkey-pita sandwich and spanikopita.

ROY POPE GROCERY & MARKET
2300 Merrick St., Fort Worth
(817) 732-2863
www.roypopegrocery.com
The oldest family grocer in Fort Worth began in 1943 and still caters to the shopper who wants personalized service and an old-fashioned setting. Imported, gourmet items are among specialties, as are hand-cut steaks and other meat. Harder-to-find exotic meats such as buffalo, venison, quail, ostrich, alligator, rabbit, goose, and squab are typically here, as is a good, small wine selection. The deli counter turns out an excellent burger, as well as take-home suppers of meat loaf, fried chicken, King Ranch chicken, soups, salads, and vegetables. There's even delivery service in nearby neighborhoods.

WHOLE FOODS MARKET
801 East Lamar Blvd., Arlington
(817) 461-9362
www.wholefoodsmarket.com
The Austin-based store specializing in natural, organic products has a small store near Six Flags in Arlington. This one has an excellent wine selection, as well as good take-home meals. A larger store is expected to open in southwest Fort Worth in late 2010 or early 2011.

Sporting Goods
BACKWOODS
2727 West Seventh St., Fort Worth
(817) 332-2423, (888) 999-6934
www.backwoods.com
Originally opened in 1973, this remarkable store moved from modest digs to a grand showplace of a home in 2008. It's a terrific place to outfit yourself for mountain climbing, kayaking adventure, fly fishing, and more. Everything in the way of adventure sports is served here, from clothing to footwear to accessories. Brand names include Patagonia, The North Face, Prana, Lole, Osprey, Marmot, Hobie, Keen, Mountain Hardware, ExOfficio, Icebreaker, as well as the new Backwoods Collection.

BASS PRO SHOPS
2501 Bass Pro Dr., Grapevine
(972) 724-2018
www.basspro.com
Get over the idea that Bass Pro Shops are just about fishing. They've grown into a place that serves everyone interested in the outdoors, whether for hunting, camping, hiking, outdoor cooking, or more. There are private appointments for gunsmithing, too, and there are workshops for golf, fly-fishing, and hunting.

CABELA'S
12901 Cabela Dr., Fort Worth
(817) 337-2400
www.cabelas.com
Found in far north Fort Worth near Alliance Airport, this is the new outpost of a national favorite. Decor includes enormous natural habitat re-creations with trophy animals and massive aquariums, and there are two ponds on-site, too. Hunting gear (ammunition, decoys, game calls), archery products (bows, cases, targets), shooting gear, dog supplies (electronic collars, dog toys), optics (eyewear, cameras, binoculars), electronics (GPS, handheld cameras), men's hunting clothes and casual clothes, women's clothing, kids' clothing, footwear, fishing gear, boating supplies, camping supplies, auto and ATV gear, home decor, and various gifts and hobbies are among merchandise. There's a restaurant and deli inside the store.

LUKE'S LOCKER
5505 Colleyville Blvd., Colleyville
(817) 849-1562
2600 West Seventh St. in Montgomery Plaza, Fort Worth
(817) 877-1448
www.lukeslocker.com
The ultimate store for runners and walking enthusiasts, Luke's sponsors a number of races and running clinics and groups.

TEXAS OUTDOORS
3821 Southwest Blvd., Fort Worth
(817) 731-3427
www.texasoutdoors.biz

This locally owned outfit sells high-quality hunting, fishing, and camping supplies, guns, knives, boots, clothes, and more. Brands represented include Beeman, Beretta, Columbia, Wolverine, Filson, La Crosse, Mossy Oak, Moore Maker, Winchester, Danner, Benelli, Browning, Buck, Daiwa, Falcon, Hodgman, Minolta, Leica, Berkley, Sage, Shimano, and Zeiss.

Thrift Stores

BERRY GOOD BUYS
1701 West Berry St., Fort Worth
(817) 921-5898
www.safehaventc.org/content/donate_items
Sales revenue from this used clothing shop supports housing and resources for domestic violence victims. There's a good selection of vintage clothing in the mix, as well as books and furniture. Donations accepted here and at the Arlington Resource Center, 401 West Sanford, Suite 1400, Arlington, (817) 548-0583.

DOUBLE EXPOSURE
1714 Eighth Ave., Fort Worth
(817) 924-8038
www.juniorleaguefw.org
Gently used clothing, often from the finest homes in town, fills this Junior League–sponsored store.

PLATO'S CLOSET
4625 Donnelly Ave., Fort Worth
817) 731-9449
5904 South Cooper St., Arlington
(817) 466-4430
www.platoscloset.com
A recycling retail store specializes in clothes for teens and twenty-somethings. Bring in your old stuff and shop for new, used goods, too.

WESTERN WEAR EXCHANGE
2809 Alta Mere Dr., Fort Worth
(817) 738-4048
www.westernwearexchange.com
Want a new pair of jeans or boots but hate breaking them in? It's already been done at this resale shop. You'll find togs from Cruel Girl, Cinch,

Wrangler, Twenty X, Resistol, Stetson, Justin, and Lucchese. Look here for pearl snap shirts.

Western Wear

FINCHER'S WHITE FRONT WESTERN
115 East Exchange Ave., Fort Worth
(817) 624-7302, (877) HAT-BOOT
www.fincherswhitefront.com
Right in the historic Stockyards, Fincher's occupies the former White Front Western Store, established in 1902. This family business, opened in 1967, stocks a complete line of western wear to clothe everyone from babies to grandmas. Look here for traditional western hats, boots, jeans, shirts, blouses, dresses, and suits, along with cowboy souvenirs and jewelry.

LEDDY'S RANCH
410 Houston St., Fort Worth
(817) 336-0800
www.leddys.com
A sister business to the Stockyards Leddy's, this location offers more in the way of fashion-forward western clothing. Snap shirts, elaborately embroidered shirts, and gorgeous blouses, skirts, pants, and boots are among the pricey goods here at the Sundance Square shop.

MAVERICK WESTERN WEAR
100 East Exchange Ave., Fort Worth
(800) 282-1315, (817) 626-1129
www.maverickwesternwear.com
Open about 20 years in the Fort Worth Stockyards Historic District in a 1905-era building, this fabulous store stocks magnificent men's and women's clothing, as well as custom-made hats, boots, and jewelry, and leather and fur coats. There are items for infants and kids, too.

M.L. LEDDY'S
2455 North Main St., Fort Worth
(817) 624-3149, (888) 565-2668
www.leddys.com
A legend since 1922, M.L. Leddy's has customers from around the world, thanks to a reputation for the finest custom work in boots, made from ostrich, alligator, and calfskin. Leddy's is also known for making saddles, as well as for stocking fine clothing, belts, buckles, and accessories.

Fast Dallas Shopping Facts

- Highland Park Village, built in 1931, was the first planned shopping center in the nation.
- NorthPark Center was the first air-conditioned mall in the country.
- Galleria Dallas offers more than 200 premier retail stores and is home to the country's tallest Christmas tree.
- Neiman Marcus was founded in Dallas, and its original flagship store remains downtown.
- At 5.5 million square feet, the Dallas Market Center is the world's largest market for wholesale merchandise.

ATTRACTIONS

I t's only fitting that explorations in Dallas should begin downtown, where one of the most striking visions is that of Old Red, the Romanesque Revival–style courthouse built in 1892. Its gargoyles and intricate detail indicate a gothic idea, and its proximity to the first pioneer's cabin and to the Texas School Book Depository, where President Kennedy's assassin fired fatal shots, remind you that Dallas history is rooted right at its physical center.

As your wanderings take you through the rest of downtown, you can't help but be impressed by the balance of old and new Dallas. There's handsome Union Station, a showplace and transportation center since 1916, and the lovely old Magnolia Hotel building, topped by the city's emblem, the flying red horse called Pegasus. The larger-than-life bronze cattle and cowboys that fill Pioneer Plaza recall a rough-and-tumble era while also posing a striking con-trast to the angular, contemporary City Hall building, one of five downtown Dallas buildings designed by the modern master architect, I. M. Pei.

Pei also designed the Morton H. Meyerson Symphony Center, a cornerstone in the renowned Dallas Arts District, known as the largest urban arts district in the nation. Alongside the Meyerson are other Arts District buildings designed by fellow Pritzker Prize winners, such as the Nasher Sculpture Center, a Renzo Piano creation; the Annette Strauss Artist Square, by Sir Norman Foster; and two landmark structures in the spanking-new Performing Arts Center, the Margot and Bill Winspear Opera House, also by Sir Foster; and the Dee and Charles Wyly Theatre, designed by Rem Koolhaas.

The downtown dichotomy continues with the Majestic Theater, a beautiful piece of yester-year, and the very modern, very kid-friendly Dallas World Aquarium. Other important places to see downtown include the Dallas Farmers' Market and the original Neiman Marcus, both of which you'll find described in the Shopping chapter, page 85. You'll see the contrasts continue as you wander to East Dallas and explore the Art Deco spread of Fair Park and the spectacular gardens at the Arboretum, and as you roam northward to see the classic Southfork Ranch and the very modern Texas Sculpture Garden.

As you head west to Fort Worth, you'll note a more pronounced look of the Old West, particularly in the Stockyards National Historic District on the north side of town, in Sundance Square in downtown, and at the Will Rogers Memorial Center in the Cultural District. It's not strictly a giddy-up scene in Cowtown, however; you'll see a remarkable wealth of art museums, here, too, as well as exquisite rose and Japanese gardens within the city's Botanic Garden com-plex, also found in the Cultural District.

Price Code Key

$...................Less than $5
$$ ....$5 to $10
$$$ .... $10 to $20
$$$$ .... More than $20

DALLAS

Downtown

**DALLAS HERITAGE VILLAGE AT
OLD CITY PARK** $
1515 South Harwood St., Dallas
(214) 421-5141
www.dallasheritagevillage.org

On the south side of downtown, find a 13-acre spread that's a living history museum. Throughout the collection of historic buildings and authentic furnishings, you'll explore the period lasting from 1840 until 1910. Shady and quiet, the setting filled with furnished log cabins, century-old shops, a Victorian bandstand, a drummer's hotel, and southern mansions is a welcome break from our rushed, concrete world of today. Programs include educational events geared for diverse audiences.

DALLAS WORLD AQUARIUM $$$
1801 North Griffin St., Dallas
(214) 720-1801
www.dwazoo.com

A fantastic ecosystem of plant and animal varieties thrives in an urban jungle, offering a rich escape from downtown life. Thrills come from exploring Borneo through the presence of Matschie's tree kangaroos; Orinoco, thanks to birds, a 40-foot waterfall, manatees living in a 200,000-gallon river, a crocodile, and red howler monkeys; a predator aquarium stocked with green moray eels and sharks; a British Columbia exhibit starring a giant Pacific octopus; the Maya exhibit, with hummingbirds, owls, jaguar, sharks, and rays; and the Cape of Good Hope, with its little blue penguins. Onsite, find three restaurants and a great gift shop.

DEALEY PLAZA FREE
Houston at Elm streets, Dallas

This is the area through which the motorcade was passing when President John F. Kennedy was assassinated. At this National Historic Landmark you can always find tourists looking at important sites within the parklike setting, pointing up at the Texas School Book Depository building (now the Sixth Floor Museum) where the assassin was perched and at the famous grassy knoll. The 1940 WPA park is presided over by a statue of early *Dallas Morning News* publisher George B. Dealey.

KENNEDY MEMORIAL FREE
500 Main St., Dallas
(214) 653-6666

In the Dallas County Historical Plaza, to the immediate east of Old Red (below), this open-air place of reflection was designed by architect Philip Johnson, a Kennedy family friend. In marked contrast to the ornate old courthouse and the elaborate skyscrapers around it, this white square contains a granite block with the inscription, "John Fitzgerald Kennedy."

MAJESTIC THEATRE VARIED
1925 Elm St., Dallas
(214) 880-0137
www.liveatthemajestic.com

Opened in 1921, this handsome landmark is listed on the National Register of Historic Places and has hosted vaudeville shows and performances by the likes of Harry Houdini. A movie house in the 1930s, it was a premiere site visited by John Wayne and other stars promoting films. Today, the renovated showplace hosts performing arts, dance, music, and theater presentations from the Russian ballet to Bill Maher.

OLD RED COURTHOUSE $$
100 South Houston St., Dallas
(214) 571-1300
www.oldred.org

At Main and Houston, facing Dealey Plaza, this Romanesque Revival structure looks like something conceived in a Hollywood film. The imposing redbrick structure dating from 1892 features gargoyles and other otherworldly details. Extensively updated and remodeled in recent years, it's a must-see site and home to a Dallas Convention & Visitors Bureau information center with 40 kiosks. Traveling history exhibits are always on display, too.

An interactive education center lets you "build" a Big D skyscraper and play video history games, participate in mock trials, and learn about Dallas.

🔍 Close-up

Oak Cliff

Immediately southwest of downtown Dallas is North Texas's own little O.C. That stands for Oak Cliff, a very cool, old neighborhood that's new and hot again.

Whereas much of Dallas is flat, Oak Cliff dips and climbs over a hilly landscape covered by trees. One area with striking mid-century modern homes is Kessler Park, and another is a rolling section called Stevens Park. Plan a lengthy afternoon to explore the whole area, beginning with the Bishop Arts District, a century-old section where Bishop Street intersects Eighth Street, which includes:

- Fabulous food at Eno's Pizza Tavern (407 North Bishop Ave.; 214-943-9200, www.enospizza .com), such as Eno's super-thin supreme pizza with sausage, onion, pepper, mushroom, and black olive; Hattie's (418 North Bishop Ave.; 214-942-7400, www.hatties.net), a lovely Southern-style restaurant with shrimp and grits and buttermilk fried chicken; La Palapa Veracruzana (118 West Jefferson Blvd.; 214-946-9925, www.lapalapaveracruzana.com), serving seafood and moles from deep within Mexico; or Tillman's Roadhouse (327 West Seventh St.; 214-942-0988, www.tillmansroadhouse.com), a rustic grill and bar with exceptional food, such as venison Frito pie and make-your-own S'mores.

- Kicky shops and galleries such as the Soda Gallery (408 North Bishop Ave., 214-946-7632, www.thesodagallery.com), selling more than 200 varieties of sodas (Tahitian Treat, anyone?), including 28 kinds of root beer; Decorazon (417 North Bishop Ave., 214-946-1003, www.decorazongallery.com), a contemporary gallery showing work from local and international artists; Bishop Street Market (419 North Bishop at Seventh, 214-941-0907), gifts in the way of tablewares, really nice "coffee-table" books, fabulous candles from Caldrea, and body products from Niven Morgan, as well as interesting little items like a pink leather flask; Indigo 1745 (370 West Seventh St., 214-948-1745, www.indigo1745.com), a boutique with men's and women's clothing and great accessories, like hats, brushes, handbags, and jewelry; and Zola's Everyday Vintage (414 North Bishop Ave., 214-943-6643,www.zolaseverydayvintage.com) stocked with fun and affordable vintage clothes, house decor, jewelry, and all manner of kitschy goodies.

But there's much more to Oak Cliff than Bishop Arts. Here are other reasons to hang around this groovy hood and explore.

Shop and eat at Bolsa (614 West Davis St.; 214-367-9367, www.bolsadallas.com), occupying a former auto garage, with a fabulous outdoor patio and shelves laden with locally sourced gourmet goods.

While away the afternoon at Jack's Backyard (2303 Pittman St.; 214-741-3131, www.jacks backyarddallas.com) a hidden casual hangout behind the bulk mail center, with solid food, Wii bowling, darts tournaments, and casual conversation in the bar or garden.

Play a round at Stevens Park Golf Course (1005 North Montclair Ave., 214-670-7506, www .stevensparkgolf.com), a municipal course with 18 holes and a deli with happy hour.

Spend the night at Belmont Hotel (901 Fort Worth Ave., 214-393-2300, www.belmontdallas .com) a renovated mid-century hotel oozing retro-chic, with poolside parties in the spring and summer, a great patio for drinking and nibbling, and a restaurant called Smoke, where everything is cooked over hardwood fires.

PIONEER PLAZA   **FREE**
Young Street at Griffin Street, Dallas
(214) 953-1184
A 4.2-acre park offers some exceptional, pure Texan photo opportunities. The focal point of this historic site is a larger-than-life-size bronze of cowboys driving more than 40 longhorn cattle along the range. Also in the park, find a historic cemetery, all in the shadows of a modern convention center.

**THE SIXTH FLOOR MUSEUM
AT DEALEY PLAZA**   **$$$**
411 Elm St., Dallas
(214) 747-6660
jfk.org
Located in the former Texas School Book Depository, where accused assassin Lee Harvey Oswald fatally shot the president, this excellent museum honors the fallen leader and memorializes a seminal event in American history. Self-guided tours are enhanced with an audio unit that explains permanent exhibits and details some 35,000 artifacts relating to the events leading up to and including JFK's death on November 22, 1963. Private footage is especially interesting. Open daily except Christmas and Thanksgiving.

UNION STATION   **FREE**
400 South Houston St., Dallas
unionstationdallas.com
Opened in 1916, this elegant white-brick building immediately south of Dealey Plaza is a Dallas landmark and was the major portal through which visitors once entered the city. It still serves Amtrak and DART (Dallas Area Rapid Transit), and it's a special events center, too, served by Wolfgang Puck Catering.

Arts District

CROW COLLECTION OF ASIAN ART   **FREE**
2010 Flora St., Dallas
(214) 979-6435
crowcollection.org
Housed within the Trammel Crow Center Pavilion, this delightful surprise in a big office build-ing represents a lifetime's collection by the late real estate tycoon and his wife, Margaret. More than 600 paintings, metal and stone objects, and architectural pieces come from China, Japan, India, and Southeast Asia. Among rare finds is the sandstone facade of an 18th-century residence from India. A lovely gift shop is on-site, too.

**DALLAS CENTER FOR THE
PERFORMING ARTS**   **$$–$$$**
2403 Flora St., Dallas
(214) 954-9925, (214) 880-0202
www.dallasperformingarts.org
Within this stunning new complex, opened in late 2009, are four venues staging myriad enter-tainment. There's the Margot and Bill Winspear Opera House, home to the Dallas Opera and Texas Ballet Theater, as well as touring Broadway shows and the like; the Wyly Theatre, designed by Pritzker Prize–winning architect Rem Koolhaas, serving as home for the Dallas Theater Center, Dallas Black Dance Theatre, and Anita N. Martinez Ballet Folklorico; the Elaine D. and Charles A. Sammons Park, a performance space spreading over 10 acres with gardens, trees, and a reflect-ing pool; and the Annette Strauss Artist Square, another outdoor performance space. Dining options include the Winspear Opera House Café and various concession areas.

DALLAS MUSEUM OF ART   **$$**
1717 North Harwood St., Dallas
(214) 922-1200
www.dallasmuseumofart.org
Here's another design from famed architect I. M. Pei. Since 1903, the DMA has been dedicated to collecting and preserving arts from around the globe, spanning times from ancient days to the present. Now a storehouse of more than 23,000 works of art, the DMA is home to pieces from every corner of the world. Among favorite areas is the Wendy and Emery Reves Collection of more than 1,400 works from the Impressionist and post-Impressionist periods, with paintings, sculpture, works on paper, and decorative arts objects among the treasures.

ℹ️ The Dallas Arts District Friends docents lead a free, one-hour guided walking tour of the Dallas Arts District at 10:30 a.m. on the first Saturday of the month. Book a place by calling (214) 953-1977.

MEYERSON SYMPHONY CENTER $$–$$$$
2301 Flora St., Dallas
(214) 670-3600
meyersonsymphonycenter.com

Typically there are 325 concert hall events staged annually at this I. M. Pei–designed showplace, which is home of the Dallas Symphony Orchestra, Turtle Creek Chorale, the Dallas Wind Symphony, and the Greater Dallas Youth Orchestra. The magnificent Lay Family Concert Organ is among the lures. You can dine at Opus, the more elegant restaurant, or at Allegro, offering a buffet.

NASHER SCULPTURE CENTER $$
2001 Flora St., Dallas
(214) 242-5100
www.nashersculpturecenter.org

Begun more than a half-century ago with the private collection of benefactors Ray and Patsy Nasher, this extraordinary museum offers 54,000 square feet of exhibit space in a building designed by the renowned Renzo Piano. Among 300 pieces in a steady rotation are ones that have been shown at far-flung places like the Forte di Belvedere in Florence, Italy, and the National Gallery of Art in Washington, DC. It's hard to believe you're downtown in this marvelous haven, with indoor and outdoor spaces that transport you. Works range from early modern period to postwar and include those by Pablo Picasso, Joan Miró, Alexander Calder, and Henri Matisse.

North and Park Cities

MEADOWS MUSEUM $
5900 Bishop Blvd. at Southern Methodist University
(214) 768-2516
smu.edu/meadows/museum/index.htm

One of the world's largest collections of Spanish art outside of Spain covers periods from the 10th to 21st centuries. Begun in 1962, the museum houses magnificent pieces that include paintings by Picasso and Miró, as well as first-edition sets of Goya's four great print series, *La Tauromaquia*, *Los Disparates*, *Los Caprichos*, and *Los Desatres de la Guerra*. Additional interests are the Meadows' Renaissance altarpieces, sensational baroque canvases, rococo oil sketches, modernist abstracts, and much more.

SOUTHERN METHODIST UNIVERSITY   FREE
Hillcrest Road between Mockingbird Lane and University Blvd., Dallas
(214) 768-2000
smu.edu

Often referred to as an Ivy of the South, this stately collection of 76 redbrick buildings sits on 210 acres in one of the gracious, old, monied neighborhoods, University Park. On campus, SMU's 10 libraries house the largest private collection of research materials in the Southwest.

Some 11,000 students attend school here as undergrads and in graduate programs offered in the law and business schools. Altogether, SMU offers 123 undergrad degrees, 127 graduate and professional degrees, and 25 doctorates. In 2013, it will become home to the George W. Bush Presidential Center, as W has again become a Dallas resident since leaving the White House. The campus is home to McFarlin Auditorium, a pleasant venue for small music, dance, comedy, and theater productions.

Fair Park (East Dallas)

Just east of downtown, Fair Park stands as a 70-year-old monument to the Texas Centennial. A spectacular, 277-acre collection of Art Deco buildings erected to celebrate the state's birthday in 1936, the park is home to a number of museums and hosts the annual State Fair of Texas in October. A National Historic Landmark, Fair Park can take a whole day to explore. The Dallas Children's Aquarium, a function of the Dallas Zoo and formerly called the Dallas Aquarium, is being renovated and will reopen in 2010 in Fair Park. Among fun facts: The "Texas Star" Ferris wheel on the Midway remains the tallest in North America; and the 52-foot "Big Tex" statue, who greets you as you walk through the center of the Fair, is known as the tallest cowboy in Texas.

In addition to the Cotton Bowl Stadium and Superpages.com concert venue, here's what you'll find there.

AFRICAN-AMERICAN MUSEUM $
3536 Grand Ave., Dallas
(214) 565-9026
www.aamdallas.org
One of the rare modern buildings at Fair Park, this cross-shaped museum of ivory-colored stone stands out not just for its beautiful contemporary design but also for its commitment to the preservation and exhibition of African-American materials of artistic, cultural, and historical value. Among noted collections is the Billy R. Allen Folk Art Collection.

DALLAS FIREFIGHTERS MUSEUM $
3801 Parry Ave., near Fair Park, Dallas
(214) 821-1500
www.dallasfiremuseum.com
Everyone is fascinated with firefighters. See more than 100 years of city history at the Dallas Firefighters Museum. The museum is housed in a restored 1907 fire station that includes an 1884 horse-drawn steamer and a 1936 ladder truck among the many historical displays and exhibits. An interesting gift shop is located in the old horse stalls.

HALL OF STATE $
3939 Grand Ave., Dallas
(214) 421-4500
www.hallofstate.com
Crafted from Texas limestone for the Texas Centennial Exposition, this handsome building serves as the home to the Dallas Historical Society and pays tribute to Texas history with an impressive number of collections. Throughout the hall are designs that symbolize Texas, from cactus and oil wells to lariats. The Hall of Heroes holds large

bronze sculptures of Texas founders, including Stephen F. Austin, the father of Texas. The Hall of State was recently restored as part of a $12 million renovation project in Fair Park.

MUSEUM OF THE AMERICAN RAILROAD $
1105 Washington St., Dallas
(214) 428-0101
www.dallasrailwaymuseum.com
A museum for young and old, this collection of rolling stock illustrates the history of the railroad and shows its continuing value today. There are 30 pieces of railroad equipment that can make a train buff of just about anyone. Note that around the end of 2010, the museum is moving north to the town of Frisco, where it will be covered by a giant shed fashioned to look like train stations of the late 19th century.

MUSEUM OF NATURE AND SCIENCE $$
3535 Grand Ave. and 1318 South second Ave., Dallas
(214) 428-5555
www.natureandscience.org
The recent merging of three museums—the Dallas Museum of Natural History, established in 1936; the Science Place, established 1936; and the Dallas Children's Museum, established 1995—continues to expand at an impressive rate. It's an entertaining place where kids have loads of fun while learning about everything from art to spying to the space shuttle to dinosaurs. There's an IMAX theater and a planetarium on-site, too.

MUSIC HALL AT FAIR PARK VARIED
909 First Ave., Dallas
(214) 565-1116
www.liveatthemusichall.com
Since 1925, this elegant hall of Spanish-Baroque-Moorish design has been a favorite destination for Broadway touring shows, opera, ballet, pop music shows, and comedian performances. It's home to the Dallas Summer Musicals, too.

Close-up

Fair Park's Unique Architecture

An unexpected treat awaits the architecture buff at Fair Park, barely 2 miles east of downtown Dallas. There, within the 277-acre National Historic Landmark built to celebrate Texas's Centennial in 1936, you'll find the nation's largest collection of 1930s Art Deco exposition-style architecture. So many people came to experience the Centennial, in fact—there were six million, including President Franklin D. Roosevelt—that Dallas was able to heave itself out of the Depression. If you love the art of structures, you'll want to spend a full morning or afternoon wandering the site, and you'll be glad you brought a camera or sketchpad along.

Here are the highlights, guaranteed to make you dawdle. (Find a map at fairpark.org).

On Parry Avenue, check out the Main Gate, where tan columns offer classic art decor from architect George Dahl, who added elements of Southwestern art onto existing and new buildings. This bas-relief styling is found throughout the park, with three-dimensional murals frequently noted, like those on the gate columns that depict the arrival of pioneers in Texas.

On the Esplanade, find a 700-foot-long reflecting pool, flanked by six sculptures of women. Dahl commissioned artists to honor periods of Texas history and the six flags that have flown over the territory and state. To the north side you'll see Lawrence Tenney Stevens's sculptures representing Texas, the Confederacy, and Spain; and to the south, the sculptures by Raoul Josett represent Mexico, France, and the United States. The Esplanade and its fountains were recently renovated as part of a $12 million improvement project in this area of the park.

Visit the Centennial Building (which has also been called the Transportation Building and Chrysler Building) to look at eight murals. From west to east, these portray ideas of speed, traction, railroad transportation, navigation, future transportation, transportation of the past, air travel, and automobile travel.

The Women's Museum awaits within a 1910 building that first served as Dallas's coliseum and that Dahl renovated in 1935 with a new Deco facade. The gorgeous *Spirit of the Centennial* sculpture of a woman on its front made it the perfect choice for the Women's Museum, which opened in 1994. Note also the *Fish Fountain* sculpture over a reflecting pool in front.

The Hall of State, which cost $1.3 million at its construction for the Centennial, was the focal point for the celebration of Texas. The exquisite bas-relief carvings of marching soldiers on the Texas limestone columns, the gorgeous bronze doors with details of Texas industry and architecture, and the interior's rooms filled with murals, gold-leaf medallions, and artifacts are all breathtaking. The Hall, which serves as home to the Dallas Historical Society, was reopened after a massive restoration for the State Fair of Texas in September 2009.

The Pan American Building Complex was another building renovated by Dahl; its facade features animal murals, appropriate in that part of the complex is home to the Dallas Police Mounted Unit.

The Swine Building has an oddity you shouldn't miss. It's called the *Woofus,* and you'll see it atop a 16-foot-high pedestal. This creature is sculptor Lawrence Tenney Stevens's fantasy composite of a sheep's head, horse's neck, hog's body, duck wings, turkey feathers, and 10-foot-wide set of longhorns, the ultimate Texas animal.

The Tower Building was considered the Centennial's centerpiece. It reaches nearly 180 feet high and exhibits murals with Texas history, inside and out.

East Dallas

DALLAS ARBORETUM $$
8525 Garland Rd., Dallas
(214) 515-6500
www.dallasarboretum.org
Spreading over 66 acres on the shores of White Rock Lake, this public botanical garden contains some of the more gorgeous floral displays in the nation. Four times a year, the displays undergo significant changes to capture the spirit and beauty of the new season. There's a Holiday Show at the historic DeGolyer mansion, and 450,000 bulbs are planted for spring blooming, which is a spectacle to melt even the hardest heart. It's a lovely place for quiet walks and meditation, for getting babies out into nature for the first time, or for taking someone with whom you need to reconnect.

DEEP ELLUM FREE
Primarily Main, Commerce, and Elm streets, east of downtown, between US 75 and Exposition Avenue
A historic district just east of downtown, this intriguing quarter was initially settled by former slaves after the Civil War. It grew in the early 20th century to a center for blues and jazz and as a cultural center in general for African-American residents. A warehouse area that can be a bit rough around the edges, it's been a destination in recent years for nightlife and the occasional dining find. Loft apartments have become popular, as have art galleries. More than a few retail businesses are tattoo parlors. The Deep Ellum Arts Festival is an outdoor street party staged over three days each April.

SWISS AVENUE HISTORIC DISTRICT FREE
(214) 821-3290
www.sahd.org
Lying a few minutes east of downtown, near the Baylor Medical Center complex, this district encompasses the bulk of the finest old homes in Dallas. It's a magnificent collection of homes listed on the National Register of Historic Places, including an estimated 200 carefully preserved

and restored homes noted for architectural styles such as Mediterranean, Spanish, Georgian, Prairie, Craftsman, Neoclassical, Italian Renaissance, Tudor, and Colonial Revival. Every Mother's Day weekend, there's a tour of seven or eight homes, typically along Swiss Avenue and on Bryan Parkway, Worth, and Live Oak, among other streets. It's a lovely place to drive around at any time of year.

North and North-Central Dallas

CAVANAUGH FLIGHT MUSEUM $
4572 Claire Chennault, Addison
(972) 380-8800
www.cavanaughflightmuseum.com
Take a self-guided tour or book ahead for a guided look through a remarkable collection of vintage aircraft housed in a 50,000-square-foot, four-hangar display area. The museum is committed to restoring, operating, and exhibiting important aircraft from various periods in history. One plane here, the Fokker D-VII, was featured in the Martin Scorsese film *The Aviator*.

FRONTIERS OF FLIGHT MUSEUM $$
Love Field
6911 Lemmon Ave., Dallas
(214) 350-1651
All aircraft eras through history are represented, from the first flight through World War II and into space exploration time. In 100,000 square feet of exhibit space, you'll find 25 aircraft, 20 interactive displays, a cool kids' section, educational workshops, and even a flight school for students who can learn to build and fly model planes. For the plane freak, there's one of three existing prototypes of the Lear Fan 2100.

Irving

This one-time suburb of Dallas has grown into its own as a business and medical center, perched in an enviable position between northwest Dallas and DFW Airport. There are a handful of interesting destinations and diversions awaiting you in Irving.

MUSTANGS OF LAS COLINAS   FREE
5205 North O'Connor Blvd., Irving
(972) 869-9047
www.mustangsoflascolinas.com
The largest equine sculpture in the world, this masterpiece lies in the Las Colinas business center called Williams Square Plaza. Take your camera.

NATIONAL SCOUTING MUSEUM $
1329 West Walnut Hill Lane, Irving
(972) 580-2100
www.nationalscoutingmuseum.org
Found near the national scouting headquarters, this educational center is so large it would take 3.2 million merit badges to cover the floor space. The single largest collection of Norman Rockwell's scouting artwork lives here.

South Dallas

DALLAS ZOO $$
621 East Clarendon Dr., Dallas
(214) 670-5656
www.dallaszoo.com

Other than some charming older residential neighborhoods and one cool retail/dining area called Bishop Arts District, there hasn't been a wealth of appeal in Oak Cliff, just south of downtown. The big exception is the Dallas Zoo, a 95-acre preserve noted on I-35 South by a towering bronze of a giraffe. It's the largest zoo in Texas, home to a new family of cheetahs and the domain of Jenny, the 33-year-old elephant and beloved zoo icon. (Note: There is a passionate movement underway to have Jenny moved to a larger sanctuary where she will socialize more with other elephants.) A new elephant habitat is in the works now, and large mammal areas already operating include those for an endangered tiger species. There's a family zoo with pony rides and a bird-feeding area, as well as a Wilds of Africa exhibit with a gorilla conservation research center.

Far North
Frisco
Another exploding community grown from a town once notable mostly for its feed stores and

---

Cattle Baron Mansions

In Fort Worth, you can visit a bygone era of wealth and luxury by touring two extraordinary cattle baron mansions. The more famous of the pair is Thistle Hill at 1509 Pennsylvania Ave. (817-332-5875, www.historicfortworth.org), home to Historic Fort Worth, Inc. An opulent home that has been restored to its 1910 grandeur, Thistle Hill was crafted in an area once called Quality Hill. It was built by Albert Buckman Wharton, who married Electra Waggoner, the daughter of North Texas rancher W. T. Waggoner. The home was designed by famous Texas architect Marshall Sanguinet and cost all of $46,000 at its construction. You'll see an interior of bog oak, white oak, curly maple, bird's eye maple, mahogany, and local soft pine. Public rooms include a parlor, library, billiard room, dining room, and conservatory, along with a wide staircase with a huge stained-glass window. It will come as no surprise that it's one of the most popular places in town for weddings.

Just a few blocks away, the Ball-Eddleman-McFarland House at 1110 Penn St. (817-332-5875, www.historicfortworth.org) rises on a bluff overlooking the Trinity River, with a stunning view to the west. The elegant 1899 home was designed by English architect Howard Messer and belonged to only two families through its life. Mostly unchanged through the years, it exhibits wonderful turrets, gables, copper finials, a slate-tile roof, and a porch crafted from red sandstone and marble. A fairy-tale setting, this is another home often rented for weddings.

Close-up

Recent and Future Dallas Developments

Newest among Dallas developments is Park Lane, a mixed-use center in near North Dallas facing NorthPark Center. Park Lane is a $750 million, 33-acre project with 700,000 square feet of retail, restaurant, and entertainment space, including a Whole Foods Market, with an additional 740,000 square feet of office space, 600 apartments, a 78,000-square-foot sports club, and a 250-room hotel. When it's complete in 2010, there will be a pedestrian passage with fountains, all connected by sidewalks and tree-lined streets. It's to be easily accessed by the DART light-rail line.

Planned in Dallas in the coming years:

In 2011, the first major component of the Trinity River Corridor Project, just west of downtown, is to be realized. This will be the Margaret Hunt Hill Bridge, one of three planned signature bridges to span the Trinity River. The bridge designs are by the renowned architect Santiago Calatrava.

In 2011, the Woodall Rogers Park, a 5.2-acre urban park, will tie Uptown and Downtown and the Arts District together with an open, urban green space at its center. The $100 million project will cover the existing Woodall Rogers Freeway and will incorporate an acoustical performance stage with lawn seating for up to 3,300, a dog park, a children's garden and playground, and a 25-foot-tall water sculpture.

In 2013, the Museum of Nature and Science should open a new venue on a 4.7-acre site within Victory Park, next to downtown. It's to be designed by Pritzker Prize laureate Thom Mayne.

Also in 2013, DART will complete its $3.3 billion expansion, adding 45 miles of light-rail lines and a new station at DFW Airport.

In 2014, the Trinity River Corridor Project will complete its signature bridges and offer more than 8,000 acres of park, forest, and lakes with hiking and biking trails and neighborhood upgrades.

pretty pastures, this small city now brings sports fans and art lovers, as well as shoppers, to town. There's a beautiful Westin Stonebriar Resort, complete with a gorgeous golf course, too. For all Frisco information, see www.visitfrisco.com.

PIZZA HUT PARK $-$$
9200 World Cup Way, Frisco
(214) 705-6700
www.pizzahutpark.com, www.fcdallas.com
A $64 million soccer stadium will wow you, whether or not you're a soccer fan. Home to FC Dallas, a major league soccer team, it's also a great place to catch World Cup game broadcasts.

TEXAS SCULPTURE GARDEN FREE
6801 Gaylord Parkway, Frisco
www.texassculpturegarden.com

Hall Office Park serves as home to a remarkable public garden adorned with big and mightily impressive works by 41 Texas artists.

Plano
Just north of Dallas, this former farmland mushroomed into one of the fastest-growing cities in the nation in the 1980s. As you drive north from Big D, you cannot tell where Dallas ends and Plano begins. The sprawling suburban mass offers everything in the way of residential, office, and retail development, but there are ways to find links to simpler times, too. Here are places to explore.

HERITAGE FARMSTEAD $
1900 West Fifteenth St., Plano
(972) 881-0140
www.heritagefarmstead.org

This 1891 farmhouse and surroundings were treated to a $1.2 million update to create a place that introduces you to the local past on this patch of the Blackland Prairie.

SOUTHFORK RANCH $$
3700 Hogge Rd., Plano
(800) 989-7800
southforkranch.com

Fans of the series *Dallas* will remember this country estate as the Ewing Mansion, home to many a big-haired gal, rouge cousins, and one famous villain. Plenty of memorabilia from the show remains on exhibit, while Texas longhorn cattle and myriad horses roam the grounds. Guided tours are offered daily. If you have a group, book a Chuck Wagon Dining Experience, complete with singing cowboys.

FORT WORTH

Downtown Fort Worth

FIREHOUSE NO. 1 FREE
Second and Commerce Streets, Fort Worth
(817) 255-9300

A stately old firehouse near Sundance Square houses a museum (an extension of the Fort Worth Museum of Science and History in the Cultural District) that details Fort Worth's first 150 years. The building itself has good stories from its service as the original city hall and, for more than a century, as a fire station.

FORT WORTH WATER GARDENS FREE
1502 Commerce St., Fort Worth
(817) 871-5755

A contemporary and refreshing oasis surrounded by the hard lines of downtown buildings, this neighbor of the Fort Worth Convention Center is a design by famed architect Philip Johnson. A stair-step design with rushing water and three pools, the urban park was created with relaxation and reflection in mind. (Swimming is forbidden, and measures have been taken with the construction of railings to prevent any temptation after three drownings a few years ago.)

SID RICHARDSON MUSEUM FREE
309 Main St., Fort Worth
(817) 332-6554
www.sidrmuseum.org

Widely known as one of the most important collections of western art in the nation, this recently expanded and reopened treasure trove exhibits an astounding assortment of the work of Frederic Remington, Charles M. Russell, and other artists. If you're looking for a single place to examine art from the American West, you can't find anything better than the paintings and sculpture amassed by the oilman and philanthropist for whom the museum is named. A lovely painting is *The Love Call*, a dreamlike, 1909 work in which a lone Indian plays his flute by moonlight, a radically different sort of depiction and a departure from the often tragic, violent images in the genre. The gift shop is excellent.

i If you have a passion for architecture, take a self-guided walking tour of downtown Fort Worth, as mapped and described at www.fortwortharchitecture.com. There are more than 100 sites on the tour, with favorites including the Burk Burnett Building at 500 Main St. (1914), the Flatiron Building at 1000 Houston St. (1907), and the Texas and Pacific Railway Terminal at Throckmorton and Lancaster (1931).

SUNDANCE SQUARE FREE
www.sundancesquare.com

The name is a reference to the Sundance Kid, buddy to Butch Cassidy of the infamous Hole in the Wall Gang who are said to have been visitors to the nearby area that was called Hell's Half Acre. The handsome quarter extends south from the beautiful old Tarrant County Courthouse, re-creating a late-19th-century look. Many of the buildings in the 20-block district have been lovingly restored, and others are new structures made to fit into the overall design. Within Sundance Square, find two live theaters, a handful of museums and art galleries, a cinema complex, comedy club, plenty of shopping, dining, and nightlife, and the glorious Bass Performance Hall. Parking is free on weekends and after 5 p.m. on weekdays. Be sure to check out the Chisholm Trail Mural at Main and Fourth Street, with a magical 3-D effect.

TARRANT COUNTY COURTHOUSE   FREE
100 East Weatherford St., Fort Worth
(817) 884-1111
tarrantcounty.com
One of the more picturesque (and photographed) county courthouses in Texas, this 1893 master-piece perched on a bluff high above the Trinity River at the north end of downtown was crafted of pinkish-red granite and boasts a four-faced Seth Thomas clock in the tower. Tours are free.

Fort Worth Stockyards, North Side

COWTOWN CATTLEPEN MAZE $
145 East Exchange Ave., Fort Worth
(817) 624-6666
www.cowtowncattlepenmaze.com
The ages-old wooden cattlepens serve as frame-work for this game, perfect for families. It's a great way to work off a big Mexican food or barbecue lunch devoured in one of the Stockyards Station restaurants.

COWTOWN COLISEUM $$$
121 East Exchange Ave., Fort Worth
(817) 625-1025
www.cowtowncoliseum.com
Home of the world's first indoor rodeo, this 1908 landmark is where you still go to see a rodeo every Friday and Saturday night, year-round. Over the years, this building has hosted far more than rodeo; it's even been an opera venue. A thorough overhaul made it much more comfortable than in its early days, with air-conditioning possibly the biggest boon. The one-hour Pawnee Bill's Wild West Show on weekends brings the Wild West to life with trick roping and riding, cowboy music, and more.

LIVESTOCK EXCHANGE BUILDING   FREE
131 Exchange Ave., Fort Worth
(817) 626-2334, (817) 625-5082
www.fortworthstockyards.org, www
.stockyardsmuseum.org

A stately 1902 building that was erected as the business center for cattle traders, this is now the home of the North Fort Worth Historical Society Museum, dedicated to sharing the heritage of the storied Stockyards area. You'll learn about the cowboys who drove hundreds of thousands of head of cattle through here en route to the markets up north in the earlier years, and you'll hear about the period when cattle were brought to the slaughterhouses that eventually opened here. The district wasn't just where beef was traded; there was all manner of commerce at saloons, boardinghouses, and bordellos, too. This particular building was the headquarters for an area once known as the Wall Street of the West; its lawn is the setting for a number of events, including a fantastic chuck-wagon cooking com-petition every October.

STOCKYARDS STATION   FREE
130 East Exchange Ave., Fort Worth
(817) 625-9715
www.stockyardsstation.com
If you sign up for a guided tour (fees involved), you'll start here at the old train station in the Stockyards. Inside the station, find more than 25 shops and businesses, including art galleries, sou-venir stands, a winery, and several restaurants. For self-guided touring, you can rent an audio tour in multiple languages.

If you want to ride the restored train, you'll board the Grapevine Vintage Railroad (www .grapevinetexasusa.com), which operates on a seasonal schedule with trips to Grapevine, north-east of Fort Worth, near DFW Airport, or to the south side of Fort Worth and back; tickets are $10 to $20.

While you're wandering Stockyards Station, be on the lookout for the twice-daily cattle drive that ambles at a leisurely pace down Exchange Avenue. The Herd, as it's called, is a group of 15 Texas longhorns that mosey down the brick road, driven by cowboys and caballeros in period costume. The Herd will wander past at 11:30 a.m. and 4 p.m.

TEXAS COWBOY HALL OF FAME $
128 East Exchange Ave. #A, Fort Worth
(817) 626-7131
www.texascowboyhalloffame.com
Inductees in this hall of honor include rodeo stars like Don Gay and Ty Murray, as well as music men George Strait and Don Edwards, but you'll find folks whose contributions to the cowboy culture were less flashy, too. Inside the hall, find the Sterquell Wagon Collection, John Justin Trail of Fame, Chisholm Trail Exhibit, History of the Mexican Charro, Texas Cowboy Hall of Fame, Zigrang Bit Collection, Adventures of the Cowboy Trail, and a gift shop and old-fashioned photography parlor. There's plenty of hands-on action for the kids, too.

i On a pretty afternoon, you can take a drive through the lovely Elizabeth Boulevard Historic District in Fort Worth, found south of downtown and north of Berry Street, along Elizabeth Boulevard between Eighth and College Avenues. This exceptional street, which is listed on the National Register of Historic Places, was the central thoroughfare lined with grand homes built by cattlemen and oil barons between 1920 and 1930. The building boom ended with the Great Depression, but you'll see extraordinary beauty in most of the lovingly restored homes.

TEXAS TRAIL OF FAME   FREE
www.texastrailoffame.org
Along the sidewalks in the Stockyards National Historic District, you'll notice bronze markers laid in the concrete. These note individuals whose contributions to the preservation of western culture have been called significant. Honorees include Stephen F. Austin, Amon G. Carter, Davy Crockett, Sam Houston, M. L. Leddy, Annie Oakley, and Sid Richardson.

West Fort Worth/Cultural District

AMON CARTER MUSEUM   FREE
3501 Camp Bowie Blvd., Fort Worth
(817) 738-1933
www.cartermuseum.org
The late newspaper publisher for whom the museum is named spent years collecting paintings and sculpture by Frederic Remington and Charles M. Russell and was a fan of all American art. These treasures live in a modern building designed by Philip Johnson, opened in 1961 and expanded recently to accommodate a growing inventory. Mr. Carter didn't live to see the final product, but its magnificent design was described in one book, *150 Years of American Art: The Amon Carter Museum Collection*, as "a simple, elegant design that combined the warmth and richness of bronze with the creamy, intricately patterned surface of native Texas shellstone." You'll find work by Eliot Porter, Georgia O'Keeffe, and others noted for creations throughout American history. Admission to the permanent collection is free but there will be a fee for special attractions. The gift shop is excellent.

BOTANIC GARDEN $
3220 Botanic Garden Blvd., Fort Worth
(817) 871-7686
www.fwbg.org
Texas's oldest botanical garden covers more than 100 acres in the middle of town, giving you a chance to escape from the world into a verdant oasis. Sheltered with nature's gifts, the gardens lie next to the interstate—but you don't know it, once you're inside. Rose gardens, butterfly oasis, a Japanese garden, a conservatory, and quiet places of reflection await. Take a book or a journal and sit quietly, waiting for a rabbit to appear. A favorite setting for weddings, the site is home to the wildly popular Concerts in the Garden, a nightly music fest from early June through early July, complete with fireworks. The Gardens Restaurant is a busy lunch and Sunday brunch place.

CHRISTIAN ARTS MUSEUM $
3205 Hamilton Ave., Fort Worth
(817) 335-1522
www.cacmuseum.org
Opened in the fall of 2009, this small but impressive religious art museum provides a new home to a wax sculpture of the Last Supper. The art-

work's beginning dates to the 1920s when artist Katherine Stubergh was asked to create a full-size replication of Da Vinci's famous painting. The piece wasn't realized until the 1950s when oil tycoon William Fleming backed the work. It was on display in a shopping center until 1965 before finding a longtime home at the Southern Baptist Radio and Television building until 1997. In 2004, the Christian Arts Commission in Fort Worth began working on building the artwork a permanent home, raising money to construct this fine, small addition to the Cultural District.

FORT WORTH MUSEUM OF SCIENCE
AND HISTORY $$
1600 Gendy St., Fort Worth
(817) 255-9300
www.fortworthmuseum.org
Replacing a humble, 50-year-old museum long outgrown, the new and grand Fort Worth Museum of Science and History was unveiled in late 2009. The utterly overhauled favorite measures 166,000 square feet in multiple levels of space; all that remains of the original version is the Omni Theater, where IMAX films have brought visitors in drove on a daily basis for years. The museum's dramatic new design, a contemporary complex of massive, colorful square shapes, comes from the Mexican architect Legorreta + Legorreta. Magnificent new spaces house the revered Museum School; Dino-Labs and DinoDig; Energy Blast!; an interactive gallery for younger visitors called Children's Museum; a cluster of five learning spaces for tweens, teens, and adults called Innovation Studios; a cafe called Stars; the Fort Worth History Gallery; the Cattle Raisers Museum; Noble Planetarium; and the museum store called Too! Perhaps most impressive are the main courtyard, shaded by a giant live oak with sitting areas, and the Urban Lantern, a 76-foot-high structure made of nearly 100 500-pound glass panels, that functions as the museum entrance.

FORT WORTH ZOO $$$
1989 Colonial Parkway, Fort Worth
(817) 759-7500
www.fortworthzoo.com

Texas's oldest zoo began in 1909 with a single lion, a pair of bear cubs and the assorted alligator, coyote, and peacock. Today, this zoo ranks among the nation's top 10, serving as home to more than 5,000 native and exotic beasts, birds, and critters. In a dozen exhibit areas, you find everything from penguins to primates, raptors to big cats, flamingos to meerkats, koalas to elephants, snakes to prize-winning Texas cattle. There's lots of food in various concession stands; just outside the zoo gates, find a miniature train ride taking kids and grown-ups throughout Trinity Park.

KIMBELL ART MUSEUM   FREE
3333 Camp Bowie Blvd., Fort Worth
(817) 332-8451
www.kimbellart.org
Widely known as a leading art museum in America, the Kimbell is also among the most richly endowed of all privately held museums. It evolved from the private collection of a wealthy local entrepreneur in the fields of agriculture, real estate, and petroleum named Kay Kimbell. He and wife Velma Kimbell established the Kimbell Art Foundation in the 1930s. Upon his death in 1964, the considerable art collection was passed to the foundation with instructions to give Fort Worth one of the finest art museums in the nation. The master architect Louis I. Kahn created the modern building, opened in 1972, and an addition planned for 2012 or 2013 will be designed by Renzo Piano to complement the original. In roughly 350 words, there are European masterpieces such as those by Fra Angelico, Caravaggio, Cézanne, Matisse, and others, along with important works from Egypt, Greece, Asia, and Africa. There is admission charged for special exhibitions, and blockbuster exhibits are not unusual. Make time to have lunch at the lovely Buffet Restaurant inside the museum, serving Friday dinner, too. (See Restaurants, page 51.)

LOG CABIN VILLAGE $
2100 Log Cabin Village Lane, off University Drive, Fort Worth
(817) 392-5881
www.logcabinvillage.org

Fort Worth's Cultural District

Between 2008 and 2010, the face of Fort Worth's Cultural District changed almost daily. If you've been away and returned and hadn't seen the massive renovations and reconstruction of the cluster of museums and surrounding environs, you wouldn't recognize it today.

The skyscape of construction cranes has come and gone, leaving behind—among a long list of shiny new things—an enormous new Science & History Museum to replace the modest, 50-year-old original. Nearby, uninspired buildings holding outdated stores and myriad offices have disappeared, with a boutique hotel and chic new bistros coming to replace them. Run-down warehouses just to the east of University Drive continue to vanish, with ultramodern complexes of restaurants, cocktail lounges, yoga studios, and fashionable townhomes taking over.

Despite the economy, development around the beloved quarter, a stone's throw west of downtown, has boomed, adding to Fort Worth's longtime cowboys-and-culture lure. Here's a look at the evolving Cultural District, with five of the more exciting developments detailed, moving from west to east.

- Along Montgomery Street, next to the National Cowgirl Museum and Hall of Fame, the Fort Worth Museum of Science and History reopened in November 2009. No longer the humble little sister keeping company with giants like the Kimbell, Amon Carter, and Modern Art museums, the utterly overhauled favorite measures 166,000 square feet in multiple levels of space; all that remains of the original version is the Omni Theater, where IMAX films have brought visitors in drove on a daily basis for years. The museum's dramatic new design, a contemporary complex of massive, colorful square shapes, comes from the Mexican architect Legorreta + Legorreta. Magnificent new spaces will house the revered Museum School, with high-tech classrooms and a courtyard, the latter graced by a sculpture called *Happy Family*, a creation from Fort Worth artist Barrett DeBusk; DinoLabs and DinoDig, where life-sized re-creations of dinosaurs found in North Texas, including the Texas State Dinosaur, the *Paluxysaurus jonesi*, feature actual fossils; Energy Blast!, with a 4-D theater technology that illustrates the physics of energy exploration and production in North Texas; an interactive gallery called the Children's Museum, where patrons from infants through eight years old enter through the mouth of a dragon; a cluster of five interactive learning spaces for tweens, teens, and adults called Innovation Studios; a lunch cafe called Stars; the Fort Worth History Gallery, telling Cowtown's story since the 1870s; the Cattle Raisers Museum, a 9,000-square-foot center detailing the history of cattle and ranching in Texas, Oklahoma, and New Mexico; Noble Planetarium, where you'll travel 13.7 billion light-years from home; and the museum store called Too! Perhaps most impressive are the main courtyard, shaded by a giant live oak with sitting areas, and the Urban Lantern, a 76-foot-high structure made of nearly 100 500-pound glass panels, which functions as the museum entrance.

- Museum Place, facing the Kimbell and Modern Art museums at the busy intersection of University, Camp Bowie, Bailey, and Seventh Street, covers 11 acres with angular structures crafted from shimmering glass and sleek metal and stone. Among the earliest tenants, Eddie V's Prime Seafood, already a big hit in Austin and instantly the busiest restaurant in town, owes much success to its cool vibe and nightly live music offerings. Domain, a posh home furnishings store, relocated here, and a boutique hotel will open in late 2010 or early 2011, along with Café San Miguel (tacos al pastor, lobster enchiladas, and quail in pumpkin mole are specialties) and Social House (catering to a young adult crowd with brews, fish and chips, and burgers), two hot Dallas restaurants looking to expand westward. Across the street, in front of a new post office, you'll see a piece of art created by nature: the 2000 tornado that ripped through Fort Worth wrestled a billboard off its base, leaving four giant steel poles bent almost to a 90-degree angle. Left as a piece of public sculpture, the poles point toward the inscription on the post office wall that reads, "Neither snow nor rain nor heat nor gloom of night stays these couriers from the swift completion of their appointed rounds."

- Steadily replacing an aged spread of industrial warehouses and auto repair yards, a 13-acre mixed-use development called West 7th lies immediately east of the museums. Apartments and offices will occupy more than half of the space, with a wealth of restaurants and retail comprising the balance. Foodies will choose between pasta at Patrizio, pizza from Fireside Pies, gelato at Paciugo, fish and chips at Delaney's, and steaks at Bailey's Prime Plus. There's a Movie Tavern, too, a place for watching first-run flicks while servers bring you pizza, burgers, and buckets of longnecks. On the east end, Foch Street offers a stretch of new businesses that replace a length of empty warehouses. Locals have quickly taken to the elegant cheesecakes and decorated cookies at J. Rae's Bakery, yoga classes at Bikram, wine tastings at Times Ten Cellars, fajitas at Mi Familia, and cutting-edge fashion for chic men and women at Dean-Kingston, a funky boutique with a turquoise 1964 Cadillac (the real thing) perched on the rooftop. A half-block west, facing Seventh Street, Backwoods offers every possible necessity and toy for outdoors-sporty types, from kayaks and hiking boots to ski goggles and fleecewear in a showplace of a store.

- The enormous white building that strikes a tricky balance between formidable and elegant, Montgomery Plaza occupies the 1928 structure formerly known as the largest Montgomery Ward in the southwest. The first of the new renovations along Seventh Street, this landmark contains million-dollar loft dwellings on its upper floors and assorted retailers and eateries on the ground floor. The big hits to date have been a runners' supply store called Luke's Locker; a contemporary art decor shop called Uncommon Angles; a steak joint and cocktail bar called Mac's; a feminine clothing boutique called Dolce Vita; a sports bar called BoomerJack's; and a Salvadoran/Tex-Mex restaurant from Dallas called Gloria's.

- Facing Montgomery Plaza, a 25-acre destination called So7—named for its location South of Seventh—consists largely of townhomes, condos, and a 150-room Residence Inn. So7 also delivers dining that promises to be a big hit, thanks to its prime location a few feet from the lush green space of Trinity Park. Opened in summer 2009, Love Shack brought the idea of stylish burger dining to Seventh Street, serving a delightfully messy ground prime steak burger topped with a quail egg, best washed down with a jalapeño-cucumber margarita. Keeping company with Love Shack, So7 Bistro will be an intimate French cafe, and Chuy's, an Austin favorite, will offer Tex-Mex food and drink in a sprawling space overlooking the park. An easy stroll away, the handsome Police and Firefighters Memorial, dedicated earlier this year, anchors the north end of Trinity Park. A serene place to end a tour of the Cultural District, the memorial brings to mind again Fort Worth's enduring sense of civic pride—and a reminder that new can be good, after all.

For all details, contact the Fort Worth Convention & Visitors Bureau, (800) 433-5747, or visit www.fortworth.com.

Situated a stone's throw from the zoo, this city-owned ode to yesteryear heritage brings the pioneer age to life. You'll see 19th-century Texas on display in authentic homes, with staffers dressed in period clothing to tell the story of a simpler, yet enormously challenging time. Among exhibits are a water-powered gristmill, one-room schoolhouse, blacksmith shop, herb garden, and several log home settings.

MODERN ART MUSEUM $$
3200 Darnell St., Fort Worth
(817) 738-9215
www.themodern.org
Known around the world by art lovers, this museum houses one of the greatest collections of modern and contemporary art in the country. More than 3,000 pieces in the permanent collection include those by Robert Motherwell, Pablo Picasso, Jackson Pollock, Gerhard Richter, Susan Rothenberg, Richard Serra, Andres Serrano, Cindy Sherman, Andy Warhol, and others from the post–World War II era. As important as its contents is the building, designed by Japanese architect Tadao Ando, who crafted it as five long, flat-roofed pavilions sitting beside a 1.5-acre pond. You can get lost in shopping at the Modern Shop, with its educational books and toys, posters, T-shirts, jewelry, and items for the garden and home. Fabulous food is offered at lunch and Sunday brunch at Café Modern. Museum admission is free on the first Sunday of every month and every Wednesday, and admission to the shop and cafe is always free. (See Restaurants, page 51.)

NATIONAL COWGIRL MUSEUM
AND HALL OF FAME $$
1720 Gendy St., Fort Worth
(817) 336-4475
www.cowgirl.net

The world's first museum honoring women of the American West offers an unusual look at our past. Originally established in the Panhandle town of Hereford, Texas, the museum moved to its gorgeous new home in 2002. A storehouse of more than 3,000 rare pictures and thousands of artifacts belonging to ranching women, trick riders, and other cowgirls, this museum inducts new honorees into its hall of fame each autumn. You can visit five gallery areas, two theaters, a research library, and a wonderful store.

WILL ROGERS COLISEUM VARIED
3401 West Lancaster Ave., Fort Worth
(817) 392-7469
www.fortworthgov.org
A much-photographed bronze of the nation's favorite humorist, riding atop his horse Soapsuds, stands before the 1936 coliseum bearing his name. Rogers was a good friend of Fort Worth philanthropist and newspaper publisher Amon G. Carter, and Carter felt this landmark honoring the Texas centennial should also honor the love for cowboy culture that Rogers shared with the world. Over the years, the 2,856-seat auditorium has played host to everyone from Jack Benny and the Vienna Boys Choir to the Rolling Stones. The adjacent coliseum hosts some 900,000 rodeo fans each year during the three-week Southwestern Exposition and Livestock Show, held in January and February. Adjacent buildings serve as an important equestrian center, bringing fans of the cutting horse, paint horse, and Arabian horse to town throughout the year.

THE ARTS

Occasionally, newcomers to Texas are just the tiniest bit surprised to find out how much folks here love music, theater, and all performing arts. Perhaps you expected to find that our passions run only to football and rodeo? While it's true that country music remains a favorite, the good people of Dallas and Fort Worth appreciate far more than the banjo and steel guitar. Once you examine all these options, you'll find that the level of artistic sophistication has been underrated. (Note: find museums in the Attractions chapter, page 106.)

The nation's largest urban arts district is the Dallas Arts District, where five venues have been designed by Pritzker Prize–winning architects: the Morton H. Meyerson Symphony Center by I. M. Pei, the Nasher Sculpture Center by Renzo Piano, the Margot and Bill Winspear Opera House and the Annette Strauss Artist Square by Sir Norman Foster, and the Dee and Charles Wyly Theatre by Rem Koolhaas. So not only are you treated to great art within, but you're blessed with seeing magnificent art on the outside, as well.

DALLAS

Choirs

TURTLE CREEK CHORALE
3630 Harry Hines Blvd. at Oak Lawn, Dallas
(214) 526-3214
www.turtlecreek.org
The 225-voice men's choir has had three decades of success, spending hundreds of hours in rehearsal annually and working at as many as 50 benefits each year. Frequently playing to audiences in Europe, the choir specializes in a mix of classical and popular music and calls the Morton H. Meyerson Symphony Center its Dallas home.

Dance Troupes

DALLAS BLACK DANCE THEATRE
2700 Flora St., Dallas
(214) 871-2376
www.dbdt.com
The oldest dance company in town performs contemporary modern ballet with 12 professional dancers in the troupe. Dancing to a mix of modern, jazz, ethnic, and spiritual music, the company often works with schoolchildren.

TEXAS BALLET THEATER
2100 Ross Ave., Dallas
(214) 369-5200
www.texasballettheater.org
The foremost professional classical dance company in North Texas, TBT is based in Fort Worth but performs in both Dallas and Fort Worth for audiences of 100,000 people annually. The dual programs each year play at Fort Worth's Bass Performance Hall, Dallas's Music Hall at Fair Park, and the historic Majestic Theatre in downtown Dallas, and has become the resident company for the new Margot and Bill Winspear Opera House at the Dallas Center for the Performing Arts. Traditional and modern performances typically fill the season, with *The Nutcracker* production a favorite during the winter holidays.

(The two cities have shared a ballet company since Dallas's ballet folded several years back. It performs in both cities. See listing under Fort Worth, below.)

Education

THE ART INSTITUTE OF DALLAS
8080 Park Lane, Suite 100, Dallas
(800) 275-4243
www.artinstitutes.edu/dallas

A Class Act

Don't look for cheerleaders at Booker T. Washington High School for the Performing and Visual Arts, founded in 1976. The school was the first structure to open within the Dallas Arts Distirct and remains the only school there. Occupying a 1922 high school, which was Dallas's first black school, Booker T. Washington became a technical-vocational school in 1955.

With desegregation, the Dallas Public Schools decided to make Booker T. Washington the magnet school for gifted artists. It grew to a place recognized throughout the nation for its exceptional programs and with famous graduates that have included Grammy winners such as R&B vocalist Erykah Badu, pianist and singer Norah Jones, jazz trumpeter Roy Hargrove, and members of the gospel group God's Property. Other renowned alumni are dancer Jay Franke, cellist John Koen, visual artists Chris Schumann and Chris Arnold, drummer Aaron Comess, and musician/singer Edie Brickell of the New Bohemians. A new building opened in the Arts District in 2008, and today, some 150 graduating seniors will pursue college degrees with between $1.5 million and $8.5 million in scholarship money. For details, visit www.dallasisd.org/btw.

You can work toward an associate's degree in the culinary arts, fashion design, video production, Web design, photography, graphic design, and restaurant management, as well as toward a bachelor of fine arts in many of those same disciplines at this growing school. Students can receive financial aid and obtain health care, too.

SOFIA ART ACADEMY
14856 Preston Rd., Dallas
(972) 980-1717
www.sofiaacademy.com
Specializing in European-style classic art, the school teaches children and adults the Old Masters technique. You can work on your portfolio, too. Private classes and workshops are available.

Film

DALLAS INTERNATIONAL FILM FESTIVAL
1155 Broom St., Dallas
(214) 720-0555
www.afidallas.com
Associated with American Film Institute, this eight-day festival is one of the largest in the Southwest, bringing an international competition of features, documentaries, and shorts to judges, media, and the public. Held in the spring, the festival offers viewings at NorthPark AMC and Magnolia Theater.

KD STUDIO
2600 Stemmons Freeway, Suite 117, AFI
(214) 638-0484
www.kdstudio.com
From a modeling agency grew this film production program, led by Andrew Stevens, producer of such films as *The Whole Nine Yards*. Students learn writing, project develoment, production, directing, lighting, editing, cinematography, sales, marketing, and distribution. There's an acting program as well, along with summer camps.

Music

DALLAS CHAMBER ORCHESTRA
(214) 321-1411
www.dallaschamberorchestra.org
A small orchestra frequently heard on National Public Radio's *Performance Today,* this group is led by Ronald Neal, formerly of the New York String Orchestra, and performs at the Meyerson and various university campuses and churches.

ℹ️ When you're wandering around downtown Fort Worth, take time to visit Bass Performance Hall, if only to see the pair of 48-foot-tall, cream-colored angels that frame the entrance to the extraordinary building. Since the hall's inception, people have been smitten by the heavenly duo, gigantic images of grace and perfection. The two were crafted over a three-year period by Hungarian artist Marton Varo, who calls them "the embodiment of human creative impulses, and humanity's guardians."

DALLAS OPERA
Campbell Centre I
8350 North Central Expressway, Dallas
(214) 443-1000
dallasopera.org
Chartered in 1957, the opera stages productions of the classics, from *Madame Butterfly* to *La Bohème*, as well as newer works, such as Heggie's *Moby-Dick*. New is the performance space, the Winspear Opera House in the Dallas Center for the Performing Arts complex downtown.

DALLAS SYMPHONY
2301 Flora St., Dallas
(214) 871-4000
www.dallassymphony.com
The Southwest's largest performing arts organization is led by conductor Jaap van Zweden, who has taken the symphony on a European tour and has launched several premieres with modern and classic composers' works. With a history dating from 1900, the DSO hosts a pops series, too, with artists such as Elvis Costello, Linda Ronstadt, and LeAnn Rimes. You'll hear the orchestra also with the Dallas Summer Musicals. The DSO is at home at the Meyerson.

Theater

DALLAS CHILDREN'S THEATER
5938 Skillman St., Dallas
(214) 740-0051
www.dct.org
A nationally ranked theater for youth productions, this company uses two venues, the Rosewood Center for Family Arts, found at 5938 Skillman St., and El Centro College Theater, 801 North Main St. Productions range from heavy, such as *The Night They Came For Me*, pertaining to the Holocaust, to sweet and traditional, such as the puppet show version of *The Tale of Peter Rabbit*.

ℹ️ *Time* magazine named the Dallas Children's Theater one of the top five theaters in the nation performing for children and their families in 2004. It was designed by legendary architect Frank Lloyd Wright, and it is the only freestanding theater built to his design that is still operating today.

DALLAS THEATER CENTER
3636 Turtle Creek Blvd., Dallas
(214) 526-8210
www.dallastheatercenter.org
Often offering productions at the Kalita Humphreys Theater, a Frank Lloyd Wright design, the company moved to its new home at the Dee and Charles Wyly Theater at the Dallas Center for Performing Arts recently. A 50-year-old theater group, DTC produces contemporary and classic works, as well as traditional holiday programs.

KITCHEN DOG THEATER
3120 McKinney Ave., Dallas
(214) 953-1055
www.kitchendogtheater.org
A theater guided by a social conscience, productions tend to focus on justice and morality. The name comes from Beckett's *Waiting for Godot*, in which the kitchen dog symbolizes the victim and participant in "our society's seemingly endless cycle of ignorance and injustice."

THEATRE THREE
2800 Routh St., Dallas
(214) 871-3300
www.theatre3dallas.com
Early in their careers, Pulitzer Prize–winning playwrights Beth Henley and Doug Wright performed at this modern, small theater. Making its home in the Quadrangle in Uptown, Theatre Three produces classics, musicals, and modern shows.

Close-up

Summer at the Museums

The long days of summer are an especially good time to take advantage of the area museums' extended hours and concerts. Free admission on some nights and free concerts in some cases make it even more appealing. Add fine cuisine on-site at most museums, and you have the makings for an evening out.

The offerings range from hands-on art classes to outdoor concerts under the stars.

A note about outdoor concerts in Texas: The museums are open, so you can duck inside if you get too hot. But if you choose an outdoor concert option elsewhere, check with the venue to see whether you can bring in drinks. If not, be sure to bring extra cash for drinks and stay hydrated—and not just with beer.

The Texas heat is serious business, especially if you're not acclimated. We've seen newcomers spend the bulk of a daylong concert in the first-aid tent, overcome by near heatstroke. And Texas summer nights are just about as hot as the days.

Admission prices listed here are subject to change, so check with the museum to be sure.

Fort Worth

- The stunning Modern Art Museum of Fort Worth has special evenings on First Fridays that include jazz concerts, special cocktails, and docent-led tours. Executive Chef Dena Peterson changes up the First Friday menu at Café Modern every month, using the freshest ingredients available at the time.

The concerts are free, and admission to galleries is $10.

More information: Modern Art Museum of Fort Worth, 3200 Darnell St.; (817) 738-9215, www.themodern.org. For reservations at Café Modern, (817) 840-2174.

- The Kimbell Art Museum in Fort Worth stays open late both Fridays and Saturdays. Admission is half-price on Saturdays, when there are special exhibitions and live music with dinner at The Buffet. Hours on Second Saturdays are 5:30 p.m. to 7:30 p.m. for gallery tours, cocktails, and music.

More information: The Kimbell Art Museum, 3333 Camp Bowie Blvd., Fort Worth, (817) 332-8451, www.kimbellart.org. Admission to the permanent collection is always free. Exhibitions run around $14 for adults.

Dallas

- The Nasher Sculpture Center has Saturday Nights in the City from June through September, with outdoor concerts in just about every genre.

The concerts generally end about 11 p.m., but gallery tours are available beforehand. And if you're hungry, Wolfgang Puck in the Garden serves its signature pizza or a three-course meal with entrees like cumin-roasted chicken breast with cilantro mint vinaigrette.

More information: The Nasher Sculpture Center, 2001 Flora St., (214) 242-5118, www.nashersculpturecenter.org. Admission to Saturday Nights in the City is $10 for adults. Bring a blanket to sit on. No outside furniture, food, or drink is permitted. For reservations at Wolfgang Puck in the Garden, call (214) 242-5144.

- The Dallas Museum of Art is a busy place all summer. The agenda includes Arts and Letters Live on Tuesday evenings; Thursday Night Live evenings with free classes and live jazz; and Late Nights each third Friday, when the museum is open until midnight.

More information: Dallas Museum of Art, 1717 North Harwood St., (214) 922-1200, www.dallasmuseumofart.org.

WATER TOWER THEATRE
15650 Addison Rd., Addison
(972) 450-6232
www.watertowertheatre.org
Home to this company is the 32,000-square-foot Addison Theatre Centre, where productions of dramatic, comedic, and musical works have plenty of impact, thanks to modern set design and technology. Favorite works have included *Indoor/Outdoor*, a story seen through the eyes of a house cat; and *Doubt, a Parable*, examining a nun's suspicion when a priest takes a special interest in a student.

FORT WORTH

Choirs

TEXAS BOYS' CHOIR
3901 South Hulen St., Fort Worth
(817) 924-1482
www.texasboyschoir.org
Founded in 1946 to give all boys of all economic and ethnic backgrounds a solid environment, this choir is legendary. Artistic training comes in an accredited academic institution where experienced teachers teach not only English, math, and science but also "self-discipline, self-confidence, decorum, patriotism, and leadership." Following the traditional European church choirs, boys train from a young age, working in music of the early Renaissance and Baroque periods. Performances also include popular American music and that of other countries and cultures. The prize-winning choir has appeared on national TV numerous times, has sung for the pope, presidents, and other heads of state. Over the years, it has traveled to Australia, Japan, England, Mexico, Latvia, and Germany. Students must audition and interview to be accepted.

TEXAS GIRLS' CHOIR
4449 Camp Bowie Blvd., Fort Worth
(817) 732-8161
www.texasgirlschoir.org
Founded in 1962, this is the nation's first chartered girls' choir. Each year, the choir tours the

U.S. and goes abroad, entertaining audiences by the hundreds. Auditions are held twice a year for girls between the ages of 8 and 12.

Dance Troupes

CONTEMPORARY DANCE
3901 South Hulen St., Fort Worth
(817) 922-0944
www.cdfw.org
Fort Worth's first professional modern dance company, this repertory troupe offers works by regionally and nationally recognized choreographers. Its goal is to bring dance programming to underserved communities with performances, teaching residencies, workshops, and master classes in schools, community centers, workplaces, shopping centers, museums, parks, festivals, and landmarks throughout North Texas.

TEXAS BALLET THEATER
6845 Green Oaks Rd., Fort Worth
(817) 763-0207
www.texasballettheater.org
The foremost professional classical dance company in North Texas, TBT is based in Fort Worth but performs in both Dallas and Fort Worth for audiences of 100,000 people annually. The dual programs each year play at Fort Worth's Bass Performance Hall, Dallas's Music Hall at Fair Park, and the historic Majestic Theatre in downtown Dallas, and has become the resident company for the new Margot and Bill Winspear Opera House at the Dallas Center for the Performing Arts. Traditional and modern performances typically fill the season, with *The Nutcracker* production a favorite during the winter holidays.

Film

LONE STAR INTERNATIONAL FILM FESTIVAL
2501 Forest Park Blvd., Fort Worth
(817) 924-6000
www.lsiff.com
A celebration of art and the cinema industry is staged for five days in November in Fort Worth. Big names attending the festival to date have included Martin Sheen, T-Bone Burnett, Robert

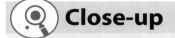 # Close-up

Arts Venues for the Ages

Both Dallas and Fort Worth have beautiful, world-class performing arts venues, where the lineups are as sophisticated or as casual as your heart desires. Here's a look at Bass Performance Hall in Fort Worth and the AT&T Center for the Performing Arts in Dallas.

AT&T Center for the Performing Arts

The AT&T Center for the Performing Arts is the new gem in Dallas's well-developed arts scene, having opened its four venues in 2009. An outdoor performing space, opera house, theater, and hall make up the sleek, contemporary complex, which sits on Sammons Park, 10 acres in the city's Arts District.

Annette Strauss Artist Square has a concrete, glass, and steel pavilion for festivals, family programs, and other events. The 26,500-square-foot performance lawn holding an audience of 5,000 slopes down to the main stage. Partly sunken walls around the edges help shield performances from the sound of nearby Wood Rodgers Freeway.

Winspear Opera House at the front of the park is home to the Dallas Opera and Texas Ballet Theater. The opera house's Margaret McDermott Performance Hall is inside the big, red-glass-sheathed drum that is one of the most striking works of architecture in the complex. It holds 2,200 to 2,300 in a space designed by a London architect and described in press materials as "a 21st-century interpretation of the classical horseshoe configuration." A 60-foot-high glass facade encloses the lobby, with a large section retractable to open the lobby, cafe, and a restaurant to Sammons Park.

Across the street from the opera house, Wyly Theatre will hold about 600 for performances of groups such as the Dallas Black Dance Theater, Anita N. Martinez Ballet Folklorico, and Dallas Theater Center. While typical theaters are built with support spaces around the sides of the stage, the Wyly's are above and below the auditorium, making it more flexible for different types of performances. The sharply vertical 12-level theater is designed to lift both seating and stage to accommodate different productions.

The City Performance Hall holds 750, and was designed for smaller arts organizations in Dallas.

Sammons Park is designed with trees, reflecting pools, and a series of gardens and walkways.

Opening season performances at the center included productions by the resident companies, as well as shows by Billy Crystal and others.

For more information: (214) 880-0202 or www.dallasperformingarts.org.

Rodriguez, Harry Dean Stanton, Bill Paxton, and Fred Durst, and as many as 50 screenings, including features, documentaries, and shorts have been presented in a single festival. Red carpets, premieres, and more Hollywood-style excitement grace the event, which plays out at AMC Palace Theatre, the Four Day Weekend Theatre, and the Scott Theatre, as well as the Norris Conference Center, Modern Art Museum, and Kimbell Art Museum.

Q CINEMA FESTIVAL
(817) 723-4358
web.me.com/qcinema
Fort Worth's gay and lesbian international film festival takes place at the Rose Marine Theater on North Main Street, near the Stockyards. Over four days in July, the festival presents international dramas, comedies, documentaries, animation, and short films to "provide a voice for gay, lesbian, bisexual, and transgendered persons."

Bass Performance Hall

Time spent here is time well spent, a respite from the world, no matter which of the performing arts stirs your soul.

The 48-foot angels sculpted of limestone on the grand facade take visitors by surprise—most aren't expecting to find one of the world's great halls in a place nicknamed Cowtown. The hall, which occupies an entire city block, holds 2,056 beneath its immense dome, in seats from orchestra level to the topmost in the upper gallery. Boxes line the U-shaped main hall, tiered like an opulent cake up to the dome. But it's not just a pretty face.

Bass Hall possesses some of the world's finest acoustics and sight lines. A pianist's softest notes are clear and true, a symphony's crashing passion surrounds you, a singer could be sitting right next to you.

The hall, built with private monies in 1998, is home to the Fort Worth Symphony Orchestra, Texas Ballet Theater, the Van Cliburn International Piano Competition and Cliburn concerts, and the Fort Worth Opera.

You can dress to the nines and have an elegant night out at the symphony—or wear jeans and take the kids to a musical. Local group Casa Mañana regularly stages performances of hits like *Grease* and *Little Shop of Horrors*.

The calendar here is wildly eclectic. One night redneck comedian Jeff Foxworthy might be onstage, followed by Russian Masters leaping and pirouetting the next. Both the hall and the adjacent McDavid Studio stay busy with Texas artists such as the Austin Lounge Lizards and Bruce Robison; big names such as Rufus Wainwright (think "Hallelujah" in *Shrek*) or Yo-Yo Ma; and oldies like the Doobie Brothers and Frankie Valli and the Four Seasons. On other nights, tributes to the likes of Abba or Elvis might be on tap.

You might see busloads of children trooping into the hall during the school year—educational programs bring kids in free from area school districts. Master classes also let high school students and their teachers work together with internationally known artists.

Bass Hall opened in 1998, the culmination of a downtown revitalization that attracted national attention. Muse-Maddox Center, which houses offices, and the Van Cliburn Recital Hall and McDavid Studio for more intimate performances and practice for the resident companies, opened in 2001. Dozens of area organizations and businesses use the hall for special events.

Tours are available, if you're interested in how those fabulous acoustics are achieved.

More information: (817) 212-4200 or www.basshall.com.

Music

FORT WORTH OPERA
1300 Gendy St., Fort Worth
(817) 731-0726
www.fwopera.org

Three ladies hatched a plan over coffee in 1946 to launch an opera company, and today their efforts remain a cornerstone in Fort Worth's fine arts. The oldest such company with continuous operation in Texas and one of the 14 oldest opera companies in the United States, the FWO employs more than 500 people for a three-performance season. Traditional works are staged, as well as world premieres, such as the 2007 production of *Frau Margot* by composer Thomas Pasatieri.

FORT WORTH SYMPHONY
330 East Fourth St., #200, Fort Worth
(817) 665-6500
www.fwsymphony.org

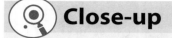

Close-up

Classical Magic

The year was 1958, and Russia had pulled ahead in the Cold War by launching *Sputnik*, the first manmade object flung into orbit around the Earth. Confident in its technological superiority, the Bear decided to prove its dominance in the arts as well with the First Tchaikovsky International Competition in Moscow.

But at the competition finale, the audience instead stood in a long, passionate ovation for a tall, lanky young man from the small East Texas town of Kilgore. Van Cliburn's performance of Tchaikovsky's Piano Concerto No. 1 and the Rachmaninoff Piano Concerto No. 3 shattered the Cold War barriers for a moment, uniting East and West in the joy of music-making.

Cliburn, now in his 70s, lives in Fort Worth today. He is retired from the international touring circuit that made him something of an ambassador for decades after that glorious moment in Moscow. But plenty of music is being made here in his name. The Van Cliburn International Piano Competition, repeated every four years since 1962, draws the best young pianists in the world to Bass Performance Hall.

A spell falls over Fort Worth during the Cliburn. The audiences in the Hall and half the city seem wrapped up in who will advance, which pieces they will play. Favorites develop, and fans who can't make it to performances sit riveted to the live Webcasts—the entire competition has been streamed live the last two times, with audience votes tallied.

The competition is several years in the making. First, a panel of judges travels around the world to select competitors. Finally, in Fort Worth, they walk onstage in evening gowns and tuxedoes, first alone with the grand piano; then, together with a quartet; and, finally with a symphony orchestra. The strain of the competition is nerve-wracking, and the stakes can be high. For many of these young pianists, this is a once-in-a-lifetime opportunity.

The winners get cash prizes, concert management services, and international engagements. Despite tremendous talent and drive, some of them are barely scraping by teaching piano in Russia or elsewhere.

At the last Cliburn in 2009, 29 pianists competed in the preliminary round; 12 remained for the semifinals; and 6 competed in the finals. The young pianists stay with Fort Worth families, practicing on their pianos for countless hours, sometimes bandaging their fingers against the continual playing.

Growing into one of the more successful companies of its size in the nation, the FWSO presents to an audience of 250,000 each year. Led by musical director Miguel Harth-Bedoya, the symphony offers exciting productions of classical and pop music each year at the Bass Performance Hall. The company's wildly popular summer program is Concerts in the Garden, a five-week outdoor party with a nightly show, changing productions, and a fireworks finale each night at about 10 p.m. An outreach program reaches some 60,000 people each season through free or low-cost performances, too.

VAN CLIBURN PIANO COMPETITION
2525 Ridgmar Blvd., Fort Worth
(817) 738-6536
www.cliburn.org

Held every four years in late May and early June, this world-renowned piano event bears the name of the famous Fort Worth artist who helped warm the hearts of many international foes during the Cold War. More than 100 applicants perform for juries around the world to claim a spot in the international competition. Contestants are auditioned in China, Germany, Switzerland, Russia, New York, and Fort Worth, and about 30 are

These are brilliant pianists—superlative technique goes without saying. In other words, you're not waiting to hear a missed note because there usually aren't any. Instead, the differences come in interpretation and style, and in rapport with the audience.

Some amazing moments take place in the Hall during the competition. Richard Rodzinski, who was president and executive director of the Van Cliburn Foundation for 20 years (the foundation organizes and puts on the competition), talks about one in particular. Competitor Stanislav Ioudenitch, who shared the gold medal with another Russian pianist, Olga Kern, in 2001, was playing with a string quartet. The intensity of the music just stopped everyone in their tracks. Rodzinski says the foundation staff, which was working downstairs, began to slowly drift upstairs to listen. The audience was spellbound, struck silent and almost unable to applaud after the piece ended. Such moments in music join performer and audience in a powerful experience that can't be duplicated. No background in classical music is necessary to grasp it, probably the reason why Fort Worth fills the hall as the competition nears its final round.

For the few weeks of the Cliburn, the pianists become Fort Worth's own celebrities, their stories common knowledge. Ioudenitch's first Cliburn was particularly heartbreaking—the young pianist was an audience favorite, and scalded his hand making a pot of tea before a round, ending his chances for that year.

Pianists who have been eliminated from competition stay in the area and play recitals, sometimes at area schools and other venues. The foundation has an educational component that lets schools "adopt" a pianist, hear a mini-recital, and follow him or her through the competition.

In non-competition years, the Musical Awakenings program brings pianists into schools, includes lessons for some students, and provides teachers with study guides.

The foundation also hosts its International Competition for Outstanding Amateur Pianists every two years at Texas Christian University, using a YouTube contest to help select competitors. Cliburn winners return to Bass Hall and other Fort Worth venues for recitals, and the foundation maintains a strong concert series, bringing in world-class classical musicians such as cellist Yo-Yo Ma and many others.

For more information about the Cliburn Competition and associated events, call (817) 738-6536 or go to www.cliburn.org.

invited to the Fort Worth event. Classical music lovers in the city can buy tickets to attend performances. The next competition will be in 2013.

Theater

ARTES DE LA ROSA
Rose Marine Theater
1440 North Main St., Fort Worth
(817) 624-8333
www.rosemarinetheater.com
The theater company Artes de la Rosa promotes and preserves the Latino community with pro-

ductions that incorporate theater and film presentations. The 1920s-era theater opened as a movie house and has been restored, earning a listing on the National Register of Historic Places.

CIRCLE THEATRE
230 West Fourth St., Fort Worth
(817) 877-3040
www.circletheatre.com
Found in Sundance Square, Circle offers contemporary plays in a space seating about 125 people. There's a strong cultural diversity to the pro-

ductions, which include comedies and dramas presented year-round. Shows often come from Texas playwrights.

i Close to DFW Airport in the Irving district called Las Colinas, find one of the most sensational sculptures anywhere in Texas. *The Mustangs of Las Colinas* is an exquisite, realistic bronze sculpture of nine wild mustangs, whose ancestors brought Spanish explorers through these parts centuries ago. The horses—created by Nairobi-born sculpture Robert Glen, who is noted for his African wildlife art—are seen galloping across a granite-based stream in Williams Square Plaza, itself surrounded by shining granite buildings. Sculpted at one and a half times actual life size, the mustangs make up the largest equestrian sculpture in the world. See them at 5205 North O'Connor Rd. in Irving.

HIP POCKET THEATER
1950 Silver Creek Rd., Fort Worth
(817) 246-9775
www.hippocket.org
Fort Worth's only outdoor theater has launched more than 200 productions, including 150 world premieres, in 30-plus years. Shows may incorporate dance, music, puppetry, projections, and mime; you'll never be bored at this adventurous theater. The season generally lasts from June through October. Music, food, beer, and wine are offered in the theater's Backyard prior to and following each performance.

JUBILEE THEATRE
506 Main St., Fort Worth
(817) 338-4204
www.jubileetheatre.org
A renowned African-American theater company, the Jubilee has expanded beyond its production of plays and musicals to offer a music series, a reading series, and an educational outreach program. Immensely popular productions are staged in a cozy, 100-seat space in downtown Fort Worth, featuring the work of established and up-and-coming creators.

STAGE WEST
821 West Vickery Blvd., Fort Worth
(817) 784-9378
stagewest.org
For about three decades, this theater company has presented everything from classic American and world drama to Shakespeare and Shaw, contemporary Broadway plays and musicals, and new works by new playwrights. Each season features between six and eight productions.

THEATRE ARLINGTON
305 West Main St., Arlington
(817) 275-7661
www.theatrearlington.org
Since 1973, this theater company has offered stage productions for mainstream and youth audiences. Nine shows usually fill a season, offering musicals, comedies, dramas, and kid programs. Classes are offered for ages four to adult, too.

PARKS AND RECREATION

Because you can count on one hand the number of times you need to put on a heavy coat each year in the Dallas–Fort Worth area, you can also count on being able to play outside much of the time. Sure, we'll have the wildly weird occasional ice storm or snow-dusting every few Januarys, but the great outdoors is primarily a place to enjoy most of the year. Even if the mercury soars to 100 degrees in summer, the sunshine still invites you to get out into the fresh air.

Although Dallas and Fort Worth sit at the foot of the plains, you just need to look beyond skyscrapers and shopping centers to discover the wealth of natural wonders for you to treasure. The vast supply of parks, lakes, and preserves gives you and your family endless opportunities to stretch your legs, play games, and work on your fitness regime.

As our society tries to embrace again the importance of activity as it pertains to health, you'll find that parks in Dallas, Fort Worth, and the surrounding suburbs offer more hiking, walking, biking, jogging, and skating paths than ever. And most cities' parks departments provide a calendar of scheduled activities, too, including league play for softball, soccer, hockey, and basketball, often for all ages and skill levels.

The abundance of golf courses and tennis courts in the Dallas–Fort Worth area is remarkable as well. If you like the water, you'll find lakes with myriad boat rentals, including some geared to windsurfing and sailing. If you're new to town and looking for people who share your passion for cycling, scuba, or running, you'll find shops that can put you in touch with local groups.

DALLAS AREA

City Parks

DALLAS DEPARTMENT OF PARKS AND RECREATION
1500 Marilla St., Room 6F North, Dallas
(214) 670-4100
www.dallasparks.org
Dallas's parks department cares for more than 21,000 acres, with 17 lakes, more than 17,000 acres of greenbelt, and more than 61 miles of bike and running trails at 24 spaces around town. Dallas has ramped up offerings for residents interested in fitness. Trails for walking, running, biking, and skating have improved in recent years; inquire with the parks departments about the free Dallas Trails Map and the $6.50 street bicycle map. Or you can download color maps from the Web site above.

If you want to help beautify your city, join in the Morning After Program that cleans up after a weekend of picnics, sports, and events in the parks.

Among parks to note are the following.

ARBOR HILLS NATURE PRESERVE
6701 West Parker Rd., Plano
(972) 941-7250
http://plano.gov/departments/parksand recreation/parks/pages/arbor_hills.aspx
A 200-acre park in Plano offers walking, jogging, and biking trails, nature trails, an off-road cycling trail, and a pavilion you can reserve. A wildlife habitat certified by the National Wildlife Federation, this park includes three eco-regions—Blackland Prairie, Riparian Forest, and Upland Forest, which may surprise some newcomers who think there's just bare prairie in North Texas.

REVERCHON PARK
3505 Maple Ave., Dallas
(214) 670-1491
The 46-acre Uptown/Oak Lawn area park offers a baseball field, basketball and tennis courts, playgrounds, and hiking trails, including access to the hugely popular, newish Katy Trail, which courses through North Dallas on an old railroad bed. Reverchon's 40-odd programs include volleyball leagues, yoga classes, health screenings, tutoring, and after-school activities.

SAMUELL-GRAND PARK
6200 East Grand, Dallas
(214) 670-1374
Enter this 78-acre East Dallas jewel through a grand old entrance to play at one of 20 fenced tennis courts, served by a pro shop. Plenty of walking, running, and biking trails crisscross the rolling hills, and you'll find golf nearby at Tenison Park. There's an amphitheater, too, hosting the summertime Dallas Shakespeare Festival.

WHITE ROCK LAKE
8300 East Lawther Dr., Dallas
(214) 670-8740
Six miles east of downtown, this natural haven brings the outdoors lovers to bike, cycle, and skate pretty much year-round. Nature fans arrive in droves on weekends, so be prepared for big crowds around the 1,015-acre lake, which happens to be a birding/wetlands site designated by the Audubon Society. Don't be surprised if you come across some of the wildlife in quiet hours, as White Rock is home to squirrels, rabbits, skunks, raccoons, possums, bobcats, red foxes, minks, and more.

While motorized boats are banned, there are plenty of sailing opportunities from the Corinthian Sailing Club and White Rock Boat Club. If Fido needs to come out and play, bring him to White Rock's Mockingbird Point, a one-acre dog park on the northwestern shore, where he can go off-leash (see Dog Park, below).

Proof that Dallas has a quirky side is found in a special, unofficial attraction at White Rock. That's the Free Advice Guys, two men who show up in nice weather on the lake's western shore, near Jackson Point, to dispense free advice on whatever problems you want to share.

Families gather at six playgrounds, including Tee Pee Hill (see Kidstuff, page 160). For picnics, check out shady areas with stone park tables, but be warned that kids come with skateboards to take over Flag Pole Hill, which has a great lake view. For a peaceful interlude, visit the Arboretum (see Attractions, page 113).

There's easy arrival with a DART White Rock Lake station at Northwest Highway and West Lawther Drive.

Dog Park
WHITE ROCK DOG PARK
At White Rock Lake
8300 East Lawther Dr., Dallas
(214) 670-8740
www.whiterockdogpark.com
Find three different sections for your dog's size, including a swimming area for the water babies. Rules are posted and must be followed; they're enforced and punishable by fines. Most important, if your dog is aggressive, leave him or her at home. Park opens at 5 a.m. but is closed for maintenance on the second and fourth Mondays of each month.

Lakes
LAKE LEWISVILLE
Elm Fork of the Trinity River, near Lewisville
www.cityoflewisville.com
This 23,280-acre lake with 233 miles of shoreline offers 9,000 acres of parkland, too. People love it for its fishing, waterskiing, swimming beaches, and good picnic and camping areas. There are four marinas and 16 boat ramps, so be prepared for boat noise.

LAKE RAY HUBBARD
Interstate 30, Rockwall
www.tpwd.state.tx.us/fishboat/fish/
recreational/lakes/ray_hubbard/
A 22,745-acre lake formed by the damming of the Trinity River northeast of Dallas, this massive

lake appeals primarily to anglers in search of the big bass catches. You can learn to sail here, too, through outfits like Sail with Scott (www.sailwith scott.com) or you can charter the company's 40-foot catamaran for a party. Take a staycation at the Hilton Bella Harbor with its lakeside pool or shop at the 120,000-square-foot Bass Pro Shops Outdoor World on the lakeshore.

WHITE ROCK LAKE
(See entry under City Parks, above)

Recreation
Baseball
DALLAS PARKS AND RECREATION
(214) 670-8740
www.dallasparks.org/Facilities/baseball.aspx
The city parks department maintains 30 diamonds, some with bleachers and lights, with Samuell-Grand the most popular. Kiest Park has a softball complex with national tournaments played here. Call to reserve a field for a family reunion or to find out about league play.

PREMIER BASEBALL ACADEMY OF DALLAS
2621 Summit Ave., Plano
(972) 398-3676
www.premierbaseballacademy.com
More than 18,000 square feet of air-conditioned baseball space includes large batting cages and a party room.

Basketball
DALLAS METROPOLITAN YMCA
(214) 329-1821
ymcadallas.com
Throughout Dallas, the YMCA branch locations offer basketball league play. Call to find out more about schedules and fees.

DALLAS PARKS AND RECREATION
www.dallasparks.org/Facilities/basketball
.aspx
Throughout the city, most parks have basketball courts. These are not reserved and are first-come, first-served. Visit the Web site to find a map of parks.

Bowling
DALLAS BOWLING ASSOCIATION
(972) 644-7746
http://dallasbowling-usbc.org
The motto of this league is "friendship is the best part of bowling," so you know this is a good way to find new pals. A list of bowling facilities is online, and there's information about tournaments, too.

Cycling
Some DART rail trains and buses are equipped with external bike racks, or you can put your bike in the designated handicap area, if it's not in use. Tips and instructions for loading and unloading your bikes on the bike ramp can be found at www.dart.org/riding/bike.asp#rail.

DALLAS BIKE WORKS
6780 Abrams Rd., Dallas
(214) 341-8921
www.dallasbikeworks.com
Here's a shop to outfit you for whatever biking adventures you're planning.

DEBO CYCLE SPORTS
4400 Matlock Rd., Arlington
(817) 557-3326
www.debocyclesports.com
This 30-year-old business will sell you bikes and gear or tune up your old bike.

Dance, Music, Arts
DALLAS DEPARTMENT OF PARKS AND RECREATION
1500 Marilla St., Room 6F North, Dallas
(214) 670-4100
www.dallasparks.org
The parks department offers Crafty Adults and Seniors, a six-week ceramics session. There are also preschool arts and crafts program for kids ages three to six.

Fitness Centers
BAYLOR TOM LANDRY FITNESS CENTER
411 North Washington St., Dallas
(214) 820-7872
www.baylortomlandryfitnesscenter.com

Numerous sophisticated, medically directed programs will steer you toward getting started and living with healthy fitness and eating practices. The 12-week weight management program provides tools for maintaining a healthy weight through fitness training sessions, dietitian meetings, and health screenings, with Pilates classes thrown in. Special aquatic programs are geared to a variety of members, and Moms on the Move teaches safe exercise for pregnant women.

COOPER AEROBICS CENTER
12200 Preston Rd., Dallas
(972) 560-COOP (2667), (866) 906-COOP
(2667)
www.cooperaerobics.com
Dr. Kenneth Cooper coined the word *aerobics,* and at his Dallas fitness facility, he employs an aerobic point system that keeps your exercise program in line. At this Preston Road location, find an indoor track, outdoor trails, fitness studios, two pools, game court, steam room and whirlpool, and a highly qualified personal training staff. There's an on-site spa and cafe, too. At the Craig Ranch in McKinney, a 10,000-square-foot training area, you'll find an Olympic-size pool, indoor and outdoor tracks, exercise studios, a full-sized basketball court, tennis, and sand volleyball, with spa and cafe. You can sign up for workshops, lectures, and nutritional coaching, as well.

DALLAS METROPOLITAN YMCA
(214) 329-1821
ymcadallas.com
At 23 branches in seven counties you will find community centers with workout rooms, swimming pools, aerobics and weight-training classes, sports leagues, personal training, and more.

THE TEXAS CLUB FITNESS
800 Main St., 15th floor, Dallas
(214) 761-6300
www.thetexasclubfitness.com
A downtown fitness club, this one pampers with free parking, towel service, dozens of fitness classes, racquetball courts, and a Circuit Express Studio, the latter for fast, effective workouts.

Golf
COWBOYS GOLF COURSE
1600 Fairway Dr., Grapevine
(817) 481-7277
www.cowboysgolfclub.com
This jewel is believed to be the world's first NFL-themed golf club. A sports-fan favorite noted for stone markers that proclaim various Dallas Cowboy achievements, it covers 159 acres. It's an 18-hole course with private lessons and plenty of pretty scenery.

FOUR SEASONS HOTEL AND RESORT
4150 North MacArthur Blvd., Irving
(972) 717-0700, (800) 819-5053
www.fourseasons.com/dallas
Among the finest of all Dallas-area lodgings, the Four Seasons is home to the prestigious Byron Nelson Classic, a favorite stop on the PGA tour. It's also one of the most posh destinations for golf in North America. The TPC Four Seasons is an 18-hole, par-70 course that recently underwent a major redesign in 2009 directed by championship player D. A. Weibring. The resort's other course is Cottonwood Valley, an 18-hole, par-71 course with recently rebuilt greens, tee boxes, and bunkers that follow the rolling hills of Las Colinas. The signature hole is shaped like Texas and has a bunker in the shape of Oklahoma and a lake resembling the Gulf of Mexico. The Four Seasons also has a driving range, sand bunker practice area, putting and chipping greens, private lessons, group clinics, shoe and club rentals, and fabulous locker rooms in the resort's spa.

HACKBERRY CREEK
1901 West Royal Lane, Irving
(972) 869-2631
www.clubcorp.com
A prestigious 7,013-yard-long, 18-hole course co-designed by the late local legend Byron Nelson, this park also has junior clinics, as well as lighted tennis courts and a fitness facility.

STEVENS PARK
1005 North Montclair Ave., Dallas
(214) 670-7506
www.stevensparkgolf.com

Open since 1922, this municipal course in a hilly, historic section of Oak Cliff is among the favorite of all Dallas golf courses. It's an 18-hole, par-71 championship course with a length of 6,005 yards. Reservations are a must. There's a deli with happy hour, too.

TENISON PARK
3501 Samuell Blvd., Dallas
(214) 670-1402
www.tenisonpark.com

A gorgeous spread in East Dallas, this park has two courses, Tenison Glen and Tenison Highlands, with a driving range and PGA and LPGA golf pros. The Golf Academy of Dallas is home here, with 41 practice stations. There's a grill and a pavilion area, too.

TOUR 18
8718 Amen Corner, Flower Mound
(817) 430-2000
www.tour18-dallas.com

The great courses from around the country—Pebble Beach, Augusta, and so forth—are simulated here. No plane ticket required, but reservations are a must.

Hockey
LEAGUE PLAY
www.hockeydallas.com

Dallas-area leagues are covered at www.hockey dallas.com. Some are faith-based, collegiate-level, club or team organizations. The Dallas Junior Hockey Association (www.djha.com) is the state's largest youth hockey association, with private lessons available.

Running
DALLAS RUNNING CLUB
(214) 432-6619
www.dallasrunningclub.com

The largest running club in DFW organizes races and runs, along with social events. You can also volunteer to work at running events; all skill levels are welcome.

LUKE'S LOCKER
3607 Oak Lawn, Dallas, (214) 528-1290
5717 Legacy Rd., Plano, (972) 398-8660
2600 West Seventh St., Montgomery Plaza, Fort Worth, (817) 877-1448
5505 Colleyville Blvd., Colleyville, (817) 849-1562
www.lukeslocker.com

Want to learn proper running technique? Luke's teaches great workshops for three levels—casual walkers, advanced walkers, and those runners who want to boost their 5k and 10k running skills. Dedication and good footwear are required.

Scuba
THE SCUBA SOURCE
(214) 213-1408
www.thescubasource.com

This program offers flexible instruction with optional fast-track, works around your schedule, and will use the PADI modular program for your home-study portion. Learn diving in a heated pool, with private sessions available. Open-water certification takes place at Athens Scuba Park, 70 miles from Dallas, over two days.

Skating
ICE TRAINING CENTER
522 Centennial Blvd., Richardson
(972) 680-7825
www.icetrainingcenter.com

Men and women of all ages are invited to join a hockey league here, and you can join a workshop. Just want to skate? Practice sessions are available. Skate rentals, party areas, arcade games, and dining available, too.

Soccer
DALLAS TEXANS SOCCER CLUB
2013 Wing Point Lane, Plano
(972) 738-9988
www.dallastexans.com

A youth soccer group takes kids to championship titles. This was the first youth group in the nation to win the Super Group U-19 Championship and to Gothia Cup and Dana Cup in the same year. Kids wanting to find college scholarships can get help here. There are soccer camps, too.

NORTH TEXAS PREMIER SOCCER ASSOCIATION
903 North Bowser, Richardson
(972) 238-9668
www.ntpsa.org
Men play in 20 divisions and four age groups, broken into skill levels. Metropolitan tournaments take place across Dallas.

Softball
DALLAS SOFTBALL MANAGERS ASSOCIATION
(214) 670-8898
www.dsma.com
Dallas Parks and Recreation organizes adult softball (men, coed, and senior) leagues through most of the year, playing at the Samuell-Grand, Fair Oaks, Churchill, and Kiest Park complexes. Levels of competition (from fun to rather serious) will vary.

Swimming
DALLAS AQUATIC MASTERS
(214) 219-2300
www.damswim.com
Olympic triple gold medalist Jim Montgomery began this swim school in 1981, teaching students 18 and older, from beginners to serious swimmers, in lessons lasting about one hour. Group and private lessons offered. Prerequisite: students should be able to swim one pool length in freestyle stroke.

DALLAS PARKS AND RECREATION
(214) 670-8400
www.dallasparks.org/facilities/swimming
.aspx
Dallas city parks offer 21 pools total; check the Web site for locations and hours. Among the more popular ones are Kidd Springs in southwest Dallas for a pretty setting with a softball field; Fretz, on the Dallas-Richardson border; and Lake Highlands North, with a great baby pool.

DOLFIN SWIM SCHOOL
(214) 361-4542
www.dolfinswimschool.com

Red Cross–certified instructors teach kids to swim, starting at three months, making swimming fun with toys and games. The Dallas Dolfin swim team includes kids ages 5 to 17 and teaches competitive swimming technique. Locations include the Midway-Walnut Hill Lane area; Preston-Walnut Hill; Meadow Road at Hillcrest; Northwest Highway and Marsh; Lemmon and North Tollway; LBJ Freeway at Hillcrest; Walnut Hill at Inwood Road.

FRISCO ISD NATATORIUM
7411 First St., Frisco
(469) 633-6160
www.friscoisd.org/natatorium
An indoor pool for swimming and diving lessons for all ages and skill levels, this is also a popular site for swim meets. Family swim times are offered, too.

JACK CARTER POOL
2800 Maumelle, Plano
(972) 208-8081
An outdoor, 50-meter pool with waterslide, diving board, wading pool, water playground, and adjacent playground. Check www.planoparks.org for all pool information.

SOUTHERN METHODIST UNIVERSITY BARR POOL
SMU Perkins Natatorium, Dallas
(214) 768-2200
smumustangs.cstv.com/facilities/pool-hours
.html
Nice outdoor and indoor pools are open to the public for reasonable fees. Swimming lessons available.

Tennis
DALLAS PARKS AND RECREATION
tennisindallas.net
Dallas parks offers full-service tennis centers with lessons, refreshments, and a pro shop with retail and repair services. Courts can be reserved for games and tournaments and league play and clinics are available. Courts include:
Samuell-Grand, 6200 East Grand, (214) 670-1374
Fretz, 14700 Hillcrest Rd., (214) 670-6622

Fair Oaks, 7501 Merriman Parkway., (214) 670-1495
L.B. Houston, 11223 Luna Rd., (214) 670-6367
Kiest, 2324 West Kiest Blvd., (214) 670-7618

HIGH POINT PARK TENNIS CENTER
421 West Spring Creek Parkway, Plano
(972) 941-7170, ext. 5
www.highpointtennis.com

Lessons are offered and leagues play on 21 lighted outdoor tennis courts with a practice wall, playground, and fully stocked pro shop with restrooms and dressing facilities. There's a junior tennis camp, too.

Volleyball
VOLLEYBALL INSTITUTE OF PLANO
1909 Tenth St., Suite 400, Plano
(469) 229-0700
www.volleyballplano.com

Lessons and camps are available, with low coach-to-player ratio. Several courts are available.

FORT WORTH AREA

City Parks

The Parks and Community Services Department oversees and keeps up more than 200 parks and public spaces citywide. Some 25 miles of paved hike-and-bike trails run beside the Trinity River and some of its tributaries; its southwestern end is in Pecan Valley Park near Memorial Oak just north of the Benbrook Lake Dam. Check out this section, with a beautiful canopy of trees covering the trail. You can connect from this trail to the river trail that goes northeast to the downtown area and beyond, or to the park roads, US 377, and state and county roads around Benbrook Lake and in southwest Tarrant County. Special parks of note follow here.

BEAR CREEK PARK
400 Bear Creek Parkway, Keller
(817) 743-4050
www.cityofkeller.com

A 44-acre space built around Big Bear Creek, this play space gives you a pond, two playgrounds, hike-and-bike trails, sandbox, picnic tables and grills, sand volleyball courts, basketball court, inline hockey rink, soccer fields, baseball fields, fire pit, drinking fountains, gazebos, pavilions, and a wild-scape garden with waterfall. Festivals and events are frequently staged at the park.

BOYS RANCH, BEDFORD
2801 Forest Ridge, Bedford
(817) 952-2323
www.ci.bedford.tx.us

Within a 24,000-square-foot center, you'll find a full-court gymnasium, fitness room, meeting room, and classroom. A busy calendar offers a monthly schedule of Jazzercise, arts and crafts, basketball, yoga, and tai chi. There's a good fitness room with contemporary equipment offered to residents 16 and older.

Around the center, a number of fields host soccer, baseball, softball, and volleyball league play. There's also an inline hockey rink and a huge swimming pool with an aquatics program in summer.

EAGLE MOUNTAIN LAKE
On the West Fork Trinity River, Fort Worth

At Fort Worth's northeast corner, the 8,738-acre lake brings crowds for waterskiing, fishing, and swimming. Marinas are found along the 200 miles of shoreline, and there are hiking-and-biking trails on the east side at Eagle Mountain Park.

FORT WOOF DOG PARK
Gateway Park, north of I-30 between Beach Street and Oakland Boulevard
www.fortwoof.org

Fort Worth's first fenced off-leash dog park sits on the east side of the city. Two large fenced areas for dogs to roam include one for dogs 40 pounds and more and a separate area for dogs weighing less than 40 pounds. People sit at picnic areas (but no food is allowed in the park) or at park benches while pups play. There are water stations for two- and four-legged visitors, as well as numerous poop-disposal locations supplied with plastic bags. Rules are strictly enforced; check the Web site for the list, which includes keeping dogs on-leash until they're inside the entry and making sure dogs wear current vaccination and city tags.

(Q) Close-up

Lakes

Ask a native of Dallas–Fort Worth where they spend quick weekends away, and more often than not you'll hear "the lake." If you're an outdoors type thinking of relocating—or just a sweating visitor in the summer—you'll want to see whether any of the area lakes offer the kinds of activities you enjoy. Lake Grapevine, Joe Pool Lake, and Lake Ray Hubbard are all Texas-sized favorites (we're talking 22,000 acres of surface area in the case of Ray Hubbard) in or near cities. It's not at all necessary to own a lake house, a boat, or really any gear other than a swimsuit to take a locals-style break from the heat. All three have equipment rental from kayaks to sailboats and some have cruises, including Lake Grapevine's unconventional Duck Ride. (Note: all lake sizes are as of 2009. Levels can vary depending on rainfall and other conditions.)

Here's a rundown:

Lake Grapevine

This 8,000-acre lake is minutes from downtown Grapevine, which is about 22 miles from both Dallas and Fort Worth. The two marinas are Scott's Landing and Silver Lake Marina, and rentals are available to suit every need: party barges, personal watercraft, ski boats, pontoon boats, and sailboat charters. Or try something completely different with a Duck Ride—an amphibious World War II military vehicle takes you to the lake and plunges in.

The lake has 146 miles of shoreline and nine miles of wilderness trails, many paved for biking or easy stroller-pushing. To get a quick look, take the dam road, Fairway Drive, off Northwest Highway in Grapevine for an overview of the Grapevine side of the lake.

Rentals: Just For Fun Watercraft Rental (www.jff.net; 817-310-3000) at Scott's Landing Marina (www.scottslandingmarina.com; 817-481-4549) has a houseboat named *Lone Star Lady*, Waverunners, and everything in between including ski boats, pontoon boats, and party barges. Prices run from $55/hour for pontoon boats (2-hour minimum) to $650/hour for the *Lone Star Lady* (3-hour minimum). The prices include safety equipment and unlimited fuel, and in the case of ski boats, waterskis, safety belt, and pull rope.

Duck rides: The DUCK is an amphibious vehicle built for World War II. Grapevine's DUCKS, Quack 1 and Quack 2, were manufactured in 1945, just as the war ended, so they never saw action. But they're getting plenty now. The DUCKS depart from Grapevine Mills mall and Gaylord Texan Resort on Lake Grapevine, or a shuttle will pick you up at the front of Great Wolf Lodge in Grapevine. Prices: $19.94 for adults, $15 for children. Visit www.duckriders.com or call 817-421-DUCK.

Hiking, biking, swimming: The trails wind past secluded areas where you might spot a cardinal, shoreline where herons have been known to hang out, and parks for picnics or people-watching. Besides the paved parts, single-track trails are marked for mountain bikers or hikers. Several city-maintained parks—Lakeview, Oak Grove, and Katie's Woods—offer picnicking, and there is a swimming beach along the shore. Check out www.grapevinetexasusa.com or call 888-329-8993.

FORT WORTH NATURE CENTER & REFUGE
Confederate Park Road at
Jacksboro Highway
(817) 392-7410
www.fwnaturecenter.org
Barely inside the city limits, the FWNC&R surprises

with its wilderness qualities. You'll discover forest, prairie, and wetlands here on 3,600 acres, with a wealth of native flora and fauna and unlimited opportunities to revel in the countryside. Wander on more than 20 miles of hiking trails, where you'll see dozens of bird species, buffalo, and the

Camping: The Vineyards Campground on Lake Grapevine (www.vineyardscampground.com; 888-329-8993) has snug cabins outfitted with linens, kitchen utensils, cable television, and Wi-Fi. Campground amenities also include RV and tent sites and a group pavilion, all with lake access.

Fishing: Bass (largemouth, spotted, and white), white crappie, and channel catfish. For more information, see www.tpwd.state.tx.us.

Joe Pool Lake

About 4 miles south of Grand Prairie, which is outside Arlington, Joe Pool Lake draws people from all over the Metroplex in the summertime, in part because it's close in and easy to access.

Rentals: Fishing boats (starting at $60 for four hours); pontoon boats (starting at $120 for two hours); ski/wakeboard boats (starting at $160 for two hours); and tubes, skis, and kneeboards (all starting at $10/hour) are all available for rental at Lynn Creek Marina, www.lynncreekmarina.com, (817) 640-4200.

Hiking, biking, swimming: The city of Grand Prairie maintains several big parks around the lake for swimming, boating, camping, and hiking: Loyd Park, 791 acres in the west shore with picnicking, camping, hiking, volleyball, and more, open 24 hours a day all year; Lynn Creek Park, swimming and playground, closed November through February; and Britton Park, with boat launches and good access to fishing holes. Information about all three is at www.fungp.org; (817) 467-2104.

Camping: Loyd Park, see details above.

Information about the lake in general can be found at www.grandfungp.org; (817) 467-2104.

Lake Ray Hubbard

This big, urban lake (I-30 crosses over it) is 21,671 surface acres east of Dallas near the city of Rockwall. While a good deal of Lake Grapevine has been developed with parks, Ray Hubbard's 111 miles of wooded shoreline has more commercial action, including a Bass Pro Shops on the southwest shore near I-30 in Garland and a Hilton in Rockwall (www.theharboratrockwall/hilton).

Rentals: Enjoy a peaceful cruise on a 40-foot wooden catamaran, $25/person for an hour and 45 minutes, through Sail with Scott (214-803-0025; www.sailwithscott.com); Jet Skis ($65/hour) and kayaks ($20 for two hours) are available from Rockwall Watersports (www.rockwallwatersports.com; 877-RWS-4FUN); or try a full-moon cruise ($70/person for three hours) with Foxy Roxy Sails (www.foxyroxysails.com; 214-869-0364).

Hiking, biking: Parks in Rockwall provide some areas for outdoor recreation near the lake. Check www.rockwall.com/parks and www.ci.garland.tx.us to take a look.

Camping: None on the lake.

Information is available at www.tpwd.state.tx.us.Lakes

occasional raccoon and possibly fox. Naturalists on staff at the on-site Hardwicke Interpretive Center will give you pointers and help you make the most of your visit. The center sponsors canoe trips, too.

HORSESHOE TRAILS, SNAKY LANE PARK
2099 Hood Lane, Grapevine
www.grapevinetexas.govindividualdepartments/parksandrecreation
A 119-acre park unfolds along Lake Grapevine through the woods, with ribbons of walking trails

and mountain-biking paths coursing through. There are picnic tables on one end of the park and soccer fields at adjacent Oak Grove Park.

LAKE BENBROOK
7001 Lakeside Dr., Benbrook
(817) 292-2400

Lying just off Fort Worth's southwest side, the U.S. Army Corps of Engineers lake was created by damming the Clear Fork of the Trinity River, about 15 river miles above its confluence with the West Fork of the Trinity in downtown Fort Worth. There's plenty of camping, with utility hookups available in Holiday Park and the Bear Creek Campground of Mustang Park. Table sites without utilities are found in the Mustang Point Campground of Mustang Park and Rocky Creek Park. Picnic sites can be found everywhere, and swimming is allowed everywhere except in boat launch areas. You'll find designated swimming beaches at North Holiday Park and Mustang Point, as well as at Baja Beach in Dutch Branch Park. The 1.5-mile-long crest of the Benbrook Lake dam is popular for joggers and bicyclists; anywhere you look, you'll find birding, too. Bring your fishing gear as well.

LAKE GRANBURY
On the Brazos River, downtown Granbury

An 8,500-acre lake about 40 minutes southwest of Fort Worth, Lake Granbury is big for fishing, camping, and picnicking. Its shoreline has become the setting for many a retiree's dream home.

LAKE GRAPEVINE
110 Fairway Dr., Grapevine
(817) 481-4541

This is the huge body of water you see when landing at DFW Airport. Around the 8,000-acre lake, look for campgrounds, picnic areas, numerous boat ramps, fishing spots, marinas, and hiking-and-biking trails and trails for horseback riding along 146 miles of shoreline.

RANDOL MILL PARK
1901 West Randol Mill Rd., Arlington
(817) 459-5474
www.arlingtontx.gov/park

Northwest Arlington's favorite green space provides tennis and basketball courts, picnic areas, playground, pavilion, softball complex, and a swimming pool. There's fishing in Randol Mill Pond and pleasant walks to take on the nature trail winding around the pond. Big flowerbeds remain an attraction, too.

RIVER LEGACY PARK
701 Northwest Green Oaks Blvd. at Cooper Street, Arlington

Covering 1,300 acres along the Trinity River in north Arlington, this green space offers eight miles of paved trails, forest, greenbelt, soccer fields, picnic tables, a meditation area, water fountains, playground, canoe launch, and a pavilion. An unusual find is the Devil's Cigar, known to exist only in Texas and Japan; the 3-inch-long fungus lives almost forever and makes a hissing sound.

TRINITY PARK
Entrances on University Drive near I-30 and on West Seventh Street near the Trinity River, Fort Worth
(817) 392-5757
www.fortworthgov.org/pacs

The city's favorite may be Trinity Park, winding along the Trinity River between the Cultural District and downtown. The trails that span the entire park have hosted such annual events as the American Heart Walk and Mayfest. It's where you feed feathered friends at the Duck Pond and ride the miniature train.

Recreation

Baseball
MEN'S SENIOR BASEBALL LEAGUE
2450 Cold Springs Rd., Fort Worth
(817) 707-9057
www.fortworthmsbl.com

Eight teams with players 25 and older play at fields all over the city, such as at Country Day School, LaGrave Field, and TCU.

YOUTH BASEBALL
(817) 732-9600
www.yscfortworth.org, www.fortworth athletics.com
The City of Fort Worth coordinates with the city's Youth Sports Council to offer free league play for children ages 5 to 17. The season lasts from March through May.

Basketball
ADULT BASKETBALL
(817) 871-7690
www.fortworthathletics.com
The city's Athletics Section offers two adult men's basketball seasons, spring and fall. You must join a team to play in the 10 regular-season games and the following playoffs. Choose between recreational league play on Monday night and competitive league play on Wednesday night.

YOUTH BASKETBALL
(817) 732-9600
www.yscfortworth.org, www.fortworthath letics.com
In summer and winter, there is league play for kids 5 to 17. A state tournament follows the winter season.

Cycling
BICYCLE CENTER OF FORT WORTH
5434 River Oaks Blvd., Fort Worth
(817) 377-1925
www.bicyclecenteroffortworth.com
Buy a bike and all the necessary accessories here; brands include Bianchi, Schwinn, GT, Raleigh, Easton, Look, Profile Design, Avenir, Shimano, Vittoria, Michelin, Continental, Snafu, Odyssey, Primo, Sarris, Louis Garneau, Bell Weather, and Maxxis. Want a skateboard? This shop carries Baker, Element, Zoo York, Speed Deamon, and more.

BIKES ON THE BUS
The T, Fort Worth's city bus system, offers bike racks on all bus fronts.

COLONEL'S BICYCLES
3053 South University Blvd., Fort Worth
(817) 924-1333
www.colonelsbikes.com
An elite independent shop, this where you buy and maintain your bike. Brands include Orbea, Moots, Giant, Bianchi, Scott USA, Electra, Surly, and Demo.

FORT WORTH CYCLING & FITNESS CENTER
3315 Cherry Lane, Fort Worth
(817) 244-7911
fwcycling.com
Products include those by Trek, Cannondale, Kuota Bicycles, Mirraco BMX, and Redline BMX. Look for all equipment, as well as technology that properly fits you to a bike.

PANTHER CITY BICYCLES
1306 West Magnolia Ave., Fort Worth
(817) 348-0660
www.panthercitybicycles.com
A cool shop near the medical district, this is the place for all-terrain bicycles, children's bicycles, comfort bikes, communter/town bikes, cross/hybrid bikes, cruiser/classic bikes, road bikes, and tandem bikes. Brands include Haro, Fuji, Jamis, MASI, Breezer, and KHS.

Fitness Center
DOWNTOWN YMCA
512 Lamar St., Fort Worth
(817) 332-3281
www.ymcafw.org
The most exciting development in years has been the opening of a new, state-of-the-art fitness facility at what had become a tired YMCA. The new center offers beautiful equipment, many loaded with TVs, and an expanded staff of fitness specialists. Classes include those for traditional aerobics to yoga, cycling, martial arts, and Cross-Fit, the latter a bootcamp-like program. Several water fitness classes are offered in two swimming pools, too. Ask about the assortment of free fitness programs geared for strength training, as well as personal training options, which cost extra. Child care is offered as well.

Golf

HAWKS CREEK
6520 White Settlement Rd., Fort Worth
(817) 738-8402
www.hawkscreek.com
Formerly the golf course at Carswell Airforce Base, this 18-hole favorite is a par-72 course decorated with plenty of mature trees and lovely water hazards.

LOST CREEK GOLF CLUB
4101 Lost Creek Blvd., Aledo
(817) 244-3312
www.lostcreekgolf.com
A par-72 course covered in Bermuda grass, this course has a putting green, chipping green, and a driving range. The landscape has a gentle roll with lots of trees for shade.

MEADOWBROOK GOLF COURSE
1815 Jenson Rd., Fort Worth
One of the city's pretty golf courses, this one on the east side provides 18 holes of par-71 play on a course measuring 6,363 yards. A pro shop and snack shop are on-site.

PECAN VALLEY GOLF COURSE
6400 Pecan Valley Dr., Fort Worth
(817) 249-1945
Two 18-hole courses are separated by the Clear Fork of the Trinity River. Both are served by a snack shop and a driving range.

TEXAS STAR GOLF COURSE
1400 Texas Star Parkway, Euless
(817) 685-7888
www.texasstargolf.com
Close to DFW Airport, this beautiful course winds through 275 acres of rolling landscape around Hurricane Creek, with stacked rock ponds, waterfalls, and plenty of woodlands. It's a par-71 course measuring 7,000 yards in length. A popular restaurant is on-site, too.

Running

FORT WORTH RUNNERS CLUB
www.fwrunners.org

Each month, this group sponsors a walk and a run for individuals and families. There's a newsletter and a calendar of social events, too.

LUKE'S LOCKER
2600 West Seventh St., Montgomery Plaza, Fort Worth
(817) 877-1448
5505 Colleyville Blvd., Colleyville
(817) 849-1562
www.lukeslocker.com
Luke's does much more than sell running gear. Want to learn proper running technique? Luke's teaches great workshops for three levels—casual walkers, advanced walkers, and those runners who want to boost their 5k and 10k running skills. Dedication and good footwear are required. Luke's also has an advanced shoe-fitting practice, guaranteeing that your performance will be at its best and your feet will be treated properly as you run.

Scuba

SCUBA DIVING SCHOOL OF FORT WORTH
3807 Southwest Blvd., Fort Worth
(817) 732-5761
www.scubadivingfortworth.com
With more than 35 years in the business, this is the dive shop with classes for certification, equipment, and dive trips. Training begins for ages 10 to 15. Book trips with this outfit to Cozumel, the Bahamas, Fiji, and, closer to home, diving lakes around Texas.

Skating

ARLINGTON SKATIUM
5515 South Cooper St., Arlington
(817) 784-6222
www.arlingtonskatium.com
A roller-rink open year-round, the facility offers classes, rentals, birthday parties, and other private functions. It's also the home rink for Dallas Derby Devils roller derby league.

Soccer

FORT WORTH ADULT SOCCER ASSOCIATION
5043 Trail Lake Dr., Fort Worth
(817) 346-0150
www.fwadultsoccer.com

Coed league play for 18 and up, with divisions according to age. Three soccer seasons stretch over the course of a year.

FORT WORTH UNITED SOCCER LEAGUE
www.fortworthunited.com
The city's oldest and largest competitive soccer club teaches skills to young men and women and organizes season and tournament play.

NORTH FORT WORTH ALLIANCE SOCCER ASSOCIATION
www.nfwasa.org
A youth soccer outfit serves the area of northern Tarrant County. Seasonal play stretches from early fall through early May.

YOUTH SOCCER
(817) 732-9600
www.yscfortworth.org, www.fortworth athletics.com
Free league play is offered to all youth ages 5 to 17 years old, with a free youth sports clinic prior to the season.

Softball
AMATEUR SOFTBALL ASSOCIATION
Gateway Park
1701 North Beach St., Fort Worth
(817) 838-9765
www.asasoftball.com
Softball tournaments take place at Gateway Park, which hosted the 2008 Women's Olympic Gold Medal Team's national tour.

CITY ADULT LEAGUE
(817) 871-7690
www.fortworthathletics.com
There's recreational and competitive play every night of the week at Gateway Park, on Fort Worth's east side, during winter and fall seasons.

CITY YOUTH LEAGUE
(817) 732-9600
www.yscfortworth.org, www.fortworth athletics.com

The city coordinates with the Youth Sports Council of Fort Worth to give girls ages 5 to 17 league instruction and play.

Swimming
BAD KONIGSHOFEN OUTDOOR FAMILY AQUATIC CENTER
Stovall Park, 2800 West Sublett Rd., Arlington
(817) 459-5223
www.arlingtontx.gov
Among the newest public pools in the Fort Worth area, this grand water play place has a shallow-water play pool, four-lane swim pool, diving board, water slides, pavilions, and showers. You can take swimming lessons here, too.

DOVE POOL
1509 Hood Lane, Grapevine
(817) 410-8140
www.grapevinetexas.gov
You can swim laps here early on Monday and Wednesday mornings. There are swimming lessons, a kids' pool, diving board, and more.

EMLER SWIM SCHOOL
280 Commerce, Suite 180, Southlake
(817) 552-SWIM (7946)
www.iswimemler.com
Small group and private lessons are taught in indoor pools constructed specifically for swim instruction. Students can be as young as six months.

FOREST PARK POOL
2850 Park Place Ave., Fort Worth
(817) 924-8248
An Olympic pool was recently renovated. There are diving boards, waterslides, and a bathhouse.

FORT WORTH FAMILY SWIM SCHOOL
43 County Rd. East, Fort Worth
(817) 939-8759
fwfamilyswimschool.com
Kids ages two and up and adults can learn to swim. For special needs individuals, there are private lessons for all ages and disabilities. For really little ones, 3 months to 30 months, there are Mom/Dad 'n Me lessons.

KELLER POINTE POOL

405 Rufe Snow Dr., Keller
(817) 743-4386
www.cityofkeller.com

A 16,970-square-foot aquatics center has it all—two pools, a hot tub, two lazy rivers, three vortex pools, three water slides, and two sets of water-playground equipment, with amenities divided between indoor and outdoor spaces. Water aerobics, scuba classes, swimming lessons, lifeguard training, and more are offered.

TCU POOL

Stadium Drive at Bellaire Drive, Fort Worth
(817) 257-PLAY
www.campusrec.tcu.edu

Texas Christian University's outdoor pool is open in summer to members and guests. The indoor pool is open at certain hours, depending on the TCU swim team schedule. Ask about family swimming lessons.

Tennis

BAYARD H. FRIEDMAN TENNIS CENTER AT TCU

3609 Bellaire Dr. North, Fort Worth
(817) 257-7960
www.tennis.tcu.edu/tennispublic

Play on 16 outdoor, lighted courts and five indoor courts. Lockers and shower facilities are on-site.

HURST TENNIS CENTER

700 Mary Dr., Hurst
(817) 788-7330
www.ci.hurst.tx.us/departments/recreation/
tenniscenter

Ten outdoor, lighted courts can be rented, and there are lessons and league play, too.

MCLELAND TENNIS CENTER

1600 West Seminary Dr., Fort Worth
(817) 921-5134
www.mclelandtennis.com

Private and group lessons are taught on 14 outdoor and 2 indoor courts. There's a pro shop on-site, too.

NORTH RICHLAND HILLS TENNIS CENTER

7111 Northeast Loop 820, North Richland Hills
(817) 427-6680
www.nrhtx.com/dept_parks_rts

In addition to 16 courts, there's a pro shop, locker rooms, and concessions area. Ask about lessons and league play.

Volleyball

TEXAS ADVANTAGE VOLLEYBALL

4302 Buckingham Rd., Fort Worth
(817) 545-4551
www.ascvb.com

Sign up for lessons or tournament play with this junior program affiliated with USA Volleyball.

STATE PARKS

The Texas State Parks system offers well more than 90 spaces of land for your pleasure. To go outside and play for many people means truly leaving the freeways behind. In these preserves, often with water, hiking trails, fishing shores, and room to unwind, you can actually see the stars at night and hear yourself think at all hours. These are parks within an hour and a half drive from either Dallas or Fort Worth. Find all parks information at www.tpwd.state.tx.us.

ACTON STATE HISTORIC SITE

30 miles southwest of Fort Worth
FR 167 at FR 4
(512) 463-7948

A former state park, this tiny park in northeast Hood County is the burial ground of Elizabeth Crockett, Davy's second wife. It's pretty in spring when bluebonnets cover the site. Her monument is touching, as she appears to be looking into the distance, waiting for him to return from the Alamo.

CEDAR HILL STATE PARK

15 miles southwest of Dallas
1570 West FR 1382
(972) 291-3900

A favorite for mountain bikers, this park has 15 miles of biking trails built by the Dallas Off Road Bicycle Association. Occupying the site of a 19th-century farm, the park holds several restored buildings that re-create the Penn Farm farmstead. The park has 300 acres with walk-in campsites and 10 boat ramps giving you access the 7,500 Joe Pool Lake.

CLEBURNE STATE PARK
60 miles south of Fort Worth
Park Road 21 at US 67
(817) 645-4215
A 500-acre state park with camping, hiking-and-biking trails, fishing, boat rentals, and a park store offers an easy escape from the city.

DINOSAUR VALLEY STATE PARK
64 miles southwest of Fort Worth
TX 205 at Park Road 59
(254) 897-4588
Immensely popular with kids and adults alike, this park became famous when dinosaur footprints were discovered in the Paluxy riverbed rock some years ago. A replica of the prints is in an exhibit, along with dinosaurs donated. There are wonderful hiking trails in this wooded, rolling parkland.

LAKE MINERAL WELLS STATE PARK
46 miles west of Fort Worth
Park Road 71 off US 80
(940) 328-1171
A favorite destination for rock climbing and rappelling on cliffs, this pretty park on a 646-acre lake provides a hilly, forested setting that's surprisingly serene. There are more than 100 picnic sites, access to a 20-mile-long trailway for hiking, biking, and horseback riding, as well as assorted programs, such as cowboy poetry and stargazing.

LAKE RAY ROBERTS STATE PARK
60 miles north of Dallas, 57 miles north of Fort Worth
FR 455 at Park Road 4137
(940) 686-2148
There are actually five units to this park, all with access to the 30,000-acre lake. You can find campsites, boat ramps, a marina, group pavilions, a lodge with hotel-style rooms, mountain bike trails, equestrian trails, and good fishing. Canoe and kayak rentals are available at the Greenbelt Corridor Unit, too.

LAKE TAWAKONI STATE PARK
60 miles east of Dallas
10822 FR 2475
(903) 560-7123
Among newer parks in the state system, this 376-acre reserve lies on the eastern shore of the 36,700-acre lake, popular for fishing, waterskiing, and camping. You'll find 78 campsites, 40 picnic areas, and more than 5 miles of hiking trails, along with 40 acres of native prairie grasslands, good for trying to spot some 130 species of birds noted here.

LAKE WHITNEY STATE PARK
72 miles south of Fort Worth
FR 1244 at Park Road 47
(254) 694-3793
A fabulous fishing lake boasts a 1,315-acre park on its north shore, where you can camp, rent screened shelters, hike, and swim. There's even an airstrip, so fly on in.

MERIDIAN STATE PARK
72 miles south of Fort Worth
TX 22 at Park Road 7
(254) 435-2536
A beautiful and well-kept secret, this woodsy, 500-acre park sits on a 72-acre lake loved by those trying to catch catfish, bass, and crappie. Birding and hiking are popular, particularly on hidden limestone ledges overlooking the water. Camping and picnicking are fine here.

SPECTATOR SPORTS

People coming to the Dallas–Fort Worth area from places that don't have a big sports-fan base may be utterly shocked at the fanaticism thriving here. It's about more than going to games; every sporting event seems to serve as the cause for a major party. Naturally, football is king, thanks to the wealth of good high school football (check out Friday night games at Highland Park High School, Carter High School, and Plano High School in the Dallas area and Trinity Bell High School and Southlake Carroll High School in the Fort Worth area) but also due to the worldwide popularity of the Dallas Cowboys.

The Cowboys weren't especially successful when they first got going in the early 1960s, but since Don Meredith got things rolling, they've been perennial favorites. In fact, the sun has risen and set on America's Team for decades now, and expectations are particularly high with the 'Boys playing in a new billion-dollar stadium, which opened in Arlington in 2009 and will serve as host for the North Texas Super Bowl XLV in 2011. Adding to the local sports scene excitement are the Dallas Mavericks, the NBA team owned by colorful billionaire Mark Cuban, and the Texas Rangers, the baseball team for which Hall of Fame pitcher Nolan Ryan serves as president. Whatever your sport, you can find a team to watch here.

AUTO RACING

TEXAS MOTOR SPEEDWAY
I-35W at Highway 114, Fort Worth
(817) 215-8500
www.texasmotorspeedway.com
Be sure to bring your earplugs to the loudest sports venue in North Texas. It's fast, too, because this is where NASCAR and IndyCar racing is done. Billed as the nation's second-largest sports and entertainment facility, it has a capacity of 200,000 spectators and brings drivers and fans from every part of the map. Through the year, the big races include the Lone Star Nationals Goodguys Rod & Custom Show in early October; 7-Eleven Qualifying Day for the NASCAR Camping World Truck Series, early November; the O'Reilly Challenge, a NASCAR Nationwide Series race, early November; Dickies 500, a NASCAR Sprint Cup Series race, early November; ARCA/REMAX Series Race & Sprint Cup Series Qualifying Day, O'Reilly 300, and Samsung Mobile 500, mid-April; and WinStar World Casino 400K and IndyCar Series, early June. Don't leave your hat, sunscreen, and binoculars

behind. You can bring a cooler in, as long as it's no larger than 14 x 14 x 14 inches.

BASEBALL

FRISCO ROUGH RIDERS
Dr Pepper Ballpark
7300 Rough Riders Trail, Frisco
(972) 731-9200
The Double-A affiliate of the Texas Rangers plays in an especially family-friendly setting, which really feels like a park, complete with lovely landscaping and even a rock-lined swimming pool. There are great sight lines throughout the park and plenty of play spaces for kids. There's lots of good food at concession stands. Tickets are moderately priced.

FORT WORTH CATS BASEBALL
300 Northeast Sixth St., Fort Worth
(817) 877-3152
www.fwcats.com
The Cats play in an independent minor league, hosting games at La Grave Field, which—ages

Texas Motor Speedway

You can do more than watch the races at Texas Motor Speedway. You can actually get on the track and learn by enrolling in the Team Texas NASCAR Sprint Cup Driving School, the nation's only Stock Car Driving School using real spring cup race cars, operating year-round when races aren't scheduled. This is great for companies; contact Team Texas High Performance Driving School at (940) 648-1043 or visit www.team texas.com.

There's also the Skillz For Life Program, a one- or two-day driving class that gives teenagers knowledge and experience for dealing with emergency driving situations. A safe, closed venue at the speedway is used for teaching real-life skills, such as dealing with skids on icy or wet roads, tailgating, and using the ABS braking system. This is done in the newest Audi A4 Quattro models. Find out more at (817) 430-4343 or www .texasdrivingexperience.com.

The Texas Rangers baseball club hit a home run in 2009 when it hired its beloved retired pitching Hall of Famer Nolan Ryan to be its president. Since being drafted by the New York Mets in 1965, Nolan played for the California Angels and the Houston Astros before signing as a free agent with the Rangers in 1988. And he was magical with the Rangers, throwing two of his seven no-hitters for the club, one in Oakland in 1990 and one at home, against Toronto, in 1991. He was also the winning pitcher in the 1989 All-Star Game in Anaheim, and he was the oldest pitcher in baseball history to win that game. Ryan retired in 1993 and was elected to the Baseball Hall of Fame in 1999, going in as a Ranger.

ago—hosted a different Cats team that was part of the Brooklyn-then-Los Angeles Dodgers club. Games are geared toward family fun, and tickets are inexpensive.

GRAND PRAIRIE AIRHOGS
1600 Lone Star Parkway, Grand Prairie
(972) 504-9383
www.airhogsbaseball.com
Not affiliated with a major league team, this independent professional baseball team belongs to the American Association of Professional Baseball teams, as do teams from El Paso; Lincoln, Nebraska; Pensacola, Florida; Shreveport, Louisiana; Sioux City, Iowa; Sioux Falls, South Dakota; St. Paul, Minnesota; and Wichita, Kansas. The AirHogs are managed by Pete Incaviglia, former star for the Texas Rangers. The stadium, which sits near Lone Star Park, is an 87,000-square-foot covered facility and includes a Kids Zone play area, grill, swimming pool, cocktail bar, and soda fountain. There is seating for 6,000, including 2,000 lawn seats.

TEXAS RANGERS
1000 Ballpark Way, #400, Arlington
(817) 273-5222
www.texasrangers.com
Playing in the American League West, this Major League Baseball team hosts games in a beautiful stadium built in 1994 to look like stadiums of old. There are 49,292 seats in a spectacular creation of red brick and granite, with a facade that features 35 cast-stone steer heads and 21 cast-stone stars, along with enormous frieze sculptures illustrating baseball images as well as scenes from Texas history. Look for a cattle drive, the Alamo, oil wells, and the Texas Rangers lawmen, the latter the namesake of the team. There's an office building and a baseball museum in the park, along with an adjacent youth baseball complex and 12-acre pond. Tickets are moderate to expensive.

Close-up

Tailgating Alternatives

If you're looking for a sit-down meal before going to a Texas Rangers baseball game or Dallas Cowboys football game, you'll find plentiful non-chain dining options in the area around the stadiums, which sit next to one another in Arlington. Some restaurants are within a few blocks and will let you leave your car parked there, allowing you to walk to your game, and some even offer shuttle service.

For a family outing, visit Tom's Burger Grill (1530 North Cooper St., 817-459-9000, www .tomsburgersngrill.com) for a burger topped with sautéed mushrooms and melted Swiss on a buttered, toasted brioche bun or all-day breakfast; Marquez Bakery and Tortilla Factory (1730 East Division St., Arlington, 817-265-8858, www.marquezbakery.com) for La Carmelita, a super-sized fresh flour tortilla filled with chorizo, ground beef, pork, or barbacoa with beans, rice, lettuce, tomato, sour cream, and cheese; or New Yorker Pizza and Pasta (1310 North Collins St., Arlington, 817-461-1950) for Brooklyn-style, thin-crust supreme pizza, loaded with pepperoni, sausage, hamburger, green peppers, mushrooms, onions, and olives or a meatball sub.

Going with the guys? Head to BJ's Brewhouse (201 East I-20, Arlington Highlands, 817-465-5225, www.bjsrestaurants.com), where house-brewed beers, Thai-style shrimp lettuce wraps, halibut tacos, and stuffed baked potatoes help fill a big menu; or Humperdink's (700 Six Flags Dr., Arlington, 817-640-8553, www.humperdinks.com), home of microbrews like McMurray's Irish Stout and Pawtucket Pale Ale and a menu of baby back ribs, grilled salmon over linguine, and club sandwiches.

If you're making a date night of a trip to the game, think about My Martini (859 Northeast Green Oaks Blvd., Arlington, 817-461-4424, www.mymartinibistro.com), a cozy place for a Lemontini or a glass of Malbec to go with shrimp dumplings or steak Oscar; Piccolo Mondo (829 Lamar Blvd. East, Arlington, 817-265-9174, www.piccolomondo.com), a place for angel-hair pasta or beef tenderloin medallions with lobster tail; or Olenjack's Grille (770 Rd. to Six Flags, 817-226-2600, olenjacksgrille.com), a casual place for sophisticated food like tequila brown sugar–glazed shrimp and short ribs with garlic mashed potatoes, as well as a Cowboys game-day tailgate party.

BASKETBALL

DALLAS MAVERICKS
American Airlines Center
2500 Victory Ave., Dallas
(214) 221-8326, (214) 747-MAVS

Established in 1971, this NBA team has gained respect in recent years with frequent playoff appearances. The Mavs broke fans' hearts in the 2006 NBA finals, losing to the Miami Heat. Games are extremely exciting, and not just for the NBA action; the sexy Mavs Dancers attract at least as much attention. And you can always watch Mavs' lively owner, billionaire Mark Cuban, too, who can be counted on to be yelling about a ref's

call or just cheering for his team. Crowd celebs frequently include the Cowboys' Tony Romo, and you may even see Hollywood visitors, such as George Clooney, who has had the occasional business deal with Cuban. There's always a party on Victory Plaza, in front of the Double A-C, before the game begins. Tickets are expensive.

FOOTBALL

DALLAS COWBOYS
900 East Randol Mill Rd., Arlington
(817) 892-5000, (817) 892-4161
www.dallascowboys.com

Almost since its beginning, this is a team comprising and creating legends. Don Meredith,

Close-up

Cowboys Packages at Area Hotels

Visitors headed to Dallas Cowboys games at the new stadium in Arlington can plan the trip without having to worry about transportation to the game, in some cases, and nearly all the hotel packages include breakfast to help with the next-day football and beer hangover. Rates are subject to availability.

Gaylord Texan Hotel & Convention Center
1501 Gaylord Trail, Grapevine
(817) 778-2000
www.gaylordhotels.com
Starting at $259/night double, this Cowboys package includes one night's stay; breakfast for two adults at the hotel's casual dining venue, Riverwalk Café; round-trip transportation to games; and 15 percent off merchandise at the resort's Southwest Spirit retail store. Resort fee is included in the package price, but tickets to the game are not. The Gaylord's rooms are rather typical hotel rooms, but the resort itself is built around an enormous atrium that houses restaurants, a faux Alamo, and more.

Hyatt Regency DFW
Dallas/Fort Worth International Airport
(972) 453-1234
www.dfwhyatt.com
If you want to enjoy the game and wake up ready to fly back home, this is your answer. The package includes one morning's break-

fast buffet for two at Jacob's Spring Grille, complimentary covered parking, transportation to and from airport entrances, and access to the 24-hour Hyatt gym. Round-trip transportation to the game is $50 more, and must be reserved 48 hours in advance. Doubles start at around $129/night. The rate is available one night before the game and on game night. Guests must show a game-day ticket at check-in. The Hyatt was recently renovated, enlarging guest rooms and adding flat-screen HDTVs, wireless Internet, iHome stereos, and Hyatt Grand Beds.

Hilton Arlington
2401 East Lamar Blvd., Arlington
(817) 640-3322
www.hilton.com
From $149/night double, the Cowboys Fan package includes overnight accommodations, a stadium blanket, chips and salsa, two Shiner Bock beers, two pralines in a cowboy hat, breakfast buffet, free parking, and 3 p.m. late checkout.

Roger Staubach, Troy Aikman, Bob Lilly, Emmitt Smith, and Michael Irvin are just the start of a list of players who have defined America's Team. The Cowboys have won five of their eight Super Bowl appearances, taking home the world championship in 1971, 1977, 1992, 1993, and 1995. The Dallas Cowboys Cheerleaders have an identity nearly equal to that of the team they support. And now, the Cowboys enter a new era of bigger-than-life magnitude, with the 2009 opening of Cowboys Stadium in Arlington. The $1 billion structure, which will host the 2011 Super Bowl, seats about 80,000 and can accommodate crowds of about 105,000. It was the site of the 2010 NBA All-Star Game, too. The Jumbotron's massive size boggles the mind and you'll find yourself looking at it almost more often than you look at the field. Stadium parking lots open four to five hours prior to the games, so you have plenty of time to throw a tailgate party. You'll find Bank of America ATMs located on the concourses, as well as the Cowboys Pro Shop on the northwest side of the stadium at Entry A or from the Main Concourse behind Section 242. The Pro Shop is open 10 a.m. until 6 p.m. Monday through Saturday and 11 a.m. until 5 p.m. Sunday.

Cowboys Stadium

Cowboys Stadium, the new $1 billion football showplace in Arlington, will host the North Texas Super Bowl XLV in 2011. Here's what football fans visiting the stadium will find:

- The largest enclosed stadium in the NFL, built with more than 26,000 tons of steel and 19 million pounds of trusswork
- The tallest movable glass wall in the world, measuring 120 feet high and 180 feet wide, taking nine minutes to open or close
- The largest domed roof in the world, 660,800 square feet, opening in about 12 minutes
- Twenty-two escalators, 18 elevators, and 10 major stairways
- An exterior covered by more than a half-million square feet of glass and stone.
- More than 1,600 toilets
- More than 800 point-of-sale locations for concessions, inluding mobile carts
- A center video board hanging 90 feet over the field and measuring 72 feet high by 160 feet wide, reaching from one 20-yard-line to the other 20-yard-line
- A party deck with a $29 admission ticket, with standing room only and no guaranteed field view
- The $14 Cowboyrita, a frozen margarita in a tall souvenir glass

GOLF

BYRON NELSON CHAMPIONSHIP
Tournament Players Course (TPC)
Four Seasons Resort and Club Las Colinas
4150 North MacArthur Blvd., Irving
(972) 717-1200, (214) 742-3896
www.hpbnc.org
Nearly 250,000 golf fans show up to see the PGA's top competitors play four days of golf during the third week in May. Named for one of the most beloved golfers of all time, the late Byron Nelson lived nearby and supported this tournament and its charities until he was well into his 90s. Tickets are expensive, but the event is great fun.

COLONIAL GOLF TOURNAMENT
3735 Country Club Circle, Fort Worth
(817) 927-4201
www.crownplazainvitational.com
Played on the home course of the late, great Ben Hogan, this invitational tournament began in 1946 and remains one of the fine smaller tour-naments on the PGA tour. Winners through the years have included Sam Snead, Jack Nicklaus, and Arnold Palmer. Tickets are expensive but crowds love the golf, the skimpy clothing seen in the gallery, and the margaritas that help ward off the late-May heat.

HOCKEY

DALLAS STARS
American Airlines Center
2500 Victory Ave., Dallas
(214) 221-8326
stars.nhl.com
A popular team in the NHL, the Stars bring a world of excitement to the ice and a special brand of thrills to a part of the country where hockey wasn't always available. Locals have taken to the sport in a huge way, and transplants from the Midwest and northern reaches of the country are delighted to find their favorite pastime close at hand. Tickets are expensive.

TEXAS BRAHMAS
NYTEX Sports Center
8851 Ice House Dr., North Richland Hills
www.brahmas.com
The 2009 Central Hockey League champions play in a 2,400-seat stadium. Tickets are inexpensive.

HORSE RACING

LONE STAR PARK
1000 Lone Star Parkway, Grand Prairie
(972) 263-7223
www.lonestarpark.com
Feeling lucky? Head to Grand Prairie, halfway between Dallas and Fort Worth, and bet on the ponies at this fabulous track. You'll see live thoroughbred racing from April through August and quarter horse racing from late September through November. If you don't bet but you love the horses, visit the paddock area. And no matter what, there's always simulcast racing in the Pavilion, which has plenty of food and beverage options.

RODEO

COWTOWN COLISEUM
121 East Exchange Ave., Fort Worth
(817) 625-1025
www.cowtowncoliseum.com
The Stockyards Championship Rodeo takes place every Friday and Saturday night at 8 in a rodeo venue built in 1908. It's been air-conditioned in recent years, but the coliseum still offers a yesteryear feel. A bonus is Pawnee Bill's Wild West Show, an authentic reenactment of the original show, offering trick roping, trick shooting, trick riding, and cowboy songs. Tickets are moderately priced.

FORT WORTH RODEO AND STOCK SHOW
Will Rogers Coliseum
3400 Burnett Tandy Dr., Fort Worth
(817) 877-2400, (817) 877-2420
www.fwssr.com
Formally known as the Southwestern Exposition and Livestock Show, this may be the single big-

Lincoln Square

Lincoln Square, a modern, redbrick retail complex in Arlington a few short blocks from the Texas Rangers Ballpark and Cowboys Stadium, reaches from I-30/Copeland Road at Collins Street south to just across the Road to Six Flags, taking up one very big block. On Cowboys game days, you can park and walk to the game if you place a receipt on your dashboard that shows a purchase of $40 or more at any of the businesses here. Here's a tip: Your purchases can be at more than one place; for example, $20 at a restaurant and $20 at another retailer. On Texas Rangers game days, there are shuttles taking diners between restaurants and the Ballpark. Dining choices in Lincoln Square include familiar chains like Black-Eyed Pea, TGI Friday's, Jason's Deli, Simply Fondue, and Colter's BBQ. Independent restaurants include Olenjack's Grille, a popular destination for steaks, lamb chops, and fish; Social Bakehouse and Coffee (formerly Celebrity Bakery), serving soups, sandwiches, and sweets; Swamp Daddy's, a smoky bar with fried gator tail, boiled shrimp, and crawfish po'boys; Birraporetti's, an Italian-accented bar and grill; Hibachi 97, with Japanese cooking tables; Sprouts Spring Roll and Pho, with fresh Vietnamese dishes; and Sherlock's Baker Street Pub, a British-themed bar and grill with tailgate parties planned for game days. www.lincolnsquarearlington.com.

gest excitement in Cowtown during the winter. Nightly rodeo action brings the toughest bull riders, bronc riders, and steer-wrestling cowboys to town. (See Annual Events, page 167.)

MESQUITE RODEO
1818 Rodeo Dr., Mesquite
(972) 285-8777
www.mesquiterodeo.com
An especially family-friendly rodeo, with lots of fun for the kiddies, takes place every Friday and Saturday evening, June through August. It's all air-conditioned, and there's dining and a full bar on-site. Tickets are inexpensive to moderate.

RUNNING

COWTOWN MARATHON
3515 West Seventh St., Fort Worth
(817) 735-2033
www.cowtownmarathon.org
Running enthusiasts just call it "the Cowtown," and since its founding in 1979, it's become exceptionally popular. Entries for the 50K (yes, people actually run that far), full marathon, half-marathon, 10K, and 5K total about 18,000 runners, who gather for the annual race on the last Saturday in February.

WHITE ROCK MARATHON
4950 Keller Springs Rd., Suite 240, Addison
(972) 839-DWRM (3976)
www.runtherock.com
On the second weekend in December each year, some 20,000 runners hit the streets of Dallas for an event that's been named the state's top marathon and half-marathon by *Competitor Texas* magazine. The route includes a 10-mile loop around scenic White Rock Lake and attracts

some 150,000 spectators who cheer the runners on. This one is a qualifier for the Boston Marathon, and the race benefits the Texas Scottish Rite Hospital for Children in Dallas.

SOCCER

FC DALLAS
Pizza Hut Park
6000 Main St., Frisco
(214) 705-6700
This MLS team, formerly the Dallas Burn, has a huge following, and games at this 145-acre stadium complex are exciting, to say the least. Tickets are moderate.

COLLEGE SPORTS

SMU ATHLETICS
(214) SMU-GAME
smumustangs.cstv.com
In Dallas, Southern Methodist University athletics include football, men and women's basketball, cross-country, equestrian, golf, rowing, soccer, swimming and diving, tennis, track and field, and volleyball.

TCU ATHLETICS
(817) 257-FROG
www.gofrogs.com
In Fort Worth, Texas Christian University men's athletics include football and baseball (both of these Horned Frogs' teams have been nationally ranked in recent years), basketball, cross-country, track and field, tennis, golf, and swimming and diving. Women's sports include golf, track and field, basketball, tennis, cross-country, equestrian, rifle, soccer, swimming and diving, and volleyball.

KIDSTUFF

When you realize that the whole Six Flags concept was born in the Dallas–Fort Worth area—remember, the prototype was Six Flags Over Texas—you understand that this is a place where kids have been having fun for ages. But as any seasoned parent knows, you don't have to take your child to an amusement park to find enjoyment. Thanks to abundant good weather that's mild most of the year, the great outdoors supplies plenty of spaces for families to play together.

For guidance about places such as the Dallas Zoo, Fort Worth Zoo, and science and history museums—you know, all the places that make learning fun for children and adults alike—turn to the Attractions chapter (see page 106). In this chapter, however, you'll find a bounty of destinations designed specifically for kids' entertainment or for helping them learn how to have more fun by being active and expanding their own creative talents. If you're searching for ways to get your young ones off the couch and away from video games and TV, here's where to start in the Dallas–Fort Worth area.

Read on here to learn about places where your children can pursue music, theater, art, and cooking, as well as reading programs, horseback riding lessons, and nature study. Several area museums offer exhibits of interest to young patrons, of course. There are camps, too, that cover all the familiar, general interests, and there are specialized camps for kids who want to focus on zoology, art, acting, singing and dancing, or the environment. Kids who like arcade games will find plenty of places to spend their allowance, too.

Sporting events are easy to find in our area, as well, with professional sports aplenty. The Dallas Cowboys play football and the Texas Rangers play baseball next door to one another in Arlington, Fort Worth's neighbor in Tarrant County, and the Dallas Stars play hockey and the Dallas Mavericks play basketball in the American Airlines Center in Dallas.

For extensive coverage on what to do with the kids in Texas, be sure to pick up our sister guide, *Fun with the Family Texas*, which offers hundreds of ideas for family fun and vacations throughout the state of Texas.

DALLAS AREA

Art, Theater, Creative Programs, and Classes

CENTRAL MARKET
5750 East Lovers Lane, Dallas
(214) 234-7000
320 Coit Rd., Plano
(469) 241-8300
www.centralmarket.com/cooking-school
.aspx

Throughout the summer and during the winter holiday and spring breaks, cooking classes are offered specifically for kids. Age groups are usually 5 to 8, 9 to 12, and 13 to 17, with sessions as brief as two hours or as long as half-days on successive days. Themes are the key here, and hands-on participation is always a hit. Classes may focus on chocolate, Italian food, breads and pastries, or a Hawaiian luau menu—they're ever-changing.

⊙ Close-up

Fair Park and the State Fair of Texas

For three weeks in September and October, your family can delight in the State Fair of Texas (214-565-9931; www.bigtex.com), a gigantic event with livestock and food competitions, arts and crafts and food booths, a huge carnival, all sorts of entertainment, and the giant Big Tex, welcoming visitors with a hearty "Howdy!"

Constructed for the 1936 Texas Centennial Exposition and recognized as a national historic landmark for its Art Deco architecture, Fair Park (located at Cullum Boulevard at Fitzhugh Avenue in the center of Dallas; 214-670-8400; www.fairpark.org) features year-round attractions, including the following:

Children's Aquarium at Fair Park
(214) 670-6826
www.dallaszoo.com
At press time, Children's Aquarium at Fair Park—formerly the Dallas Aquarium at Fair Park, which is administered by the Dallas Zoo—was expected to reopen on Memorial Day Weekend, 2010, after extensive renovation. It's a smaller facility than some, making it a perfect place for younger kids. New, colorful exhibits and features promise to intrigue little patrons. Anticipated exhibits include brightly hued fish, exotic coral, tidal touch pools, and programs to engage the senses.

Hall of State at Fair Park
3939 Grand Ave., Fair Park
(214) 421-4500
www.hallofstate.com
This stately limestone building made its debut in 1936 as part of the Texas Centennial Exhibition and was the most expensive building, per square foot, in Texas at the time. It's a magnificent tribute to Texas. Best for ages six and up.

Museum of the American Railroad
1105 Washington St., Fair Park
(214) 428-0101
www.dallasrailwaymuseum.com
See preserved old locomotives, cars, and memorabilia. The gift shop is housed in the restored 1905 Houston and Texas Central Depot.

The Museum of Nature and Science
3535 Grand Ave., Fair Park
(214) 421-3466
www.natureandscience.org
A combination of three former museums—the Dallas Museum of Natural History, the Science Place, and the Dallas Children's Museum— this has hundreds of hands-on exhibits and displays about natural history, zoo science, energy, and health, as well as a 79-foot, domed IMAX theater and a planetarium show. Separate fees for exhibits, IMAX theater, and planetarium; combination tickets available.

Music Hall at Fair Park
909 First Ave., Fair Park
(214) 565-1116
www.liveatthemusichall.com
The Music Hall is home to Dallas Summer Musicals, fun performances during the summer. Best for ages eight and up.

Texas Discovery Gardens at Fair Park
3601 Martin Luther King Jr. Blvd.
(214) 428-7476
www.texasdiscoverygardens.org
Here's a seven-acre urban garden area with botanical collections and a special Garden for the Blind, featuring plants noted for their textures or scents. Special gardening events and classes.

The Women's Museum
3800 Parry Ave., Fair Park
(214) 915-0860
www.thewomensmuseum.org
A contemporary, 70,000-square-foot museum in a gorgeous old building, this operates in association with the Smithsonian Institution and pays tribute to the contributions and achievements of women throughout history. Best for ages six and up.

DALLAS MUSEUM OF ART
(214) 922-1822
dallasmuseumofart.org/family/familyevents/
index.htm
Child magazine named this one of the nation's
10 best museums for kids, thanks to a bevy of
programs that include a monthly late-night event
for kiddos, art creation events on the first Tuesday
of the month, a regular adventure program, and
an outreach program in local elementary schools.
Ask about summer camps, too.

DALLAS THEATER CENTER SUMMERSTAGE
(214) 252-3918
When school's out, this theater program can keep
your children busy and prompt them to build
confidence and learn about the performing arts.
Acting and Musical Theater for ages 7 to 12 tells
stories through song and theater in two-week
programs. Pre-College Actor Training Program for
the 13- to 18-year-old is suited for more serious
would-be thespians, giving students a chance to
work with actors and directors.

Camps

CAMP GRADY SPRUCE
(940) 779-3411, (866) 391-7343
www.campgradyspruce.org
A popular YMCA overnight camp on Possum
Kingdom Lake, the summer offerings are for boys,
girls (ages 7 to 12), and co-ed (ages 13 to 16). Kids
water-ski, sail, ride horses, learn archery, hike, and
work at arts and crafts. Dances, campouts, games,
and cookouts are typical.

DALLAS ZOO CAMP
(214) 670-7501
www.dallaszooed.com/kidcamps/anim_
adventure.html
Zoo camps are available as single-day options or
week-long day camp sessions. All sessions work
on socialization and zoo exploration, with kids
split into age-appropriate groups, starting with
three- and four-year-olds and continuing to K
through 8. Themes range from Animal Art to the
African Savanna.

MERRIWOOD DAY CAMP
2541 West Campbell Rd., Garland
(972) 495-4646
www.merriwoodranch.com/camp.htm
Weekly sessions are offered in June and July for
girls. Activities include English horseback riding,
horse care, barn management, swimming, and
tennis.

MUSEUM OF NATURE AND SCIENCE SUMMER CAMP
3535 Grand Ave., 1318 South Second Ave.,
Fair Park
(214) 428-5555
www.natureandscience.org/discovery_
camp/default.asp
Day camp programs cover a variety of age
groups. Typical options include Discovery Camp
for ages 3 to 4 and 5 to 12, a week-long session
offered eight times during the summer, each
with a different theme, such as Under the Sea
or Dallas B.C.; and CSI Dallas, a 2½-day camp for
ages 13 to 17, where kids work with a real forensic
professional to gather clues.

Games and Amusements

ADVENTURE LANDING
17717 Coit Rd., Dallas
(972) 248-4653
www.adventurelanding.com/dallas/index
.html
Miniature golf, laser tag, arcade, go-karts, batting
cages, teddy-bear factory, bumper boats, birthday party areas, and plenty of food make this a
destination.

CELEBRATION STATION
4040 Towne Crossing Blvd., Mesquite
(972) 279-7888
www.celebrationstation.com
All under one roof, find more than 100 video
games, batting cages, go-karts, laser tag, an
18-hole miniature golf course, paintball, and
more.

MALIBU SPEEDZONE
11130 Malibu Dr., Dallas
(972) 247-7223
www.speedzone.com
See who's fastest in your family at Malibu Speedzone. The facility has differently powered racing cars for children or adults, including a two-seater. Or play the exciting video games. Best for ages six and up.

Kid-Friendly Museums

AFRICAN-AMERICAN MUSEUM
3536 Grand Ave., Fair Park
(214) 565-9026
www.aamdallas.org
The African-American Museum has one of the largest—and best—collections of African-American folk art in the country, as well as cultural and historical exhibits. The interior of the building is also impressive. Best for ages six and up.

CAVANAUGH FLIGHT MUSEUM
4572 Claire Chenault Dr. at Addison Airport, Addison
(972) 380-8800
www.cavanaughflightmuseum.com
More than 30 planes from both world wars, the Korean War, and the Vietnam War are displayed, along with an aviation art gallery and gift shop. Best for ages six and up.

DALLAS FIREFIGHTERS MUSEUM
3801 Parry Ave., near Fair Park, Dallas
(214) 821-1500
www.dallasfiremuseum.com
Everyone is fascinated with firefighters. See more than 100 years of city history at the Dallas Firefighters Museum. The museum is housed in a restored 1907 fire station that includes an 1884 horse-drawn steamer and a 1936 ladder truck among the many historical displays and exhibits. An interesting gift shop is located in the old horse stalls. Best for ages four and up.

DALLAS HERITAGE VILLAGE AT OLD CITY PARK
1515 South Harwood St., Dallas
(214) 421-5141
www.dallasheritagevillage.org
Take a quick step back in time into furnished log cabins, century-old shops, a Victorian bandstand, a drummer's hotel, and southern mansions. Best for ages four and up.

DALLAS MUSEUM OF ART
1717 North Harwood St., Dallas
(214) 922-1200
www.dallasmuseumofart.org
The Dallas Museum of Art features an extensive collection of pre-Columbian art along with American and European masters and special traveling exhibits. Best for ages 10 and up.

FRONTIERS OF FLIGHT MUSEUM
6911 Lemmon Ave., adjacent to Love Field, Dallas
(214) 350-3600
www.flightmuseum.com
The Frontiers of Flight Museum chronicles the history of aviation from early balloon flights to the space program through a number of exhibits and displays. Best for ages six and up.

INTERNATIONAL MUSEUM OF CULTURES
7500 West Camp Wisdom Rd., Dallas
(972) 708-7406
www.internationalmuseumofcultures.org
Through life-size and miniature exhibits, the museum portrays cultures from around the world. The diversity here is almost overwhelming. Best for ages four and up.

SIXTH FLOOR MUSEUM AT DEALEY PLAZA
411 Elm St., Dallas
(214) 747-6660
www.jfk.org
Unfortunately, one of the things Dallas is best known for is being the place where President John F. Kennedy was killed. The Sixth Floor

Museum honors JFK with exhibits on his life and death, including photographs, artifacts, and a film. The museum is housed on the sixth floor of the former Texas Schoolbook Depository Building at Houston and Elm Streets, where Lee Harvey Oswald allegedly fired his fatal shots. Nearby, at Main and Market Streets, are a cenotaph and memorial park dedicated to Kennedy. Best for ages 10 and up.

Library

DALLAS PUBLIC LIBRARY
1515 Young St., Dallas
(214) 670-1400
dallaslibrary.org/childrenscenter/kids.htm
Every branch of the library system offers a summer reading program and most branches offer storytime programs, too. An impressive program during the school year is the library's Dallas After-School Homework Help, an online system that provides live help via the Internet. It's available to students grades K through 12, between the hours of 3 p.m. and 10 p.m. Kids can get help with math, science, English, and social studies, and they can have their papers proofed and reviewed.

i The Dallas Public Library permanently displays one of the original copies of the Declaration of Independence, printed on July 4, 1776, and the First Folio of William Shakespeare's *Comedies, Histories & Tragedies.*

Outdoors and Nature

CEDAR RIDGE PRESERVE
7171 Mountain Creek Parkway, Dallas
(972) 709-7784
www.audubondallas.org
Cedar Ridge Preserve (formerly Dallas Nature Center) is a 360-acre park with picnic areas, a butterfly garden, and 7 miles of hiking trails around Joe Pool Lake. The area is the habitat for many animals and birds, including some rare ones like the black-capped vireo. The visitor center has a number of educational exhibits. Best for ages four and up.

DALLAS ARBORETUM AND BOTANICAL GARDENS
8525 Garland Rd., Dallas
(214) 515-6500
www.dallasarboretum.org
Relax in 66 acres of spectacular natural beauty at the Dallas Arboretum and Botanical Gardens. The gardens have more than 2,000 varieties of azaleas among the thousands of blooming plants and ferns. Two historic mansions and scenic White Rock Lake are also on the grounds. Best for ages two and up.

DALLAS WORLD AQUARIUM
1801 North Griffin St., Dallas
(214) 720-2224
www.dwazoo.com
The Dallas World Aquarium is one of two nice aquariums in Dallas. This one features sea life from the world's oceans, including corals, giant clams, sharks, and stingrays. Best for ages two and up.

DALLAS ZOO
650 South R. L. Thornton Freeway, Dallas
(214) 670-5656
www.dallaszoo.com
Your family can see thousands of animals, including the world's largest rattlesnake collection, at the Dallas Zoo. Among the highlights are the 25-acre Wilds of Africa exhibit and a monorail that will take you on a bird's-eye tour. The facility also has picnic areas and a miniature train. Best for ages two and up.

TEXAS DISCOVERY GARDENS
3601 Martin Luther King Jr. Blvd., Dallas
(214) 428-7476
www.texasdiscoverygardens.org
Kids can come to Fair Park year-round to get their hands dirty while learning about the environment. There are outdoor learning and service projects for grades K through 8, as well as for scouts, science clubs, and others. Check out after-school and summer offerings.

Parks and Playgrounds

The Dallas Parks Department maintains more than 180 playgrounds across the city. Among the most popular is Tee Pee Hill at White Rock Lake in East Dallas, where families enjoy fishing, hiking and biking, as well as picnicking at a pavilion. Visit www.dallasparks.org for more playground information. See more parks detail in the Parks & Recreation chapter (page xx).

Performing Arts

Dallas is renowned for its performing arts companies, many of which offer productions that young audiences can appreciate. Most are best for ages 10 and up.

THE ANITA N. MARTINEZ BALLET FOLKLORICO
(214) 828-0181
www.anmbf.org
This ballet performs at various venues including the restored historic Majestic Theatre, 1925 Elm St., Dallas.

THE DALLAS BLACK DANCE THEATRE
(214) 871-2376
www.dbdt.com
This group performs in the Dee and Charles Wyly Theatre in the new Dallas Center for the Performing Arts, 2100 Ross Ave., Dallas.

THE DALLAS OPERA
(214) 443-1000
www.dallasopera.org
The opera performs at the Margot and Bill Winspear Opera House at the new Dallas Center for the Performing Arts, 2100 Ross Ave., Dallas.

THE DALLAS SYMPHONY
(214) 692-0203
www.dallassymphony.com
The symphony plays in the Morton H. Meyerson Symphony Center, 2301 Flora St., Dallas.

THE DALLAS THEATER CENTER
(214) 522-8499
www.dallastheatercenter.org

This group performs in the Dee and Charles Wyly Theatre in the new Dallas Center for the Performing Arts, 2100 Ross Ave., Dallas. The company presents several plays specifically for children and teenagers during the summer.

Sporting Events

DALLAS MAVERICKS
Administrative office at 2909 Taylor St., Dallas
(214) 747-MAVS
www.nba.com/mavericks
The ever-popular Dallas Mavericks of the National Basketball Association play in the fan-friendly American Airlines Center (www.americanairlines center.com) at 2500 Victory Ave., Dallas. Best for ages four and up.

DALLAS STARS
2601 Avenue of the Stars, Frisco
(214) 387-5500, (214) GO-STARS (ticket line)
www.dallasstars.com
Always contenders in National Hockey League play, the Dallas Stars are also residents of the American Airlines Center (www.americanairlines center.com). Best for ages six and up.

FORT WORTH AREA

Art, Theater, and Creative Programs

AMON CARTER MUSEUM FAMILY FUNDAY
3501 Camp Bowie Blvd., Fort Worth
(817) 989-5030
Art-making and exploration are among activities the museum offers on selected Sundays to let kids and parents learn more about the special exhibits and permanent collections at this renowned museum.

CENTRAL MARKET
4651 West Freeway, Fort Worth
(817) 377-9307
1425 East Southlake Blvd., Southlake
(817) 310-5600
www.centralmarket.com/cooking-school
.aspx

Throughout the summer and during the winter holiday and spring breaks, cooking classes are offered specifically for kids. Age groups are usually 5 to 12 and 13 to 17, with sessions as brief as two hours or as long as half-days on four successive days. Themes are the key here, and hands-on participation is always a hit. Classes may focus on chocolate, Italian food, breads and pastries, or a Hawaiian luau menu—they're ever-changing.

CHILDREN'S THEATER AT CASA MAÑANA
3101 West Lancaster, Fort Worth
(817) 332-2272
From September through May, the professional theater company at Fort Worth's primary musical stage offers productions for kids. A typical season may include *The Jungle Book*, *Cinderella*, *Peter Pan*, and *Santa Claus Is Coming to Town*.

KIDS WHO CARE
1300 Gendy St., Fort Worth
(817) 737-5437
www.kidswhocare.org
A year-round musical theater company for kids ages 6 to 20 brings together children from around Texas, the U.S., and the world to sing, dance, and act. Productions are in the works throughout the school year, and there are intensive programs in summer, too, all with public performances at the programs' conclusion.

Camps
ART CAMP AND SUMMER ART STUDY
Modern Art Museum
3200 Darnell St., Fort Worth
(817) 738-9215
www.themodern.org
Kids 5 to 13 can attend Art Camp and ages 14 to 16 go to Summer Art Study, programs that teach through art observation and activities that explore the works in current exhibitions. Area artists frequently participate, leading art activities in the galleries, giving kids a chance to make

art and talk about the process. At camp's end, families come to see what the kids have learned and produced.

CAMP CARTER
6200 Sand Springs Rd., Fort Worth
(817) 738-9241
www.campcarter.org
A popular YMCA summer camp since 1948, this value- and activity-based residential and day camp works for kids ages 6 to 16. Activities played out on 300 acres include sailing, swimming, archery, horseback riding, outdoor living, computer lab, team sports, hiking, biking, and more. Overnight camps for boys and girls last one and two weeks. There's also a dedicated equestrian camp with 22 horse stalls and a covered riding arena for kids wanting to learn horse care and riding skills.

CAMP CASA
Casa Mañana Theatre
3101 West Lancaster, Fort Worth
(817) 332-2272
For children ages 8 to 14, there is a three-week day camp, Monday through Friday, giving kids time to audition, rehearse, and produce a show that they'll perform for two nights at camp's end. It's fun and constructive.

LIVE GREEN CAMP
Bedford Boys Ranch
2801 Forest Ridge, Bedford
(817) 952-2323
www.ci.bedford.tx.us
A week-long day camp for kids 6 to 12 provides plenty of outdoor adventure and hands-on learning activity that achieves two goals—that of promoting physical fitness and teamwork and that of emphasizing care for the land and the equipment we use on it. Kids will understand more about learning to live in a planet-friendly way while having fun at swimming, games, and nature exploration.

SUMMER ZOO CAMP
Fort Worth Zoo
1989 Colonial Parkway
(817) 759-7500
www.fortworthzoo.com
Week-long camps for ages three through the sixth grade are offered through the summer. Each has a different theme, such as Amazon Adventures, Zoo Explorers, Desert Creatures, and Wild in the Water. Camp tuition includes a T-shirt, guided zoo tours, animal presentations, chats with animal keepers, snacks, craft activities, and more.

YOUNG ARTISTS' WORKSHOP, SUMMER CAMP AT THE KIMBELL
3333 Camp Bowie Blvd., Fort Worth
(817) 332-8451
www.kimbellart.org
Ages 12 to 15 participate in a four-day afternoon workshop that allows them to work with professional artists and educators to look at new ideas for producing art. Ages 6 to 12 attend camp, a four-day afternoon session that takes them through the galleries and prompts them through art activities in different mediums.

Games and Amusements

GAMEWORKS AT GRAPEVINE MILLS MALL
3000 Grapevine Mills Parkway, Grapevine
(972) 539-6757
www.gameworks.com
Admission is free at this massive play space for young and not-as-young. Games include virtual bowling, Deal or No Deal, UFO Catcher, Sega Rally 3, and much more, plus darts and pool, too. There's a full restaurant and bar, as well.

LASER QUEST
7601 Blvd. 26 North, North Richland Hills
(817) 281-0360
www.laserquest.com
Need a place for a birthday party, soccer team get-together, or day camp? This one is good for anyone who likes a good game of hide-and-seek. You play tag with lasers in a huge, multi-level space with specialty lighting, fog, and throbbing music.

PUTT-PUTT FUN CENTER
7001 Calmont Ave., Fort Worth
(817) 737-2242
Northeast Loop 820 at Hwy 183, North Richland Hills
(817) 589-0523
2004 West Pleasant Ridge Rd., Arlington
(817) 467-6565
www.putt-puttgolf.com
Miniature golf, batting cages, an arcade with video games and pinball, plus a snack bar. The North Richland Hills location has two go-kart tracks, carnival rides, bumper boats, mini-bowling, and a more elaborate game room, as well as freshly baked pizza, ice cream, nachos, and sodas.

Six Flags Over Texas

In its history, Texas has been part of six countries. The flags or seals of those nations are commemorated all over the state, from the amusement park of the same name in Arlington to the mosaic tiles in the floor of the state capitol in Austin.

Spain: 1519–1685 and 1690–1821
France: 1685–1690
Mexico: 1821–1836
The Republic of Texas: 1836–1845
The United States of America: 1845–1861 and 1865 to the present
Confederate States of America: 1861–1865

SIX FLAGS OVER TEXAS
At I-30 and Hwy 360, Arlington
(817) 530-6000
www.sixflags.com/parks/overtexas
Six Flags Over Texas is the most popular tourist attraction in the state. Opened in 1961 by Dallas real estate magnate Angus Wynne Jr., at a price of $10 million, it served as a template for theme parks for decades. The park is full of gravity-

defying roller coasters, including the top-rated wooden Texas Giant coaster. It also features a parachute drop, a number of thrill and entertainment shows, and Looney Tunes characters roaming the grounds. One of the best attractions here is called the Right Stuff, a virtual-reality ride that creates the full sensation of supersonic flight. Best for ages four and up.

Kid-Friendly Museums

AMERICAN AIRLINES C. R. SMITH MUSEUM
4601 Hwy 360, at FAA Road near the DFW Airport, Fort Worth
(817) 967-1560
www.crsmithmuseum.org
You'll discover all kinds of things about passenger airplanes at the American Airlines C. R. Smith Museum. Named for the "Father of American Airlines," the museum has a number of interactive displays, films, videos, and hands-on exhibits. Best for ages six and up.

AMON CARTER MUSEUM
3501 Camp Bowie Blvd., Fort Worth
(817) 738-1933
www.cartermuseum.org
Fine art at the Amon Carter Museum includes one of the largest collections of western art in America, featuring works by Charles Russell and Frederic Remington. The museum also showcases exceptional traveling exhibits, hosts educational and homeschooling programs, and has an extensive research library. Best for ages six and up.

BC VINTAGE FLYING MUSEUM
At Meacham International Airport, Fort Worth
(817) 624-1935
www.vintageflyingmuseum.org
Want to see more airplanes? Go to the BC Vintage Flying Museum at the south end of Meacham International Airport, where you'll see lots of World War II memorabilia and a B-17 Flying Fortress. Best for ages six and up.

i Mayfest in Fort Worth's Trinity Park (817-332-1055; www.mayfest.org) is a massive gathering early in May, with hundreds of arts-and-crafts and food booths, sports activities, competitions for all ages, continuous entertainment, a special children's area, and a concert by the city symphony.

BUREAU OF ENGRAVING AND PRINTING
9000 Blue Mound Rd., Fort Worth
(817) 231-4000, (866) 865-1194
www.moneyfactory.gov
See billions of dollars being printed! Take a fascinating 45-minute guided tour or watch the video, see the exhibits, and visit the gift shop. Security screening to enter facility. Best for ages 10 and up.

CATTLE RAISERS MUSEUM
1501 Montgomery St., Fort Worth
(817) 332-8551
www.cattleraisersmuseum.org
The brand-new 10,000-square-foot state-of-the-art museum opened in late 2009 as part of the new Fort Worth Museum of Science and History in Fort Worth's cultural district. Find out what Fort Worth was all about at this very kid-friendly place. The colorful history of Texas ranching is portrayed with photos, cowboy artifacts, and interactive displays and video games. Best for ages four and up.

MUSEUM OF SCIENCE AND NATURAL HISTORY
1501 Montgomery St., Fort Worth
(817) 255-9300, 888-255-9300
www.fortworthmuseum.org
Have more family fun at the Museum of Science and Natural History in air-conditioned comfort. The huge museum complex allows kids to dig for dinosaur bones or learn about the wonders of science or history in a number of hands-on, interactive exhibits. Observe the night sky and experience other stellar phenomena at the Noble Planetarium. Then experience the ultimate in sight

and sound at the Omni Theater, an 80-foot dome that envelops viewers. Best for ages four and up.

NATIONAL COWGIRL MUSEUM AND HALL OF FAME
1720 Gendy St., Fort Worth
(817) 336-4475, (800) 476-FAME
www.cowgirl.net
It wasn't just cowboys who won the West. Women played just as important a role. The Cowgirl Hall of Fame honors those women who helped make the West great—the pioneers, the performers, the rodeo stars, and the ranch owners. The Cowgirl Hall of Fame moved into a new, impressive facility in the museum district of Fort Worth, and it's full of stuff that will take hours to see. Best for ages six and up.

Library
FORT WORTH PUBLIC LIBRARY
500 West Third St., Fort Worth
(817) 871-7745
www.fortworthlibrary.org
All library branches maintain a summer reading program, administered by the mayor's office. The libraries also offer storytimes, and the Central Library sponsors an area called Our Place, where teens gather to study, hang out, read, work on computers, and receive homework help.

Outdoors and Nature
BOTANIC GARDEN
3220 Botanic Blvd., Fort Worth
(817) 871-7686
www.fwbg.org
The Botanic Garden in Trinity Park is a showcase of 150,000 plants in both formal and natural settings. Small waterfalls, ponds, and pathways abound for a relaxing visit. The conservatory houses hundreds of exotic tropical plants. The Japanese garden is a six-acre garden with a pagoda, moon deck, teahouse, and meditation garden.

FORT WORTH NATURE CENTER AND REFUGE
9601 Fossil Ridge Rd., Fort Worth
(817) 392-7410
www.fwnaturecenter.org
Not far from the gardens is the Fort Worth Nature Center and Refuge, just west of the Lake Worth Bridge. The 3,500-acre refuge offers an interpretive center, picnic areas, and hiking and self-guided nature trails. Some trails are wheelchair-accessible. The kids will love seeing the bison herd or the white-tailed deer. There's even a prairie-dog town. Best for ages four and up.

FORT WORTH ZOO
1989 Colonial Parkway, Fort Worth
(817) 759-7555
www.fortworthzoo.com
The Fort Worth Zoo is a first-class attraction. Your family will go wild over this place, where you can get face-to-face with gorillas, orangutans, and chimpanzees at the World of Primates or watch eagles flying above and around you in Raptor Canyon. Step back into old-time Texas at a one-room schoolhouse, ranch house, and other buildings around which the deer and the antelope do play and the buffalo do roam. Stroll tree-shaded paths that wind around the grounds so you can see more than 5,000 exotic and native animals in natural-habitat exhibits. The kids will enjoy the Yellow Rose Express Train Ride at the zoo. Two ornate miniature trains carry passengers between the Safari Depot and the Texas Wild exhibit. Best for ages two and up.

RIVER LEGACY LIVING SCIENCE CENTER
703 Northwest Green Oaks Blvd., Arlington
(817) 860-6752
www.riverlegacy.org
You'll find a wide range of interactive environmental education exhibits here, including a simulated raft ride down the Trinity River. Open Tuesday through Saturday 9 a.m. to 5 p.m. Best for ages six and up.

Close-up

Fort Worth Stockyards

The Stockyards Historic Area, a National Historic District, captures the Old West with a number of shops and restaurants along Exchange Avenue. A new handheld GPS multimedia computer "tour guide" is available for rent in several languages at the Stockyards Visitor Center. Stockyards Station (817-625-9715) is a large western festival market housed in the renovated hog and sheep pens of the original stockyards. It's the perfect place to buy souvenirs. To see authentic cowboys waxing poetic, make an effort to attend the annual Red Steagall Cowboy Gathering in October at the Stockyards. The three-day event is filled with western songs, lore, and poetry. Best for ages four and up.

Here are the primary family-friendly things to do in the Stockyards.

Cowtown Rodeo
121 East Exchange Ave., Fort Worth
(817) 625-1025, (888) COWTOWN
Everyone enjoys a rodeo, and Fort Worth puts one on every Friday and Saturday night at 8 p.m. in the Stockyards Historic District at the Cowtown Coliseum, site of the first indoor rodeo in 1908. In addition to regular rodeo events, Pawnee Bill's Wild West Show features trick roping, riding, and cowboy songs and stories in the summer. Occasionally they feature "Free Kids on Fridays" specials, so check it out.

The Fort Worth Herd
East Exchange Avenue in the Historic Stockyards District
(817) 336-HERD
www.fortworthherd.com
Watch the world's only daily cattle drive! Bring your camera! Watch genuine cowboys drive a herd of authentic Texas Longhorn cattle down Exchange Avenue twice a day (at 11:30 a.m. and 4 p.m.) to and from their grazing grounds. Educational and family programs are offered throughout the year. Best for ages two and up.

Grapevine Vintage Railroad
130 East Exchange Ave., Fort Worth
(817) 625-7245
www.gvrr.com
The vintage steam train makes round-trip excursions from Grapevine to Fort Worth's Stockyards Historic District on weekends, except in January when it's closed for maintenance. You may purchase a one-way ticket at the Stockyards Station Depot or take a short afternoon excursion ride in Fort Worth. Best for ages two and up.

Parks and Playgrounds

The Fort Worth Parks and Community Services Department maintains more than 200 parks and public spaces across the city, many with playgrounds. Among the most popular is Trinity Park, along University Drive between I-30 and Seventh Street, where families enjoy fishing, hiking, biking, picnicking, feeding ducks on a pond, playing on playground equipment, riding on a miniature train, and, during the first weekend in May, a four-day outdoor party called Mayfest. Visit www.fortworthgov.org/pacs for more playground information. See more parks detail in the Parks & Recreation chapter (page 139).

DYNO-ROCK INDOOR CLIMBING GYM
608 East Front St., Arlington
(817) 461-3966
www.dynorock.com
Now here's an unusual place where your children can be entertained and get exercise at the same time. And what kid doesn't like to climb? Here they do so safely, in a controlled environment. Best for ages six and up.

HURRICANE HARBOR
1800 East Lamar Blvd., across the freeway from Six Flags, Arlington
(817) 530-6000
www.sixflags.com/hurricaneharbortexas
This huge, 47-acre water park (formerly Wet 'n' Wild) is one sure way to beat the Texas heat. You'll find waterslides, tube rides, lagoons, and a special area for families with small children that is like a park within a park. Best for ages two and up. (Open daily May through Labor Day, weekends only through mid-September.)

Performing Arts

BRUCE WOOD DANCE COMPANY
(817) 927-6500
www.brucedance.org

THE FORT WORTH OPERA
(817) 731-0726
www.fwopera.org

THE FORT WORTH SYMPHONY
(817) 665-6000
www.fwsymphony.org

THE TEXAS BALLET
(817) 212-4280
www.texasballettheater.org
For a bit of culture, catch a show by one of the city's excellent fine arts companies; most productions are geared for ages 10 and up. These and other organizations perform at several venues including the Nancy Lee and Perry R. Bass Performance Hall in Sundance Square, the downtown Convention Center, and The W. E. Scott Theatre in the Cultural District.

Fine theater productions may also be seen at Casa Mañana (817-332-2272; www.casamanana.org), Hip Pocket Theater (817-246-9775; www.hippocket.org), or Stage West (817-784-9378; http://stagewest.org).

Sporting Events

DALLAS COWBOYS
900 East Randol Mill Rd., Arlington
(817) 892-5000, (817) 892-4161
www.dallascowboys.com

The Cowboys have won five of their eight Super Bowl appearances, taking home the world championship in 1971, 1977, 1992, 1993, and 1995. The new $1 billion stadium, which will host the 2011 Super Bowl, opened in 2009, with seating for about 80,000 and expandable for crowds up to 105,000. Kids will especially love its space-age look. You'll find 286 concession places; more than 1,600 toilets; and a pro shop. Tickets are expensive.

i Now more than 100 years old, the Fort Worth Rodeo and Stock Show (also called the Southwestern Exposition and Livestock Show and Rodeo) in Fort Worth (817-877-2400; www.fwstockshowrodeo.com) is a major family event running for three weeks from mid-January into early February. There's a downtown parade, livestock judging, a carnival, headliner entertainers, and a professional rodeo. Located at the Stock Show Grounds at the Will Rogers Memorial Center, 1 Amon Carter Square.

TEXAS MOTOR SPEEDWAY
On Highway 114, at I-35W., Fort Worth
(817) 215-8500
www.texasmotorspeedway.com
A state-of-the-art track north of Fort Worth showcases NASCAR and Indy Car races on the big track, Legends Cars on the quarter-mile oval, and auto shows and concerts. Racing takes place spring through summer. Best for ages eight and up.

TEXAS RANGERS
1000 Ballpark Way, off I-30 at Highway 157, Arlington
(817) 273-5222
www.texasrangers.com
The American League Texas Rangers play at a ballpark that combines a very traditional look with modern comforts and conveniences. Behind the bleacher area are several gift shops, an art gallery, and the Legends of the Game Museum (817-273-5600). Best for ages four and up.

ANNUAL EVENTS

If you can't find a party going on in some corner of the Dallas–Fort Worth Metroplex on any given weekend, you're not trying very hard. Rain or shine, in January or June, there's always a big selection of festivals and special events that give you a reason to celebrate, enjoy the arts, spend time outdoors, or explore Texas culture.

People in North Texas spend ample time finding parties that showcase rodeos, headline-making football contests, African-American and Hispanic heritage, good food and drink, fun and games in the park, great music, and fit friends who run 26.2 miles. And you can bet that there's celebration aplenty when it comes to holidays that honor romance, the Irish, independence, and Christmas.

Dallas and Fort Worth play host to lots of these gatherings; to see a complete listing, month by month, visit www.visitdallas.com and www.fortworth.com and click on Events Calendar. Other cities with a full schedule of special events include Addison and Grapevine; see those calendars at www.addisontexas.net (click on Events/Festivals) and www.grapevinetexasusa.com (click on Event Calendar). Here are highlights of some of the biggest events of the year.

JANUARY

AT&T COTTON BOWL CLASSIC
Cowboys Stadium
One Legends Way, Arlington
(817) 892-BOWL, (888) 792-BOWL
www.attcottonbowl.com
The 2010 Cotton Bowl classic, played on New Year's Day or thereabouts, is the first in the tradition's 73-year history not played in the Fair Park stadium. Moving to its new home at the Cowboys Stadium, it remains the college football contest—usually played close to New Year's Day—between teams from the Big 12 and Southeastern conference. Tickets sell out and are usually expensive.

FORT WORTH RODEO AND STOCK SHOW
Will Rogers Memorial Center
3400 Burnett Tandy Dr., Fort Worth
817-877-2400, 817-877-2420
www.fwssr.com

The official name for this three-week cowboy shindig and showcase for the world of ranching and farming is the Southwestern Exposition and Livestock Show. Begun just over 100 years ago, the nation's longest-running such event begins in mid-January and lasts until early February, bringing thousands of exhibitors to town. An exposition for young and old patrons, the stock show fills massive halls at the Will Rogers complex with farm and ranch exhibits and more furred and feathered creatures than you can imagine. Kids from around the state bring the livestock they've raised for show and competition, with the junior steer show bringing well over $1 million in sales at auction. There's a midway carnival, petting zoo, shopping by the acre, and lots of friendly folks in cowboy hats and boots. Plenty of beer and food—at concession stands and at Reata at the Rodeo, a sit-down steak house—keep the crowds well fueled. There's a nightly rodeo, with matinees on weekends (see Spectator Sports, page 153).

🔍 Close-up

What to Eat at the Fort Worth Rodeo and Stock Show

When the annual stock show and rodeo blow into town every January, you can bet some cold weather is likely to come with it. In fact, a little sleet is bound to fall over the Will Rogers Memorial Complex once during the three weeks that the big show takes. But there are plenty of ways to stay warm and keep your belly happy at the same time.

Burritos, steaks, and burgers are plentiful, and there's a lot of soup—always good on those coldest days—and way more than enough sweets to keep your dentist and personal trainer busy for the coming year.

But as there are five places to eat practically every 10 yards you walk at the Stock Show, it's hard to know what's best for your noshing dollar. So we'll cowboy up and make the decision for you. Here's what you shouldn't miss this season.

Chili. Buy a bowl of it, or ask for it in a Frito pie or on hot dogs, burgers, and french fries. The guys at the Burger and Chili Shack inside Round Up Inn serve a classic Texas recipe that's also a favorite at the Houston Rodeo in February and March and the Cotton Bowl football game in January. You can also find nachos and homemade lemonade at the Shack, too.

Cowboy burrito. Look outside the west entrance to the Moncrief Building to find the Texas Skillet, a stand with a seven-foot-wide frying pan. There, cooks will whip up a signature burrito stuffed with grilled steak, skillet potatoes, tomatoes, bell peppers, and cheese. This showy effort is also a hit at Fort Worth's Main Street Festival and the Houston Rodeo, so chances are you're going to like it, too.

Hot breakfast. Lucky you! You have good options for sitting down to a plate of bacon and eggs—and more. The Texas Skillet offers a menu of pancakes, breakfast tacos, breakfast quesadillas, and breakfast sandwiches on croissants, as well as bacon, eggs, and toast. The perennial favorite, of course, is the Stockman's Café, found in Cattle Barn No. 2. The only 24-hour operation during the run of the Stock Show, this place feeds as many as 800 or more per mealtime, which speaks volumes about its homey scrambled eggs, bacon, sausage, biscuits, and cream gravy. You may like it so much that you'll return at lunch for chili, hot dogs, or a cheeseburger, the latter topped with grilled onions.

Barbecue. Look at the food court in Round Up Inn for a stand selling sliced and chopped brisket sandwiches, as well as plates laden with brisket, sausage, and all the trimmings. In

MARTIN LUTHER KING BIRTHDAY PARADE
City Hall Plaza
1500 Manilla Dr., Dallas
(214) 670-8438
The parade usually begins at 10 a.m. on the Saturday prior to MLK Day to commemorate the late Dr. King's legacy. The parade brings floats, bands, and community, civic, and church groups together in a march through downtown Dallas, past the MLK Community Center to Fair Park.

FEBRUARY

COWTOWN MARATHON
www.cowtownmarathon.org
(817) 735-2033
Usually held on the last Saturday in February, this massive marathon race is a qualifier for the Boston Marathon. The race begins and finishes in downtown, with routes for the whole and half-marathons, as well as the 5K and 10K races, coursing through the city.

the Justin Arena and at the Centennial Room in the Moncrief Building, you can buy sliced or chopped sandwiches. Head to the Amon G. Carter Jr. Exhibits Hall for a pulled pork sandwich at the Whole Hog Café stand.

Kid food. Little ones will surely be dragging you to the Exhibits Hall, where concession stands sell their very favorite foods. Your choices there include thick slices of Mama's Pizza, hand-dipped corny dogs, popcorn, burgers, and French fries.

Mexican food. Always a popular stand, the Margaritaville booth on the north wall of the Exhibits Hall dispenses an astounding volume of beef and chicken fajitas, fajita nachos, and wine-based margaritas each year. These wash down well with freshly made iced tea, too, if you're the designated driver.

Sugary treats. Cheesecake-on-a-stick is a huge seller inside Round Up Inn. But if you're a traditionalist and can't image a Stock Show visit without funnel cake, you'll be glad to know this is as widely available as ever. Jake's Cakes is a favorite stand inside the Poultry Barn; other vendors are found near the rodeo arena inside Will Rogers Coliseum and several places on the midway.

Bakers. The longest lines near the noon hour are often found at stands dispensing baked potatoes—and for good reason. These big boys—roughly 1¼ pounds each—are more than a meal, especially when you load them up with margarine, sour cream, cheese, bacon bits, and chives. Find them at the cinnamon roll stands in the cattle barns.

Cinnamon rolls. Here's the one thing that's guaranteed to demolish even the best-kept New Year's fitness resolutions. They're nothing short of a big mound of warm, sweet sin, and anyone who's had even a bite knows this is no exaggeration. Visit the Crown Cinnamon Roll stands in the Exhibits Hall, Justin Building, and cattle barns. Go ahead and get the works with icing and chopped nuts.

Soup, soup, soup. If you're looking for a sure way to warm up on those chilly days, there are several places ready to help. The cinnamon roll booth in Cattle Barn No. 2 sells bread bowls filled with hot concoctions, with daily changing offerings that may include chili, beef stew, broccoli-cheese, clam chowder, chicken noodle, and more. In the Poultry Barn, the soup kiosk dispenses bowls of spicy chicken tortilla, chili, chicken and dumplings, and broccoli-cheese, among others. Look in Round Up Inn and just outside the cattle barns for the Cajun stand, where you'll find bowls of jambalaya as well as red beans and rice, too.

SWEETHEARTS DESSERT FANTASY
(817) 255-2500
www.lenapopehome.org

Usually held in latter February, this romance-themed annual event extends Valentine's Day a bit for those who love sweets and want to contribute to a great cause. It's a mega-tasting of signature desserts and fantasy cakes by independent restaurants and chefs from around Fort Worth, benefitting the children and families of Lena Pope Home, a facility that provides preventive and rehabilitative services for improved family life. Attendance is often more than 500, bringing between $75,000 and $90,000 in fundraising.

MARCH

COOKING FOR KIDS
Kids Who Care
300 Gendy St., Fort Worth
(817) 737-5437
Kidswhocare.org/support_cookin

A celebrity chef cook-off event usually held in very early March benefits the musical theater group called Kids Who Care. The venues in recent years have included the Fort Worth Club and the Fort Worth Stockyards. Cooking teams consist of local chefs paired with local celebrities, with the twosomes whipping up something magical from a box of mystery ingredients. They have 45 minutes to do so over a camp stove with a tabletop, cutting board, and a few pieces of cookware as their only tools. Attendees watch the cooking, taste the competitive dishes, and drink wine, as well as watch the kids perform. Tickets are moderately priced.

DALLAS IRISH FESTIVAL
Fair Park, Dallas
(214) 821-4173
www.ntif.org
A gigantic festival held the first weekend in March brings more than 60,000 to celebrate the Emerald Isle and its heritage. There is a huge schedule of music and dance, and you can find plenty of souvenirs, beer, and Irish food, too.

SAVOR DALLAS
(866) 277-7920
www.savordallas.com
Food lovers convene for a gastronomic adventure over a full weekend in early March. Programs are offered all over downtown and in the Arts District, including a wine stroll in the Dallas Museum of Art, the Meyerson Symphony Center, and the Nasher Sculpture Center; various wine seminars; and a grand tasting, at which you can sample dishes from some of the great restaurants around the city. Tickets are moderate to expensive.

ST. PATRICK'S DAY PARADE
Greenville Avenue, Dallas
(214) 368-6722, (972) 480-0621
www.greenvilleave.org
Over 30 years, this has become an enormously popular event, drawing some 90,000 people to the near-east Dallas neighborhood. Bars, restaurants, boutiques, and other merchants throw the bash, leading with a parade of more than 100 floats. It's a free party and families come in droves, but it becomes rowdier into the night. A

band may play a little after noon—in 2009, it was the Old 97s—and that event carries a moderate charge. Parking can be an issue, so try to take the DART Light-Rail to the Park Lane or Lovers Lane station.

APRIL

BIG TASTE OF FORT WORTH
Big Brothers/Big Sisters
(888) 887-BIGS
www.bbbs.org/taste
The premier food-tasting event in Fort Worth benefits Big Brothers/Big Sisters. Now more than 30 years old, the party takes place in late April, typically at a country club or downtown hotel. The popularity is such that the event keeps outgrowing its venues, as several hundred people will show up for this one-night eating extravaganza. Restaurants and catering companies from around the region donate the food, with chefs coming to prepare and dispense their best work. Numerous wines are sampled, too. Ticket prices are on the high end of moderate.

GRAPEVINE NEW VINTAGE WINE AND ARTS FESTIVAL
(800) 457-6338
www.grapevinetexasusa.com
The wine-centric town by DFW Airport throws many a party each year, and this one's always a huge hit. You'll taste wines from the growing stash of vineyards and wineries in town, hear music, shop, eat, and ride the vintage train over a weekend of grape-fueled merriment in mid-April. Ticket prices vary.

MAIN STREET ARTS FESTIVAL
(817) 336-2787
www.mainstreetartsfest.org
Fort Worth's downtown bash over four days in mid-April brings tens of thousands of people together to celebrate the visual arts, entertainment, and fabulous food. There's a juried art fair, live concerts throughout the day on various stages, and much more. Admission is free.

USA FILM FESTIVAL
6116 North Central Expressway, Dallas
(214) 821-3456
www.usafilmfestival.com
A prestigious gathering of film fans and film stars for eight days in April has grown to international significance. Films screened for members have included *Valkyrie, Julie and Julia, Slumdog Millionaire, Stop-Loss,* and *The Hangover.* Year-round events are offered, as well.

MAY

MAYFEST
Junior League of Fort Worth
Trinity Park, Fort Worth
(817) 332-1055
www.mayfest.org
Begun in 1973 to help beautify Trinity Park, the river areas, and greenbelts, Mayfest continues to take place in Trinity Park over the first weekend in May. Thousands of patrons of every possible age and description show up for the fun, which includes dance and musical performances, an art show, face-painting, kids' games, and loads of food and beverages.

TASTE OF ADDISON
www.addisontexas.net
(972) 450-2851
A two-fisted punch of great food and music takes place on the grassy town green near Addison Circle over a weekend in early May. Several dozen restaurants whip up food to dispense from booths, and there's an ample amount of beverages for all ages to wash it down. Day and night, find music and dance performances happening on various stages.

JUNE

CONCERTS IN THE GARDEN
Botanic Garden
3151 Rock Springs Rd., Fort Worth
(817) 332-8780
The Fort Worth Symphony kicks off a month of musical celebration in early June with nightly concerts. The symphony plays at the beginning and

end of the series, with musical groups varying from country to jazz to pop music. Bring a picnic and blanket to spread out over the lawn, beneath the stars. The show ends nightly with fireworks. Tickets are moderately priced.

SHAKESPEARE FESTIVAL, SHAKESPEARE DALLAS
3630 Harry Hines Blvd., 3rd Floor (event office)
(214) 559-2778
www.shakespearedallas.org
Stretching over a season lasting from late June into October, Shakespeare in the Park includes three or more presentations on the amphitheater stage in Samuell-Grand Park. It's not Shakespeare as usual, however: in 2009, presentations included *The Taming of the Shrew* as an 1850s western, for example. Productions since the company began in 1971 have been top-shelf. Bring a blanket to watch under the stars in a lovely old park. Ticket prices are inexpensive to moderate.

TEXAS SCOTTISH FESTIVAL AND HIGHLAND GAMES
Maverick Stadium, UTA Campus, Arlington
(800) 363-7268
Golfers dressed in kilts are among the revelers taking part in a happy celebration of Scottish heritage in early June. The weekend-long party includes dance contests, athletic competitions, musical performances, and much consumption of food and drink.

JULY

Q CINEMA FESTIVAL
(817) 723-4358
web.me.com/qcinema
Fort Worth's gay and lesbian international film festival takes place at the Rose Marine Theater on North Main Street, near the Stockyards. Over four days in July, the festival presents international dramas, comedies, documentaries, animation, and short films to "provide a voice for gay, lesbian, bisexual, and transgendered persons." (See The Arts, page 128.)

Close-up

Cinco de Mayo and Dieciseis de Septiembre

More than a quarter of the DFW area's population is Hispanic, which brings a rich and colorful diversity to the fabric of life here.

The Mexico connection has roots as deep as cowboy culture. The first cowboys in Texas were, in fact, the Mexican vaqueros, who had been rounding up cattle for Spanish patrones or ranchers for probably centuries when Anglo ranchers appeared on the scene.

The vaqueros were known for their horsemanship and cattle working skills, and passed their techniques to the young cowboys who came to the new ranches. Vaqueros' equipment—the type of saddle, lassos, sombreros, chaps, etc.—gradually lost their Mexican ties and just became part of any cowboy's standard gear.

Today, tamales are almost as common at Christmas as turkeys, and of course almost everyone is addicted to Tex-Mex. It's not uncommon to hear conversations in Spanish, and the Fiesta grocery chain sells everything from tortilla presses to the masa to make the tortillas to put on tacos after you're done. Events in both Dallas and Fort Worth cities mark traditional Mexican holidays.

For Cinco de Mayo, for example, Dallas typically has celebrations at Fair Park with bands on several stages and a parade in the Oak Cliff neighborhood. Events in the city also include Ballet Folklorico performances. In Fort Worth, a downtown celebration is put on by the city's chapter of the National Latino Peace Officers Association.

But newcomers who are unfamiliar with Mexican culture should know that despite the widespread misconception, Cinco de Mayo is not Mexican Independence Day. September 16, Dieciseis de Septiembre, is closer to our own Independence Day. May 5 is not a national holiday in Mexico, where it's celebrated regionally, and primarily in the state of Puebla.

But the date does commemorate an important victory for Mexico in 1862, when an outnumbered Mexican army defeated the French at the Battle of Puebla. The crucial triumph came during a difficult and violent time in Mexico's history. The country had gained independence

---

FOURTH OF JULY
1300 Robert B. Cullum Blvd., Dallas
(214) 670-8400
www.fairpark.org
Dallas's Fair Park hosts a free family event at the recently renovated Cotton Bowl stadium. There's a patriotic program, musical performances, games, and fabulous fireworks. Admission to Fair Park museums is free on July 4, too.

TASTE OF DALLAS
West End Historic District, Dallas
(214) 741-7180
www.tasteofdallas.org
In mid-July, omnivores show up in the downtown district for a weekend of eating. The largest out-door food festival in town brings 350,000 to graze on edibles from restaurant booths and to hear music on two stages. There are kids' play areas and a carnival midway, as well as arts and crafts. Admission is free and tastings are inexpensive.

AUGUST

KRLD RESTAURANT WEEK
(214) 330-1396
www.krld.com
Several dozen top-rate restaurants across the Dallas–Fort Worth area join together with the all-news radio station and with Central Market stores to offer three- and four-course dinners at prices you cannot find otherwise. During Restaurant Week, in mid-August, you can eat at participating

from Spain in 1821, only to be beset by the Mexican-American War from 1846 to 1848 and the Mexican Civil War in 1858. The wars had left the country deeply in debt to England, Spain, and France. England and Spain negotiated agreements, but France was interested in empire-building, and wanted to install Archduke Maximilian of Austria as ruler of Mexico. Using the unpaid debt as grounds, the French invaded Mexico along the Gulf coast at Veracruz, and started marching toward Mexico City. U.S. President Abraham Lincoln was sympathetic to Mexico, but unable to help because the U.S. was in the midst of its own Civil War.

Some 6,500 French troops encountered about 4,500 soldiers led by General Ignacio Zaragoza Seguin near Puebla, and the outnumbered and less well-equipped Mexicans prevailed, ending the invasion. Although the French eventually invaded successfully, the triumph at Puebla on May 5 was a victory that gave Mexico a sense of unity after so many divided years.

Dieciseis de Septiembre, on the other hand, does celebrate Mexican independence from Spain, although Spain didn't recognize it on that day. September 16, 1810, was the date Father Miguel Hidalgo y Costilla in the town of Dolores gave the Grito de Dolores (literally "cry from Dolores"), the cry for Mexican independence. The Spanish crown didn't recognize Mexican independence, though, for 10 more years.

Both Dallas and Fort Worth have a smattering of Dieciseis celebrations.

Finally, El Dia de los Muertos, or Day of the Dead, November 1 and 2, also gets its due here. The holiday has roots in Aztec culture, and is also tied to All Saint's Day and All Souls' Day. November 1 is traditionally for departed children, while November 2 remembers adults. The days typically include an altar with offerings to the dead at cemeteries, often along with plenty of liquor and funny stories about the departed.

In Dallas, the holiday has included an exhibit of Day of the Dead art at the Bath House Cultural Center (214-670-8749, www.bathhousecultural.com) and activities at the Latino Cultural Center (214-671-0052, www.dallasculture.org). In Fort Worth, the Modern Art Museum has an extensive collection of Day of the Dead material and also hosts a celebration (817-738-9215, www.themodern.org).

restaurants for $35, not including beverages and tip. The fund-raiser benefits the North Texas Food Bank and the Lena Pope Home. Some restaurants extend the generous offer for one and two weeks beyond the official Restaurant Week, too.

SEPTEMBER

GALLERY NIGHT
www.fwada.com/spring-gallery-night
(817) 870-2717
The Fort Worth Art Dealers Association presents an afternoon and evening of gallery browsing in mid-September. There's lots of wine flowing, the better to prompt you to spend money on art. Thousands of people attend, so expect crowded spaces at the free event.

i The 52-foot "Big Tex" statue that greets visitors at the annual State Fair of Texas is the tallest cowboy in Texas. The State Fair has been held in the same location since 1886.

STATE FAIR OF TEXAS
3921 Martin Luther King Blvd., Dallas
(214) 565-9931
www.bigtex.com
For decades, this has been one of the state's favorite events, bringing in thousands of attendees from everywhere. It lasts for 24 days, beginning in mid- to late-September and covering Fair Park's grounds like a blanket. Big-name music performers on the various stages have included Pat Green, Willie Nelson, the Jonas Brothers,

(Q) Close-up

What to Eat at the State Fair of Texas

Once the team of Carl and Neil Fletcher introduced their Corny Dog (you may call it a corned dog or corn dog, but in Texas, we say "corny dog") around 1940, the future of fatty foods at the great State Fair of Texas was cemented. Fried foods of every description have surfaced at the fair in the years since, with spiral-cut curly french fries among the most popular for several years.

But then in 2005, the fried frenzy reached such a fever pitch that fair officials decided to organize the Big Tex Choice Award. This food fight among fair concessionaires determines who has the best among the new food offerings—and they're almost always fried, fried, and fried. A committee reviews the proposed new items and looks at recipes, often taste-testing before choosing the finalists for the competition. On Labor Day, about three weeks before the Fair begins, the contest happens and the new favorites are predicted.

Each year, awards are given in the Most Creative and the Best Taste categories. In 2005, Viva Las Vegas Fried Ice Cream won Most Creative, and Best Taste went to the Fried PB, Jelly, and Banana Sandwich. In 2006, the awards for Most Creative and Best Taste went to Fried Coke and Fried Praline Perfection, respectively. In 2007, winners were Deep Fried Latte and Texas Fried Cookie Dough. In 2008, Fried Banana Split and Chicken-Fried Bacon were the winners. In 2009, Deep Fried Butter and Deep Fried Peaches & Cream took the top honors.

Among other intriguing new additions to the concession-stand offerings in 2009 were Deep Fried Peanuts, Stuffed Wings on a Stick, BBQ Stuffed Wings, Texas Bar-B-Q Boomerangs (hickory-smoked brisket, chopped and mixed with special sweet, smoky flavorful barbecue sauce, scooped into a wonton wrapper, and fried), Fried Apple and Peanut Butter on a Stick, Banana Praline Waffles, Deep-Fried Pizza, Fried Chocolate Jalapeño, Fried Peanuts in Shells, Frozen Turtle Cheesecake on a Chocolate Stick, Chili Cheese Dog Pot Pie, Southern Fried Fajitas, and Texas Pig Candy (sweet, spicy cocktail sausages glazed with brown sugar, raspberry-chipotle sauce, and cayenne pepper).

and many more. There are shows for everything from cars to cows, cooking contests and demonstrations, a huge midway with carnival games and rides, and hundreds of good things to eat, including the enormously famous Fletcher's corn dog (called "corny dogs" in Texas). The Texas vs. Oklahoma football showdown takes place during the State Fair at the Cotton Bowl. Tickets are moderate for the fair and expensive for the football game.

OCTOBER

KOMEN DALLAS RACE FOR THE CURE
NorthPark Center
Northwest Hwy at North Central Expressway
(214) 361-6345
www.komen-dallas.org/race

The Susan G. Komen Foundation is based in Dallas and the race, now almost 30 years old, brings overwhelming participation. There's a 1K and a 5K run/walk, all raising money to heighten awareness and educate the public about breast health and to celebrate breast cancer survivors. The race takes place in mid-October. There's a modest registration fee.

RED STEAGALL'S COWBOY GATHERING AND WESTERN SWING FESTIVAL
Fort Worth Stockyards District
(817) 444-5502
www.redsteagallcowboygathering.com
An annual celebration in mid-October in the Fort Worth Stockyards National Historic District, this full-on cowboy experience includes a ranch rodeo, trail ride, wagon train, chuck-wagon cook-

ing competition, cowboy music, cowboy poetry, horse cutting, and much more. Tickets are moderately priced.

NOVEMBER

HOLIDAY AT THE ARBORETUM
8525 Garland Rd., Dallas
(214) 515-6500
www.dallasarboretum.org
Beginning the day after Thanksgiving and lasting through December, the already-gorgeous gardens become a fantasyland for the holidays. The magnificent DeGolyer home and gardens simply sparkle and shine.

TRAINS AT NORTHPARK
1030 NorthPark Center
(214) 361-6345
www.rmhdallas.com/trains/index.html
Since 1987, NorthPark turns into Santa's spectacle with an assortment of 35 0-gauge toy trains running in holiday scenery in the shopping center. It's not just for kids—adults are wild about this holiday special, too. Benefitting the Ronald McDonald House, the train event lasts until just after New Year's Day.

DECEMBER

CHILDREN'S PARADE
1321 Commerce St., Dallas
(214) 742-8200, (214) 456-8360
www.childrens.com/parade/index.cfm
Neiman Marcus and the Adolphus Hotel have teamed up to offer a magical holiday parade on the first Saturday in December. Not unlike the famous Macy's Thanksgiving Day Parade, this one thrills with marching bands, fabulous floats and balloons, acrobats, and Santa's arrival. Crowds number about 350,000 and there is bleacher seating available. You can even inquire about having breakfast with Santa, too.

WHITE ROCK MARATHON
2401 North Houston, Dallas
(214) 303-5572
www.runtherock.com
A qualifier race for the Boston Marathon, this race registers 20,000 participants and always fills up. There are various categories, including marathon, half-marathon, five-person relay, corporate relay, and 5K fun-run options. The route courses through east and downtown Dallas; there's a big post-race party with food and local music at the American Airlines Center in Victory Park, and the whole event benefits the Scottish Rite Hospital for Children. Registration fees are moderate.

DAY TRIPS AND WEEKEND GETAWAYS

When the daily stress of carpools, deadlines, and traffic pile up, nothing cures like a road trip. Getting away from the concrete jungle means heading down two-lane highways, losing and finding yourself on a hiking trail, or waking up to the sound of nothing in a small country inn.

Some of these trips can be done in a day and a night, but why not stretch that out over three to four days? After all, it takes time to find restoration, and besides, you'll want to go at a leisurely pace as you gaze through all these windows to the past.

Before setting out on your road trip, make a list of everything you and your travel companions want to do, and be sure to note the order of importance. For some, finding the best food and wine are at the top of the list. For others, going on the best hike possible outweighs all other activities. Some will put shopping above all else. And so on.

Then do your homework. Scour the blogs and travel Web sites for information on your destination. See if postings on tripadvisor.com, yelp.com, and urbanspoon.com steer you toward or away points of interest, hotels, or restaurants.

Get out a road map, plan your path, and print it out; you can't always trust your GPS not to put you into a lake. Or call AAA (please, if you're not a member, join already!) and ask them to route your drive. Just be sure to ask for the backroads, because the interstate will generally bore you to tears. How many cookie-cutter shopping centers do you need? None! Find the local color that sits on smaller highways; chances are, by skipping the interstate traffic, you'll get where you're going just as quickly.

Bear in mind that crowds will typically be larger in the afternoon and that can be a buzz kill. Several of the more popular state parks (like Enchanted Rock and Lost Maples, see below under Hill Country) will limit entry when the day is busy, so early arrival may be imperative. And if you put more active pursuits on the morning schedule, leave the latter part of the day free for massages, followed by eating and sipping.

Find out if the spas and restaurants you're most eager to visit require booking well in advance. And if you're staying at an inn with personalized service, ask the staff to help with those reservations. But take care to not over-plan. By leaving air in the schedule that allows for discovery and impromptu adventure, you could find yourself doing your best Lucy impression in a grape-stomp at a winery or getting a behind-the-scenes tour at an artist's new studio. And remember to enjoy yourself, not just check things off a list.

DAY TRIPS

Wanderers who most enjoy these routes are those needing a break from urban sprawl. Away from the city, you'll feel as though you're light-years from malls and freeways and amusement parks, and you'll have a chance to discover a more authentic Texas. Small towns often offer just the restoration you need.

Denton and Gainesville

It's just 30 miles north from Dallas or Fort Worth on I-35 to the town of Denton, an esteemed center of education and home to the renowned One O'Clock Lab Band at the University of North Texas. A few blocks away, Texas Woman's University boasts a DAR Museum, where a collection of first ladies' gowns show the fashion acumen of state leaders' wives since the Republic of Texas period. Nearby, find Little Chapel in the Woods, a handsome place of serenity designed by O'Neil Ford and dedicated by Eleanor Roosevelt in 1939.

A gorgeous 1895 courthouse, housing a fine little history museum, presides over downtown and its collection of art galleries, cafes, and boutiques, as well as a vintage hardware store. Area saloons provide a steady supply of live Texas music.

Another half-hour north, past dozens of beautiful horse farms, Gainesville is home to the Frank Buck Zoo; historical exhibits at the Morton Museum of Cooke County; a driving tour past graceful,19th-century homes along Church, Denton, and Lindsay streets; and the Fried Pie Company, a worthwhile stop for sinful pastries stuffed with fruit. From Gainesville, head west on U.S. Highway 82 to Muenster, founded in 1899 by immigrants from Westphalia, Germany. Today it's a great stop for excellent German food and for exploring the town's early heritage at the Muenster Museum. Be sure to visit the very ornate St. Peter's Church, which looks as though plucked from a village in the Black Forest.

Information: Denton, www.discoverdenton .com, (888) 381-1818; and Gainesville, www .mortonmuseum.org, (940) 668-8900.

Granbury and Glen Rose

To investigate turn-of-the-century townships, with a bit of the Wild West thrown in, take US 377 southwest of Fort Worth about 40 minutes to Granbury, one of the first towns in Texas to undergo a massive courthouse square restoration back in the 1970s that put this site on the National Historic Register. Today's offerings include a delightful opera house with a full schedule of musical and dramatic productions, a wealth of antiques stores and boutiques, and a restaurant called Café Nutt, tucked inside an old hotel called the Nutt House, serving fancy versions of down-home, Southern favorites. Other good dining on Granbury's Hood County square includes the Merry Heart Tea Room and Babe's Chicken House.

Crossing Lake Granbury, you'll take Texas Highway 144 southeast about 15 minutes to Glen Rose, the Somervell County Seat, perched prettily where the Paluxy and Brazos rivers meet. You can rent an inner tube for floating or a canoe for paddling, enjoy a bluegrass jam session, take a driving tour past hundreds of exotic and endangered animals at Fossil Rim, and see dinosaur tracks in riverbed rock at Dinosaur Valley State Park. If you're hungry, stop for barbecue at the Ranch House in Glen Rose or head just south of town for barbecue or chicken-fried steak at Lone Coyote. Another 20 minutes south along US 67 and Texas 220, you'll reach the town of Hico, famous for an artisan chocolate maker, a coffee shop with the biggest and best meringue pies in Texas, and a Billy the Kid Museum. There's good shopping in Hico's cool little boutiques, too.

Information: Granbury, www.granburytx .com, (800) 950-2212; and Glen Rose, www.glen rosetexas.net, (888) 346-6282.

Waxahachie, Corsicana, and Ennis

Roughly a half-hour's drive south of Dallas along I-45, Waxahachie's first claim to fame was the construction of its exquisite Ellis County Courthouse, built in 1894 to 1895. One of the Italian craftsmen imported to carve the intricate relief details fell in love with a local lady who, ultimately, didn't return his affection. Look carefully and you'll see her face change in a series of depictions from lovely to hideous. The whole of downtown is a wonder, as well; have a poke around the Ellis County Museum to learn more of the town's history, then see changing exhibits at the Webb Gallery or have lunch at one of the cute, local cafes.

In your inspection of Waxahachie, you'll see a spectacular collection of Victorian architecture in this brick-street burg, which is showcased each June during the Gingerbread Trail Tour. Some homes have been used as locations for such movies as *Tender Mercies*, *The Trip to Bountiful*, and *Places in the Heart*. The pink, purple, and white blooms you see in summer are celebrated during the Crape Myrtle Festival, and there's a late-spring

⊕ Close-up

Where to Eat on a Wildflower Trip

You know that spring has truly sprung when bluebonnet patches sprawl along the roadsides, and Indian paintbrush and black-eyed susans have never been more radiant. It's usually a bumper crop of wildflowers to be enjoyed around North Texas, often from March through May, and spring fever will make you positively woozy. When it's high time to hit the road, remember that road-trippers cannot live by blooms alone. All that energy expended on oohs and ahhs, and the time spent doubling back to take photos, will work up a powerful appetite after a spell. But where are the must-stop places to eat?

Down-home cafes account for the bulk of these recommendations, but you'll find a few of them serving food as flowery as those highway views. Again, we're steering you away from the interstate as often as possible, but you'll still find that most of these distances are fewer than two hours from Dallas–Fort Worth. Remember to take your camera, as well as a good appetite.

Oh, and to find the good flowers, call the state highway hotline at (800) 452-9292 or visit www.txdot.gov/travel/flora_conditions.htm to find out which roads have the best blooms the day you're planning your drive.

Heading North

The Center Restaurant (603 East Highway 82, Muenster; 940-759-2910; www.thecenterrestaurant.com): Deciding which of the longtime favorite German restaurants in this Teutonic town to visit? Go for one providing a little more ambience. Open nearly fifty years, the Center, serving three meals a day, charms with its hand-painted Bavarian designs and pampers with a vast menu of tender schnitzels and famous Pagel family sausages, with good spicy red cabbage and fresh yeast rolls alongside. It would be tough to find better German potato salad anywhere, and the ample dessert selection even includes a sugar-free coconut pie. The bonus is a sunny beer garden with the occasional live music offering.

Clark's Outpost (101 US 377 at Gene Autry Dr., Tioga; 940-437-2414; www.clarksoutpost.com): Sort of a ramshackle wooden building on the outside, the cheery interior is generally full of savvy diners who know where to pull in for serious hickory-smoked vittles. Good eats include favorites such as smoked ruby red trout, as well as smoked German sausage and fried quail legs. Lamb fries can be paired with pork ribs. Best sides include collard greens and jalapeño-spiked black-eyed peas. Good beer list, too. Open and lunch and dinner.

Ranchman's Cafe (110 West Bailey St., Ponder; 940-479-2221; www.ranchman.com): Open since 1948, this creaky joint along Farm Road 156 may be the purest throwback in business. That whine you hear coming from the kitchen is your steak being cut per your order. Favorite picks include T-bones topped with grilled onions or mushrooms, grilled quail, calf fries, and fresh-cut french fries. Be sure to call ahead to reserve your baker. Pies and cobblers are big hits, too. It's open at lunch and dinner.

Looking South

Line Camp (4610 Shaw Rd., Tolar; 254-835-4459; www.linecampsteakhouse.com): Way back off the highway sits a newish steak house that just seems like it's been around a while. Named for the cattle camps that ruled the range before barbed-wire fencing marked ranch property, this friendly place for good eating and happy imbibing does a good job with a smart, short menu. You can get a beef tenderloin filet, strip, or rib eye, but we love the flatiron steak, topped with butter and a roasted green chile and the chicken-fried boneless pork chop. On the second Sunday of the month, there's an open jam session on the stage out back, where families gather at 1 p.m. for country gospel and acoustic music.

Let's Eat (28602 US 377 North, Bluff Dale; 254-728-3635): A big surprise for a little cafe, Let's Eat occupies an old, unassuming white building on the roadside. Inside awaits the unlikely tableau of people crammed into booths and seated cheek to jowl at a long community table. Lunch favorites include plates of pork chops, meat loaf, and fried shrimp; at dinner, try the New York strip with creamed potatoes. Families feel at home here, as do adults toting bottles of wine and six-packs of fancy beers. Take-out casseroles include King Ranch chicken, chile relleno, and beef lasagna; orders required 24 hours in advance.

Ranch House (1408 Northeast Big Bend Trail (US 67), Glen Rose; 254-897-3441): Begun as a tiny barbecue shack, this town favorite has evolved into quite the meeting and eating place. Even in the middle of the afternoon, it's full, a testament to the pecan-smoked goodness of the foods served in generous quantities. Two people can easily split a three-meat plate, best composed of tender pork ribs, crusty but tender beef brisket, and smoked sausage. Sides include sensational jalapeño potato salad and homey pinto beans. On Friday and Saturday nights, you can opt for pecan-grilled pork chops and rib eye steaks. Do not pass up the buttermilk pie—truly to die for.

Rough Creek Lodge (Country Road 2015, south of Glen Rose; 254-965-3700; www.roughcreeklodge.com): Chef Gerard Thompson has a gift for rendering elegant works of things like grilled Texas quail and cheese grits, and a quesadilla graced with heirloom tomato, bacon, Stilton, and arugula pretty much has no equal. Over the years we've been rocked by his pheasant potpie and his chocolate angel food cake with macadamia nut ice cream; just when it seemed impossible to find anything better, his pastry team came up with the most sublime breakfast breads on the planet. Yes, you'll pay premium prices for these eats, but each bite is worth every penny. After such a fabulous meal, you'll be ready to collapse in a dreamy bed in one of the lodge's divine rooms. Serving three meals daily.

Koffee Kup (US 281 at TX 6, Hico; 254-796-4839; www.koffeekupfamilyrestaurant.com): A popular stop en route south on US 281 to San Antonio, this old-fashioned coffee shop is where folks gather to swap stories and check up on each other. Veteran customers drive from near and far for the mile-high meringue pies. Chocolate and coconut are favorites, but don't overlook the peanut butter. The burger and fries are plenty good, too. Visit at breakfast, lunch, and dinner.

Driving West

Wildcatter Ranch (6062 TX 16 South, Graham; 940-549-3555; www.wildcattersteakhouse.com): Be sure to take a table by the window—or out on the patio, if the weather's welcoming—so you can look out at the tree-cloaked hills reaching toward the horizon at this Young County steak house. Bob Bratcher, a cowboy cook from farther West Texas, does a mean porterhouse, perfect for two to share and best when paired with smoked creamed corn, grilled asparagus, and a bottle of McPherson cabernet from the Panhandle. There's a kids' menu, too, as well as lots of appetizers if you just want to snack awhile. If you want to make it a sleepover, the ranch has 16 fabulously appointed cabins and lodge rooms, too.

Scarborough Faire Renaissance Festival just outside of town.

Southeast about 40 miles, Corsicana honors one of its own who made the big time; at the Lefty Frizzell Country Music Museum, you'll see the handprints of Merle Haggard in the sidewalk in front of the Lefty's statue. If your sweet tooth's acting up, head over to the Collin Street Bakery for one of its world-famous fruitcakes, a double-chocolate pecan cake, pecan pie, apricot-pecan pound cake, or pecan praline cookies, all baked using renowned Navarro County nuts.

Information: Waxahachie, www.waxahachie chamber.com, (972) 937-2390; Corsicana, www .visitcorsicana.com, (877) 648-2688; and Ennis, www.visitennis.org, (972) 878-4748.

Waco and Bryan-College Station

Possibly one of the easiest fast getaways lies in a jaunt down to Waco, roughly 90 minutes south of Dallas–Fort Worth along I-35 and a popular travelers' stop since the Chisholm Trail cattle-drive days. Once there, you can perch on a stool at a 1940s soda fountain, sipping an icy-cold Dr Pepper at its very birthplace. Crafted by a Waco pharmacist, the soft drink is honored at its very own museum housed within its original bottling plant. Nearby, you can soak up local history at the Cotton Museum, then learn about the most famous of all American lawmen at the Texas Rangers Museum before exploring the lives of Lone Star athletes such as Nolan Ryan, Tom Landry, George Forman, and Babe Didrikson Zaharias at the Texas Sports Hall of Fame.

If you're a photo buff, don't miss the famous Suspension Bridge, the first bridge built over the Brazos River and one that continues to serve as a dramatic city landmark. Make time to visit Baylor University, the world's largest Baptist university, home to magnificent stained-glass windows and a remarkable collection of poetry at the Armstrong-Browning Library.

It should be noted, of course, that Waco was the scene of an enormous tragedy in the 20th century. On April 19, 1993, 76 people died after a 51-day siege by the ATF on the Branch Davidian compound at Mount Carmel, a few miles northeast of Waco. Trees were planted in memory of the David Koresh followers who died there, and a memorial stands in honor of the ATF officers who died there, as well.

An 85-mile drive beyond Waco takes you through pastoral scenery along TX 6 to Bryan–College Station, also known as Aggieland, home of Texas A&M University. There, look for the beautiful Albritton Bell Tower, with 49 bells cast in France weighing 17 tons in all; and the Sam Houston Sanders Corps of Cadets Center, honoring the Aggie cadet corps members of all time. Don't miss the George Bush Presidential Library and Museum, honoring the 41st president, where you're taken on a virtual White House tour by Bush family dogs Millie and Ranger, and where you'll see the former president's Camp David and *Air Force One* offices, a computerized family photo album and scrapbook, a restored Avenger similar to the one Bush flew as a World War II Navy pilot, and exhibits detailing his careers as U.N. Ambassador, CIA director, and president. Don't leave Bryan without visiting Messina-Hof Winery to taste wines and enjoy a leisurely lunch or dinner.

Information: Waco, www.wacocvb.com, (800) 922-6386; and Bryan–College Station, www .visitaggieland.com, (800) 777-8292.

Weatherford and Mineral Wells

Take a trip back in time on a short jaunt west from Dallas–Fort Worth along US 180. To appreciate the rewards in two storybook towns out that way is to abandon the interstate and follow the four-lane highway that rumbles and rolls over rocky swells in the raw topography. In Weatherford, the nation's Cutting Horse Capital, stop to rummage through the antiques shops and browse the stands at the old, stucco farmers' market just east of the town square. You can pick up honey and jams from local makers, and in summer, pick up the famous Parker County peaches and astonishingly large watermelons. Another two blocks west, the exquisite, red-roofed Parker County Courthouse rises like a giant wedding cake crafted from white limestone in 1886. Lunch at the Downtown Café or the Chicken Scratch Bistro will fortify you for the day.

In spring and summer, travelers through Weatherford enjoy prowling the grounds of Chandor Gardens, created in 1936 by the portrait artist Douglas Chandor, for whom sat such dignitaries as Queen Elizabeth II and Winston Churchill. Settling here with his Texan wife, he crafted from a barren hill this sensational spread of waterfalls, Chinese meditation sites, grottos, and blooming gardens.

About 15 miles west of Weatherford, look for the turn-off to Lake Mineral Wells State Park, a 3,000-acre, woodsy sanctuary surrounding the serene reach of lake. The park is regionally famous among rock climbers for its Penitentiary Hollow Climbing Area, and it's a great jumping-on spot for the 22-mile Rails to Trails pathway, a new trail for cyclists, hikers, and equestrians built over an old railbed.

In Mineral Wells, pay a visit to the Famous Water Company, a business established in 1904 to sell rejuvenating local waters that made the town, well, famous. Pick up some water, enjoy an ice cream, buy some locally made soaps. Then wander over to the abandoned Baker Hotel, a giant, yellow-brick masterpiece that once brought celebrities like Judy Garland, Clark Gable, Will Rogers, and Harpo Marx to town.

For information: Weatherford, www.weatherford.com, (888) 594-3801; and Mineral Wells, www.mineralwellstx.com, (940) 325-2557.

Abilene and Albany

Remnants of the Old West can be uncovered a short drive west through a stretch of landscape that marks the end of the flat North Texas prairies, giving way to the craggy golden and white rocks of the Palo Pinto Mountains, carpeted in twisted, aged live oak and forbidding, thorny mesquite trees. As you make your way two to three hours away from home, you can't help but gain appreciation for the determined spirit of pioneers who made a new life all those years ago in this lonely land.

Stay on US 180 west to Albany, the Shackelford County Seat and home to a wealth of western heritage. At the center of town is the elaborately ornamental 1883 courthouse, which is surrounded by fantastically restored historic buildings. Among them, the Lynch Building is now occupied by an excellent bookstore filled with Texana, and the Old Jail Art Center houses an astounding art museum within the 1878 jailhouse. Just off the square, too, is the Ice House, a good place for Mexican food, and the Beehive and Mercantile, a saloon and steak house of renown.

Fifteen miles north of town via US 283, Fort Griffin State Park spreads on lands just above the Clear Fork of the Brazos River. The park, which is home to the official Texas Longhorn herd, encompasses ruins of an 1867 fort where buffalo hunters, cattle drivers, and gunslingers ranging from Billy the Kid and Pat Garrett to Bat Masterson stopped off. Also called the Flat, so named for its positioning beneath a mesa, it was known as the "wickedest place on earth" due to its 34 on-the-street killings and the presence of notable gamblers and outlaws.

Today that illustrious past is celebrated in the annual bash called the Fort Griffin Fandangle, a two-weekend party in latter June showcasing a delightful outdoor drama at the expansive, grassy Prairie Theater. Thousands flock to Albany annually for this 40-year-old tradition, booking rooms months in advance.

Just south of Albany, Abilene offers elements for war and history buffs, art lovers, and children, all housed within the Grace Museum. You can find masterpieces in military flying machines at Dyess Air Force Base, and you can explore beautiful ruins at Fort Phantom Hill. In town, one of the most interactive heritage experiences in the state awaits at Frontier Texas!, a new museum that puts loads of drama in your investigation of the Texas Forts Region. Information: Albany, www.albanytexas.com, (325) 762-2525; and Abilene, www.abilenevisitors.com, (800) 727-7704.

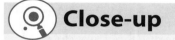

Close-up

Texas Fall Foliage

It often comes as a surprise to newcomers that Texas can enjoy a brilliant fall foliage season—because, surprise!, the state isn't barren, after all. Occasionally, heavy summer rains will wash away chances for the most luscious leaves, but there's no harm in hoping for the best. Botanists and other expert prognosticators refuse to make promises, but we do know where to go should the leaves deliver their annual autumn dance.

Surveying state parks and other destinations traditionally offering good color, we know that prime time for wandering country roads in search of turning leaves is typically late October through at least mid-November and possibly even Thanksgiving. For an overview of state parks with a history of good foliage, visit www.tpwd.state.tx.us/spdest/parkinfo/seasonal/foliage.

We like these picks for areas with seasonal beauty.

In the Hill Country: Lost Maples State Park, about 330 miles southwest of Dallas–Fort Worth and 86 miles northwest of San Antonio.

What to see: One of the prime spots for hikers seeking moderate challenges, this rocky, hilly park becomes one of the most popular destinations in Texas in autumn, thanks to the isolated stands of big-tooth maples that have no kin within hundreds of miles. These magnificent trees glow with gorgeous reds and golds while changing, keeping company with yellowing walnut and pecan trees.

What to do: In addition to hiking the park, be sure to drive one of the most scenic ribbons of pavement anywhere, the stretch of Ranch Road 337 that reaches from Vanderpool (5 miles south of the park) to Leakey (pronounced "LAY-kee"). Hairpin turns give you dramatic views of craggy, scrubby hills, some reaching 2,100 feet high. Find good home cooking at Lost Maples Café in the town of Utopia, just south of Vanderpool, and at Frio Canyon Lodge in Leakey.

Where to stay: Frio Canyon Lodge (www.friocanyonlodge.com, 830-232-6800) is a renovated 1941 motor lodge covered in limestone. Neal's Lodges (www.nealslodges.com, 830-232-6118) has been a favorite place to rent a cabin on the Frio River since 1926.

Details: Lost Maples State Park, (830) 966-3413, www.tpwd.state.tx.us. Check out the foliage report, updated weekly, at www.tpwd.state.tx.us/spdest/findadest/parks/lost_maples/foliage.phtml. Note that the park will only accommodate 250 vehicles at once, so either plan to arrive early in the morning on weekends or visit during the week. For campsite reservation, call (512) 389-8900, 9 a.m. to 6 p.m. Monday through Friday.

In East Texas: The Piney Woods region, with four national forests and the country's only

Austin

Point the car south on I-35, driving about 200 miles to the state capital. You'll better appreciate the Lone Star State after a visit to one of the state's finest museums, the impressive Bob Bullock Texas State History Museum, named for the late lieutenant governor and filled with a raft of ever-changing exhibits that tell the story of Texas. The beautiful State Capitol building,

glorious in pink granite, is where you can watch the legislature (if in session) or simply revel in the rotunda's exquisite design. Nearby, the Lyndon B. Johnson Library and Museum offers a fascinating look at the life and service of an enigmatic national leader, while the George Washington Carver Museum showcases African-American history in Austin and Travis County. On Congress Avenue, leading south away from the Capitol, natural preserve, covers a wide sweep of landscape east of Dallas to the Louisiana state line and from the Red River clear down to Beaumont. You're guaranteed breathtaking drives throughout that quarter of the state any time of year; when the hardwoods change color in the midst of all those evergreens, it's magical. Some drives into the area from Tarrant County can take three to four hours, while others can easily fill a couple of days.

What to see: To see photos of last year's glory, including cardinal-red sumac and crape myrtles gone scarlet everywhere, visit the East Texas Tourism Association's Web site coverage at www.easttexasguide.com/fallfoliage/destinations.html. Heading northeast from Fort Worth, you can look for sweetgums turning coppery around Winnsboro and Lake Bob Sandlin State Park (130 miles from Dallas–Fort Worth) and yellow hickory near Linden and Daingerfield State Park (about 130 miles east of Dallas–Fort Worth). You might catch rusty dogwoods around Palestine (130 miles southeast of Dallas–Fort Worth) and a profusion of orange, gold, and red among the pines in Big Thicket National Preserve–area towns like Livingston (225 miles southeast of Dallas–Fort Worth) and Woodville (another 33 miles east of Livingston).

What to do: You can fish, camp, and take nature walks through the woods and around the water at Daingerfield and Lake Bob Sandlin state parks and on secluded trails through the dense Big Thicket forest. On driving tours, make stops for shopping at Canton during First Monday Trade Days, the full weekend prior to the first Monday of each month; at Mineola to buy beautiful, handcrafted goods at Pine Mills Pottery; and to eat the famous double-fudge pound cake and Texas pecan cake at Eilenberger Bakery in Palestine and big family-style meals starring fried chicken and corn bread at the Pickett House near Woodville.

Where to stay: For camping reservations at the state parks, call (512) 389-8900, 9 a.m. to 6 p.m. Monday through Friday. Perennial lodging favorites in the Piney Woods include the Excelsior House in Jefferson (www.theexcelsiorhouse.com, 800-490-7270) and the Woodbine Hotel in Madisonville (www.woodbinetexashotel.com, 888-966-3246).

In near West Texas: Palo Pinto, about 75 miles west of Dallas–Fort Worth via US 180, is a little town lying 12 miles west of Mineral Wells and smack in the middle of a scenic highway that usually becomes its most gorgeous in November. TX 4 reaches north from Palo Pinto toward Graford and south toward Santo; follow the two-lane road's rises and dips and twists as it burrows through a little range called the Palo Pinto Mountains, which most fans will tell you rivals the famous Hill Country's beauty.

What to do: In addition to the drive, you can hike and rock-climb in nearby Mineral Wells State Park, which has a great lake beside which to picnic. Hungry travelers will be delighted to learn that the Palo Pinto Cafe has reopened, too.

Where to stay: Try the Silk Stocking Row B&B in Mineral Wells (silkstockingbb.com, 940-325-4101) or Wildcatter Ranch at Graham (www.wildcatterranch.com, 940-549-3500).

find the Austin Museum of Art and the Mexic-Arte Museum, both showcasing the work of multiethnic artists from around the state. While you're on Congress, stop for a glass of wine at Cork & Co., or for a massive burger at the Roaring Fork, the ground-floor restaurant at the Stephen F. Austin Hotel.

If your artistic soul needs nourishment, explore the Jack S. Blanton Museum of Art within the Harry Ransom Center on the University of Texas campus. Then head over to Lamar Street to pick up some handcrafted treasures at Clarksville Pottery and Gallery before soaking up the sun beside the always-cooling waters at Barton Springs, the vintage, rock-bottom pool inside Zilker Park. While away the evening hours first by watching the world's largest colony of Mexican free-tailed bats take flight at dusk from beneath

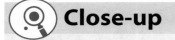

Close-up

Buffalo Gap

Out west of Dallas–Fort Worth, in an area just south of Abilene, there's a great little hideout that's good for an overnighter. If you hang your hat in Buffalo Gap, a cozy little burg that's hardly more than a wide spot in the road, you'll be glad you brought your appetite along. That's because you'll want to tuck into one of the spectacular meals at Perini Ranch Steakhouse—there are few things better than cowboy cook Tom Perini's smoked prime rib and green chile hominy, nor his Sunday fried chicken—and then you won't want to leave Buffalo Gap right away.

That's why Tom and wife Lisa Perini opened their Perini Ranch Guest Quarters, so you don't have to go home too quickly. There are two fabulously appointed houses that sit less than a half-mile from the steak house; the showplace of the pair is the Main House, an 1885 farmhouse, original to the ranch, which has been painstakingly restored and transformed into a place anybody would happily call home. One of the two bedrooms sleeps three people, and the other has a queen for two. The bathrooms are simply gorgeous, and the comfy living room—complete with HD-TV and satellite—overlooks an expansive deck, which has a fire pit. Decor is casual chic instead of the overdone ranch theme, with antique prints and lithographs providing much of the art. You'll want to sit on the porch rockers for hours on end, gazing out at the rocking, rolling landscape in this topography called the Callahan Divide. (The second, smaller house has a kitchenette, comfy bedroom, and pretty bathroom; it sleeps three.)

There's wireless Internet connection, too, as well as a well-appointed, fully-stocked kitchen and big bowls of fresh fruit. A wonderful kitchen accessory is the microwavable egg poacher from local artist George Holland at nearby Buffalo Gap Pottery. You can pick one up on the way out of town, along with a set of bowls or a wine cooler.

Don't miss the chance to explore Buffalo Gap Historic Village, one of the best places to investigate life in pioneer Texas. Relocated authentic buildings show you how the doctor, blacksmith, banker, livery folk, and other early settlers worked and lived. In the bookstore, you can find terrific volumes on Texana, too. Call Perini Ranch at (800) 367-1721; www .periniranch.com. Contact Buffalo Gap Pottery, 534 Vine St. in Buffalo Gap, at 325-572-5056. Contact Buffalo Gap Historical Village at 325-572-3365 or www.buffalogap.com.

the Congress Avenue bridge, then head down South Congress for live music at the Continental Club, a plate of tacos at Guero's, and a scoop of ice cream at Amy's.

Information: www.austintexas.org, (866) GO-AUSTIN.

Hill Country

An hour west of Austin and about four to five hours southwest of Dallas–Fort Worth, the topography turns to wildflower-covered land swells and scrub-dusted valleys. This magical, scenic region has stolen hearts for a century or so; many of her captives will testify that once you've been smitten, you'll never be able to put the Hill Country out of your mind. Benevolent with wild beauty and serene spirit, this region urges you to adopt a footloose attitude. As you wander from town to town, seduced by spring-fed rivers and lakes, the shade of age-old cedars and live oaks, and the craggy reassurance of ancient limestone bluffs, you'll be tempted to toss your cell phone out the window.

The best-known of the mid-19th-century towns carved by scrupulous German immigrants is Fredericksburg, where long blocks in every direction are lined with limestone buildings crafted in an original design called fachwerk. The Pioneer Museum tells the story of this town's early settlers, while a memorial to the

Pacific Theater side of World War II is explored at the marvelous Admiral Nimitz Museum, a state historical park named for the navy commander from Fredericksburg. Main Street bustles with boutiques and gift shops, bakeries and brewpubs, wine tasting rooms and cafes growing more elegant all the time.

Use Fredericksburg as a jumping-off point to explore the region. Hike the wondrous Enchanted Rock, a huge granite uplift just north of Fredericksburg, and go wander the trails at the deeply wooded Lost Maples, near Vanderpool, west of Fredericksburg. Visit winery tasting rooms at the vineyards scattered throughout the Hill Country; you're likely to take home wines from Becker Vineyards at Stonewall, just east of Fredericksburg, and from Sisterdale, about 20 minutes southeast of town. Down in Kerrville, about 25 minutes south of Fredericksburg, visit the Cowboy Artists of America Museum and go see the exotic wildlife roaming the wide open spaces at the Y.O. Ranch. If you're an early riser, book a cowboy breakfast with one of the dude ranches down in Bandera, where you can ride horses along the bucolic Medina River.

Just a short drive east of Fredericksburg, Johnson City is best known for the LBJ National Park, which includes the famous LBJ Ranch and the childhood home of Lyndon B. Johnson. Perhaps most beautiful is Pedernales Falls State Park, with breathtaking waterfalls tumbling over enormous limestone boulders. If all this exploration makes you hungry, stop at the Hill Country Cupboard in Johnson City for a chicken-fried steak and a piece of pie.

Information: www.fredericksburg-texas.com, (888) 997-3600.

Jefferson and Marshall

Heading east toward the forested Piney Woods region, your first stop is about three to four hours from Dallas in Marshall, the Confederates' center of government during the Civil War after the fall of Vicksburg and a lovely, Victorian town filled with historical architecture. Downtown, find wonderful surprises in the Michelson Art Museum, which features the work of the late Russian-American post-impressionist, Leo Michelson. You'll need a trailer to haul away the great deals on glazed pots, dishes, mugs, and bowls at the beloved Marshall Pottery, which also sells garden statuary. On Marshall's downtown square you'll find the small but interesting Harrison County Historical Museum within the remodeled and striking former county courthouse, which is bedecked in millions of lights at Christmastime.

Just a few minutes north on US 59, you'll come to Jefferson, a genteel little town that drawls in a fashion far more Southern than Texan. It recalls a gracious era of plantation life, cotton riches, and riverboat adventure, much of which is palpable even now. The brick streets of downtown are lined with plenty of quaint shops selling antiques, gifts, clocks, and more, but you might just choose to survey the town aboard a carriage tour, during which your guide will acquaint you with the rich history of this old riverport landing, or aboard a boat tour on the Big Cypress Bayou. Among good places to eat downtown is the Hamburger Store, known for its homemade pies.

Be sure to visit the Jefferson Historical Society Museum, within the giant red Old Federal Building, and the Excelsior House, a historic inn that was visited by Ulysses Grant, Rutherford B. Hayes, and Oscar Wilde. Among several of the graceful, 19th-century homes open for tours is House of the Seasons, a magnificent creation blending Victorian and Greek Revival designs. Allow a whole day to explore the vast, primeval wonders of nearby Caddo Lake, about 15 miles east of town toward the Louisiana state line. You can rent a canoe for paddling among the giant, ancient cypress trees or join a lake cruise aboard a paddlewheeler replica. Rent a cabin under the massive pines at Caddo Lake State Park or at one of the fishing camps, where you can hire fishing guides to show you where the best catches are found.

Information: Marshall, www.marshall-chamber.com, (903) 935-7868; and Jefferson, www.jefferson-texas.com, (903) 665-2672.

Round Top

Between three and four hours southeast of Dallas–Fort Worth via US 77 and 290, you'll find a tiny town tucked into the rolling, live oak–covered landscape about midway between Austin and Houston called Round Top. The sign reads population 81, but that might refer simply to the number of people in a couple of shops on the quaint town square at any given moment. A boomtown of cozy proportions in Fayette County, Round Top dates from 1835 and has become famous in spite of its small size. That's because visitors come in droves to attend classical music concerts at the lauded Festival Hill Institute, and in the spring and fall, at almost a frenzied pace, to the cluster of antiques fairs that happen over one weekend in early April and October. Shoppers know this is where the real stuff, never junk, is found: Whatever vintage wash basin, armoire, quilt, lamp, door, bed, stove, or vase you seek is here, rest assured.

If it's not antiques fair weekend, not to worry. On the Round Top square alone are wonderful little shops like PJ Hornberger Folk Art Gallery and Old Stone Brewery Antiques, plus little shops that offer soaps and bath crystals made in the 19th-century fashion, reproductions of antique Texas maps, old and new cookbooks, and whimsical home decor items from jeweled picture frames to handpainted footstools. For steaks, catfish, barbecue, and Sunday noon fried chicken, head to Klumps Restaurant, in an old tinsmith shop on the square; and for exceptional pies, go to Royer's. And at nearby Washington-on-the Brazos State Park, you'll find a great little museum where copies of the Texas Declaration of Independence and other early Texas history keepsakes are sold.

Information: www.roundtop.org, (979) 249-4042.

RELOCATION AND RETIREMENT

Throughout North Texas, individual cities offer information and varying degrees of assistance or guidance for relocating individuals and families. And these days, every good real estate agent is a relocation specialist, helping you navigate your way through the selection of neighborhoods and the offerings therein, depending on your need for schools, retail, and city services.

Having a car is important in this region. Few people living in North Texas rely wholly on mass transit, although light-rail is finally, but slowly, on the grow. Oddly, some cities don't have any bus service, but these are typically cities with easy access to freeways and toll roads. If you want to ride the bus or light-rail to work, it's best to look for housing close to either downtown Dallas or Fort Worth, although there are park-and-ride lots in many suburbs, too.

When consulting the relocation departments of the offices listed below, you can also find information regarding economic and demographic profiles of the cities you're considering. Keep in mind that Dallas and Tarrant Counties are home to numerous municipalities. Laws and regulations vary from city to city; check with the relocation offices in each of the following chambers of commerce for specific information pertaining to utilities, automobile registration, driver's license offices, property taxes, pet licenses, and voter registration. Most of the Web sites below offer extensive, detailed information to ease your move to the area.

CHAMBERS OF COMMERCE AND SIMILAR RESOURCES

Dallas Area

DALLAS REGIONAL CHAMBER OF COMMERCE
700 North Pearl St., Suite 1200, Dallas
(214) 746-6600
www.dallaschamber.org
Visit the Web site and click on About the Area, then click on Newcomer. You will find the immensely helpful *Newcomer & Relocation Journal*, a quarterly publication, accessed also at www.yournewcomerguide.com.

Here are similar contacts in the Dallas area.

METROCREST CHAMBER OF COMMERCE
(972) 416-6600
www.metrocrestchamber.com/relocation-resources.html
This office serves the cities of Addison, Carrollton, and Farmers Branch.

NORTH DALLAS CHAMBER OF COMMERCE
(214) 368-6485
www.ndcc.org/magazine/relocation.html
Representing a wide swath of the northern part of the area.

Fort Worth Area

ARLINGTON CHAMBER OF COMMERCE
www.arlingtontx.com/relocating-to-arlington
Check out this Web site for information on the post office, city hall, schools, property taxes, and utilities.

DESTINATION DFW
www.desinationdfw.com
An online relocation guide to Dallas and Fort Worth gives you information from business and housing to health care, senior living, and education.

FORT WORTH CHAMBER OF COMMERCE
www.fortworthchamber.com/about_fw/moving.html

The Lovely New World of Condos

You're too tired to walk the dog or cook dinner? In desperate need of a mani-pedi or a massage? Laundry piling up? All of it can be handled for you at home without lifting a finger, if you buy into the hottest new housing market in Dallas and Fort Worth: upscale condominiums attached to luxury hotels.

These high-end high-rise homes fitted with over-the-top kitchens, sparkling glass tile, or beautiful stone baths—and some with tall windows framing miles and miles of Texas—attract professional singles and empty-nesters who want to live the good life without having to leave home. Most are located in or near the city centers, so they're less attractive to families with kids who need to get to school. For families interested in the condo lifestyle, a new urbanism development in Southlake, between Dallas and Fort Worth, is just the ticket.

Dallas

You can practically live at the Ritz, at the Tower Residences at the Ritz-Carlton, Dallas, 95 homes in a 23-story Regency-design building downtown next to the hotel. Homeowners enjoy 24-hour Ritz concierge service from a priority phone, private entrance and underground parking, an outdoor pool and fitness center, plus private wine storage and a la carte access to hotel dining and housekeeping.

Here, you're close to the Central Business District, American Airlines Center, the West End's eateries, and the cultural arts district.

The one- to three-bedroom homes run $800,000 to $6.2 million. Information: (214) 855-2020, www.theresidencesdallas.com.

Also in downtown Dallas, hard by American Airlines Center, are the W Dallas Victory Residences, at the W Dallas Victory. If you choose to cook instead of using your VIP access to Victory Park restaurants, order your grocery list purchased and delivered, and then whip something up on the Varenna kitchen system. Or have a chef brought in to prepare your meal at home.

The residences also offer Woof/Meow pet services, weekly botanical services, car valet, and 24-hour maintenance as part of its Whatever/Whenever services. Exclusive access to the Bliss spa goes without saying. Homeowners also receive special rates and VIP services at W hotels worldwide.

Prices start at $349,000 for a one-bedroom and $699,000 for two bedrooms. Information: (214) 777-4321 or www.victoryresidences.com.

In nearby exclusive Turtle Creek, the Plaza Turtle Creek is the residential counterpart of the beloved Rosewood Mansion of Turtle Creek. Though the Plaza is not owned or developed by Rosewood, it is managed by the hotel and touts a "concierge lifestyle." The amenities include a conservatory, a wine cave, a library, fitness center, and pool, with access to hotel services similar to those offered at the Ritz and W condos. Kitchens are equipped with Sub-Zero appliances, and bathrooms finished with limestone and tumbled marble.

Properties start at about $460,000 for 1,546 square feet. Or, lease one starting at $5,400/month for 1,932 square feet. Information: (214) 850-4914 or www.theplazaturtlecreek.com.

Fort Worth

In Cowtown, the 1301 Throckmorton Omni Residences rise above the Omni Hotel, the city's newest luxury lodging.

Here, the 24-hour concierge service will bring you steaks from Bob's Steak and Chop House (a highly regarded steak house in a state full of them), cooked or ready for you to prepare.

The units in the 30-story building are designed so that all the major rooms have a wall of floor-to-ceiling glass—from some you can see all the way to Dallas, some 50 miles away.

Interiors can be chosen in traditional, transitional, and contemporary, all outfitted with Viking gas ranges, Ann Sacks tile, and motorized, remote-controlled blinds.

Residents have a 16th-floor rooftop infinity edge pool, 24-hour controlled access, and concierge services; a Zen garden and outdoor fire pit; a resident-only fitness center; parking; an entertainment area with a gourmet kitchen; and other perks including signing privileges at the Omni's Mokara Spa, Cast Iron Grill, Wine Thief, Whiskey and Rye Sportsbar, and Starbucks, all in the hotel.

Again, a concierge service will make dining and entertainment reservations; shop for groceries and deliver them; take care of pets, housekeeping, and plants; and even plan a party for you. Residents will receive special rates at the Omni hotels worldwide.

The 12 floor plans range from 873 square feet with no terrace, starting at $402,500, to a 4,500-square-foot penthouse for $2.65 million. Information: (817) 535-6665; www.1301throckmorton.com.

Southlake

New urbanism—a kind of re-creation of small-town living in the midst of big-city amenities—is a concept that became a happy reality in this city north of Dallas and Fort Worth and an easy commute to both.

The development began with Southlake Town Square, where City Hall and a library rub shoulders with shopping that includes a Coach store, an Apple store, Crate and Barrel, and dozens more, big and small. Next came a multiplex movie theater and residences, called brownstones after the venerable homes in New York City.

Planners had originally envisioned empty nesters moving into the condominiums, but instead a surprising number of families are calling them home. Children who live here attend the Carroll Independent School District, where all 11 schools are rated "exemplary" by the state, and the high school sports teams consistently win regional and state honors.

Originally, 48 units were built, and those resell from $500,000 to $1 million when they come on the market. The condos are three-story units, typically with living, dining, and kitchens on the first floor; bedrooms on the second; and a large family or game room on the third. In response to surveys of potential buyers, developers plan to build about 50 two-story units with the master suites downstairs.

Besides the school district, some of the appeal here comes from the European-style atmosphere in the town square. In the evenings, teenagers waiting for movies to start sit around a big fountain talking, or haunt the Starbucks in Barnes & Noble. Couples window-shop, and families with strollers go for walks.

The dining ranges from several seafood spots to pizza to Tex-Mex and Italian, just a few minutes' walk from the condos. Visitors can stay at the Hilton on Town Square.

The square also stays busy with family-oriented festivals in summer and fall, and around the holidays.

Information: (817) 310-1093 or www.lifeinthesquare.com.

Close-up

A Relocation Primer

Are you a hip twenty-something looking for an apartment with great nightlife and the edgiest eateries? A young family hunting for good schools and a big backyard? Or discriminating empty nesters seeking both sophistication and fun? It's all here.

The trick is finding what you want without running yourself ragged. Home purchasing and rental in the DFW is a big job. Remember that this is a huge area. The suburbs, which contain hundreds of housing developments, sprawl in all directions from both Dallas and Fort Worth. The solution: plan, plan, plan. We can give you some tools, and offer the kind of rough idea that you might get from a friend about what's available where.

Time spent on research—whether it's on the Internet or talking to someone familiar with the area—is time and money saved on the ground. Nothing can be more annoying than landing for a house-hunting trip, wasting gasoline getting lost, finally finding the X on the map . . . and disliking the area once you get there. Here, you're also in danger of choosing 10 homes to view that just happen to be so far apart you can only get to three in the day you'd planned to see them all.

Also keep in mind that Texas is different from the rest of the nation when it comes to real estate. Buoyed by the natural gas industry, the unemployment rate has stayed steadier than it has elsewhere, and therefore so have real estate markets. The average home price in Dallas toward the end of summer 2009 was $211,400; in Fort Worth it was $146,900. The big bargains on foreclosures that were available elsewhere during the recession are not nearly as prevalent here.

Two Internet sites will help you get started. One is www.realtor.com, which provides tons of photos of homes on the market, and all the essential basic information about those homes including schools and Realtor contact information. The other is the cache of all Texas real estate numbers, the Real Estate Center at Texas A&M University, www.recenter.tamu.edu. Numbers freaks will love this site, where you can access market reports, housing affordability figures, and population data, and read *Tierra Grande*, the center's journal.

Then, when the time comes to contact an agent, consider using a buyer's agent. They represent you instead of the seller, and it doesn't cost you a penny more. Some of the buyer's agents in this area have been here awhile and know the market well. Whomever and whatever kind of agent you choose, find out how long they've been working this market and which parts of it they know. An agent who knows Fort Worth might just actively dislike Dallas, for example, and vice versa.

And consider renting for a little while, if you're not already. Families with children who are in a position to buy will hate the idea, because kids will get established in school and uprooting them again is not ideal. Experience shows that might happen anyway, because there's no way to get a real feel for all of these diverse and widespread areas without spending some time there.

For either buying or renting, certain criteria are a given: proximity to work and schools, safety. But you need to know more than that. What's the neighborhood like? What else is around it? How old are the homes? What's the difference between, say, Keller and McKinney? The way to learn, and we can't stress enough that learning is key before setting out, is to ask questions, looking both online and talking to someone who lives here.

Here are some general ideas about where to find certain kinds of homes.

Charming and Older

These are nearly all within the city limits of Dallas and Fort Worth. Very few suburbs are old enough to have quaint Victorians or sweet 1920s bungalows.

Both cities, though, have long-established areas like this that tend toward the high end of the price range. The homes have the usual drawbacks that go along with being old and gorgeous—few bathrooms and closets, frequent maintenance problems, and sometimes questionable plumbing and electrical unless they've been updated. A good building inspector can find a lot of this before you buy.

Both cities also have older homes in areas that are up-and-coming and therefore more affordable. Because these areas can shift over time, it's best to contact someone you know, or an agent, to find out what's hot when you're searching.

Keep in mind that the big-city school districts, while improving, are not necessarily the best in the area.

Lofts

Lofts in the heart of the action are easy to find in both cities. In Dallas, Deep Ellum is one place to look. While the city's music and nightclub scene can be rowdy and the area a little rough around the edges, this is a hot spot for restaurants, shops, and general coolness. Both apartments and warehouse-style spaces—wide-open traditional lofts—are for sale and for rent.

In Fort Worth, the loft market is relatively new, and nearly all of it is downtown or nearby. The homes here tend more toward condos than rentals, and are usually high-end spaces with quality finishes—lovely condos with mind-blowing views all the way to Dallas, for example, are on the market.

New Homes, Tract Houses

These are largely in the suburbs. The ones nearer Dallas will almost always be more expensive. A lot of developments have open space (required in some cities), with swimming pools and jogging trails a part of the package, often with an annual homeowners association fee.

The developments range from opulent and large custom homes (in Southlake, for example) to the suburban cookie cutter feel. But sometimes the tradeoff for tract housing is worth it—in Keller, for example, an elementary school sits right in the middle of one such development, which makes life a lot easier on everyone in the family.

New Urbanism

The mixed retail/residential concept, a kind of urban re-creation of small-town life, has proven successful in several places: Southlake Town Square (www.southlaketownsquare.com), between Dallas and Fort Worth, and Frisco Square (www.friscosquare.com), almost due north of Dallas, are two. While developers had originally thought they'd attract empty nesters, families are also finding these appealing.

The vision was European-style open-air strolling, shopping, and eating, and it's happening. Both developments contain city halls and libraries, along with tons of shopping and restaurants, and in Frisco's case, a couple of museums. In Southlake, the homes are "brownstones," essentially townhome-style condos, and Frisco also has townhomes and plans apartments.

Both developments plan a variety of festivals and fairs throughout the year with live music, family activities, and booths selling food and artisans' wares.

Visit this Web site for links and information educating you on setting up your water account, finding child care and hospitals, automobile tags, property taxes, churches, and much more. There's a glossy, full-color *Newcomer's Guide* available, too.

GRAPEVINE CHAMBER OF COMMERCE
www.grapevinechamber.org
From this site, you can order a relocation packet that will be sent within 10 days.

KELLER CHAMBER OF COMMERCE
www.kellerchamber.com/keller-info
Here's how to find all information about neighborhoods, city services, schools, and organizations in Keller.

SOUTHLAKE CHAMBER OF COMMERCE
www.southlakechamber.com/southlake-relocation.aspx
This Web site provides extensive information regarding utilities, garbage and recycling services, schools, voter registration, child care, health care, churches, and organizations.

RELOCATION SPECIALISTS

COLDWELL BANKER DFW
Relocation Services
2801 Gateway Dr., Suite 180, Irving
(800) 527-7028
www.cbdfw.com/relocate/services.asp
Among the biggest firms in Dallas–Fort Worth, this one employs a team of certified relocation specialists.

EBBY HALLIDAY REALTORS
(972) 980-6600
www.ebby.com/relocation/moving.shtml
One of the oldest firms in Dallas has offices all over the Metroplex, with lots of relocation help available.

AREA SUPPORT GROUPS

Adjusting to life in a new city can be tricky, especially if you're dealing with special issues. Here are support groups that may prove helpful to you as you settle into your new home, and beyond.

ALCOHOLICS ANONYMOUS
(214) 887-6699
www.aadallas.org
(817) 332-3533
www.fortworthaa.org

AL-ANON FAMILY GROUPS
(214) 363-0461
www.dallasal-anon.org, www.texas-al-anon
.org/ftworth

DIABETES SUPPORT GROUP OF DALLAS
(972) 566-7106

EATING DISORDER GROUP
(214) 345-2791

GILDA'S CLUB NORTH TEXAS
(214) 219-8877

HIV POSITIVE SUPPORT GROUP
(214) 520-6308
(817) 336-2492

PET GRIEF COUNSELING SUPPORT GROUP
(214) 461-5131
www.gildasclubtx.com

SENIOR SCENE AND RETIREMENT

The Dallas–Fort Worth area isn't one typically chosen as a retirement destination. A lot of people who relocate for retirement choose areas with less urban surroundings, and those choosing Texas typically move to destinations several hours south of Dallas–Fort Worth, such as San Antonio, the Hill Country, or the Rio Grande Valley. That said, there are some very nice retirement communities in North Texas and excellent activity centers for senior citizens.

Dallas Area
Retirement Communities
CARUTH HAVEN COURT
5585 Caruth Haven Lane, Dallas
(214) 368-8545
www.caruthhavencourt.com
Here is possibly Dallas's most desirable assisted-living community. Sitting at the edge of the Park Cities, just off of North Central Expressway, Caruth Haven Court has one-bedroom apartments, small suites, a pretty dining room, a full menu of services, and a whirlpool spa. Among activities are lunch outings to restaurants, daily exercise classes, excursions to plays and musicals, and bridge and bingo games.

EDGEMERE
Northwest Highway at Thackery in Dallas
(214) 265-9100
www.edgemeredallas.com
This is your destination if you're looking for an upscale, resort-style community. Spreading over 16 acres, it's for people age 62 and older and offers a residential section with an emphasis on wellness and activity with lots of services and events. It's also a place with assisted living and private nursing available.

GRACE PRESBYTERIAN VILLAGE
550 East Ann Arbor Dr., Dallas
(214) 376-1701
www.gracepresbyterianvillage.org
Since 1962, this has been one of the premier retirement facilities in Dallas. In a setting of 27 woodsy acres in Oak Cliff, this faith-based community offers residential cottages, garden homes, and apartments; assisted living with nursing and rehab services; and qualified care for residents with Alzheimer's and dementia. Ample activities are planned for those who want to take advantage of such.

Senior Centers
Many activity centers for senior citizens are administered by city parks and recreation departments. You can usually count on finding various programs to keep active residents, typically over 60 years old, moving and stimulated. Activities range from yoga, stretching, and aerobic exercise classes to music, dance, or arts and crafts, as well as weekly or monthly social gatherings, like potluck lunch or supper. It's a great way for older residents to stay socially and physically active, and most activities are free or bear a very small charge.

ALLEN SENIOR RECREATION CENTER
451 East St. Mary, Allen
(214) 509-4820
www.cityofallen.org

CEDAR CREST SENIOR CENTER
1007 Hutchins Rd., Dallas
(214) 819-2000

GARLAND SENIOR ACTIVITY CENTER
600 West Ave. A, Garland
(972) 205-2769
www.ci.garland.tx.us

GOODBAR SENIOR CENTER
3000 Concord, Mesquite
(972) 279-6881
www.cityofmesquite.com

MCKINNEY SENIOR RECREATION CENTER
1400 South College, McKinney
(972) 547-7491
www.mckinneytexas.org

PLANO SENIOR CENTER
401 West Sixteenth St., Plano
(972) 941-7155
www.plano.gov

RICHARD HSU ACTIVITIES CENTER
2129 East Arapaho Rd., Richardson
(214) 819-2000

SENIOR CENTER AT FRISCO SQUARE
6670 Moore St., Frisco
(972) 292-6550
www.friscofun.org

🔍 Close-up

Volunteering

Retirees who want to give back to the community through volunteering have hundreds of options. Whether it's serving as a "grandparent" to a child, using carpentry skills, or greeting people at Dallas/Fort Worth International Airport, you're bound to find a good fit.

Here are some of the biggest programs and clearinghouses for volunteer opportunities:

Dallas/Fort Worth International Airport Ambassadors

The airport's Ambassadors are especially visible. They help passengers find connecting flights or baggage claim; provide current information about hotels and attractions; offer translation services for international visitors; and just about anything else. They've been known to provide Band-Aids for a hurt finger, and will go out of their way to find someone to help if they don't have an answer themselves.

Ambassadors attend three hours of orientation, plus classroom and on-the-job training, and receive a manual. They're asked to work at least one four-hour shift a week and make a yearlong commitment. Ambassadors get free airport parking and have social events and field trips.

For information, call the Ambassador manager at (972) 574-1492 or go to www.dfwairport .com/ambassadors.

RSVP

A major clearinghouse for senior volunteer opportunities, the Senior Source's RSVP is linked to almost 200 nonprofit agencies in the area. They'll match volunteers 55 and older with jobs they want. Some examples: staffing a holiday train at a mall; working at the Texas State Fair; disaster response; ushering at a children's theater; tutoring; making small home repairs; serving as museum guides and docents; building computers for the disabled or impaired; bulk mailing; and stuffing goody bags.

RSVP provides free supplemental liability insurance for its volunteers.

For more information, call the RSVP director at (214) 823-5700 or go to www.seniorsource .org.

Volunteer Center North Texas

This nonprofit clearinghouse has been operating for almost 40 years, making nearly 80,000 volunteer referrals a year. It has more than 1,000 member agencies. Volunteers can register online and browse a list of projects.

An example of the selection: administrative help at the Salvation Army; help with a variety of needs including child care, a baby supplies drive, GED instruction, and mentoring young moms at Alley's House, an organization that helps teenage mothers; helping at the American Airlines C. R. Smith Museum; transporting blood for the American Red Cross; working with hospice; animal care; business consulting; and many more. The list numbers in the hundreds.

For more information, call (214) 826-6767 or go to www.volunteernorthtexas.org.

Hospitals

Most area hospitals need volunteers to greet, answer phones, work with children, or staff information desks. Contact the hospital you're interested in for more information.

Museums

Many area museums recruit volunteers, both skilled and unskilled, to help. For example, the Dallas Museum of Nature and Science looks for volunteers to work with children, demonstrate science experiments, and help with clerical work, as well as skilled individuals with paleontology backgrounds to work with fossils.

City Government

Cities also need volunteers. The city of Fort Worth has a Citizens Fire Academy in which residents take courses to learn more about how the department works; and a Code Rangers program, in which residents are trained to recognize and report suspected code violations in their neighborhoods. Dallas's ServiceWorks! program places volunteers in every department, doing office work, landscaping, customer service, research, and other jobs.

Information: For Fort Worth Citizens Fire Academy, call (817) 392-6862; Code Rangers, (817) 392-6574.

The Dallas ServiceWorks! program uses Volunteer North Texas to find volunteers, or you can call the city at (214) 670-3579.

Animal Shelters

Operation Kindness, a large no-kill shelter in Carrollton, always needs volunteers to clean cages, walk dogs, help train dogs, help with fund-raising, enter data, and more. Information: (972) 481-PAWS or www.operationkindness.org.

The Humane Society of North Texas, with two Fort Worth locations, looks for volunteers to work at least four hours per month. The volunteer enrollment fee is $25. The shelter also places pets in foster homes and needs volunteers for special events.

Information: (817) 332-4768, ext. 119, or www.hsnt.org.

AARP Create the Good

The American Association of Retired Person's Web site at www.createthegood.org will search your zip code for opportunities. If transportation is a problem, this site is a good choice, since it finds nearby opportunities. Some that turned up in the DFW area in a search: tax aid; teaching people how to prepare for emergencies; teaching fraud prevention; repairing medical equipment for hospice patients; grant writing; helping with a fund-raising barbecue; and helping with a fund-raising chili cook-off.

Volunteer Match

Another Internet service, Volunteer Match (www.volunteermatch.com) also lets you search by zip code, and will come up with still more opportunities. Some of them included art therapist; advisor to people with intellectual and developmental disabilities; cooking meals for HIV/AIDS patients; helping at a regional conference for foster teens; and bringing pets to hospice patients.

Fort Worth Area

Retirement Communities

JAMES L. WEST CENTER
1111 Summit Ave., Fort Worth
(817) 877-1199
www.jameslwest.com
On the edge of downtown, this nonprofit residential center and adult day program for seniors specializes in care for those with Alzheimer's and related dementia. Activities and programming are extensive, with the goal of keeping residents and clients involved, comfortable, and confident.

TRINITY TERRACE
1600 Texas St., Fort Worth
(817) 338-2400
www.retirement.org
This complex of high-rise apartment homes on the edge of downtown overlooks the Trinity River. Residents can choose between independent living, extended living, and skilled nursing care. All residents can take advantage of temporary stays in the Health Care Center, too, when necessary. The Recreation Department keeps a full schedule of activities ready for the taking.

WATERMERE
302 Watermere Dr., Southlake
(817) 748-8000
www.watermere-at-southlake.com
This new master-planned luxury, gated retirement community markets to residents 55 years and older. This is upscale living, with golf and tennis, clubhouse, walking trails, and beautiful landscaping surrounding villa homes and condos. Also on-site, the Isle at Watermere has assisted living with Alzheimer's and dementia care among specialties.

Senior Centers

Senior centers in the area offer various programs, often including yoga, aerobic exercise, music, dance, and arts and crafts, as well as weekly or monthly social gatherings, like potluck lunch or supper. In Hurst, regular activities include weekly dances (big band sound and country-western), exercise, line dance classes, bridge, ceramics, tai chi, china painting, tap dance, porcelain dolls, needlecraft, quilting, NARFE and AARP meetings, travel opportunities, special events, and field trips. In Euless, there's dominoes, billiards, shuffleboard, and cards every day. And that's just a sampling. Activities are typically free of charge or bear a minimal fee.

ARLINGTON SENIOR CENTER
1000 Eunice St., Arlington
(817) 277-8091

BEDFORD/HURST SENIOR CENTER
2817 R. D. Hurt Parkway, Bedford
(817) 952-2325

COLLEYVILLE SENIOR CENTER
2512 Glade Rd., Colleyville
(817) 283-7648

FORT WORTH SENIOR CENTER
8211 White Settlement Rd., Fort Worth
(817) 246-6619

GRAPEVINE SENIOR ACTIVITIES CENTER
421 Church St., Grapevine
(817) 410-8130

KELLER SENIOR ACTIVITIES CENTER
660 Johnson Rd., Keller
(817) 743-4370

SIMMONS SENIOR CENTER
508 Simmons Dr., Euless
(817) 685-1670

EDUCATION AND CHILD CARE

Finding places to gain an education in North Texas couldn't be easier. The menu of colleges and universities in and around Dallas and Fort Worth suits any and all appetites for learning, with hundreds of options ranging from associates' degrees to doctorates.

The list of more recognized university names starts with Southern Methodist University in Dallas, initially founded in 1911 by the Texas Educational Commission, which was composed of representatives from the five annual conferences of the Methodist Episcopal Church, South, in Texas. Perkins School of Theology is among SMU's attractions, too. It opened with an enrollment of 706 in 1915 and is now a beautiful collection of 73 buildings, enrolling 9,000 students.

Thirty-odd miles west in Fort Worth, Texas Christian University grew from Add-Ran College, founded in 1873. In 1914, Brite College of the Bible was added at TCU, and it remains a popular entity called Brite Divinity School.

The two universities competed in athletic contests in the old Southwest Conference for several decades; today, SMU competes in Conference USA and TCU is in the Mountain West Conference. Students interested in nursing, nutrition, ranch management, and theology will find TCU a good fit, and those looking at dance, fine arts, and theology will like SMU. Both schools have exceptional MBA programs, and SMU is known for its law school, as well.

The University of Texas at Arlington went through a boom in the 1970s, making it a place that now provides exceptional education in architecture, biomedical engineering, social work, nursing, and international studies. Other specialized programs in the area include the law school at Texas Wesleyan University in Fort Worth; music, interior design, and hotel and restaurant management at the University of North Texas in Denton; and education degrees at the Univeristy of North Texas and Texas Woman's University in Denton.

Several of the public school systems for kids in kindergarten through 12th grade have earned high marks. If you're in the market for a private school education for your child, your choices are numerous among parochial schools. And when it's time to put the little one into child care, some excellent choices await parents who want socialization and preliminary educational stimulus for their toddlers and preschoolers.

HIGHER EDUCATION

Major Colleges and Universities

SOUTHERN METHODIST UNIVERSITY
6425 Boaz Lane, Dallas
(214) 768-2000
www.smu.edu

With a gorgeous campus of Georgian redbrick buildings in the elite neighborhood of University Park, this private school with about 11,000 students offers undergraduate, graduate, and professional programs through seven schools, specifically humanities and sciences; business; the performing, visual, and communication arts; engineering; education and human development; law; and theology. Additional campuses are in Plano and Taos, New Mexico. Of special interest is the statistic that SMU's 10 libraries house the largest private collection of research materials in the Southwest; SMU was recently ranked in Forbes magazine as the 13th best university in the United States; and it houses a superior collection of Spanish art at the internationally acclaimed Meadows Museum. Founded in 1911,

SMU is nonsectarian in its teaching. SMU's athletic teams are the Mustangs.

TEXAS CHRISTIAN UNIVERSITY
2800 South University Dr., Fort Worth
(817) 257-7000
www.tcu.edu
A private university founded in 1873, TCU has an enrollment of 8,700 students pursuing studies in 116 undergraduate, 16 graduate, and 13 doctoral areas. The student-faculty ratio is 14:1. The campus spreads around University Drive on the near south side of town and across the 106-acre area called Worth Hills, which was once a golf course but is now taken up by various athletic fields and the wonderful TCU tennis center. Among interesting specialty areas is the Starpoint School, a speech and hearing clinic and school for elementary children with learning disabilities. The Horned Frog football team, which won major championships in the 1920s, 1930s, and 1950s, has become a top-ranked entity again in the 21st century. Among choice scholastic disciplines is communications study at the Schieffer School of Journalism, named for honored J-school grad, Bob Schieffer.

TEXAS WESLEYAN UNIVERSITY
1201 Wesleyan St., Fort Worth
(817) 531-4444
www.txwes.edu
Founded in 1890 in Fort Worth, this Methodist liberal arts and sciences school offers a Weekend/Evening Program and a law school, the latter fully accredited by the American Bar Association. Texas Wesleyan had about 3,200 students enrolled in 2009.

TEXAS WOMAN'S UNIVERSITY
304 Administration Dr., Denton
(940) 898-2000
www.twu.edu
The nation's largest university primarily for women, TWU offers programs in business, education, and general studies at Denton, Dallas, and Houston campuses and online. Enrollment totals about 12,500, with more new nurse and health care graduates than any school in Texas. While the university has admitted men since 1972, its mission originally was and still is "to provide a liberal education and to prepare young women 'for the practical industries of the age' with a specialized education."

UNIVERSITY OF DALLAS
845 East Northgate Dr., Irving
(800) 628-6999; (972) 721-5266
www.udallas.edu
A private, Catholic liberal arts college founded in 1956, this elite school has an enrollment of about 1,300 undergraduate and 1,700 graduate students from numerous states and countries. Classes are small, and degree programs are offered in several disciplines. There were 10 National Merit Scholars in the 2008 freshman class, and the university has a Phi Beta Kappa chapter.

UNIVERSITY OF NORTH TEXAS
1155 Union Circle, Denton
(940) 565-2000
www.unt.edu
About 30 miles north of Dallas and Fort Worth, UNT distinguishes itself as one of just nine public universities in the country enrolling more than 4,000 Hispanics and 4,000 African Americans among its total of 33,300. Among honors is a recent citation by the *Princeton Review*, which named UNT a "Best in the West" college. The university offers 97 bachelor's, 101 master's, and 49 doctoral degree programs within the university's 11 colleges and schools. The music school is among the best in the nation, giving rise to the renowned One O'Clock Lab Band, an honored jazz ensemble. Among other prestigious schools within UNT is the College of Visual Arts and Design, with progams in Communication Design and Interior Design.

UNIVERSITY OF NORTH TEXAS HEALTH SCIENCE CENTER
3500 Camp Bowie Blvd., Fort Worth
(817) 735-2000
www.hsc.unt.edu
The UNT Health Science Center sits on 33 acres in the Fort Worth Cultural District and houses the

University Newspapers

The larger universities in the Dallas–Fort Worth area publish good newspapers that give you a view into university life and concerns. Among the papers to read are:

The Shorthorn covers the University of Texas at Arlington. During the fall and spring semesters, it publishes Tuesday through Friday and twice a week, Tuesday and Thursday, in summer. Interestingly, the paper's 65 to 70 staffers come from about 20 different majors. Circulation is about 25,000.

The *SMU Daily Campus* publishes Tuesday through Thursday and select Fridays and Saturdays during the fall and Tuesday through Friday in spring. Circulation is about 5,000.

The *TCU Daily Skiff*, sponsored by the Schieffer School of Journalism, publishes Tuesday through Friday in fall and spring, with a circulation of about 6,000.

Texas College of Osteopathic Medicine; Department of Physician Assistant Studies; Graduate School of Biomedical Sciences; School of Public Health; and School of Health Professions. *U.S. News & World Report* has ranked the Texas College of Osteopathic Medicine one of the top medical schools in the nation for primary care for eight consecutive years. More than 1,200 students are enrolled.

UNIVERSITY OF TEXAS AT ARLINGTON
701 South Nedderman Dr., Arlington
(817) 272-2011
www.uta.edu
A booming school with 25,000 students and a richly diverse enrollment, UTA offers 180 bachelor's,

master's and doctoral degrees within 10 colleges and schools. UTA went through impressive growth in the 1970s, when the school's four colleges were joined by the Institute of Urban Studies and schools of social work, architecture and environmental design, and nursing, each of which generates its own undergraduate and graduate programs. UTA's School of Architecture offers hands-on training, internships, international exchange programs, and bachelor's degrees in architecture and interior design and master's degrees in architecture and landscape architecture.

UNIVERSITY OF TEXAS AT DALLAS
800 West Campbell Rd., Richardson
(972) 883-2111
www.utdallas.edu
UTD offers more than 125 academic programs across its seven schools, with undergraduate and graduate programs found in Arts and Humanities; Behavioral and Brain Sciences; Economic, Political, and Policy Sciences; Engineering and Computer Science; Interdisciplinary Studies; Management; and Natural Sciences and Mathematics. Enrollment is about 15,000 students.

Theology

DALLAS THEOLOGICAL SEMINARY
3909 Swiss Ave., Dallas
(800) DTS-WORD
www.dts.edu
Begun in 1924, this nondenominational Bible college has grown from 13 students to an enrollment of 2,050 today. This seminary was a pioneer in creating a four-year course for a master's degree in theology. As it's grown, the school offers courses in practical theology, missions, church history, Christian education, and much more. Find it in the beautiful old historic neighborhood in East Dallas, near downtown.

SOUTHWESTERN BAPTIST THEOLOGICAL SEMINARY
2001 West Seminary Dr., Fort Worth
(817) 429-4971
www.swbts.edu

Grown from Baylor University's theology department, the school was founded in 1907 at the Baylor University campus in Waco but moved to its present home in 1910 and operates under the Southern Baptist Convention. Much like a university in its function, it's divided into three schools, those of theology, educational ministries, and church music, each offering its own degree programs and staffed by its own faculty. Well more than 40,000 graduates have been sent into the world of worship and ministry.

Community Colleges

DALLAS COUNTY COMMUNITY COLLEGE
1601 South Lamar St., Dallas
(214) 378-1824
www.dcccd.edu
County-wide, this school system enrolls more than 64,000 students on seven campuses—Brookhaven, Cedar Valley, Eastfield, El Centro, Mountain View, North Lake, and Richland. An associate degree is awarded in more than 100 career programs. Among the more popular choices is the culinary arts program at the El Centro campus in downtown Dallas.

TARRANT COUNTY COLLEGE
1500 Houston St., Fort Worth
(817) 515-8223
www.tccd.edu
More than 37,000 students are enrolled in TCC's associate degree and technical programs at five campuses, including those in Hurst, northwest and south Fort Worth, Arlington, and the Trinity River Campus in downtown Fort Worth. There are three degrees offered, including the Associate of Arts, Associate of Arts in Teaching, and Associate of Applied Science.

PUBLIC SCHOOLS

Dallas Area

DALLAS INDEPENDENT SCHOOL DISTRICT
3700 Ross Ave., Dallas
(214) 841-4941
www.dallasisd.org

The nation's 12th-largest school district enrolls more than 160,000 students and employs 19,000. Dallas's diversity is reflected in the total student body, which speaks nearly 70 different languages at home.

FRISCO INDEPENDENT SCHOOL DISTRICT
6942 Maple St., Frisco
(469) 633-6000
www.friscoisd.org
Among the fastest-growing school districts in the state with a growth rate of up to 30 percent annually for the past decade, Frisco has about 34,000 students and adds two to six new schools each year. The district covers 75 square miles and serves residents of Frisco, some parts of Plano, McKinney and Little Elm, and people in parts of Collin and Denton County.

HIGHLAND PARK INDEPENDENT SCHOOL DISTRICT
7015 Westchester Dr., Dallas
(214) 780-3000
www.hpisd.org
This district has 6,300 students in an area encompassing one high school, one middle school, one intermediate school, and four elementary schools. The prestigious high school was listed among top high schools in the nation in a 2008 *Newsweek* report. About 98 percent of graduates pursue a college education. The school district serves only residents in the cities of Highland Park and University Park, where school tax rates are very high.

LEWISVILLE INDEPENDENT SCHOOL DISTRICT
1800 Timber Creek Rd., Flower Mound
(469) 713-5200
www.lisd.net
More than 50,000 students go to schools in a 127-square-mile district, and the district grows by up to 2,000 students annually. LISD serves all of or portions of 13 municipalities, including Argyle, Carrollton, Copper Canyon, Double Oak, Flower Mound, Frisco, Grapevine, Highland Village, Hebron, Lewisville, Plano, and The Colony.

PLANO INDEPENDENT SCHOOL DISTRICT
2700 West Fifteenth St., Plano
(469) 752-8100
www.pisd.edu
Plano ISD covers 66 square miles and has 69 schools altogether with an enrollment of more than 54,000.

RICHARDSON INDEPENDENT SCHOOL DISTRICT
400 South Greenville Ave., Richardson
(469) 593-0000
www.richardson.k12.tx.us
This northern Dallas County district covers almost 39 square miles and enrolls more than 34,000 students in four high schools, eight junior high schools, one freshman center, 41 elementary schools, and one alternative-learning center. About 90 percent of graduates attend college.

Fort Worth Area

ARLINGTON INDEPENDENT SCHOOL DISTRICT
1203 West Pioneer Parkway, Arlington
(682) 867-4611
www.aisd.net
Arlington's ISD enrolls more than 63,000 students in 74 schools, including nine high schools, 13 junior high schools, and 52 elementary schools. It's the eighth-largest district in Texas.

FORT WORTH INDEPENDENT SCHOOL DISTRICT
100 North University Dr., Fort Worth
(817) 871-2000
www.fortworthisd.org
There are nearly 80,000 students in 80 elementary schools, 24 middle schools and sixth-grade centers, 13 high schools, and 27 special campuses.

GRAPEVINE-COLLEYVILLE INDEPENDENT SCHOOL DISTRICT
3051 Ira E. Woods Ave., Grapevine
(817) 251-5200
www.gcisd-k12.org

Covering more than 54 square miles, the Grapevine-Colleyville ISD offers 17 traditional schools and two alternative campuses, with a total attendance of about 14,000 students. There are 11 elementary schools, four middle schools, two high schools, two alternative schools, and one early childhood development center. The high school graduation rate is 95 percent.

i The TAKS or Texas Assessment of Knowledge and Skills test is taken by students in grades 3 through 11 and is a requirement for promotion at some levels and in some subjects. A bill passed by the state legislature mandates that new, end of course exams be taken starting in the 2011 to 2012 school year. For more information about these tests, go to www.tea.state.tx.us.

HURST-EULESS-BEDFORD INDEPENDENT SCHOOL DISTRICT
1849 Central Dr., Bedford
(817) 283-4461
www.hebisd.edu
The district serves the city of Bedford, most of the cities of Euless and Hurst, and small parts of North Richland Hills, Colleyville, Fort Worth, and Arlington. The district operates 19 elementary schools, five junior high schools, and two high schools, enrolling about 20,000 students total. Diversity is big here, as students speak more than 60 different languages at home. This community has one of the largest Tongan populations outside of the South Pacific.

KELLER INDEPENDENT SCHOOL DISTRICT
350 Keller Parkway, Keller
(817) 744-1000
www.kellerisd.net
Here's another of the rapidly growing school districts: Keller ISD's enrollment has more than doubled over the past decade and will likely grow from the current 30,000 students to 40,000 students in the coming decade. There are 35 campuses serving a 51-square-mile area including all of Keller and parts of Colleyville, Fort Worth, Haltom City, Hurst, North Richland Hills,

Close-up

Public School Funding and Testing

Big-city public school districts have their struggles everywhere, and the DFW area is no different. Parents will want to educate themselves about the schools before deciding where to live.

Both the Dallas and Fort Worth independent school districts have had their share of problems, but they both also have pockets of excellence. Size-wise, enrollment in the Dallas district in 2009 was about 157,000, in the Fort Worth district about 80,000. Generally speaking, locals consider schools in the surrounding suburbs a better bet—and they do get higher ratings in state accountability reports. Enrollments there tend to run 15,000 and under. Keep in mind that there are hundreds of dedicated and hardworking Texas teachers who are very good at what they do. Generally, the heart of the problem is considered to be the state's school funding formulas.

Understanding the state of Texas public education funding requires a bit of background. You may or may not realize that Texas has no state income tax, which helps fund schools in some states. Here, school funding comes instead from property tax revenue, plus state and federal dollars. The original mix, back when Texas school funding was first put together in 1949, was 80 percent state, 20 percent local.

As the years passed, court decisions and time changed school funding, and eventually some inequalities emerged—in a nutshell, richer districts had vastly better schools, while teachers literally were bringing in their own toilet paper in some of the poorest areas. In 1993, the famed "Robin Hood" legislation was passed to fix all of that. The biggest bone of contention was the part of Robin Hood that said state financial aid was provided to a district inversely to the district's wealth—the state divided up property tax money so that every district didn't get all it generated in tax revenue. It was instead—like the money Robin Hood took from the rich—given to the poorer districts, with a lot of formulas and tax caps that were designed to keep things on a more equal footing.

You can imagine the wealthier districts were none too pleased, and some districts had to tax at the highest possible rate allowed just to keep the lights on. In 2005 a judge decided kids weren't getting the kind of education the Texas Constitution called for, and threw the whole thing out.

Some changes have taken place since then, and lots of improvement as measured by test scores, although the schools are still a favorite topic to complain about. Funding is still shared, though the state has taken a much larger percentage of the load, increasing cigarette and alcohol taxes and allocating all surplus funds to schools.

Several Dallas schools were named No Child Left Behind–Blue Ribbon Schools in 2009, a national designation for public and private schools that are either academically superior compared to others in the state, or show dramatic, consistent improvement in student

Southlake, Watauga, and Westlake. There are 21 elementary schools, five intermediate and five middle schools, and five high schools.

SOUTHLAKE CARROLL INDEPENDENT SCHOOL DISTRICT
3051 Dove Rd., Grapevine
(817) 949-8222
www.southlakecarroll.edu

A multitude of state awards has gone to Carroll ISD, which offers 11 schools serving nearly 8,000 students. There are five elementary schools, two intermediate schools, two middle schools, and two high schools. Roughly 98 percent of graduating seniors go to college. The football program has been enormously successful, winning several state titles in recent years.

achievement. (None of the other area schools were on that year's list, although many have been in the past.) The 2009 schools recognized were George Bannerman Dealey International Academy, George Peabody Elementary, the School of Health Professions, and Victor H. Hexter Elementary.

On the state level, Texas measures school performance with the Texas Assessment of Knowledge and Skills test, the TAKS, which schoolchildren here dread almost as much as having their cell phones taken away. The individual school and district ratings are based on TAKS scores, which generates a whole book's worth of debate over teachers "teaching to the test." We're going to stay out of that, and instead pick some pertinent numbers to give you a rough idea of what some DFW-area districts are doing, test-wise. For very detailed reports on these scores sorted in all kinds of ways—by district, by region, by school, etc.—plus reams of other data on the schools, go to the Texas Education Agency's Web site, www.tea.state.tx.us.

Here's a snapshot of a few districts from the state's 2009 accountability reports, bearing in mind that some schools in the districts are not included for various reasons. What you don't see in the list is that overall the districts with the highest tax base are the ones that performed best on the TAKS. And, for context, state ratings break down this way: exemplary, 9.5 percent of schools; recognized, 37.2 percent; academically acceptable, 45.4 percent; and academically unacceptable, 7 percent. The TEA figures listed by district in alphabetical order (schools' individual ratings are also on the TEA Web site):

Arlington: Exemplary—6, Recognized—32, Academically acceptable—28, Academically unacceptable—2

Birdville: Exemplary—11, Recognized—11, Academically acceptable—9, Academically unacceptable—0

Carroll (Southlake area): Exemplary—all 11 schools

Coppell: Exemplary—11, Recognized—3, Academically acceptable—0, Academically unacceptable—0

Dallas: Exemplary—46, Recognized—82, Academically acceptable—73, Academically unacceptable—22

Fort Worth: Exemplary—12, Recognized—43, Academically acceptable—49, Academically unacceptable—12

Grapevine-Colleyville: Exemplary—10, Recognized—5, Academically acceptable—2, Academically unacceptable—0

Highland Park: Exemplary—all 7 schools

Hurst-Euless-Bedford: Exemplary—11, Recognized—14, Academically acceptable—1, Academically unacceptable—0

Irving: Exemplary—3, Recognized—14, Academically acceptable—14, Academically unacceptable—0

Keller: Exemplary—17, Recognized—15, Academically acceptable—2, Academically unacceptable—0

PRIVATE SCHOOLS

Dallas Area

EPISCOPAL SCHOOL OF DALLAS
4100 Merrell Rd., Dallas
(214) 358-4368
www.esdallas.org

A 30-year-old school, ESD has grown quickly into a prestigious college prep school. The main campus has 39 acres, a new stadium, and an arts and humanities center. AP courses are offered in English, calculus, statistics, biology, chemistry, physics, U.S. government, economics, U.S. history, European history, world history, Latin, Spanish, French, art history, studio art, 2D art, 3D art, music theory, and computer science.

HOCKADAY SCHOOL
11600 Welch Rd., Dallas
(214) 360-6311
www.hockaday.org

An all-girls school established in 1913 enrolls students from pre-K through 12th grades and includes a boarding school. The college prep school covers 100 acres in north Dallas and enrolls about 1,050 students.

ST. MARK'S OF TEXAS
10600 Preston Rd., Dallas
(214) 346-8000
www.smtexas.org

Established in 1906, this elite school for boys enrolls about 850 currently. Approximately 19 percent attend on scholarship; the school is competitive in scholastics and athletics.

Fort Worth Area

ALL SAINTS' EPISCOPAL SCHOOL
9700 Saints Circle, Fort Worth
(817) 560-5700
www.asesftw.org

A smaller private school, this one opened in 1951 and offers a 1:12 faculty-student ratio. Found on a 103-acre campus on the west side of town, All Saints enrolls more than 800 students, many of whom go on to school at Ivy League colleges. A full offering of athletics is found here.

FORT WORTH CHRISTIAN
7517 Bogart Dr., North Richland Hills
(817) 281-6504
www.fwc.org

Founded in 1958, this school enrolls nearly 900 students from pre-K through 12th grade, with students coming from 30 municipalities from across North Texas, including Keller, North Richland Hills, and Colleyville. Among special notes are the Campus Center, with two art rooms, music room, band room, strings room, and theater with stage, lights, sound, and projection; and full-time teachers directing band, orchestra, choir, art, and theater programs. Bible class and daily chapel services are part of the curriculum.

FORT WORTH COUNTRY DAY
4200 Country Day Lane, Fort Worth
(817) 732-7718
www.fwcds.org

This is the largest of the private schools in Tarrant County and possibly the most prestigious, with an enrollment of about 1,125. Kindergarten is a full-day program, and all students work with computers from that time. Middle school students work in community service at Habitat for Humanity, Tarrant Area Food Bank, and more. Upper school students are offered a full range of honors programs. Athletics offerings range from cross-country, hockey, volleyball, and lacrosse to basketball, football, baseball, and more.

GRACE PREPARATORY ACADEMY
3300 West I-20, Arlington
(817) 467-0057
www.graceprep.org

Grace Prep distinguishes itself as a Christian school employing a university-style schedule and a teaching approach that involves parents. Elementary students only attend classes on Tuesday and Thursday, and junior high and high school students attend on Monday, Wednesday, and Friday, spending the rest of the time with parents, who act as co-teachers under the school's direction. Character education is emphasized, along with scholastics, athletics, and clubs. Enrollment is about 450.

SOUTHWEST CHRISTIAN SCHOOL
6801 Dan Danciger Rd., Fort Worth
(817) 294-0350
7001 Benbrook Lake Dr., Fort Worth
(817) 294-9596

Founded in 1969, Southwest Christian enrolls more than 900 students on two campuses. Class sizes are small, and teaching is based on a Christian perspective. Athletics are plentiful.

TRINITY VALLEY SCHOOL
7500 Dutch Branch Rd., Fort Worth
(817) 321-0100
www.trinityvalleyschool.org

Since 1959, Trinity Valley has grown from 7 to 940 students. Today's campus covers 75 acres in southwest Fort Worth, with special offerings including Spanish and Chinese language classes for children in K through third grades; a full component of art, choir, and drama along with English, Latin, ability-driven mathematics, science, and social studies for middle schoolers; and a wide range of elective courses for students in upper school. Plenty of athletics are available, too.

CHILD CARE AND PRESCHOOLS

CRÈME DE LA CRÈME
6802 Colleyville Blvd., Colleyville
(817) 416-3683
www.cremedelacreme.com
An elite child-care center with educational activities, this one works well for families with working parents, as hours are from 6:30 a.m. until 6:30 p.m. Open to infants, toddlers, preschoolers, kindergarten students, and after-school care for ages 6 through 12, with programs in music, art, computer science, creative movement, and language. There's also a TV studio, gym, and library, along with tennis, basketball, soccer, climbing wall, and playground. Other North Texas locations are found in Frisco, Coppell, Plano, and Allen.

DALLAS MONTESSORI ACADEMY
5757 Samuell Blvd., Dallas
(214) 388-0091
www.dallasmontessori.com
Family activities are valued along with education at this school for students from preschool age through eighth grade. Through the year, events include a Fall Festival, Spring Festival, Teacher's Appreciation Luncheon, Grandparents' Day, and Dad's Breakfast.

NORTHAVEN CO-OPERATIVE PRESCHOOL
11211 Preston Rd., Dallas
(214) 691-7666
northavencoop.com
A high level of parental involvement keeps tuition down at this accredited early childhood program. In participating in the co-op, parents help out in every level of operation. The school serves kids ages two to five.

PRIMROSE
www.primroseschools.com
There are 39 preschool locations in the DFW area, all using an accredited "balanced learning" program. Children can be as young as six weeks and be as old as five years in the child-care program and may be as old as twelve in the after-school program. Safety and first aid are priorities, too.

WHITE ROCK NORTH SCHOOL
9727 White Rock Trail, Dallas
(214) 348-7410
www.whiterocknorthschool.com
Enrollment is for infants through sixth grade. For students there are courses in language arts, including grade school accelerated reading programs; mathematics; science; information technology, with a fully equipped computer lab; social sciences; environmental education; health/safety/physical education; and fine arts, including music, art, drama, and dance. There's a summer swim program, too.

HEALTH CARE AND WELLNESS

If you find yourself in need of top-rate medical care, you'll be glad you're in the Dallas–Fort Worth area. Recent research from the University of North Texas's Center for Economic Development and Research in Denton shows that the health care industry keeps the metroplex economy strong, employing nearly 170,000 people with a $4.1 billion annual payroll. What's more, the health care industry generates more than $13 billion in volume here, accounting for more than 10 percent of the area's gross product.

Across the North Texas area you'll find nearly three-dozen general-care hospitals and a vast number of outpatient clinics with the most advanced technology available. In fact, it's the fine medical care and readily available research that help give Dallas–Fort Worth its superior standard of living. Specialties for which is the area is known include trauma and burn treatment, advanced cardiac care, cancer care and treatment, spine care and surgery, neuroscience and surgery, and cosmetic surgery.

The North Texas medical and health community ranks among the nation's strongest, due in part to the presence in Dallas of the prestigious University of Texas Southwestern Medical School, which claims four Nobel laureates. On the UT Southwestern campus, there's Zale Lipshy University Hospital, a highly specialized private adult referral hospital offering up-to-the-minute research in medical applications to patients. Nearly 70 percent of dentists practicing in the Dallas–Fort Worth area are graduates of the Baylor College of Dentistry, an institution established in 1905, which also offers a prestigious school for dental hygiene training.

Hospitals in Dallas and Fort Worth known for pediatric care are Children's Medical Center of Dallas and Texas Scottish Rite Hospital for Children (Dallas) and Cook Children's (Fort Worth), with specialties ranging from cancer treatment to open-heart surgery to reconstructive surgery. All three of these hospitals have undergone impressive growth in recent years, with newly constructed facilities accommodating a huge number of patients.

You can find large and small group practices and single practitioners, whether you need treatment for asthma, depression, eczema, or thyroid problems. The local medical societies are sources of information and assistance. The Dallas County Medical Society, which was established in 1876, counts local physicians, medical students, and residents among members. Part of its work concerns addressing public health issues, including immunizations, preventing obesity, and supporting smoke-free cities. Society physicians are known nationally for their research on weighty matters such as Gulf War syndrome and Alzheimer's disease. If you're looking for a doctor, the local leading referral systems are found at the medical societies. Search the Dallas County Medical Society physician finder at www.dallas-cms.org/finder/physicianfinder.cfm and the Tarrant County Medical Society's system at www.tcms.org. If you know someone who needs but cannot afford medical care, check with Project Access Dallas, a volunteer system of 700 physicians and partner hospitals and labs that will help. You can learn more by visiting www.projectaccess.info.

Staying fit is a snap, thanks to weather that stays mild most of the time. In addition to an increasing number of parks with fitness trails, there are fitness centers on almost every corner. If you like running or walking, biking, in-line skating, playing racquetball or tennis, participating in aerobic classes, or lifting weights, there are lots of workout options available near your home or business.

HOSPITALS AND HEALTH CARE

Dallas Area

BAYLOR HEALTH CARE SYSTEMS
(800) 4BAYLOR
www.baylorhealth.com
Since 1903, this nonprofit hospital system offers 21 facilities at day-surgery centers, hospitals, primary-care centers, senior-care centers, fitness centers, imaging centers, rehabilitation centers, and more all over the Dallas–Fort Worth area. Through the Web site, you can find a physician or treatment for any sort of ailment or malady. There's a full schedule of classes and wellness events for the public, as well.

CHILDREN'S MEDICAL CENTER
1935 Medical District Dr., Dallas
(214) 456-7000
www.childrens.com
Dallas is blessed to have one of the largest and most respected pediatric health centers in the entire country. It's the only academic health care center in North Texas devoted to the care of children from birth to age 18, covering everything from eye exams and sewing up split chins to treating heart disease, cancer, and cystic fibrosis. This is also a major center for kidney, liver, intestine, heart, and bone marrow transplants for children. Connected to the prestigious University of Texas Southwestern Medical Center, this hospital has extensive therapy and after-care programs. There are 483 beds in the hospital and a Level I trauma center. There's also a new Children's Medical Center at Legacy (Plano), too.

i Parkland Hospital was named one of the best hospitals in the U.S by *U.S. News & World Report* for 2008.

METHODIST DALLAS MEDICAL CENTER
1441 North Beckley Ave., Dallas
(214) 947-8181
www.methodisthealthsystem.org
Begun as a 100-bed hospital in south Dallas overlooking 1924 downtown Dallas, Methodist has grown over the decades to be a multi-campus hospital now offering care not just in its original Oak Cliff area but also in Cedar Hill, Grand Prairie, Mansfield, Midlothian, and McKinney. Among specialties are a rehabilitation center for patients recovering from strokes or brain and spinal cord injuries; multi-trauma; neurological disorders; cardiopulmonary procedures; and complex orthopedic surgeries.

TEXAS HEALTH PRESBYTERIAN HOSPITAL DALLAS
8200 Walnut Hill Lane
(214) 345-6789
texashealth.org
Presbyterian Hospital dates from 1966 and became part of the Texas Health group in 2008. A contemporary complex in North Dallas, it has 866 beds and 1,200-plus physicians on staff, offering care in specialty areas such as cancer, cardiovascular, neurology, orthopedics, senior care, women's health, and pediatrics. Among innovative treatments at the hospital is a nonsurgical alternative to hysterectomy, which usually allows women to get back to their regular routines within seven to ten days—instead of six weeks. Among awards received, Texas Health Resources won the Best Employers for Healthy Lifestyles award from the National Business Group on Health. That means the hospital system promotes a healthy workplace and helps employees and their families make better choices about their health and well-being.

i Parkland Hospital in Dallas has a burn center, established in 1962, that has grown into one of the nation's largest civilian burn units. A 14-bed Burn Acute Care Unit and a nine-bed Burn ICU are among assets here. Nearly 1,000 burn victims are treated each year in Parkland's emergency department, and the ICU and Acute Care Unit will admit more than 500 pediatric and adult burn patients annually. Services extend to the whole family, including rehab and outpatient follow-up.

 **Close-up**

Susan G. Komen for the Cure

In the past few decades, Susan G. Komen has become nearly a household name across the nation. Possibly the most extraordinary of all cancer-fighting entities, Susan G. Komen for the Cure was established in 1982 by Dallasite Nancy Brinker in memory of her sister, Susan G. Komen, who died from breast cancer at age 36. From its inception that year, this Dallas-based pioneer in the breast cancer movement has invested more than $1 billion for the fight against breast cancer.

Shortly before she died, Susan G. Komen asked her younger sister, who was 33 at the time, to promise to find a way to stop this disease. Nancy G. Brinker—who has herself survived breast cancer since her sister's death—has done little else since giving her sister her word. Now Komen for the Cure exists as the planet's largest grassroots network of breast cancer survivors and activists, who work tirelessly to raise money to make sure there's quality care for everyone and that there's an ongoing effort to push the science community to find cures and save lives.

By 2002, Komen for the Cure had launched the Race for the Cure, a 5-kilometer run/walk, in more than 100 American cities to raise big money and create greater awareness for the fight against breast cancer. The events also celebrate breast cancer survivorship and honor everyone who has lost a battle with the disease. The year 2008 marked the 25th anniversary of the Susan G. Komen Race for the Cure, now the largest series of 5K events in the world, with more than one million participants just between 2005 and 2008.

Komen for the Cure reports important milestones resulting from its work, including impressive statistics:

- Nearly 75 percent of women over 40 years old now receive regular mammograms, the single most effective tool for detecting breast cancer early (in 1982, less than 30 percent received a clinical exam).

- The five-year survival rate for breast cancer, when caught early before it spreads beyond the breast, is now 98 percent (compared to 74 percent in 1982).

- The federal government now devotes more than $900 million each year to breast cancer research, treatment, and prevention (compared to $30 million in 1982).

- America's 2.5 million breast cancer survivors, the largest group of cancer survivors in the U.S., are a living testament to the power of society and science to save lives.

For details, visit www.komen.org.

TEXAS SCOTTISH RITE HOSPITAL
2222 Welborn St., Dallas
(214) 559-5000
www.tsrhc.org

Since 1921, Scottish Rite has been a leader among hospitals treating kids with orthopedic and other troubles, regardless of a family's ability to pay for care. Founded by a group of Texas Masons who wanted children with polio to receive care, Scottish Rite has become an outstanding provider of medical attention for kids with scoliosis, clubfoot, hand disorders, hip disorders, and limb length differences, along with certain neurological disorders and learning disorders, including dyslexia. More than 190,000 children have been treated here and more than 40,000 clinic visits are made annually by children. The hospital takes a multidisciplinary approach to care, tailoring treatment to the individual needs of each child and family. The hospital literally wrote the book on children's orthopedic care: the *Tachdjian's Pediatric Orthopaedics: From Texas Scottish Rite Hospital for Children*, now in its fourth edition, is a textbook considered the standard reference guide for orthopedic surgeons around the world.

UNIVERSITY OF TEXAS SOUTHWESTERN MEDICAL CENTER
5909 Harry Hines Blvd., Dallas
(214) 645-5555
www.utsouthwestern.org

UT Southwestern is a leader among American academic medical centers, care providers, and research facilities. Its stated mission is to improve health care here and across the country and to educate everyone in the medical community as to how to best utilize biomedical science and prevent disease and illness. Within the system are medical schools training nearly 4,400 medical, graduate, and other health students, residents, and fellows annually; federally and foundation-supported research projects numbering about 3,500 per year and costing $400 million annually; and a workforce of 10,400 to care for almost 97,000 hospitalized patients and 1.8 million outpatients each year. There are two hospitals, St. Paul's and Zale Lipshy, with UT Southwestern, along with dozens of clinics in every possible medical specialty. Although its size is massive, it's surprisingly user-friendly. Doctors and others in patient care use the same overall information system, so your care among myriad professionals is easy to track. What's more, you have access to your online file so that you can follow test results and appointments.

Fort Worth Area

BAYLOR ALL SAINTS
1400 Eighth Ave., Fort Worth
(817) 926-2544
www.baylorhealth.com

Opened in 1906, All Saints Hospital has been a mainstay in Fort Worth's medical community and joined the Baylor system in most recent years. Found in the medical district immediately south of downtown, this 537-bed hospital and the 71-bed satellite hospital in southwest Fort Worth provide care for every ailment from asthma, dia-

> **i** The University of Texas Southwestern Medical Center at Dallas is home to four Nobel laureates: three in physiology/medicine and one in chemistry.

Cosmetic Surgery

Since the 1970s, Dallas has been a leader among cities with abundant medical care in the world of cosmetic surgery. The use of computer imaging has been a boon for cosmetic surgeons in recent years, and one segment enjoying particular growth of this use in Dallas is that of facial rejuvenation. Using computer imaging, doctors show patients goals for specific procedures. A patient can better predict what the result will be after surgery for a receding chin, crooked nose, or aging skin. Advanced technology has been a boon also for the extremely popular laser resurfacing procedure, giving skin a smoother appearance, as the laser strips away outer layers of damaged skin and allows new cells to form that give a more youthful, tighter look. More available than ever are Dallas-area dermatologists and plastic surgeons whose clinics specialize in laser removal of tattoos, too. Many cosmetic surgeons and dermatologists waive the consultation fee when procedures are scheduled.

---

betes, cancer, and heart and vascular to pediatric care, spine care, urology, and women's health.

PLAZA MEDICAL CENTER OF FORT WORTH
900 Eighth Ave., Fort Worth
(817) 336-2100
www.plazamedicalcenter.com

Smaller than the more prominent hospitals, this 320-bed facility offers excellent care, comprehensive diagnostic and treatment services, surgery, and outpatient services. There's a new day-surgery center, an expanded pharmacy, new labs, a new cafeteria, and an enlarged lobby. Like at all the medical district hospitals, there is valet parking.

TEXAS HEALTH HARRIS METHODIST
1301 Pennsylvania Ave., Fort Worth
(817) 250-2000
www.texashealth.org

Since 1930, this big, redbrick hospital just south of downtown has been the go-to place for having babies, undergoing joint surgery, getting stitches from a skateboard fall, and treating cancer, heart, and other major health problems. The hospital, now part of the 14-hospital Texas Health Care, has more than 710 beds and is served by more than 800 doctors. In addition, there is a Harris branch in southwest Fort Worth, Hurst-Euless-Bedford, and Azle. The Harris Fort Worth hospital has its share of awards: It was named a Distinguished Hospital for Clinical Excellence by HealthGrades, a Colorado-based rating company. In addition, the hospital's green initiatives, which included reducing energy consumption and transforming the hospital's waste management practices, won it the 2008 Environmental Awareness Award in the corporate/business category by the League of Women Voters of Texas Education Fund.

**UNIVERSITY OF NORTH TEXAS HEALTH
SCIENCE CENTER**
3500 Camp Bowie Blvd., Fort Worth
(817) 735-2000
www.hsc.unt.edu

Opened in 1970 as the Texas College of Osteopathic Medicine (TCOM), the 1,200-student campus has grown to also include the Graduate School of Biomedical Sciences, School of Public Health, Department of Physician Assistant Studies, and School of Health Professions. The faculty provides medical care through UNT Health, now the largest multi-specialty practice in Tarrant County. The hospital and medical specialists' offices are spread over a 33-acre area in the Cultural District.

WELLNESS

Dallas Area

COOPER AEROBICS CENTER
12200 Preston Rd., Dallas
(972) 560-COOP (2667), (866) 906-COOP (2667)
www.cooperaerobics.com

UT Southwestern Medical Center

Some of the top biomedical researchers in the country are at the University of Texas Southwestern Medical Center in Dallas. More than 3,500 biomedical research projects are ongoing in a given year, funded to the tune of $400 million. Four Nobel laureates are here, including the researchers who discovered in 1985 how cholesterol is metabolized, leading to huge advances in the treatment of cardiovascular disease. The center also started three biotechnology companies looking into new treatments for congestive heart failure; genetic screening aimed at changing the way vaccines are developed (that company has since been sold but still operates in Dallas); and new cancer treatments.

Clinical trials are conducted at the Alzheimer's Disease Center, and are also part of other research projects.

UT-Southwestern trains more than 4,400 students each year at its three instititons: UT Southwestern Medical School; Graduate School of Biomedical Sciences; and UT Southwestern School of Medical Professionals.

To learn more visit www.utsouthwestern.edu.

In addition to serving as a premier fitness facility, the Cooper Center in Dallas's beautiful Preston Hollow neighborhood devotes a significant area to wellness programs for individuals and companies. Your interest may be simply to check in annually for a consultation and wellness exam and to come away with a specific, customized plan for health improvement as the result of a 4-, 6-, or 13-day program, with facilities for overnight stays. Companies can look into the 360-degree

Health Audit, working with your firm's insurance company on ways to be a more health-minded company. Individuals can take water fitness classes, run on the indoor track, work out with a trainer, or follow a specific fitness plan as directed by one of the physicians on staff who can help you deal with cardiology, cholesterol, or diabetes issues, as well as injury therapy.

DALLAS WELLNESS CENTER
2929 Carlisle St., Suite 350, Dallas
(214) 965-9355
www.dallaswellnesscenter.com
An excellent source for help in treating injuries from work or car accidents, this place also believes in using a preventative approach to health care. It's a holistic ideology, mixing chiropractic care, physical therapy, exercise programs, massage, and nutrition so that drugs and surgery are not necessary.

THE HEART HEALTH AND WELLNESS CENTER
9900 North Central Expressway, Suite 215, Dallas
(214) 750-8509
www.hearthealth.net
Taking care of the heart through preventative measures is the focus of this respected center in North Dallas.

Fort Worth Area
FEM CENTRE
709 West Leuda St., Fort Worth
(817) 926-2511
www.femcentre.com
This medical clinic near the medical district is a leader in bio-identical (natural) hormone replacement therapy and specializes in treating health issues with nutrition whenever possible. A "lifetime wellness" approach is employed to detoxify the body, balance hormones, boost the immune system, and prevent illness.

NATURAL THERAPEUTICS HOLISTIC SPA
6340 Camp Bowie Blvd., Fort Worth
(817) 738-4904
www.naturaltherapeuticshs.com

Gyms and Fitness

Fitness fanatics and yoga buffs have plenty of places to sweat and stretch here. The usual chains are abundant: Lifetime Fitness (www.lifetimefitness.com) has eight locations around the Metroplex; 24-Hour Fitness (www.24hourfitness.com) has 25; Gold's Gym (www.goldsgym.com) has eight; Larry North (www.larrynorth.com), a Texas-only health club chain, has two locations in Dallas, one in Southlake, and one in Fort Worth; Sunstone Yoga (www.sunstoneyoga.com), for hot yoga and power yoga, has 11, though some of those are in fairly distant suburbs. Some cities also have YMCAs that issue guest passes; the Downtown Dallas Y (214-954-0500, www.downtowndallasymca.org) does. The Fort Worth downtown Y does not.

Found on Fort Worth's west side, this leading center for holistic health care offers colon hydrotherapy, reflexology, foot soaks, lymphatic detox, infra-red sauna, therapeutic massage, and more in a small, relaxing office.

THE WELLNESS CENTER
2481 Forest Park Blvd., Fort Worth
(817) 926-9642
www.yogadoctor.com
Founded in 1986 by Dr. Kari Rollins, this is the leading illness-prevention facility in Fort Worth, located near TCU. This is where you find a blend of modern medicine and ancient healing arts, and it's a good place to consult with doctors who are interested in noninvasive treatment. In addition to treating health issues, the center offers yoga and meditation classes, along with educational programs for self-healing.

SPECIALIZED HEALTH CARE

AIDS/HIV

AIDS ARMS INC.
219 Sunset, #116-A, Dallas
(214) 521-5191
1907 Peabody Ave., Dallas
(214) 421-7848
www.aidsarms.org
Case management and referrals, outpatient medical care, and HIV testing.

AIDS INTERFAITH NETWORK
501 North Stemmons, #200, Dallas
(214) 943-4444 (programs)
(214) 941-7696 (administration)
www.aidsinterfaithnetwork.org
Day-care center, care-a-van, programs for Latinos and African Americans, prescription program, bus passes, interpretation.

AIDS OUTREACH CENTER OF ARLINGTON
401 West Sanford, Arlington
(817) 275-3311
www.aoc.org
Comprehensive AIDS prevention and service agency.

AIDS OUTREACH CENTER OF FORT WORTH
801 West Cannon, Fort Worth
(817) 335-1994
www.aoc.org
Offers free and/or low-cost services to HIV-positive individuals and their families.

Mental Health

MENTAL HEALTH AMERICA OF GREATER DALLAS
624 North Good-Latimer, Dallas
(214) 871-2420
www.mhadallas.org
Promoting mental health in the community, MHA works on the premise that mental illness can be effectively treated and believes that people with mental illness should have access to care on par with that of anyone with any other illness.

Mental Health

The state-run crisis hotline for Dallas County is (866) 260-8000, and the state programs here are run by the North Texas Behavioral Health Authority, www.ntbha.org.

In Fort Worth, the state-run crisis hotline is (800) 866-2465, and the programs are at Mental Health/Mental Retardation of Tarrant County, www.mhmrtc.org.

Also, in a mental health crisis including suicide prevention, contact Texas Suicide Prevention at (800) 273-TALK; www.texassuicide prevention.org. For help in a search for a therapist for an adult or child, look at the nonprofit Mental Health America of Texas's Web site, www .mhatexas.org. Links there will take you to *Psychology Today* listings that include photos and specialty descriptions of area therapists.

Poison Control

TEXAS POISON CENTER NETWORK
(800) 222-1222
If you get bitten and you don't know by what, don't hesitate to act. Texas has plenty of venomous critters, including rattlesnakes, copperheads, cottonmouths, coral snakes, black widow spiders, scorpions, and stinging caterpillars. Fire ants, common in grassy areas, build big hills, and if you see one, avoid it like the plague. Their stings won't kill you, but they are painful, and leave an ugly pustule. Poisonous plants you might run into are poison ivy and bull nettle. For photos, symptoms, and more information about poison matters of all kinds, look at www.poisoncontrol.org.

MEDIA

The Dallas–Fort Worth market intrigues in that you find two sizable cities sharing and experiencing broad and competitive coverage. Together, the cities span an area the size of Houston, yet they have their own newspapers and magazines that address the differing personalities and issues within their own cities.

That said, the media business suffers here—as it does across the nation—from the shrinking of newspapers and budget cuts at radio and TV stations. Perhaps the strangest development of this new world of media coverage is the recent concept of content sharing, which many journalists never predicted would occur. The *Dallas Morning News* and the *Fort Worth Star-Telegram*, healthy rivals for nearly a century, began sharing photographs and stories in late 2008.

Many of the media outlets offer expanded coverage on their Web sites, which is teased at on the print page or during broadcasts. Several newspapers, magazines, and radio and TV stations have good interaction with readers and a few have very amusing blogs. Check out www.guidelive.com from the *Dallas Morning News;* www.dfw.com from the *Fort Worth Star-Telegram*; www.unfairpark.com from the *Dallas Observer*; and frontburner.dmagazine.com from *D Magazine*, in particular.

On the radio, you'll find plenty of talky hosts during the morning and afternoon drive times, so you'll just have to hunt around for those that entertain you most or annoy you least. There's abundant conservative talk radio, more than adequate sports radio, and plenty of music to go around. Television programming is average for a market of this size, with the network affiliates offering local shows in the morning and lots of local news throughout the day. Spanish-language radio and TV programming is always on the grow, keeping pace with the Hispanic population.

Be warned, however, that you may find yourself just about hooked on a station when it suddenly changes format. That's happened frequently in the past couple of years as stations reinvent themselves in an effort to grab listeners who could be lured away by satellite radio. Many radio stations in the Dallas–Fort Worth market have gone high-def, too, also in an effort to keep you from devoting your time and money to satellite radio.

PRINT

D MAGAZINE
4311 Oak Lawn Ave., Dallas
(214) 939-3636
www.dmagazine.com
Dallas's monthly magazine, founded in 1974, likes to cover hot business and social types, fashion, food and wine, travel, and the occasional sports interest. Annual issues look at who lives in the most expensive homes in town, where the best school districts are, and where to find the best dining by neighborhood. Monthly circulation is about 62,000. *D* has one of the liveliest blogs in the state, found at frontburner.dmagazine.com.

DALLAS MORNING NEWS
508 Young St., Dallas
(214) 977-8222
www.dallasnews.com; www.guidelive.com
"The world at your doorstep" was the long-running motto of Dallas's surviving daily newspaper, which began publishing in 1885 and has won several Pulitzer Prize awards. Daily sections

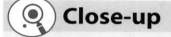 **Close-up**

In the Age of Print

In Dallas, the Dealey name has always been one heard frequently, and the Carter name in Fort Worth held similar importance. That's because those were the names of the men who are credited with building two valued newspaper companies.

The *Dallas Morning News* was launched under the Belo Corporation by George Bannerman on October 1, 1885 and began with a circulation of 5,000. It grew, leasing a special train on the Texas and Pacific Railway to carry papers to Fort Worth, and in 1887, using a special train on the Houston and Texas Central to deliver papers to McKinney, Sherman, and Denison on the morning they were printed. The *News* was printing an 8- to 12-page edition daily and 16 pages on Sunday by 1888 and built a circulation of 17,000 by 1895. The newspaper avoided controversy, but took a bold step in condemning the Ku Klux Klan in the early 1920s. Circulation rose to 86,000 by 1928. As Dallas grew, so did the paper. By the 1990s, the paper could be found all over the state, and in 2003, it had a Sunday circulation of 784,905 and a daily circulation of 525,532. Respect came, as well, as the *Morning News* received Pulitzer Prizes in 1986, 1989, 1991, 1992, 1993, and 1994. Members of the Dealey family remain at the company's publishing helm.

Thirty-odd miles west, the *Fort Worth Star-Telegram* enjoyed certain success. Founded as the *Star* in 1906 by a group of newsmen, its advertising manager was Amon G. Carter Sr. It initially published in 16 pages for a 4,500-copy free delivery. Carter and a partner bought the rival *Telegram*, an evening newspaper, in 1908 and launched a new paper, the *Star-Telegram*, in 1909. In the 1920s, Carter—a staunch supporter for Fort Worth who would take his own lunch to business meetings in Dallas, so as not to give money to the rival city—pasted a phrase on the masthead that read, "Where the West Begins," a slogan that continues today. Papers were delivered all over West Texas, some by stagecoach in the earliest days, and later they were dropped by bundles from airplanes. Carter remained the majority owner and publisher of the paper until his death in 1955 and was succeeded by his son, Amon G. Carter Jr., who died in 1982 of a heart attack, ironically in Dallas.

The *Star-Telegram* changed hands through the years, moving from the Carter family to Capital Cities, which later became Capital Cities/ABC, Incorporated, when it purchased the ABC television network; then the Disney Corporation; followed by Knight-Ridder and then McClatchy Company. The newspaper has claimed two Pulitzer Prizes; the first was in 1981 for Larry Price's photographs of Liberian officials being slain by a firing squad, and the second was in 1985 for meritorious public service following a series of stories that exposed a flaw in Bell helicopters (a Fort Worth–area company) that factored in numerous crashes. At its strongest period, in the 1990s, circulation climbed above 290,000 daily and more than 350,000 on Sundays.

Like most daily newspapers, the Dallas and Fort Worth papers struggle to keep circulation and advertising today, and some people wonder how long these will remain in business. Most newspaper fans agree that it's best that Mr. Dealey and Mr. Carter aren't around to see the demise of their work.

include coverage of metro news, business, arts and entertainment, lifestyle, and sports. Specialty coverage of food, cooking, dining, new films, theater, and museum openings usually happens weekly. Circulation is about 371,000 on weekdays and 522,000 on weekends. Interesting and entertaining blogs are found at www.guidelive.com.

DALLAS OBSERVER
2501 Oak Lawn Ave., Dallas
214) 757-9000
www.dallasobserver.com

The alternative weekly in Dallas has a circulation of 110,000 and is well liked for its investigative stories and general irreverence for anyone in an ivory tower. Coverage ranges from government and politics to business, entertainment, and sports. Dining coverage is solid, too. The Best Of coverage each year is always fun to read, with goofy topics like "Best Place to See Garbage Bags as Outerwear," along with the usual "Best Skyline View." Amusing and thoughtful blogging is found at www.unfairpark.com.

FORT WORTH STAR-TELEGRAM
400 West Seventh St., Fort Worth
(817) 390-7400
www.star-telegram.com
Fort Worth's daily newspaper has been covering news, business, sports, and lifestyle interests for more than 100 years. Today's coverage is heavy on local news and business and high school, college, and local professional sports. Dining and local arts and entertainment get attention in the Friday edition. A monthly luxury lifestyle magazine called *Indulge* offers a focus on fashion, home and garden, entertaining, and travel. Circulation is about 300,000 on Sunday.

FORT WORTH WEEKLY
1204 West Seventh St., Fort Worth
(817) 335-9559
www.fwweekly.com
Fort Worth's alt weekly newspaper publishes on Wednesday and offers local news, business, government, politics, and entertainment coverage, usually with a healthy dose of anything from skepticism to attitude. The editorial camp likes to take on the sacred cows other local media won't touch. Check out the Blotch, the weekly's blog, at the Web site.

FORT WORTH, TEXAS MAGAZINE
6777 Camp Bowie Blvd., Fort Worth
(817) 560-6111
www.fwtexas.com
Fort Worth's glossy monthly claims a circulation of nearly 75,000 and offers heavy coverage of social events and features on leaders in business, the arts, and society.

MODERN LUXURY DALLAS
2828 Routh St., #350, Dallas
(214) 880-0020
www.modernluxury.com
With a circulation of about 50,000, this fashion-centric monthly covers all areas that fall within the luxury lifestyle category. High-end trends are popular coverage, with interior design, travel, food, and wine among special interests.

360 WEST
1612 Summit Ave., Suite 201, Fort Worth
(817) 632-8100
www.360westmagazine.com
This sophisticated lifestyle magazine looks at fashion, homes, business, food, and travel, and the people who do interesting things in those areas. It's more high-end than not and offers a bit more diversity than some other slick magazines.

TELEVISION

Dallas–Fort Worth offers a number of network affiliates and independent local stations with original programming.

KDAF 33
8001 John W. Carpenter Freeway, Dallas
(214) 252-9233
www.the33tv.com
The 33 belongs to the Tribune Broadcast Company station group, along with WGN in Chicago, KTLA in Los Angeles, and WPIX in New York. It's a big hit, with top syndicated programs and offerings from the CW Network.

KDFI 27
400 North Griffin St., Dallas
(214) 720-4444
www.kdfi27.com
This is the sister station to KDFW (see below). Programming is typically popular talk shows and reruns of favorite dramas and comedies.

KDFW 4
400 North Griffin St., Dallas
(214) 720-4444
www.myfoxdfw.com

Here's the Fox affiliate, with original, local morning programming on a weekday show called *Good Day*. Visiting celebrities, authors, chefs, and others will frequently be featured on the program. The station dates back 80 years and was formerly known as KRLD.

KERA 13
3000 Harry Hines Blvd., Dallas
(214) 871-1390
www.kera.org
KERA 13 is the public television station, carrying PBS programming. It's among those with the highest ratings in the nation and there is plentiful local programming. You'll see the station working in community events and outreach, too.

KTVT 11
5233 Bridge St., Fort Worth
(817) 451-1111
cbs11tv.com
The CBS affiliate offers local coverage of news, sports, business, and entertainment. Among favorite station personalities is Babe Laufenberg, a former Dallas Cowboys quarterback who covers sports and hosts a couple of sports shows.

KTXA 21
5233 Bridge St., Fort Worth
(817) 451-1111
www.ktxa.com
This independent station is a sister station to KTVT (see below). Content tends to be paid programming and syndicated reruns.

i Research shows that the Dallas–Fort Worth area is the fifth largest media television market in the United States, with over 2.4 million households and over 6.5 million people. The DFW Metroplex is the fastest-growing TV market, too.

KXAS 5
P.O. Box 1780, Fort Worth
(800) 232-5927
www.nbcdfw.com

Channel 5, the NBC affiliate, broke ground in color broadcasting in Texas. Today it's a leader in breaking news, weather, traffic, and sports, and there's local entertainment and lifestyle coverage, too.

KXTX 39
3100 McKinnon St., Dallas
(214) 521-3900
www.telemundodallas.com
This Spanish-language station offers national, regional, and local programming.

WFAA-TV 8
606 Young St., Dallas
(214) 748-9631
www.wfaa.com
Begun as a radio station in 1922 by the Belo Corporation, which owns the *Dallas Morning News*, WFAA became a TV station in 1950. The call letters stood for "working for all alike," and by 1957 the station became the ABC affiliate. The station introduced local viewers to HDTV in 1997 and has won a raft of national news awards. *Good Morning Texas* provides local interest programming at 9 a.m. weekdays.

RADIO

Dozens of stations are found on the dial, and you can listen to them live on your computer, too. The largest listening audience is drawn to country formats, which are found at 99.5 The Wolf, or KPLX (www.995thewolf.com); The Big 96.3 KSCS (www.kscs.com); KXEZ 92.1, classic country (www.kxez.com); 95.3 The Range, KHYI (www.khyi.com); and 95.9 The Ranch, KFWR (www.959theranch.com). Classic rock is found at Lone Star 92.5, KZPS (www.kzps.com). Oldies are on KLUV 98.7 (www.kluv.com), and the classical music mainstay is WRR 101.1 (www.wrr101.com). Public radio is KERA 90.1 (www.kera.org). For sports, go to 103.3 ESPN Radio (sports.espn.go.com/stations/espn1033) and to 1310 The Ticket, KTCK (www.theticket.com). For all news, weather, and traffic, head for 1080 KRLD (www.krld.com).

WORSHIP

As though you need reminding, let us point out that the Dallas–Fort Worth area is the buckle on the Bible Belt. That means there's a high percentage of Baptist, Church of Christ, and fundamentalist and evangelical Christian churches hereabouts. But that doesn't mean you cannot find diversity in opportunities for worship. Catholic churches are plentiful, as well, as are Protestant churches, such as Episcopal, Methodist, Presbyterian, and Lutheran.

The most significant growth in recent years has been in nondenominational churches, some of which have enormous congregations (5,000 or more attending services on Sunday!), and many of these gather in repurposed buildings, such as nicely renovated former bowling alleys or industrial warehouses. There's been slow but steady growth in churches that embrace diversity; the most popular gay-friendly church of note in Dallas is Cathedral of Hope, and in Fort Worth, it's Celebration Community Church.

You can also find places of worship, of course, if you're Jewish, Buddhist, or Islamic. For interfaith information in Dallas, look to Thanks-Giving Square (1627 Pacific Ave., 214-969-1977; www.thanksgiving.org), a sanctuary and common meeting place for people of faith from around the world.

DALLAS AREA

Christian

CATHEDRAL OF HOPE
5910 Cedar Springs Rd., Dallas
(214) 351-1901
www.cathedralofhope.com
A spirit of inclusiveness prevails at this church near downtown, with two Sunday services in English and one in Spanish and a Wednesday evening service. Community outreach is an emphasis.

CHRIST THE KING CATHOLIC
8017 Preston Rd., Dallas
(214) 365-1200
www.ctkdallas.org
The church in University Park dates from the 1940s, when the parish had 500 families. Today it has more than 6,000 members. Mass is offered weekday mornings, on Saturday evening, and at four services on Sunday.

CHURCH OF THE INCARNATION EPISCOPAL
3966 McKinney Ave., Dallas
(214) 521-5101
www.incarnation.org
Dating from 1879, this church now covers five acres and offers seven Sunday services, including Choral Evensong from the 1662 prayer book. Outreach projects include helping the homeless population.

FIFTH CHURCH OF CHRIST, SCIENTIST
5655 West Northwest Highway
(214) 361-1625
www.fifthchurchdallas.com
Services and Sunday school are offered, and there's a Wednesday Testimony Meeting, too. Refer to the Web site for information on TV and radio broadcasts of services and Bible lessons.

FIRST BAPTIST CHURCH
1707 San Jacinto, Dallas
(214) 969-0111
www.firstdallas.org
Since 1872, this church in downtown Dallas has been big in the local worship community. Today

🔍 Close-up

Bishop T. D. Jakes

Whether or not you're a religious person, chances are that you've heard of Bishop T. D. Jakes. In 2005, *Time* magazine named him one of the 25 most influential evangelicals in the nation, and the *New York Times* said Jakes is "one of the top five evangelists most frequently cited by theologians, scholars, and evangelical leaders to step up to the international pulpit behind the Rev. Billy Graham."

Jakes, a native of West Virginia, is the charismatic visionary who runs the Potter's House, a multiracial, nondenominational church in southeast Dallas and a house of worship with more than 30,000 members and more than 50 active outreach ministries. The church employs almost 400 people and runs like a company, serving its members and the public at large with seminars that help build leadership and life skills for men, women, and children. His approach is one that blends spirituality with practicality.

Through the Potter's House, Jakes and the congregation focus on good works that have global impact. Among their significant efforts have been fund-raising for UNICEF tsunami relief; supplying drinking water to people and livestock, along with medical care and supplies, in Kenya; and providing aid to victims of Hurricane Katrina. In each case, contributions totaled well over $100,000 per project.

Services at the Potter's House (6777 West Kiest Blvd., Dallas, 214-331-0954) are on Sunday morning, and Christian education classes are on Wednesday evening. The church also offers youth ministry, singles ministry, and premarital and marital counseling. For details, visit www.thepottershouse.org.

---

it covers six city blocks with seven major buildings. First Baptist offers four Sunday services and several Wednesday evening activities too.

FIRST METHODIST CHURCH
1928 Ross Ave., Dallas
(214) 220-2727
www.fumcdal.org
Open downtown since 1926, this church offers worship services at two times on Sunday, with the 11 a.m. service streaming on a Webcast.

FIRST PRESBYTERIAN DALLAS
408 Park Ave., Dallas
(214) 748-8051
www.firstpresdallas.org
This downtown church has been around for 150 years and offers a diverse congregation. An emphasis is on music; on Sunday you may hear Bach, Celtic tunes, or African-American spirituals. There are two Sunday worship services. Stewpot Ministries serves a hot meal to more than 500

people daily and offers help from social workers, a medical and dental clinic, and in areas of drug rehab and psychiatry.

GRACE BIBLE CHURCH
11306 Inwood Rd., Dallas
(214) 368-0779
www.gracebiblechurch.org
The popular nondenominational church offers traditional and contemporary Sunday services and a number of groups that meet throughout the week.

HIGHLAND PARK METHODIST CHURCH
3300 Mockingbird Lane, Dallas
(214) 521-3111
www.hpumc.org
More than 90 years old, this church at the corner of the Southern Methodist University campus offers a variety of worship services, including traditional, contemporary, and Anglican, for a total of seven Sunday services.

HIGHLAND PARK PRESBYTERIAN
3821 University Blvd., Dallas
(214) 526-7457
www.hppc.org
There are four Sunday worship services at this 80-year-old church in the Park Cities.

LOVERS LANE UNITED METHODIST
200 Inwood Rd., Dallas
(214) 691-4721
www.llumc.org
Grown from a modest church on Lovers Lane to a big, contemporary place of worship, this church offers plenty of gatherings along with its worship services. Divorce Recovery, Deaf Ministry, Twelfth Step Ministry, and several others are available.

ST. THOMAS AQUINAS
6306 Kenwood Ave., Dallas
(214) 821-3360
www.stthomasaquinas.org
The East Dallas church dates back about 50 years and offers preschool and school for children kindergarten through eighth grade. Mass is offered weekday mornings; Tuesday, Thursday, and Saturday evenings; and six times on Sunday.

Islamic
ISLAMIC ASSOCIATION OF NORTH TEXAS
Dallas Central Mosque
840 Abrams Rd., Richardson
(972) 231-5698
www.iant.com
Members of the Dallas Central Mosque maintain the Web site, which lists some eight more area mosques with their locations and hours of worship, as well as schools, housing outreach, and student associations.

Jewish
CHABAD OF DALLAS
6710 Levelland Rd., Dallas
(972) 818-0770
www.chabadofdallas.com
This Shul describes itself as "one of Dallas's most unorthodox, Orthodox synagogues, a popular center for both Jews who are returning to their Jewish roots and experienced congregants." The North Dallas synagogue offers a multitude of services, studies, group activities, and gatherings for young and old.

TEMPLE SHALOM
6930 Alpha Rd., Dallas
(972) 661-1810
www.templeshalomdallas.org
A Reform congregation, the temple was founded in 1965. Today's temple dates from 1972 and sits on a beautiful, woodsy space covering 14 acres in North Dallas. There are numerous groups within the temple offering a full schedule of events.

Unitarian
FIRST UNITARIAN CHURCH OF DALLAS
4015 Normandy Ave., Dallas
(214) 528-3990
www.dallasuu.org
Organized in 1899, the church's slogan is "Whoever you are whatever you are wherever you are on your journey we bid you welcome." Found in University Park, the church offers a number of social and service groups for fellowship and volunteer work.

FORT WORTH AREA

Buddhist
INTERNATIONAL MEDITATION CENTER & BUDDHIST TEMPLE FOR WORLD PEACE
609 Truman St., Arlington
(817) 303-2700
www.meditationintexas.org
The temple is open for tours or quiet contemplation weekdays, and a lunchtime meditation is offered Monday and Wednesday at noon, with a vegetarian lunch. The Kadampa Meditation Center Texas, part of an international spiritual community dedicated to achieving world peace, is the vision of Venerable Geshe Kelsang Gyatso, Spiritual Director of the New Kadampa Tradition. Classes at the center are geared toward those in search of simple relaxation as well as those who seek lasting inner peace and contentment.

i The temple campus for one of the largest Buddhist communities in DFW was destroyed by fire in 2009. Members of a Lao-American community some 11,000 strong in northwest Fort Worth are rebuilding their temple at the Wat Lao Thepnimith complex where Buddhist monks studied and prayed. About 3,000 Lao-Americans used the campus as both a spiritual and cultural center. For information about how to help, or how to find members of the Buddhist community, call (817) 238-8543.

Christian

ALL SAINTS' EPISCOPAL CHURCH
5001 Crestline Rd., Fort Worth
(817) 732-1424
www.allsaintsfortworth.org
This diverse parish offers daily services, including four on Sunday, at one of the oldest Episcopal churches in the city. Monthly choral Evensong is popular. Monthly outreach activities include feeding the homeless at the local night shelter.

BROADWAY BAPTIST
305 West Broadway, Fort Worth
(817) 336-5761
www.broadwaybc.org
Founded just south of downtown in 1882, this church offers multiple ministries and enjoys a more liberal outlook than some in this part of the country. Especially appealing is its music program, with its Chancel Choir and 191-rank Casavant Frères organ. The annual presentation of Handel's Messiah brings in a huge, citywide audience.

CELEBRATION COMMUNITY CHURCH
908 Pennsylvania Ave., Fort Worth
(817) 335-3222
www.celebration-community-church.com
Founded in 1993, this nondenominational church in Fort Worth's medical district prides itself on its diversity and inclusive spirit. A number of ministries serve the community and members who are in need. There are two Sunday services and some midweek activities, too.

CHRIST CHAPEL BIBLE CHURCH
3740 Birchman Ave., Fort Worth
(817) 731-4329
www.ccbcfamily.org
A quickly growing, nondenominational Bible church, Christ Chapel has recently opened a big, contemporary building near the Cultural District. The ministry approach here uses what's called the Life Stage Model, spanning the phases of life from childhood to senior adult, each with its own pastor. A contemporary worship service is offered twice on Sunday as is one traditional.

FELLOWSHIP CHURCH
508 Carroll St., Fort Worth
(817) 870-0049
www.fortworth.fellowshipchurch.com
This new church near downtown is a branch of a bigger nondenominational church just north of DFW Airport. It's expansive, casual, and youthful, with three Sunday services and lots of groups for members to join. Youth ministry is a big focus.

FIRST CHURCH OF CHRIST, SCIENTIST
4705 Camp Bowie Blvd., Fort Worth
(817) 731-6891
www.christiansciencetexas.org
This church just west of the Cultural District offers a Sunday service and Sunday school, a Wednesday evening meeting, and a reading room.

FIRST METHODIST FORT WORTH
800 West Fifth St., Fort Worth
(817) 336-7277
www.fumcftw.org
Since 1930, this downtown church with a commanding presence has been among the city's most popular. Sunday school is a big deal here, both for kids and teens and adults. There's a mission nearby that helps the homeless, too. Four Sunday services are offered.

FIRST PRESBYTERIAN CHURCH FORT WORTH
1000 Penn St., Fort Worth
(817) 335-1231
www.fpcfw.org

This large, downtown church offers a lot of social activities and community outreach, as well as a good day school for young children. Three Sunday morning services are offered.

HOPE CHURCH
1750 Beach St., Fort Worth
(817) 535-5555
www.hopechurch.com
Begun in 1978, this nondenominational church on the east side of Fort Worth has grown to 800 members. It's big and laid-back but enthusiastic, with modern music and a come-as-you-are approach. Congregants wear shorts and flip-flops or their Sunday best. There are three services on Sunday.

MCKINNEY MEMORIAL BIBLE CHURCH
4805 Arborlawn Dr., Fort Worth
(817) 921-5200
www.mckinneychurch.com
A modern, nondenominational church founded in 1954, this one offers sign interpretation at one of its two Sunday morning services. Student ministries are especially popular, as is mission work.

ST. ANDREW'S CATHOLIC CHURCH
3717 Stadium Dr., Fort Worth
(817) 927-5383
www.standrewcc.org
One of the more active parishes in North Texas offers a wealth of family activities and social ministries, as well as a parish school. A children's choir sings at Saturday evening mass, and there's an assortment of traditional and contemporary music at four of the five mass services on Sunday. Weekday mass is offered on Monday, Wednesday, Thursday, and Friday.

ST. PATRICK'S CATHOLIC CHURCH
1206 Throckmorton St., Fort Worth
(817) 332-4915
www.stpatrickcathedral.org
A magnificent 1892 Gothic Revival building, this church is noted for its beautiful stained glass windows from Munich. Mass is said twice daily. Sunday masses are offered at 8 a.m., 9:30 a.m., 11 a.m., 12:30 p.m., and 5 p.m.

ST. PAUL'S LUTHERAN CHURCH
1800 West Freeway, Fort Worth
(817) 332-2281
www.stpaulfw.com
The first Lutheran church in town dates from 1893 and pulls a congregation from 60 different zip codes. There's a children's school on-site and the church offers adult Sunday school and ministries for men, women, youth, and college students, as well as two Sunday services.

TRAVIS AVENUE BAPTIST CHURCH
800 West Berry St., Fort Worth
(817) 924-4266
www.travis.org
Children's ministry is a focus here, as are ministries for married and single adults, seniors, and separate men's and women's groups. On Sunday there are three services.

TRINITY EPISCOPAL CHURCH
3401 Bellaire Dr. South, Fort Worth
(817) 926-4631
www.fortworthtrinity.org
A casual folk mass is among the five Sunday services, and there are weekday services Monday through Thursday, too. Within this busy church a block off the TCU campus, you'll find more than a dozen smaller groups with a full schedule of activities.

UNIVERSITY CHRISTIAN CHURCH
2720 South University Dr., Fort Worth
(817) 926-6631
www.universitychristianchurch.org
A lovely church on one corner of the TCU campus, UCC offers two traditional services and one alternative service on Sunday. This is the second-largest Disciples of Christ church in the country and it offers strong youth, children, and adult ministries.

WESTSIDE UNITARIAN UNIVERSALIST CHURCH
901 Page Ave., Fort Worth
(817) 924-6988
www.westsideuu.org

Westside is a young church with preaching that derives from both Unitarianism and Universalism. There's a Sunday service, as well as religious education classes for young and old on Sunday. Groups within the church meet during the week to share interests in everything from spirituality to quilt-making.

Jewish

BETH-EL CONGREGATION
4900 Briarhaven Rd., Fort Worth
(817) 332-7141
www.bethelfw.org
A Reform synagogue, Beth-El strives to provide spiritual, educational, social, and religious benefit to its members. You'll find evening Shabbat worship services on Friday, and traditional Shabbat morning services are held on Saturday for special occasions such as a Bar or Bat Mitzvah. Kabbalat Shabbat services have an earlier start time and generally are not as long as a traditional Shabbat service, and Family Shabbat service is a creative service, has an earlier start time, and is usually led by Religious School students.

CONGREGATION AHAVATH SHOLOM
4050 South Hulen St., Fort Worth
(817) 731-4721
www.ahavathsholom.org
This newer synagogue in southwest Fort Worth offers a number of services: Kabbalat Shabbat Services on Friday evenings; Shabbat Morning Services on Saturday; Torah Troop or Junior Congregation Services on Saturday mornings, twice a month during the school year; and Morning and Evening Minyan Services, Monday through Friday mornings and Sunday through Thursday evenings. The chapel offers a traditional minyan for anyone who needs to say Kaddish, meeting every morning and evening, year-round.

INDEX

A

Aardvark, The, 79
AARP Create the Good, 195
Abacus, 41
Abilene, Texas, 181
accommodations, 20
    hotels and motels, 20
    hotel spas, 26
    inns and bed-and-breakfasts, 35
Acton State Historic Site, 146
Adair's Saloon, 70
Addison Improv, 71
Adele Hunt's European Collectibles, 87
Adolphus, The, 20, 21
Adventure Landing, 159
African-American Museum, 111, 158
A Hooper, 100
AIDS Arms Inc., 212
AIDS/HIV care, 212
AIDS Interfaith Network, 212
AIDS Outreach Center of Arlington, 212
AIDS Outreach Center of Fort Worth, 212
Al-Anon Family Groups, 192
Albany, Texas, 181
Al Biernat's, 49
Alcoholics Anonymous, 192
Allen Senior Recreation Center, 193
All Saints' Episcopal Church, 220
All Saints' Episcopal School, 204
Alternative Furnishings, 87
Amateur Softball Association, 145
AMC Palace 9 Theater, 83
American Airlines C. R. Smith Museum, 163
American casual restaurants
    Dallas area, 37
    Fort Worth, 51
American upscale restaurants
    Dallas area, 41
    Fort Worth, 52
Amon Carter Museum, 118, 163
Amon Carter Museum Family Funday, 160
Amtrak, 17
Angelika Film Center, 73
Angelo's Barbecue, 56
Angry Dog, 70
Animal Crackers, 99
animal shelters, 195
Anita N. Martinez Ballet Folklorico, 160
annual events, 167
antiques, 87, 96
Arbor Hills Nature Preserve, 133
Arcodoro/Pomodoro, 47
area overview, 2
    business and industry, 2
    cowboy culture, 3
    dining and nightlife, 4
    government, 5
    language and diversity, 5
    museums and the arts, 5
    shopping, 4
    sports, 3
    statistics, 6
    tourism and conventions, 5
Arlington Chamber of Commerce, 187
Arlington Highlands, 94
Arlington Independent School District, 201
Arlington Senior Center, 196
Arlington Skatium, 144
Art Camp and Summer Art Study, 161
Artes de la Rosa, 131
Art Institute of Dallas, 123
Artisan Baking Co., 102
arts, 123
    area overview, 5
    choirs, 123, 127
    Dallas, 123

dance troupes, 123, 127
education, 123
film, 124, 127
for kids, 160, 166
Fort Worth, 127
museums, 126
music, 124, 129
theater, 125, 131
venues, 128
Asian Mint, 43
Asian restaurants
Dallas area, 43
Fort Worth, 55
AT&T Center for the Performing Arts, 128
AT&T Cotton Bowl Classic, 167
attractions, 106
Dallas, 106
Dallas arts district, 109
downtown Fort Worth, 116
East Dallas, 113
Fair Park, 110
Fort Worth Cultural District, 118
Fort Worth Stockyards, 117
Irving, 113
North and North-Central Dallas, 113
North and Park Cities, 110
north of Dallas, 114
South Dallas, 114
Aura, 72
Austin Avenue Grill and Sports Bar, 75, 90, 91,
148, 150, 187
Austin, Texas, 182
Aventino Ristorante, 62

B
Babe's Chicken Dinner House, 61
Baby Bliss, 99
Backdoor Comedy, 71
Backwoods, 103, 121
Bad Konigshofen Outdoor Family Aquatic
Center, 145
Bailey's Prime Plus, 121
Bailey's Uptown Inn, 35
Baker Street Pub & Grill, 81
Balcony Club, 73
Ball-Eddleman-McFarland House, 114
Banks Fine Art, 88
barbecue restaurants
Dallas area, 43
Fort Worth, 56
Barley House, 73

Barnes & Noble, 83, 89, 97
Bar 9, 80
bars, 70, 76
dance , 72
live music, 73, 79
piano, 80
sports, 81
wine, 76, 82
Barse, 83
baseball
professional, 148
recreational, 135, 142
basketball
profesional, 150
recreational, 135, 143
Bass Performance Hall, 77, 83, 125, 129
Bass Pro Shops, 104, 141
Bayard H. Friedman Tennis Center at TCU, 146
Baylor All Saints, 209
Baylor Health Care Systems, 207
Baylor Tom Landry Fitness Center, 135
BC Vintage Flying Museum, 163
Bear Creek Park, 139
bed-and-breakfasts
Dallas, 35
Fort Worth, 36
Bedford/Hurst Senior Center, 196
Belle Starre Carriages, 19
Benito's, 62
Berry Good Buys, 104
Beth-El Congregation, 222
Bicycle Center of Fort Worth, 143
bicycling, 135, 143
Big Taste of Fort Worth, 170
Bikes on the Bus, 143
Bikram, 121
Bill's Records, 92
Billy Bob's Texas, 78
Bishop Street Market, 108
Bistro B, 43
Bistro Louise, 60
BJ's Brewhouse, 150
Blackstone Marriott Courtyard, 28
Bliss Dallas—Victory, 26
Blue Mesa Taco & Tequila Bar, 17
Blues Jean Bar, 89
Boardroom, The, 76
Bob's Steak & Chop House, 49, 66
Bolla at the Stoneleigh, 41
Bolsa, 108
Bonnell's Fine Texas Cuisine, 52

Booger Red's, 76
Booker T. Washington High School for the Performing and Visual Arts, 124
Book Rack, 97
bookstores, 89, 97
BoomerJack's Grill, 81, 121
Borders, 89, 97
Botanic Garden, 118, 164
boutiques, 89, 98
bowling, 135
Boys Ranch, Bedford, 139
Bread Winners, 37
Brix Pizza & Wine Bar, 39, 65
Broadway Baptist, 220
Bruce Wood Dance Company, 166
Brumbaugh's Leather Gallery, 101
Bryan–College Station, Texas, 180
Bubba's Cooks Country, 47
Buddhist worship, 219
Buffalo Bros., 81
Buffet at the Kimbell Art Museum, 51
Bureau of Engraving and Printing, 163
Burger House, 45
burger restaurants
    Dallas area, 45
    Fort Worth, 56
business and industry, 2
bus service, 19
Buttons Restaurant, 61
Byron Nelson Championship, 152

C

Cabela's, 104
Cacharel Restaurant & Grand Ballroom, 60
Café Aspen, 53
Cafe Brazil, 38
Café Modern, 39, 51
Café on the Green, 41
Café San Miguel, 121
Camp Carter, 161
Camp Casa, 161
Camp Grady Spruce, 157
Campisi's Restaurant, 47
camps, 157, 161
Cantina Laredo, 16
Capital Grille, 50
Carshon's Delicatessen, 57
Caruth Haven Court, 193
Casa Mañana, 166
Cathedral of Hope, 217
Cattlemen's Steakhouse, 66

Cattle Raisers Museum, 163
Cavanaugh Flight Museum, 113, 158
CD Warehouse, 101
Cedar Crest Senior Center, 193
Cedar Hill State Park, 146
Cedar Ridge Preserve, 159
Celebration, 47
Celebration Community Church, 220
Celebration Station, 159
Center Restaurant, 178
Central Market, 92, 102, 155, 160
Chabad of Dallas, 219
chambers of commerce
    Fort Worth, 187
Charlie Palmer at Hotel Joule, 49
child care, 205
Children's Aquarium at Fair Park, 156
Children's Medical Center, 207
Children's Parade, 175
Children's Theater at Casa Mañana, 161
choirs, 123, 127
Christ Chapel Bible, 220
Christian Arts Museum, 118
Christian worship, 217, 220
Christ the King Catholic, 217
Christopher H. Martin Gallery, 88
Church of the Incarnation Episcopal, 217
Chuy's, 121
Cinco de Mayo, 172
Circle Theatre, 131
City Adult League, 145
city government, 195
City Streets, 80, 83
City Youth League, 145
Clark's Outpost, 178
Classic Carriages, 19
Cleburne State Park, 147
clothing
    kids, 90, 99
    men's, 91, 100
    western wear, 94, 105
    women's, 91, 100
Coal Vines Pizza Southlake, 65
Coldwell Banker DFW, 192
colleges, 197
Colleyville Senior Center, 196
Colonel's Bicycles, 143
Colonial Golf Tournament, 152
comedy clubs, 71, 77
community colleges, 200
concert bar venues, 71

Concerts in the Garden, 171
concert venues, 77
condos, 188
Congregation Ahavath Sholom, 222
Connections Book Store, 98
Contemporary Dance, 127
Cooking for Kids, 169
Cool River Cafe, 16
Cooper Aerobics Center, 136, 210
Cork, 76
Corsicana, Texas, 177
Cosmic Café, 50
Cotton Island, 89
country music clubs, 72, 79
Courtyard by Marriott on University, 33
Covey, The, 77
Cowboy Cool, 94
cowboy culture, 3
Cowboys Golf Course, 136
Cowboy's Red River, 72
Cowtown Cattlepen Maze, 117
Cowtown Coliseum, 117, 153, 165
Cowtown Farmers Market, 103
Cowtown Marathon, 154, 168
Cowtown Rodeo, 165
Craft, 42
Crème de la Crème, 205
Cross-Eyed Moose, 96
Crow Collection of Asian Art, 109
Crush, 76
Culver's Frozen Custard, 54
Curly's Frozen Custard, 54
cycling, 135, 143

D
Daddy Jack's, 49
Daisy Polk Inn and Cottage, 35
Dallas
    arts, 123
    attractions, 106
    condominiums, 188
    history, 8
    hospitals, 207
    hotels and motels, 20
    inns and bed-and-breakfasts, 35
    kidstuff, 155
    nightlife, 70
    parks and recreation, 133
    private schools, 203
    public schools, 200
    senior scene and retirement, 193

    shopping, 85
    wellness, 210
    worship, 217
Dallas Aquarium, 156
Dallas Aquatic Masters, 138
Dallas Arboretum, 113
Dallas Arboretum and Botanical Gardens, 159
Dallas area restaurants
    American casual, 37
    American upscale, 41
    Asian, 43
    barbecue, 43
    burgers, 45
    French, 46
    home cooking, 47
    Italian, 47
    Mexican/Tex-Mex, 48
    seafood, 49
    steak, 49
    vegetarian, 50
Dallas Arts District Friends, 110
Dallas Bike Works, 135
Dallas Black Dance Theatre, 123, 160
Dallas Bowling Association, 135
Dallas Center for the Performing Arts, 109
Dallas Chamber Orchestra, 124
Dallas Children's Theater, 125
Dallas County Community College, 200
Dallas Cowboys, 166
Dallas Department of Parks and Recreation,
    133, 135
Dallas Farmers Market, 92
Dallas Firefighters Museum, 111, 158
Dallas Fish Market, 49
Dallas/Fort Worth International Airport, 14
Dallas/Fort Worth International Airport
    Ambassadors, 194
Dallas Heritage Village at Old City Park, 106
Dallas Independent School District, 200
Dallas International Film Festival, 124
Dallas Irish Festival, 170
Dallas Marriott Suites Market Center, 24
Dallas Mavericks, 160
Dallas Metropolitan YMCA, 135, 136
Dallas Montessori Academy, 205
Dallas Morning News, 214
Dallas Museum of Art, 109, 126, 157, 158
Dallas Observer, 215
Dallas Opera, 125, 160
Dallas Parks and Recreation, 135, 138
Dallas Public Library, 157

Dallas Regional Chamber of Commerce, 187
Dallas Running Club, 137
Dallas Softball Managers Association, 138
Dallas Stars, 152, 160
Dallas Symphony, 125, 160
Dallas Texans Soccer Club, 137
Dallas Theater Center, 125, 160
Dallas Theater Center Summerstage, 157
Dallas Theological Seminary, 199
Dallas Wellness Center, 211
Dallas World Aquarium, 107, 159
Dallas Zoo, 114, 159
Dallas Zoo Camp, 157
dance clubs, 80
dance troupes, 123, 127
DART (Dallas Area Rapid Transit), 19
David Dike Fine Art, 88
day trips, 176
Dealey Plaza, 107
Dean-Kingston, 100, 121
Debo Cycle Sports, 135
Decorazon, 108
Deep Ellum, 113
Delaney's, 121
Del Frisco's Double Eagle Steak, 50
Del Frisco's Steakhouse, 66, 82
delis, 57
Denton, Texas, 176
Design & Grace, 101
Destination DFW, 187
Dh Collection, 101
Diabetes Support Group of Dallas, 192
Dieciseis de Septiembre, 172
Dino's Steak and Claw House, 52
Dirty Laundry, 100
Dixie House Café, 62
D Magazine, 213
dog park, 134
Dolce Vita, 121
Dolfin Swim School, 138
Dolly Python, 94
Domain, 120
Domain XCIV, 98
Double Exposure, 104
Dove Pool, 145
Dow Art Galleries, 96
Downtown YMCA, 143
Dragonfly at the Hotel Zaza, 38
Dream Café, The, 38
Drew's Place, 61
driving tips, 19

duck rides, 140
Dutch's Burgers & Beer, 56
Dyno-Rock Indoor Climbing Gym, 165

E
Eagle Mountain Lake, 142
Earth Bones, 83
Eating Disorder Group, 192
Ebby Halliday Realtors, 192
Eddie V's Lounge, 80
Eddie V's Prime Seafood, 65, 120
Edgemere, 193
Edmund Craig Gallery, 96
education, 197
    arts, 123
    child care and preschools, 205
    higher education, 197
    private schools, 203
    public schools, 200
8.0, 79, 83
El Asadero Mexican Steak House, 64
Elizabeth Boulevard Historic District, 118
Ellerbe Fine Foods, 51
El Sol Mexican Imports, 101
Embargo, 80
Embassy Suites, 28
Embassy Suites Market Center, 25
Emler Swim School, 145
Ennis, Texas, 177
Eno's Pizza Tavern, 108
Episcopal School of Dallas, 203
Ernest Tubb Record Shop, 102
Esperanza's Bakery & Café, 64
Etta's Place, 36

F
Fairmont Hotel, 21
Fair Park, 110, 112, 156
fall foliage, 182
Farpointe Cellar and Wine Bistro, 82
Fashion Lounge, The, 100
FC Dallas, 154
Fellowship Church, 220
FEM Centre, 211
Fiesta Mart, 92, 103
Fifth Church of Christ, Scientist, 217
film, 124, 127
Fincher's White Front Western, 105
Finn MacCool's Pub, 81
Firehouse No. 1, 116
Fireside Pies, 47, 121

First Baptist Church, 217
First Church of Christ, Scientist, 220
First Methodist Church, 218
First Methodist Fort Worth, 220
First Monday in Weatherford, 99
First Presbyterian Church Fort Worth, 220
First Presbyterian Dallas, 218
First Unitarian Church of Dallas, 219
fitness centers, 135, 143
Five Sixty by Wolfgang Puck, 43, 52
flea markets, 99
Flying Fish, 65
Flying Saucer, 76, 83
foods, specialty, 92, 102
Forest Park Pool, 145
Fort Woof Dog Park, 139
Fort Worth
    arts, 127
    attractions, 116
    chambers of commerce, 187
    condominiums, 188
    history, 10
    hospitals, 209
    hotels and motels, 28
    inns and bed-and-breakfasts, 36
    nightlife, 76
    parks and recreation, 139
    private schools, 204
    public schools, 201
    senior scene, 196
    shopping, 94
    wellness, 211
    worship, 219
Fort Worth Adult Soccer Association, 144
Fort Worth Cats Baseball, 149
Fort Worth Chamber of Commerce, 187
Fort Worth Christian, 204
Fort Worth Convention & Visitors Bureau, 121
Fort Worth Country Day, 204
Fort Worth Cultural District, 120
Fort Worth Cycling & Fitness Center, 143
Fort Worth Family Swim School, 145
Fort Worth Herd, The, 165
Fort Worth Independent School District, 201
Fort Worth Museum of Science and History,
    119, 120
Fort Worth Nature Center and Refuge, 140, 164
Fort Worth Opera, 129, 166
Fort Worth Public Library, 161
Fort Worth restaurants
    American casual, 51
    American upscale, 52
    Asian, 55
    barbecue, 56
    burgers, 56
    delis, 57
    French/European, 60
    Greek/Middle Eastern, 60
    home cooking, 61
    Italian, 62
    Mexican/Tex-Mex, 62
    pizza, 65
    seafood, 65
    steaks, 66
    vegetarian, 68
Fort Worth Rodeo and Stock Show, 153, 166,
    167, 168
Fort Worth Runners Club, 144
Fort Worth Senior Center, 196
Fort Worth Star-Telegram, 214, 215
Fort Worth Stockyards, 117
    hotels and motels, 32
Fort Worth Symphony, 129, 166
Fort Worth, Texas Magazine, 215
Fort Worth United Soccer League, 145
Fort Worth Water Gardens, 116
Fort Worth Weekly, 215
Fort Worth Zoo, 119, 164
Forty Five Ten, 89
Four Day Weekend, 77
Four Seasons Hotel and Resort, 25, 30, 136
Fourth of July, 172
Fox & Hound English Pub & Grille, 81
Foxy Roxy Sails, 141
Frankie's, 76
Freddy's Frozen Custard and Steakburger, 54
Fred's Texas Café, 56, 79
french fries, 39
French restaurants
    Dallas area, 46
    Fort Worth, 60
French Room, 46
Frisco, 114
Frisco Independent School District, 200
Frisco ISD Natatorium, 138
Frisco Rough Riders, 149
Frontiers of Flight Museum, 113, 158
frozen custard, 54

G
Gainesville, Texas, 176
Galerie Kornye West, 96

Galleria Dallas, 85, 86
Gallery Night, 173
Gameworks at Grapevine Mills Mall, 162
Garland Senior Activity Center, 193
Gaylord Texan Hotel & Convention Center, 33, 151
George's Imported Foods, 103
getting here, getting around, 13
    air, 14
    driving tips, 19
    in town, 18
    light-rail, 17
ghostbar, 72
gift shops, 89, 98
Gilda's Club North Texas, 192
Gilley's, 72, 78
Ginger Man, The, 70, 77
Glen Rose, Texas, 177
Gloria's, 64, 67, 80, 121
Goff's Hamburgers, 46
Go Fish, 49
Gold's Gym, 211
golf, 136, 144, 152
Goodbar Senior Center, 193
government, 5
Grace, 52, 53
Grace Bible Church, 218
Grace Preparatory Academy, 204
Grace Presbyterian Village, 193
Grady's, 68
Granada Theater, The, 71
Granbury, Texas, 177
Grand Hyatt DFW, 34
Grand Prairie AirHogs, 149
Grape, The, 38
Grapevine Chamber of Commerce, 192
Grapevine-Colleyville Independent School District, 201
Grapevine Mills, 102
Grapevine New Vintage Wine and Arts Festival, 170
Grapevine Senior Activities Center, 196
Grapevine Vintage Railroad, 165
Great Wolf Lodge, 34
Greek restaurants, 60
Green Papaya, 43

H
Hackberry Creek, 136
Half-Price Books, 89, 98
Hall of State, 111, 112, 156

Hard Eight BBQ, 56
Hattie's, 38, 108
Hawks Creek, 144
Head over Heels, 100
health care, 206
    hospitals, Dallas, 207
    specialized, 212
    wellness, 210
Heart Health and Wellness Center, The, 211
Hedary's Mediterranean Restaurant, 60
Heritage Farmstead, 115
Hibiscus, 39
Highland Park Independent School District, 200
Highland Park Methodist Church, 218
Highland Park Pharmacy, 39, 40
Highland Park Presbyterian, 219
Highland Park Village, 85
High Point Park Tennis Center, 139
Hill Country, 184
Hilton, 141
Hilton Anatole, 25
Hilton Arlington, 151
Hilton Fort Worth, 29
Hilton Park Cities, 25
Hip Pocket Theater, 132, 166
history
    Dallas, 8
    Fort Worth, 10
    timeline, 11
HIV Positive Support Group, 192
Hockaday School, 204
hockey, 137, 152
Holiday at the Arboretum, 175
Holiday Inn Express Hotel and Suites, 29
home cooking restaurants
    Dallas area, 47
    Fort Worth, 61
home furnishings, 101
Hope Church, 221
horse-drawn carriages, 19
horse racing, 153
Horseshoe Trails, Snaky Lane Park, 140
hospitals
    Dallas, 207
    Fort Worth, 209
    volunteering, 195
Hotel Ashton, 29
Hotel Belmont, 21, 30, 108
Hotel Indigo, 21
Hotel Lumen, 27
Hotel Palomar, 27, 31

hotels and motels
    Dallas Downtown, 20
    Dallas Market Center, 24
    Dallas Uptown, 23
    Fort Worth Cultural District, 33
    Fort Worth, DFW Airport, 33
    Fort Worth Downtown, 28
    Fort Worth Stockyards, 32
    North Dallas and Irving, 25
hotel spas, 26
Hotel St. Germain, 35
Hotel ZaZa, 23
House of Blues, 72
Hui Chuan, 55
Hulen Mall, 95
Humperdink's, 70, 150
Hurricane Harbor, 166
Hurst-Euless-Bedford Independent School
    District, 201
Hurst Tennis Center, 146
Hyatt Place Fort Worth Stockyards, 32
Hyatt Regency, 22
Hyatt Regency DFW, 34, 151
Hyena's Comedy Night Club, 77

I
Ice Training Center, 137
imports and handcrafts, 101
Indigo 1745, 108
inns
    Dallas, 35
    Fort Worth, 36
International Meditation Center & Buddhist
    Temple for World Peace, 219
International Museum of Cultures, 158
Into the Glass, 82
Inwood Theater, 73
Islamic Association of North Texas, 219
Islamic worship, 219
Italian restaurants
    Dallas area, 47
    Fort Worth, 62

J
Jack Carter Pool, 138
Jack's Backyard, 108
James L. West Center, 196
J & J Blues Bar, 79
J&J Oyster Bar, 66
Javier's, 48
Jazz Café, 61

Jefferson, Texas, 185
Jewish worship, 219, 222
J. Gilligans, 79
Jimmy's Food Store, 92
Joel Cooner Gallery, 88
Joe Pool Lake, 141
Joe T Garcia's Mexican Restaurant, 64
Joli Petite Baby Boutique, 100
Joule, The, 22
J. Rae's Bakery, 121
JR's Steakhouse, 68
Jubilee Theatre, 132
Just For Fun Watercraft Rental, 140
Justin Boot Outlet, 102

K
Kalachandji's Palace and Restaurant, 50
KD Studio, 124
Keller Chamber of Commerce, 192
Keller Independent School District, 201
Keller Pointe Pool, 146
Keller Senior Activities Center, 196
K. Flories Antiques, 97
kidstuff, 155
    clothing, 99
    Dallas area, 155
    Fort Worth, 160
    sporting events, 166
Kids Who Care, 161
Kimbell Art Museum, 119, 126
Kincaid's, 57
Kitchen Dog Theater, 125
Knox Street Pub, 71
Koffee Kup, 179
Komen Dallas Race for the Cure, 174
KRLD Restaurant Week, 172

L
Labels Designer Consignment Boutique, 94
La Bodega, 17
La Buena Vida, 83
Lake Benbrook, 142
Lake Granbury, 142
Lake Grapevine, 140, 142
Lake Lewisville, 134
Lake Mineral Wells State Park, 147
Lake Ray Hubbard, 134, 141
Lake Ray Roberts State Park, 147
lakes, 134, 140, 141
Lake Whitney State Park, 147
Lakewood Bar & Grill, 73

La Mariposa Imports, 92
Lambert's, 67, 69
L'Ancestral, 46
language, 5
Lanny's Alta Cocina Mexicana, 64
La Palapa Veracruzana, 108
La Piazza, 62
La Playa Maya, 64
Larry North, 211
Laser Quest, 162
Leddy's Ranch, 83, 105
Lee Harvey's, 71
Legacy Books, 89
Legends of the Game Museum, 166
Let's Eat, 179
Lewisville Independent School District, 200
libraries, 157, 161
Library, 77
Lifetime Fitness, 211
light-rail, 19
Lili's Bistro on Magnolia, 51
Lincoln Square, 153
Line Camp, 178
Live Green Camp, 162
Livestock Exchange Building, 117
Log Cabin Village, 119
Lonesome Dove Western Bistro, 68
Lone Star International Film Festival, 127
Lone Star Park, 153
Lost Creek Golf Club, 144
Lost Maples State Park, 182
Lotus Bar, 73
Love Field Airport, 14
Lovers Lane United Methodist, 219
Love Shack, 57, 121
Loyd Park, 141
Lucile's, 51
Luke's Locker, 94, 104, 121, 137, 144
Lynn Creek Marina, 141
Lynn Creek Park, 141

M
Mac's on 7th, 67, 121
Magnolia, 73
Magnolia Hotel, 22
Main Street Arts Festival, 171
Majestic Theatre, 107
Malibu Speedzone, 159
Malla Sadi Men's Boutique, 17
malls, 85, 94
Mansion on Turtle Creek, 42

Marquez Bakery and Tortilla Factory, 150
Marshall, Texas, 185
Martin Luther King Birthday Parade, 168
Maverick Western Wear, 105
Mayfest, 163, 171
McKinney Avenue Trolley, 18
McKinney Memorial Bible Church, 221
McKinney Senior Recreation Center, 193
McLeland Tennis Center, 146
Meadowbrook Golf Course, 144
Meadows Museum, 110
media, 213
    print, 213
    radio, 216
    television, 215
Men's Senior Baseball League, 142
mental health, 212
Mental Health America of Greater Dallas, 212
Mental Health/Mental Retardation of Tarrant
    County, 212
Meridian State Park, 147
Merriwood Day Camp, 157
Mesquite Rodeo, 154
Methodist Dallas Medical Center, 207
Metrocrest Chamber of Commerce, 187
Mexican/Tex-Mex restaurants
    Dallas area, 48
    Fort Worth, 62
Meyerson Symphony Center, 110
Michaels Restaurant & Ancho Chile Bar, 54
Mi Cocina, 48
Middle Eastern restaurants, 60
Mi Familia, 121
Milagros Frames & Gifts, 98
Milan Gallery, 83, 97
Mineral Wells, Texas, 180
Miss Molly's in the Stockyards, 36
M.L. Leddy's, 105
Modern Art Museum, 122, 126
Modern Luxury Dallas, 215
Mokara Spa, 26
Molly the Trolley, 19
Montgomery Plaza, 95
Montgomery St. Antique Mall, 97
Mountain Hideout, 94
Movie Tavern, 121
Movie Tavern at Hulen, 80
movie theaters, 73, 80
Museum of Nature and Science, 111, 115, 156
Museum of Nature and Science Summer
    Camp, 157

Museum of Science and Natural History, 164
Museum of the American Railroad, 111, 156
museums
    area overview, 5
    kid-friendly, 158, 163
    summer programs, 126
    volunteering, 195
music, 124, 129
Music Hall at Fair Park, 111, 156
music stores, 92
Mustangs of Las Colinas, 114, 132
My Martini, 150

N
Nana, 42
Nasher Sculpture Center, 110, 126
National Cowgirl Museum and Hall of Fame,
    122, 164
National Scouting Museum, 114
Natural Therapeutics Holistic Spa, 211
Neighborhood Services, 53
New Yorker Pizza and Pasta, 150
Nick & Sam's, 50
nightlife
    area overview, 4
    bars, 70, 76
    comedy clubs, 71, 77
    concert bar venues, 71
    concert venues, 77
    country music clubs, 72, 79
    Dallas, 70
    dance bars, 72
    dance clubs, 80
    Fort Worth, 76
    live music, 73
    live music bars, 79
    movie theaters, 73, 80
    piano bars, 80
    pubs, 75, 77, 81
    sports bars, 81
    wine bars, 76, 82
Nobu, 43
No Frills Grill & Sports Bar, 81
Nonna, 47
Nonna Tata, 62
Northaven Co-operative Preschool, 205
North Dallas Chamber of Commerce, 187
North East Mall, 95
North Fort Worth Alliance Soccer Association,
    145
NorthPark Center, 87

North Richland Hills Tennis Center, 146
North Texas Behavioral Health Authority, 212
North Texas Premier Soccer Association, 138
NYLO Dallas, 27, 30

O
Oak Cliff, 108
Old Red Courthouse, 107
Olenjack's Grille, 52, 150
Omni Hotel, 28, 32
Omni Mandalay Las Colinas, 27

P
Paciugo, 121
Palo Pinto, Texas, 183
Pan American Building Complex, 112
Panther City Bicycles, 143
Pappagallo Classiques, 83
Pappas Bros. Steakhouse, 50
Parigi, 41
Paris Coffee Shop, 62
Parkland Hospital, 207
Park Lane, 115
parks and recreation, 133
    city parks (Dallas), 133
    city parks (Fort Worth), 139
    dog park, 134, 139
    lakes, 134, 140, 141
    recreation, 135, 142
    state parks, 146
Parks at Arlington Mall, 95
Patrizio, 121
Pawnee Bill's Wild West Show, 165
Pearl's Dancehall & Saloon, 79
Pease-Cobb Antiques, 97
Pecan Valley Golf Course, 144
Peggy Sue BBQ, 43
performing arts, 160, 166
Pete's Dueling Piano Bar, 81, 83
Pet Grief Counseling Support Group, 192
Photographs Do Not Bend, 88
Piccolo Mondo, 150
Pierre's Mardi Gras, 66
Piney Woods region, 182
Pink's Western Wear, 94
Piola Italian Restaurant and Garden, 62
Pioneer Plaza, 109
Piranha Killer Sushi, 55
Pittet Company, The, 88
pizza, 65
Pizza Hut Park, 115

Plano, 115
Plano Independent School District, 201
Plano Senior Center, 193
Plato's Closet, 104
playgrounds, 160, 165
Plaza at Preston Center, The, 87
Plaza Del Sol Imports, 101
Plaza Medical Center of Fort Worth, 209
Plaza Turtle Creek, 188
Poag Mahone's Irish Pub, 81
poison control, 212
Poor David's Pub, 73
Porch, The, 41
preschools, 205
Primo's Bar & Grill, 48
Primrose, 205
P.S. the Letter, 98
pubs, 77, 81
Putt-Putt Fun Center, 162

Q
Q Cinema Festival, 128, 171
Quarter Bar, The, 71

R
radio, 216
Railhead Smokehouse, 56
Ranch House, 179
Ranchman's Cafe, 178
Randol Mill Park, 142
Reata Restaurant, 17, 68, 82
Red Steagall's Cowboy Gathering and Western
    Swing Festival, 165, 174
REI, 94
relocation
    relocation specialists, 192
    support groups, 192
Renaissance Worthington, 32
Republic, 71
Residence Inn, 33
Residence Inn Fort Worth Cultural District, 33
Residence Inn, So7, 121
restaurants
    area overview, 4
restaurants, Dallas area
    American casual, 37
    American upscale, 41
    Asian, 43
    barbecue, 43
    burgers, 45

French, 46
    home cooking, 47
    Italian, 47
    Mexican/Tex-Mex, 48
    seafood, 49
    steak, 49
    vegetarian, 50
restaurants, Fort Worth
    American casual, 51
    American upscale, 52
    Asian, 55
    barbecue, 56
    burgers, 56
    delis, 57
    French/European, 60
    Greek/Middle Eastern, 60
    home cooking, 61
    Italian, 62
    Mexican/Tex-Mex, 62
    pizza, 65
    seafood, 65
    steaks, 66
    vegetarian, 68
retirement
    Dallas, 192
    Fort Worth, 196
retirement communities, 193, 196
Retro Cowboy, 83
Reverchon Park, 134
Richard Hsu Activities Center, 193
Richardson Independent School District, 201
Riddell Rare Maps & Fine Prints, 88
Ridglea Music, 102
Ridgmar Mall, 95
Rios Interiors, 101
Rise No 1, 46
Ritz-Carlton, 23
Ritz-Carlton Dallas Spa, 26
River Legacy Living Science Center, 164
River Legacy Park, 142
Rockwall Watersports, 141
rodeo, 153
Rodeo Exchange, 79
Rosewood Mansion on Turtle Creek, 23
Rough Creek Lodge, 179
Round Top, Texas, 186
Roy Pope Grocery & Market, 103
RSVP, 194
Ruby, 98
running, 137, 144, 154

S

Sail with Scott, 141
Saint-Emilion Restaurant, 60
Sammy's Bar B Que, 43
Samuell-Grand Park, 134
San Francisco Rose, 41
Sardines Ristorante Italiano, 62
Savor Dallas, 170
Scat Jazz Lounge, 80
Schakolad, 83
schools, private
    Dallas, 203
    Fort Worth, 204
schools, public, 202
    Dallas, 200
    Fort Worth, 201
scuba diving, 137, 144
Scuba Diving School of Fort Worth, 144
Scuba Source, The, 137
seafood restaurants
    Dallas area, 49
    Fort Worth, 65
senior centers, 193, 196
senior scene
    Dallas, 192
Shakespeare Festival, Shakespeare Dallas, 171
Sheraton Dallas Hotel, 23
Sheraton Downtown, 32
Sheridan's Frozen Custard, 54
Shoe Gypsy, 100
shopping, 85
    antiques and fine art, 87, 96
    area overview, 4
    bookstores, 89, 97
    boutiques and gift shops, 89, 98
    clothing, kids, 90, 99
    clothing, men's, 91, 100
    clothing, women's, 91, 100
    Dallas, 85
    flea markets, 99
    Fort Worth, 94
    home furnishings, 101
    imports and handcrafts, 101
    malls and shopping areas, 85, 94
    music stores, 92
    outlets, 102
    specialty foods, 92, 102
    sporting goods, 94, 103
    thrift stores/resale shops, 94, 104
    western wear, 94, 105
Shops at Legacy, The, 87

Shorthorn, The, 199
Sid Richardson Museum, 83, 116
Silver Fox, 50
Simmons Senior Center, 196
Six Flags Over Texas, 162
Sixth Floor Museum, 109, 158
skating, 137, 144
Skillz For Life Program, 149
SMU Athletics, 154
SMU Daily Campus, The, 199
SMU Perkins Natatorium, Dallas, 138
Snookie's Bar & Grill, 77
Snuffer's Restaurant & Bar, 46
soccer, 137, 144, 154
Social House, 121
Soda Gallery, 108
Sofia Art Academy, 124
softball, 138, 145
Sonny Bryan's "The Original," 44
Sons of Hermann Hall, 72
So7, 121
So7 Bistro, 121
South Dallas Café, 47
Southern Methodist University, 110, 197
Southern Methodist University Barr Pool, 138
SouthFork Ranch, 116
Southlake Carroll Independent School District, 202
Southlake Chamber of Commerce, 192
Southlake Town Square, 96, 189
Southwest Christian School, 204
Southwestern Baptist Theological Seminary, 199
Southwestern Exposition and Livestock Show and Rodeo, 166
Spiral Diner, 68
Spoiled Pink, 98
sporting goods, 94, 103
sports
    area overview, 3
    recreational, 135, 142
sports for kids, 166
sports, spectator, 148
    baseball, 148
    college, 154
    golf, 152
    hockey, 152
    horse racing, 153
    rodeo, 153
    running, 154
    soccer, 154

Stage West, 166
St. Andrews Catholic Church, 221
State Fair of Texas, 156, 173, 174
state parks, 146
statistics, 6
steak restaurants
    Dallas area, 49
    Fort Worth, 66
Stephan Pyles, 42
Stevens Park, 136
Stevens Park Golf Course, 108
Stockyards Historic District, 165
Stockyards Hotel, 33
Stockyards Station, 117
Stoneleigh Hotel, 24, 31
St. Mark's of Texas, 204
St. Patrick's Catholic Church, 221
St. Patrick's Day Parade, 170
St. Paul's Lutheran Church, 221
St. Thomas Aquinas, 219
Studio Movie Grill, 80
Studio Sabka Fine Art Gallery, 97
Summer Zoo Camp, 162
Sundance Square, 96, 116
Sunstone Yoga, 211
support groups, 192
Susan G. Komen for the Cure, 208
Suze, 41
Sweethearts Dessert Fantasy, 169
swimming, 138, 145
Swiss Avenue Historic District, 113
Szechuan, 55

T
Taco Diner, 49
Tarrant County College, 200
Tarrant County Courthouse, 117
Taste of Addison, 171
Taste of Dallas, 172
Taste of Europe, 60
TCU Athletics, 154
TCU Bookstore, 98
TCU Daily Skiff, The, 199
TCU Pool, 146
Team Texas High Performance Driving School, 149
Team Texas NASCAR Sprint Cup Driving School, 149
television, 215
Temple Shalom, 219
Tenison Park, 137

Ten Martini Bar & Lounge, 77
tennis, 138, 146
Terra Cotta Mule, 101
Texas Advantage Volleyball, 146
Texas Assessment of Knowledge and Skills, 201
Texas Ballet, 166
Texas Ballet Theater, 123, 127
Texas Boys' Choir, 127
Texas Brahmas, 153
Texas Club Fitness, 136
Texas Christian University, 198
Texas Cowboy Hall of Fame, 118
Texas Discovery Gardens, 156, 159
Texas Girls' Choir, 127
Texas Health Harris Methodist, 210
Texas Health Presbyterian Hospital Dallas, 207
Texas Motor Speedway, 148, 149, 166
Texas Outdoors, 104
Texas Poison Center Network, 212
Texas Rangers, 148, 166
Texas Scottish Festival and Highland Games, 171
Texas Scottish Rite Hospital, 208
Texas Sculpture Garden, 115
Texas Star Golf Course, 144
Texas Suicide Prevention, 212
Texas Trail of Fame, 118
Texas Wesleyan University, 198
Texas White House, 36
Texas Woman's University, 198
Thai Tina's, 55
theater, 125, 131
Theatre Arlington, 132
Theatre Three, 125
theology schools, 199
1301 Throckmorton Omni Residences, 188
Thistle Hill, 114
360 West, 213
thrift stores, 94, 104
Tigin Pub, 17
Tillman's Roadhouse, 39, 108
Time Out Tavern, 71
Times Ten Cellars, 76, 121
Tokyo Café, 55
Tom's Burger Grill, 150
Tour 18, 137
tourism and conventions, 5
Tower Residences, 188
Trains at NorthPark, 175
Travis Avenue Baptist Church, 221

TRE (Trinity Railway Express), 19
Trinity Episcopal Church, 221
Trinity Park, 142
Trinity River Corridor Project, 115
Trinity Terrace, 196
Trinity Valley School, 204
trolleys, 18
Tu Hai Restaurant, 56
Turtle Creek Chorale, 123
24-Hour Fitness, 211
Twisted Root Burger, 46

U
Uncommon Angles, 99, 121
Union Station, 109
Unitarian worship, 219
universities, 197
University Christian Church, 221
University of Dallas, 198
University of North Texas, 198
University of North Texas Health Science
    Center, 210
University of Texas at Arlington, 199
University of Texas at Dallas, 199
University of Texas Southwestern Medical
    Center, 209, 210
University Park Village, 96
USA Film Festival, 170

V
Van Cliburn International Piano Competition,
    130
vegetarian restaurants
    Dallas area, 50
    Fort Worth, 68
Veracruz Café, 49
Vessels, 83
Vidalias, 67
Vineyards Campground on Lake Grapevine,
    141
volleyball, 139, 146
Volleyball Institute of Plano, 139
Volunteer Center North Texas, 194
volunteering, 194
Volunteer Match, 195

W
Waco, Texas, 180
Warwick Melrose, 24
Watermere, 196

Water Tower Theatre, 127
Wat Lao Thepnimith, 220
Waxahachie, Texas, 177
W Dallas Victory Residences, 188
Weatherford, Texas, 180
Weekend Flea Market at Will Rogers, 99
weekend getaways, 176
Weekends Crazy Horse Saloon, 72
wellness, 206
    Dallas, 210
    Fort Worth, 211
Wellness Center, The, 211
western wear, 94, 105
Western Wear Exchange, 104
Westin at the Galleria, 28
Westside Unitarian Universalist Church, 221
West Village, 87
Whimsey Shoppe, The, 88
White Elephant, 79
White Rock Dog Park, 134
White Rock Lake, 134, 135
White Rock Marathon, 154, 175
White Rock North School, 205
Whole Foods Market, 93, 94, 103
Wildcatter Ranch, 179
wildflowers, 178
Will Rogers Coliseum, 122
wine bars, 76, 82
Wine Styles, 83
Wine Thief, The, 53, 84
Wingfield's Breakfast & Burger, 46
Winslow's Wine Cafe, 84
Women's Museum, The, 112, 156
Woodall Rogers Park, 115
Woolley's Frozen Custard, 54
worship
    Dallas, 217
    Fort Worth, 219
W, The, 23

Y
Yellow Rose Express Train Ride, 164
YMCA, 211
Yogi's Deli & Grill, 57
York Street, 42
Young Artists' Workshop, Summer Camp at
    the Kimbell, 162
Youth Baseball, 143
Youth Soccer, 145

Z
Zambrano Wine Cellars, 84
Zoe & Jack, 100
Zola's Everyday Vintage, 108
Zubar, 73

Travel Like a Pro

To order call 800-243-0495 or visit thenewgpp.com

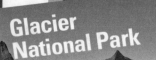